☑ W9-COH-230

What the reviewers said...

"A rich man's son from upper-class Tory Toronto who embraced relatively radical views and grew more radical with age.... His tab collars, striped shirts and double-breasted grey suits proclaimed Bay Street to the last button-hole; the words that issued from beneath the clipped moustache made Bay Street shudder."

— Christopher Young, Southam News Services

"Reveals an ongoing struggle between the conservative and progressive wings of the Liberal party, both in and out of office.

....Fascinating insight into the way the Liberal establishment works, though it's only between the lines.

...Valuable insight into our political history and a revealing portrait of the man himself."

— CBC newsman Norman DePoe

"Some frank judgments...not vicious, but neither are they sentimental.

He is in no sense a narrow or petty-minded nationalist. He does not dislike other countries. But he is convinced that, if Canada is to survive, we must take steps to ensure that we shall be able to define our own priorities as a nation.

Gordon has devoted his own political life to giving an example of courage, understanding and determination. *A Political Memoir* is a chronicle of his successes and frustrations. It deserves to be pondered by anybody interested in the future of our country."

— The *Gazette*

"The shape of our intellectual history may be symbolized by the work and lives of four figures: Harold Innis, the analyst; George Grant, the perceiver; Margaret Laurence, the story-teller; Walter Gordon, the doer."

— novelist Dave Godfrey in *Canadian Forum*

"History is not likely to forget a man who could not stop talking about foreign ownership, even for a shot at the prime ministership."

— Don McGillivray, *Report*

By the Same Author

Troubled Canada: The Need for New Domestic Policies (1961)
A Choice for Canada: Independence or Colonial Status (1966)
Storm Signals: New Economic Policies for Canada (1975)

Walter L. Gordon

A Political Memoir

Goodread Biographies

Copyright © 1977 by Walter L. Gordon

CANADIAN CATALOGUING IN PUBLICATION DATA
Gordon, Walter L., 1906-
  A political memoir

Includes index.
ISBN 0-88780-110-2

1. Gordon, Walter L., 1906- 2. Canada — Politics
and government — 1963- *I. Title

FC621.G67A36 1983 971.0643'0924 C83-098344-9
F1034.3.G67A36 1983

ALL RIGHTS RESERVED

First published in 1977 by
McClelland and Stewart Limited

Published in paperback 1983 by
Goodread Biographies
Canadian Lives series publisher: James Lorimer

Goodread Biographies is the paperback imprint of
Formac Publishing Company Limited
333 - 1657 Barrington Street
Halifax, Nova Scotia
B3J 2A1

Printed and bound in Canada

Contents

Illustrations
(between pages 200 and 201)

To Liz
with my love and gratitude

Preface

This book deals with the relatively short, but sometimes hectic, period in which I was engaged in politics. It was my practice to make notes of many of the conversations and discussions in which I participated during the time I was in Ottawa, including in some cases notes of what I planned to say in cabinet and caucus. I have relied on these notes and on copies of correspondence to refresh my memory about many of the incidents referred to and, in some cases, have quoted parts of them in the text or attached them as appendices.

The first sixteen chapters were written in the summer of 1968, immediately after I retired from politics when the events described were clear in my mind. I revised them slightly in the summer of 1969 but then, almost at the last minute, decided not to publish them at that time.

Later, Denis Smith wrote a flattering biography of me, *Gentle Patriot: A Political Biography of Walter Gordon* (Edmonton: Hurtig Publishers, 1973). In doing so, he had access to all my political papers, including the manuscript for these memoirs from which he quoted extensively. Because of this, there are many duplications in Smith's book and this one. This does not mean that Smith included everything that appears in these pages. There are, moreover, differences in our interpretations of events and also in style. That is the justification for publishing these memoirs now. The final chapter is new and deals with what I have been doing since retiring from politics nine years ago.

One of my main preoccupations for many years has been Canada's increasing dependence on the United States and whether anything can be done about it. This will be a principal theme throughout this political autobiography which covers the years from 1960 to 1968, inclusive. The purpose of the earlier chapters, covering my professional experience as a chartered accountant and management consultant as well as my work in Ottawa in wartime, is to indicate something of the background and origins of my views about the independence issue. In discussing events during the time I was actively engaged in politics, I shall mention a number of incidents in which the independence issue was highlighted. At the same time, I shall hope to demonstrate some of the difficulties of prosecuting views that run counter to the conventional wisdom of the day or which are opposed by "the establishment." This difficulty is made greater in Canada by the division of powers between the federal and the provincial governments and by the wide regional differences of opinion that exist about economic issues.

It should be said, at the outset, that I do not favour, and never have favoured, a narrow, restricted, protected role for Canada. We live and work and trade in a world that is becoming more interdependent all the time. No country, least of all Canada, could expect to prosper if it were to isolate itself from what is going on elsewhere. Canada's economy is a relatively open one, and this helps us to keep our industries more competitive than they otherwise would be.

The fact that has most bearing on the Canadian economy and on Canadian thinking is that we live next door to the most powerful nation the world has ever known. Two-thirds of our total trade is done with the United States. And our lives are influenced more than we probably realize by communications media, advertising, technology and science, business methods, politics, foreign policy, ideas, culture, values, all of which are American.

The so-called American Empire does not operate in the same way as the other empires that have preceded it, but that does not mean it is any less effective. Because of our close proximity, we are continually conscious of the thrusting, acquisitive impact of American enterprise, which is extraordinarily successful because, for the most part, it is only indirectly controlled or influenced by the United States government in Washington. The push comes from American businessmen, labour leaders, teachers, writers, philosophers, and artists in their individual capacities, as well as from the Pentagon.

There are many Canadians in positions of importance who do not believe the steady competitive pressures of our American friends can be withstood successfully. Nor do they see any good reason why they should be. These people believe that in the years ahead the Canadian economy will become increasingly integrated with that of the United States, and that this will redound to everyone's benefit and well-being. Some of those who feel this way admit that this development may reduce, to some degree, Canada's ability to manoeuvre, Canada's independence if you will. But they question whether any nation can have any meaningful independence in this nuclear age. In these circumstances, they ask, why should we try to resist a trend that may be inevitable anyway? They ask, what difference does it make whether or not Canada retains a limited degree of independence? It can be no more than that. They question whether in these circumstances it matters very much if Canada for all practical purposes becomes a part of the United States.

Perhaps Canadian independence – and by this I mean only a limited degree of Canadian independence – is not worth bothering about. Perhaps it does not matter very much if Canada's principal industries are controlled abroad; if the key management decisions are made by people in New York or Chicago or Detroit or San Francisco. Perhaps we should let the present trends continue and let nature – in this case, the natural impulse of American acquisitiveness – take its course. I have not thought so. And neither have many of the younger business executives who work for companies that are controlled abroad, some trade-union leaders, some of those in the professions, including the teaching profession, some of the new generation of civil servants, and many of the students in our universities. And so the debate about this question still continues. Obviously, it is the members of the younger generation who must decide the outcome.

W.L.G.

"Seldom Seen"
R.R. 3, Schomberg
Ontario

May 1977

Acknowledgements

Many people helped me in the preparation of this book. Six of my friends read drafts of the complete manuscript; others read sections dealing with incidents with which they were familiar. I made many changes in the text as a result of the comments and criticisms I received from them for which I record my warmest thanks.

Brian Land, Professor and Director of the School of Library Science in the University of Toronto, who was my Executive Assistant in Ottawa, spent considerable time with me during the summer of 1969 helping to pull the book into better shape. I am particularly grateful to him and also to Susan Carter, a graduate student at the University of Toronto, who was of great assistance in doing research and checking facts.

John Robert Colombo edited the manuscript for McClelland and Stewart and made many useful suggestions. I am much indebted to him. My secretary, Diana Murray, typed many drafts of the book without a whimper. She was assisted at the end by Barbara Hunter who was my secretary in Ottawa. I am grateful to them for their hard work and also for their encouragement and cheerfulness.

CHAPTER ONE

Professional Experience

Studying to become a chartered accountant; Royal Commission on Price Spreads and Mass Buying; inquiry into the automobile industry; proposal to subsidize the production of peat; early friendship with Mike Pearson; post-war expansion of the Clarkson Gordon and Woods Gordon firms; proposed Canadian holding company.

It is customary for an autobiography to begin with a recitation of the events, real or imaginary, preceding and attending the author's birth, and a colourful, sometimes coloured, account of his exploits at school and college. This is not that kind of chronicle. So far as I can recollect, nothing that occurred during my school and college days had any bearing on the happenings, policies, and ideas with which this political autobiography has to deal. Therefore, I shall begin with my enrollment as a student with Clarkson, Gordon & Dilworth, Chartered Accountants, on January 2, 1927, shortly before my twenty-first birthday.

Thomas Clarkson had founded the original Clarkson firm in 1864. He was succeeded by his son, E.R.C. Clarkson, and he in his turn by his son, G.T. Clarkson, the senior partner at the time when I became a student. Subsequently, G.T.'s son, Geoffrey, became a partner, and in 1968 Geoffrey's son – another Geoffrey – was admitted to the partnership. I mention this in passing, as it is improbable that any other professional firm in Canada has had the advantage – and I believe there is considerable advantage in such continuity – of having five generations of the same family participate directly in its work and operations.

Associated with G.T. Clarkson when I began working with the firm were my father, H.D. Lockhart Gordon, and R.J. Dilworth. These three men were quite dissimilar in their temperaments and in their outside interests. But in their professional activities they got along remarkably well together. They were all hard workers and set their standards very high. No cutting corners or sloppy work was tolerated. Theirs was not only one of the two oldest firms in Canada but the acknowledged leader in its field, and they meant to keep it that way.

G.T. Clarkson had started in the receivership and bankruptcy end of the business when he was fifteen. In a long and distinguished professional career, he had reorganized and managed many businesses. He possessed excellent judgement, and was *the* "business doctor" of his day. His advice was sought not only by bankers and businessmen but also by governments, especially by successive governments in Ontario. Indeed, there were times when he seemed to spend more time at the Parliament Buildings in Queen's Park than he did in the firm's offices on Wellington Street. His friend, Premier Howard Ferguson, a staunch Conservative, consulted him on a wide variety of questions. This did not go unnoticed by members of the official opposition who made certain that the fees paid to G.T. Clarkson for his services were given wide publicity.

At that time in Toronto, there was a sensational newspaper called *Hush* which specialized in sex and scandal. The editor of *Hush* delighted in publishing stories about Mr. Clarkson's influence in Ontario government circles. One headline read "Clarkson Known as Jesus Christ around Queen's Park." This upset Mr. Clarkson, a religious man, who thought the headline blasphemous. I met him leaving the office, red-faced and obviously flustered with the offending paper clasped firmly in his hand. He said he was going to see his friend Jack Johnston (Strachan Johnston, K.C.), Mr. Clarkson's lawyer) and get him to start libel proceedings against the editor of *Hush*. Some time later I asked Mr. Clarkson how the action was proceeding. He looked a bit chagrined and said that on reflection he was not going to sue the hated editor, much as he despised him. Then he began to laugh. He told me that Strachan Johnston had listened to his angry denunciation of *Hush* without a word until he finished. Then Johnston said, "In the present state of religious feeling in this province, no jury would think your reputation had been damaged merely because you were compared with Jesus Christ! You had better forget about a libel suit."

When I began to work for the Clarkson firm at the beginning of 1927, the starting salary for students was sixty dollars a month and the hours were very long. Theoretically, we worked a thirty-nine hour week, but in practice there was a great deal of overtime, especially in the winter months. It was quite a shock in my first week as a student to find the working hours were from 9:00 A.M. until midnight, with two hours off for meals. On Saturday, we were allowed to stop at 11:00 P.M. This made a seventy-seven hour working week. As it took an hour to get to work and another hour to get home at night, there was not much time left for other things. Fortunately, when the winter rush was over, we worked more normal hours.

For the first year or two, learning to be an auditor in those days was rather dull and monotonous. But if a student showed interest and was lucky, there were opportunities to get away from the auditing routine for extended periods, and to spend one's time on investigations and special assignments of one kind or another. I found this a fascinating way of learning what goes on behind the scenes and also of how to make individual businesses more profitable and efficient. This was the kind of work in which I wished to specialize.

I had my first taste of this other kind of work – other than regular auditing, that is – shortly after enrolling as a student. The firm was retained by the Royal Commission on Customs and Excise to examine the books and records of a wide variety of enterprises which the commission proposed to investigate. Newton W. Rowell, K.C., was chief counsel to the commission. He was a distinguished and successful lawyer who had previously enjoyed a remarkable political career, first as leader of the Liberal Party in Ontario and then as President of the Privy Council and acknowledged second-in-command in Sir Robert Borden's wartime government. Mr. Rowell, who was a confirmed teetotaller, dominated the commission and used it to launch a crusade against the bootleggers and other elements of the liquor trade. Like the United States, most of Canada at that time was suffering under Prohibition, a form of masochism much favoured by Mr. Rowell and like-minded Calvinists in English-speaking Canada.

It was my good fortune to be attached to this commission throughout its tour of Western Canada as a sort of glorified office boy. My duties were to assist Colonel A.E. Nash, the partner in charge of all the investigations being done by our firm for the commission. My job was to see that copies of reports were available on time for the commission's sittings, and to do odd jobs for all and sundry. The importance of my rather ill-defined responsibilities was brought home to me as the commission was approaching Winnipeg. I was called into private consultation by one of the commissioners, a judge of the Supreme Court of Ontario, who had impressed me at several of the hearings. He was a large man who had the ability to sleep soundly through much of the day but, at critical moments, without appearing to wake up, to ask extremely pertinent questions of the witnesses. This technique must have required much practice.

The commissioner informed me that I appeared to him to be a perspicacious young man who should go far in the profession. He then asked if I would perform a small service for him. I was much flattered by his compliments and promised to do anything I possibly could to help him. This settled, he asked that, on arrival at each city where the commission was to sit, I should seek out the most reliable bootlegger and purchase two bottles of the best available Scotch whisky. He suggested that, if I had any

15

trouble in finding a good bootlegger, I should consult the senior officer of the R.C.M.P. in the area. He added that, if I could manage to deliver to him the required necessaries of life without the knowledge of Mr. Rowell, it would spare everybody's feelings. My recollection is that I was able to carry out this mission satisfactorily.

During my four years as a student – 1927 to 1930, inclusive – I learned what was necessary about accounting theory, about auditing techniques, and about how to handle a financial or business investigation. Early in 1931, I qualified as a chartered accountant. In the meantime, my salary had been increased in modest stages but my immediate prospects for advancement were not overly encouraging, and I was restless.

At that time, the standards of the profession in the United States were not as high as they were in Canada. Because of this, a well-trained Canadian accountant could get a job very easily with any of the large accounting firms in the United States. I decided to take two weeks off in order to size up the situation for myself. I went to New York and called on about a dozen of the top firms there and was offered jobs by most of them. But after ten days I decided I did not want to work in New York no matter what the attractions might be. For one thing, the idea of spending two hours or more a day commuting was not exciting. I preferred to remain a Canadian and, if possible, help demonstrate that Canadian professional men, if given the opportunity, can be just as competent and imaginative as their counterparts in other countries. So I returned to Toronto and signed on permanently with Clarkson, Gordon & Dilworth.

A few years later, two events occurred in quick succession which provided the breaks I had been hoping for. In 1935, I was invited to become a partner in the firm. J. Grant Glassco was admitted to the partnership at the same time. He became perhaps the outstanding professional accountant of his generation in Canada, acting as President of the Institute of Chartered Accountants of Ontario, the Canadian Institute of Chartered Accountants, and the Canadian Tax Foundation. In 1960, he was appointed Chairman of the Royal Commission on Government Organization. Glassco and I had a most successful partnership which lasted for over twenty years before he left the firm to join Brazilian Light and Power Limited, of which in due course he became President.

The second event, which occurred almost immediately after I became a partner in the firm, came as the aftermath to a general election in Ontario. After twenty-one years in office, the Conservatives were defeated and the Liberals elected. One of the first acts of Mitchell Hepburn, the new Premier, was to dismiss the Clarkson firm which for many years had acted as auditors of the Hydro-Electric Power Commission of Ontario and a great many other government institutions. This was very hard on the three senior partners, Messrs. Clarkson, Gordon, and Dilworth. The work lost almost overnight accounted for nearly one-quarter of the total business of the firm. Clarkson was in his late fifties at the time. My father was over sixty, and Dilworth was nearly seventy. It was too late for them to hope to find enough new business to make up for losses of this magnitude. This meant that Glassco and I would have to do much of the work of rebuilding the business of the firm, a great opportunity for us at thirty and twenty-nine, respectively.

We decided that never again would we permit the firm to become so dependent on a single client. Rather wistfully, we set a theoretical limit of five per cent of the firm's total volume of business as the maximum we would undertake for any one client or associated group of clients. While we both thought this important if the real independence of the firm was to be safeguarded, we were inclined to smile – in the circumstances, there seemed no chance that this self-imposed limitation would ever become embarrassing. Many years later, however, we found that nearly five per cent of a greatly expanded volume of business was being done for a single client, another Conservative government in Ontario, and that we were being urged to accept still further government assignments. We concluded that our original decision had been a sound one, however, and with considerable reluctance we recommended to the government that other accountants be retained to do some of the work in question.

Glassco and I agreed that, if we were to rebuild the fortunes of the firm, we would have to do some specializing. It seemed sensible for one of us to become an expert on taxation and for the other to spend most of his time on practical business problems. The question then was to decide which of us should concentrate on what. We agreed to toss for it. It was not until the third or fourth toss that we got the answer both of us were looking for. Glassco became the tax expert.

During the thirty-five years I was in practice, I was lucky enough to work on a variety of government inquiries and investigations. I have referred, in passing, to the Royal Commission on Customs and Excise in 1927. Then, shortly after the Bennett government came to power in 1930, an inquiry was launched into current business practices with particular reference to the spread or mark-ups between producers' costs and retail prices. The examination was begun by a parliamentary committee under the chairmanship of the Minister of Trade and Commerce, the Honourable H.H. Stevens. When Parliament recessed, the inquiry was continued by the Royal Commission on Price Spreads and Mass Buying, again at the beginning under Mr. Stevens' chairmanship. The Clarkson firm was retained to assist the Royal Commission, all the work being directed by Colonel A.E.

Nash, one of the partners. I spent over a year on this work, first on an exhaustive review of The T. Eaton Co. Limited, and later on a number of other investigations, including an examination of the agricultural-implement industry.

The evidence submitted to the commission attracted a great deal of publicity, most of it unfavourable to the business community. However, this may have helped people to let off steam and perhaps to distract the public's attention at a time of great depression and suffering. The same kind of thing was happening in the United States but there the government was bringing in the New Deal legislation, control of the banks, the Securities and Exchange Commission, unemployment insurance, etc. In Canada, nothing constructive was attempted until just before the term of the Bennett government expired. And most of the legislation passed at that time was later held to be unconstitutional.

But by 1934, the Stevens commission was getting out of hand. Mr. Bennett had called on L.B. Pearson, a young member of the Department of External Affairs, to take over as secretary with the object of getting a report written and winding up the commission as soon as possible. Pearson accomplished this task with the good humour, hard work, and tact for which he was already becoming known – and with a minimum of fuss. Given the circumstances, it was a remarkably able piece of work, and he won the admiration of all those who were aware of what he had accomplished.

I had been the chief witness before the commission for a full week in connection with The T. Eaton Company's profits and volume of sales, including details of the operations of individual stores, mail-order department, and so on. Never before had the public known how big the Eaton Company was or how its business was conducted. In fact, not more than half a dozen people in the company itself knew about these matters and, understandably, everyone was very curious. So my testimony was given front-page treatment by all the newspapers in the country. As a result and quite fortuitously, I became reasonably well-known in professional circles while still in my late twenties.

Shortly after this, the firm was retained to assist the Tariff Board, whose chairman was the Honourable George Sedgewick, late of the Supreme Court of Ontario, to undertake a full-scale inquiry into the automobile industry. Colonel Nash was in charge of the work, with me as his assistant. Again, I spent nearly a full year on the job, at the end of which I believed I knew something about the industry and why it cost twenty per cent more to manufacture a low-price car in Canada (a composite Chevrolet, Ford, and Plymouth) than in the United States. The differential in retail prices was even greater due to higher taxes and transportation costs in Canada and to the higher selling and distribution costs in our much smaller and fragmented market.

Part way through this investigation, I remember going in to see Colonel Nash in considerable pain. During the weekend, I had fallen while skiing and had broken my coccyx, the little bone at the end of the spine which I suppose in another age had been the beginning of one's tail. I said I had been to the doctor who informed me there were two alternatives; I could have the bone removed, which would mean I would be laid up for three weeks, or I could buy myself a rubber cushion with a hole in it, and suffer for the next six to ten months. Nash snapped at me to go and buy a cushion. That was that.

It is true that this occurred during the Depression, a time when it was unwise to argue with one's boss. It is also true, of course, that we were in the middle of an important investigation, and Colonel Nash did not wish to contemplate a three-week delay. I spent a most uncomfortable six months and felt very foolish as I went about with my rubber cushion. I can still recall the look of astonishment on the face of the Assistant to the President of the General Motors Corporation when, as the representative of the Tariff Board of the Canadian government, I entered his office in Detroit, placed my cushion on a chair, and eased myself into it, probably grimacing as I did so. Perhaps understandably in the circumstances, this high official of General Motors was reluctant to give any information to the Canadian government about his company's costs and prices. It took a good deal of persuasion to get him to change his mind. This same official, Charles E. Wilson, later became famous when, after serving as president of his company, he became Secretary of Defence in President Eisenhower's administration. His remark, "What is good for General Motors is good for America," is not likely to be soon forgotten.

We submitted an exhaustively detailed report to the Tariff Commission on the facts and figures of the automobile industry in Canada with pertinent comparisons with those in the United States. We also prepared a private memorandum for the Commissioners in which we made suggestions respecting a new tariff structure. This included considerable emphasis on incentives in the form of duty drawbacks depending upon the amount of Canadian content in cars produced in Canada.

One of the results of the new automobile tariff, which was recommended by the Tariff Board and approved by Parliament, was the growth of machine shops throughout Ontario, many of which were called upon to expand rapidly during the war to produce munitions. This would not have been possible if the necessary technical and management skills had not been developed beforehand. Another result has been that the differential between manufacturing costs in the automobile industry in Canada and the United States has steadily narrowed.

Another job for Ottawa in the mid-1930s was in connection with a proposal to subsidize the production of peat and market it in the form of briquets. The promoter of this idea was a man called Brown who at one time had been mayor of Medicine Hat. Behind him was the Balfour family of England which had invested heavily in the project; Babcock Wilcox, also of England, which was to manufacture the equipment; and the Southam newspapers which were giving the project much publicity. Brown entertained lavishly and succeeded in getting one hundred members of Parliament to sign a petition urging the government to grant a subsidy of one dollar a ton to establish a peat industry in Canada, using the process promoted by Brown.

There was no enthusiasm for this proposal in civil service circles, but in view of the petition the government agreed that it should be looked into by the Department of Mines and Natural Resources. It was decided to send a committee of three to Europe, the committee to consist of two engineers from the Mines department and an accountant to check on the costs of production. By happy chance, I was chosen to be the accountant and invited to meet Dr. Charles Camsell, the Deputy Minister, to talk things over. Dr. Camsell, a marvellous man who was born and brought up in the Far North and had had many adventures in a long and useful life, looked a little startled when I walked into his office. I was on crutches and my foot was in a walking cast. I explained I had the gout but that the attack should be over before the committee was due to leave for England. Dr. Camsell said the two engineers would be expected to write a report on the technicalities of the process; I was to report on the costs of production; and the three of us should prepare a joint report summarizing our conclusions.

After conversations with the Babcock Wilcox people in London, we visited what we were told were pilot operations in Scotland and Ireland, only to find some peat bogs cleared of overburden but no production. It developed that the only plant actually producing peat briquets was in Denmark. Accordingly, I proceeded to Aalborg in the north of Denmark and spent two weeks examining the process and checking costs. While peat briquets were being produced in a highly complicated plant, it was by no means a commercial operation. My suspicion, later confirmed in Copenhagen, was that the Danes used this pilot plant as a talking point in their negotiations when purchasing brown coal from Germany. Theoretically, they could resort to their own peat supplies if the Germans charged them too much for coal. Apart from that, the peat project was of little practical value. I had all we needed to report back to Dr. Camsell.

20

My wife, Liz, came with me on this trip, and we stayed at the Connaught Hotel while we were in London to investigate the peat project. Mike Pearson was at Claridge's a few blocks away, as a one-man adviser to the Right Honourable R.B. Bennett, the Prime Minister. They were in London for the Silver Jubilee celebrating the twenty-fifth anniversary of George V's accession to the throne. Mr. Bennett had chosen Pearson to go with him as a reward for the good work he had done in winding up the Stevens Commission. It meant, however, that Pearson had had to put in a great deal of overtime in order to brief the Prime Minister on a wide variety of subjects. Despite this, he was in wonderful form. He had known Liz for several years and I had met him when he became secretary of the Stevens commission. During our short stay in London, Pearson visited us at the Connaught at least once a day and regaled us with jokes and stories.

It was Pearson's custom to keep a bowler hat and a rolled umbrella in a locker at Canada House. Immediately he arrived in London, he would collect what in those days were these essential articles of clothing and then appear dressed as every Englishman. We complimented him on his appearance the first time we saw him so accoutred. Mike accepted our congratulations but admitted it always took him a day or two to get used to carrying an umbrella. He went on to say that on that very morning, in running down the front steps at Claridge's, the umbrella had got stuck between his legs and he had sprawled face downwards on the pavement. He said that as a senior diplomat from the Commonwealth – or perhaps it was the Empire at that time – he felt he had cut a rather sorry figure in the eyes of the splendidly uniformed doorman who had looked down on him in horror.

One day, Mike turned up at our hotel looking just a little bit subdued. We asked what was the matter, and he replied that the Old Man (Mr. Bennett) had taken him for a walk the previous evening. As they were going through the Green Park, Mr. Bennett stopped, pushed his well-developed paunch in Mike's direction, and said: "I've put you down for an O.B.E. in the Jubilee Honours, Pearson. What do you think of that?" Without thinking, Mike replied: "I would have settled for a twenty-five-dollar-a-month raise, Sir." There was a frozen silence which was not broken for some time. Then Mr. Bennett asked what Pearson's salary was. Mike answered that it was $296 a month, but out of this he was expected to pay for quite a bit of departmental entertaining. He said that, with a wife and two children to look after, this did not leave him much to come and go on. Apparently Mr. Bennett was impressed, as Pearson got both his O.B.E. and a raise in salary.

Shortly before the Second World War began, I suggested to Douglas

Woods, a well-known industrialist, that we should merge the practice being conducted by his J.D. Woods Co. Limited, which specialized in factory management, with the more general business-reorganization work done by Clarkson, Gordon and Dilworth. This was agreed to and J.D. Woods and Gordon Limited was formed. Some years after the war, we decided to operate as a partnership, and the name was changed to Woods, Gordon & Co., Management Consultants.

It was during the early years of the war that we began to realize how much the accounting profession was changing. The large American firms, in particular, were expanding into other countries, and we concluded that when the war was over this trend would be accelerated. It was imperative for us to take steps to meet this competition. Accordingly, my father proceeded to work out a very satisfactory arrangement with Arthur Young & Co., one of the six or seven largest firms in the United States. A joint firm was formed to do Arthur Young's work in Canada and our work in the United States. The joint firm – Arthur Young, Clarkson, Gordon & Co. – has nothing to do with Arthur Young's own practice in the United States or with the practice of the Clarkson firm in Canada. Both are carried on quite independently of each other. Under the arrangement referred to, the partners of the Clarkson firm have benefited greatly by having access to all the new techniques developed by the profession in the United States and by being kept up to date on American tax law and practice. The arrangement has been equally beneficial to Arthur Young & Co. I mention this as an example of what can be accomplished without selling control of established Canadian businesses to the Americans.

Shortly after completing the arrangement with Arthur Young & Co., we proceeded to open offices in all the principal cities in Canada, usually by joining forces with local firms. The Clarkson firm's practice expanded enormously in the post-war period, and the same was true for Woods, Gordon & Co. This was what we had worked and hoped for, but the changed character of the two firms, with offices in all the principal cities and an increasing number of partners, had its disadvantages. It became necessary to formalize our principles and standards of behaviour in a way that was not necessary with only a few partners who saw each other almost daily. In particular, we emphasized the importance of partners consulting one another before expressing opinions that were at all out of the ordinary or about which there could be differences of view. This form of double check was a long-standing tradition in the firm.

Most of the work done by an accountant or a management consultant is of a confidential character and, therefore, cannot be discussed even after the lapse of many years. Much of the work done by a firm of auditors and accountants is of a routine nature and would not be worth recalling in any event. But this does not mean that a large and active practice like that of Clarkson, Gordon & Co. and Woods, Gordon & Co. did not have its lighter moments.

For example, I remember as a young accountant being asked to find out what was going wrong with the operations of a hotel in a large city in Ontario whose profits were falling off alarmingly. I spent three weeks examining the hotel's books and records, and while it was quite clear that business had fallen off rather drastically, I could not put my finger on the reason for this. Clearly, some new approach would be needed if I were going to be able to write the kind of report that would help the owners of the hotel to correct the situation. I decided to do some entertaining and proceeded to discuss the facts of hotel life with individual members of the staff. One evening the building superintendent – who doubled as the house detective – confided that he was greatly worried about what was happening to the hotel since its manager had acquired an obsession about sin. He told me that it was the practice of the manager to sit in the lobby and, when any travelling salesman turned up with one of the "local girls," he would signal the desk clerk to say there were no rooms. My friend went on to say that this was giving the hotel a very bad reputation with the travelling fraternity throughout the province, who were now transferring their custom to a rival establishment. He informed me of his great embarrassment only the night before when a traveller with a suitable local companion had been given a room while the manager was out to dinner. Apparently this was reported by one of the bellboys when the manager returned to the lobby. Immediately he ordered the building superintendent into action. This took the form of playing a fire hose through the transom upon the occupants of the room in question at a rather intimate moment. As my friend put it, this story would be all around Ontario within twenty-four hours, with the result that the business of the hotel would be reduced still further.

I had my answer. The difficulty was to write the kind of report expected from a firm of chartered accountants and, at the same time, to make it clear to the owners of the hotel what was happening. Somehow or other this was accomplished. A new and perhaps more broad-minded manager was appointed, and the hotel became a highly profitable venture once again.

A later and very different example of the kind of work done by Woods, Gordon & Co. involved Gerry Bailey, an expert in work measurement. He was the co-author with Ralph Presgrave of *Basic Motion Timestudy* which became the standard work on the subject in North America, just as an earlier book, *The Dynamics of Time Study,* by Ralph Presgrave, one of the founders of J.D. Woods and Co. Ltd., had been in its day.

Bailey, as a partner of Woods Gordon, did important work for the Canadian Post Office in streamlining the mail-sorting operations. This came to the attention of the U.S. Post Office and the U.S. Ordnance Corps, both of which approached Woods, Gordon & Co. to assist them. Strong opposition developed in the United States, however, to the proposal that two important units of the American government should employ a Canadian firm. Eventually, Bailey was retained by both of these organizations but only to assist them in training their own staffs to carry on the work. Nevertheless, it gave us considerable satisfaction to know that two departments of the American government wished to retain a Canadian firm, not for sentimental reasons but because they felt it was the most efficient in the field. This experience brought home to us the great handicap that Canadians are under in competing for work in the United States against American firms on equal terms. When the shoe is on the other foot, Canadians have a tendency to welcome American consulting firms with open arms.

Another example of the kind of work undertaken by the Clarkson and Woods Gordon firms was the reorganization of the Hydro-Electric Power Commission of Ontario in 1947. Colonel George Drew, the Premier of Ontario, telephoned one day to say he had had a row with the Chairman of the Commission and had fired him. He asked me to take the job. I said I could not leave the firm but would be glad, in a professional capacity, to supervise the kind of reorganization that was obviously called for. This was agreed to, and Dr. Richard Hearn was appointed General Manager and Chief Engineer. It was my good fortune to work closely with Dick Hearn for several years during which time the Hydro was reorganized from top to bottom. This included not only many changes in the personnel, and in the way the lines of responsibility and authority were established, it also involved the changeover of parts of the system, including thousands of consumer appliances, to a uniform sixty cycles and a complete revision of the Hydro's costing system. This reorganization enabled the Hydro to meet the challenge of a tremendous post-war expansion program. It was a fascinating experience during which I gained the greatest respect for Dick Hearn and his capacity for getting things done well and quickly. Under his direction, Ontario Hydro became as efficient in every way as any large corporation I have ever encountered, either in the public or the private sector.

There is a postscript to this story. Many years later, in 1959, I was invited to visit Red China with James S. Duncan and our wives. We spent nearly a month there and had an exhilarating time meeting many people and seeing everything we asked to see. On his retirement as President of Massey Ferguson, the farm implement company, with which he had been associated all his working life, Jimmy Duncan had succeeded Dick Hearn as Chairman of Ontario Hydro. However, he still remained very much of a "free enterpriser" in philosophy and temperament. During our time in China, we were invited to many banquets and this involved the innumerable speeches that are a mark of such occasions. After each speech, I made a practice of introducing my friend, Jimmy, as the director of the largest and most efficient socialistic enterprise in Canada. This statement was always greeted with applause by our Communist hosts, and Jim Duncan was required to take over from there. He would tell me afterwards that I could get away with such jokes at his expense in China, but if I ever repeated this kind of remark in Canada I would never be forgiven.

In the late 1930s, I began to think about the tendency, which was just beginning, for the owners of Canadian businesses to sell out to American corporations. It seemed to me this trend could be offset by forming a Canadian holding company with adequate capital which would be available as an alternative purchaser. In those days, the shares of Canadian companies, especially family-owned companies, were usually valued at much lower prices, relatively speaking, than they were in 1968. In many cases, a valuation of five or six times current earnings was not thought to be unreasonable. Moreover, many of the companies that were available to purchase had accumulated large cash balances which a holding company could withdraw without incurring any liability for tax. It was possible in this way for a holding company to acquire an existing corporation and to use the surplus cash accumulated by it to pay for a substantial proportion of the purchase price.

I made up an imposing list of the companies that might be purchased in this way and then discussed the proposition with Mr. Clarkson and my father. They gave me their blessing but said they did not believe I was well enough known to be able to raise sufficient capital on my own. I therefore approached J.Y. Murdoch, K.C., President of Noranda Mines and one of my father's friends, and asked him for his help. This he agreed to readily when I explained I hoped to raise most of the capital in England. He also believed this project would tend to offset in some degree the growing American influence in Canada. Murdoch enlisted the support of Arthur Purvis of Montreal, President of Canadian Industries Limited and a highly respected member of the business community. With these two men to back me, I went to England to see another of my father's friends, Sir Edward Peacock, the head of Baring Brothers, the investment bankers, and a Director of the Bank of England. Sir Edward encouraged me with my proposal. While it was not the kind of venture in which Barings would be interested themselves, he said he would not hesitate to recommend me and my scheme to others in the City, especially as I had the backing of two such well-known businessmen as Jim Murdoch and Arthur Purvis. This he did and after many months of negotiation I was informed that five million pounds could be raised as capital.

At the then rate of exchange, this was the equivalent of $25 million, a substantially larger sum than Murdoch, Purvis, and I had contemplated. However, we decided it would be foolish to turn this offer down, and in the early months of 1939 we agreed to proceed with a venture which might have become very big indeed. I say this because given a capital sum of that size before the war, and the technique of using the surplus cash in any companies acquired to pay for a large part of their purchase price, we would have been able to obtain control of a wide range of Canadian business enterprises. It seemed probable that I would have to devote a large part of my time to this venture. However, this was not to be.

In March 1939, I received a letter from the London underwriters saying that while they had been successful in lining up the five million pounds of capital, the Bank of England did not wish them to proceed. They informed me confidentially that while there was no formal exchange control in Britain, the officials of the Bank were convinced there would be war in Europe before the year was over, and were exerting every kind of pressure in the form of moral suasion to discourage the export of capital from Britain. In these circumstances, the underwriters concluded that our project should not be proceeded with. Thus collapsed an early attempt by private interests to offset the encroachment of American financial control of Canadian business enterprises and Canadian resources.

It was not possible to start this project over again after the war with British capital or, indeed, on anything like the scale that was contemplated in 1938 and 1939. However, with the help of Jim Murdoch, R.A. Laidlaw, Hartland Molson, and others, we managed to organize a similar venture on a modest scale which, under the able direction of Larry Bonnycastle, has had a considerable success. I refer to Canadian Corporate Management Company Limited. Originally, about seventy per cent of the capital of this company was held in the United States and thirty per cent in Canada. Now the percentages have been more than reversed, and only about fifteen per cent of the shares are held by American citizens. This has been one small exception to the general trend under which so much of the control of Canadian business has been acquired by enterprising Americans.

CHAPTER TWO

Ottawa in Wartime

Foreign Exchange Control Board; preparations in case Britain was overrun; Special Assistant to the Deputy Minister of Finance; federal-provincial tax agreements; liaison with the Department of National Defence; the first big wartime budget; Mr. King's choice of a successor to O. D. Skelton; Wartime Prices and Trade Board; post-war taxation priorities; Royal Commission on Administrative Classifications in the Public Service.

A few days after war began in September 1939, Graham Towers, the Governor of the Bank of Canada, telephoned G. T. Clarkson to ask for help in organizing the work of the Foreign Exchange Control Board. This body had just been established by Order-in-Council. Mr. Clarkson asked me if I would like to take this on and I left for Ottawa that evening.

I arrived at the Bank of Canada rather early to be greeted by Brooks, the most magnificent of receptionists, who was always immaculately dressed in striped trousers and a morning coat. Brooks had come out from England as butler to a Governor General, Lord Bessborough, and had stayed on with Mr. Bennett when the latter was Prime Minister. After that, he had moved to the Bank of Canada.

Shortly after my arrival at the Bank, the postman appeared and demanded sixty-five cents in unpaid postage. The cashier had not arrived, the petty cash fund was locked up, and it turned out that Brooks was out of money. Accordingly, he told the postman to come back in half an hour. At this point, I decided to step into the breach and offered to put up the money. Brooks assured me that this would be quite unnecessary; after all, it was the Bank of Canada. But I insisted on paying the postman after informing Brooks that, as I expected to be working there, I did not want the institution to get a reputation for being unable to pay its bills. On that occasion Brooks was not amused but later on we became good friends.

When Towers came in, he explained things to me very briefly, asked if I had anyone else in mind who might come in to help on short notice, and gave me a copy of the Order-in-Council establishing the Foreign Exchange Control Board and setting out its responsibilities. Towers said to come back to see him after I had read the Order and he would try to answer any questions. I was then despatched to a desk in a very large room in what appeared to be a more-or-less unfinished attic. As I was about to start reading the Order, I looked up to see a long line-up of businessmen who had come to Ottawa to try to find out what they had to do in order to get their normal shipments moving. I started to deal with them one after another, and somehow found solutions to their problems.

One of the men in the line turned out to be the Secretary Treasurer of Falconbridge Nickel Mines. His name was Parkinson and I knew him well as I was responsible for his company's audit work. Parkinson explained that a large shipment of nickel matte for the company's refinery in Norway was being held up in Montreal. He said that I knew very well that all the refined nickel was shipped from Norway to Britain and none of it went to Germany. He told me he had been in Ottawa for three days running from one office to another trying to get someone to release the ship at Montreal so that the refinery in Norway would not have to close down. He asked me whether I could help him.

I told him we could try, and asked one of the stenographers to take a telegram to the Collector of Customs in Montreal, reading as follows: "Please release immediately S. S. *Blank* loaded with nickel matte for Norway STOP Satisfied cargo not destined for enemy hands STOP." The girl asked me how the telegram should be signed, which was something of a poser. We decided the best thing would be to sign it simply "Foreign Exchange Control Board." Immediately after the telegram was received by the Montreal authorities, the ship was released and set sail for Norway. My friend, Parkinson, returned happily to Toronto where he told everyone he ran into that, while some Ottawa departments did not seem to know what they were supposed to do, the Foreign Exchange Control Board was marvellously efficient.

The sequel was an angry memo from Graham Towers demanding to know who had sent the telegram. I placed the memo quietly in the waste-paper basket. More memos followed on the same subject for several weeks, all of which were placed in the same receptacle. It was not until I was leaving the board some five months later that I confessed to Towers that I had been the one responsible for the telegram. He said that Hugh Scully, the Deputy Minister of Customs and Excise, one of the directors of the Foreign Exchange Control Board, had been very angry at the time. Towers then asked me why I had not let him know what had happened. I replied that if I had told him all the things I had done off the cuff during my first week or two with the board, he would have had to fire me. By that time, of course, we had got to know each other well so we could afford to be amused about the incident.

It was a big job of organization and one that had to be worked out very quickly. The Order-in-Council required permits to be obtained in connection with every export or import shipment. This was quite impracticable in the case of large corporations having hundreds or thousands of shipments every week. To overcome this difficulty, we developed a system of monthly reporting which worked out very well. A similar reporting system was devised to deal with all financial transactions with other countries by banks and other institutions, including the stock exchanges.

One of the problems to begin with was to get staff. We overcame this by telephoning everyone we could think of and asking them to come to Ottawa by the next train. We pointed out there was no authority to pay them but that this would probably be sorted out in time. If anyone hesitated, we simply replied there was a war on.

I remember going back to see Towers about ten days after I first arrived. By that time I had read the Order. We had managed to collect a preliminary staff of a dozen or two. We had been working almost day and night and things were beginning to get sorted out. He seemed surprised when I said some of his new employees, whom no one at the Bank had interviewed or even seen, would like to be paid one of these days. However, he promised to arrange it. Towers, quite apart from his clear understanding of central banking and of the principles of foreign exchange control, was one of the best organizers I have encountered. He truly believed in delegation, both in theory and in practice, something some of the other more publicized of Ottawa's wartime administrators did not.

Canadian exporters were accustomed to selling their goods for payment in Canadian dollars, and many of them found it hard to understand why they should be required to demand payment in U.S. funds. In the very early days of the Board, I was visited by two important gentlemen in their late sixties who seemed mildly outraged over the fact that a new agency of the Canadian government was presuming to tell them how they should conduct their business. The first of these gentlemen was Robert C. Stanley of New York, the President of International Nickel. He was accompanied by Britton Osler, K.C., his Toronto lawyer, a friend and contemporary of my father's. They had had a trying trip to Ottawa, and I expect were a bit put out at being interviewed by what must have seemed to them a rather young, inexperienced, and temporary civil servant occupying quarters which were bare, uncomfortable, and cramped.

But we had a good discussion and I believe that when they left Mr.

29

Stanley and Mr. Osler had got over their feeling that there was a deliberate conspiracy to frustrate their company's objectives. In any event, after that trip they turned over the job of dealing with the Board to their assistants, Henry Wingate, who at that time was Secretary of International Nickel, and Harold Mockridge, then a junior partner in Mr. Osler's firm. This made things easier all round, and I seem to recall that we were able to settle the problems of International Nickel and some of its related companies with a minimum of bother.

My part of the job of organizing the Foreign Exchange Control Board was pretty well completed by the end of 1939, and early in the following year my responsibilities were turned over to Max Mackenzie, a chartered accountant from Montreal, who after the war became Deputy Minister of Trade and Commerce under the Honourable C. D. Howe. I returned to Toronto to help sort out the firm's affairs. This was at the time of the so-called phony war in Europe. There was a complete lull in the fighting, and no one seemed to know what was going to happen. However, members of the staff were leaving at a rapid rate to join the services. Grant Glassco had left the firm and taken a position in industry about the time I had gone to Ottawa to the Foreign Exchange Control Board. And things were in something of a mess.

One of my first acts on returning to Toronto was to have a long talk with Glassco. He was unhappy in his new job, and as he wanted to return to the profession it did not take a great deal of effort to persuade him to come back to Clarkson's. I explained that in all probability I would be returning to Ottawa in one capacity or another. In the meantime, we set about to organize the firm as best we could for what looked as if it were going to be a difficult few years. Some months after my return to Toronto, the war began in earnest. In the early summer of 1940, as France was overrun, Towers asked me to come to Ottawa again. He said that while he had no authority whatever in the matter, he thought some small group in Ottawa should be doing some thinking about what would happen in Canada if Britain were invaded and knocked out of the war. He asked me if I would be willing to do this with Alex Skelton and Dean Marble, two senior officials of the Bank of Canada, on the understanding that no one would be told what we were doing and that ideally nothing would ever come of it.

I spent several months on this assignment working at the Bank of Canada. We had access to all available information about the state of the war in Europe, shipping losses, the troops in Britain equipped to repel a possible invasion (or, more accurately, the lack of them), the aircraft and air crews available to take part in what was to become the Battle of Britain, and so on. It was a most unpleasant summer. Knowing what we did, it seemed incredible that Britain would be able to survive. We did our best to think about and plan for some of the legislation and administrative changes that would be necessary if Britain were overrun. The whole thing seemed as unreal as it proved to be unnecessary – thanks, perhaps more than anything, to Hitler's failure to drive across the Channel after Dunkirk.

Life must go on, of course, and occasionally that summer had its lighter moments. I remember working very late at the Bank one Friday or Saturday evening when a worried-looking official came to my office and urged me to go and talk to Donald Gordon, the Deputy Governor of the Bank, as quickly as possible. I presumed I was appealed to as the only other person of any seniority in the building at the time, even if in my case it was quite undefined. It happened that Towers was away that weekend and Donald Gordon was in charge of things. Donald, who later made a tremendous reputation as Chairman of the Wartime Prices and Trade Board and after the war as President of the Canadian National Railways, had immense energy and a vast capacity for work. There were times, however, when he became a bit carried away and this was one of them. He told me that a French battleship with forty million dollars in gold bullion aboard was in Halifax harbour. Gordon said the Foreign Exchange Control Board was most anxious to get its clutches on the gold but that he had just received a telephone call from Halifax advising that the French warship was getting up steam preparatory to sailing off to Martinique. The gold was still on board. Gordon claimed that, as Deputy Chairman of the Board, he was authorized to prevent this from happening, and that it was his duty so to do. He said he was going to order the commander of the shore batteries at Halifax harbour to stop the French battleship from leaving. He hoped a shot across the bows would be sufficient, but if not it would be necessary to sink the ship.

I had a nasty feeling that a new role for the Bank of Canada might be in the making. As Donald was not in a mood to listen to any doubts as to his authority to order Canada's armed forces into action, another approach was called for. Accordingly, I telephoned a friendly admiral who had been very helpful to me in connection with the shipping situation. Fortunately he was at home and not yet asleep. Without disclosing what was going on at the Bank, I ascertained particulars of the relative firepower of the Halifax shore batteries and of the French battleship. I was able to report to Donald Gordon that, if the shore batteries managed a direct hit on the warship, the effect would be not dissimilar to a shot from a peashooter on the retreating back of a policeman, but that a return broadside from an irritated battleship would make the explosion in Halifax harbour in 1917 seem like a small display of fireworks. In other words, Halifax would be completely levelled and practically all its population killed. In the circumstances, I suggested the forty million dollars in gold was hardly worth it, especially as we would not get it anyway. Donald agreed to my pleading and Halifax was saved.

Sometime that summer, a delegation from the Bank of England headed by Sir Otto Neimeyer, one of the Bank's senior officers, arrived in Canada and asked for office accommodation at the Bank of Canada. This meant that many of us had to give up the offices we had been using. We did not mind this so much but all of us were curious, from Graham Towers on down, about what the Englishmen were up to. They made no move to enlighten us, and Towers remarked casually one day that if I found out he would like to know too.

Shortly after this I happened to be in New York. Walking up Fifth Avenue, I ran into one of Neimeyer's assistants looking very depressed and lonely. He greeted me effusively, and we went around the corner to the bar at the Algonquin. I ordered martinis, whispering to the barman that my companion was an Englishman who liked his on the warm side, to make his doubles, and to keep our glasses filled. It was not long before my companion confided the reason for his despondence. He had a mistress he was very fond of in Brussels and had received no word from her since the German occupation. He asked if I could help him. I said that, if we changed her status to fiancée, I could ask Sir Edward Peacock, a director of the Bank of England, if he would be willing to make the necessary inquiries. My friend was very grateful, especially later when Sir Edward reported that the girl was safe and sound.

It was then my turn to ask questions. At just the right moment in a rather liquid afternoon, I inquired what the visiting Englishmen who had acquired our offices were doing. He told me. They were making preparations in case parts of the British establishment, including the Bank of England, were forced to flee to Canada. There was really nothing secret about this but my friend said that Neimeyer and his colleagues were reluctant to speak about such an embarrassing possibility. And in any event they assumed we knew what they were up to. When I got back to Ottawa, I passed this information on to Towers, and everyone seemed pleased that no longer was there any need for secrecy or silence.

On several occasions during the fall of 1940, I called in to see the Honourable J. L. Ilsley, the Minister of Finance, whom I had first met when he was a young opposition member on the Stevens Committee. The Department of Finance was planning for a federal-provincial conference to be held early in 1941, at which it was expected to obtain approval from the provinces of the recommendations of the Rowell-Sirois Commission. I informed Ilsley that from all I heard in Toronto, Mitch Hepburn, Premier of Ontario, would never agree to the Rowell-Sirois proposals. Hepburn hated Mackenzie King and was preparing to frustrate the federal government at the conference. In the circumstances, I urged that the conference should be called off – unpopular advice which was not heeded.

I was very considerably surprised, therefore, when Ilsley telephoned me in late November or early December and invited me to join the Department of Finance in a temporary wartime capacity. He said they had some eminent academics on the staff but needed someone with some practical experience in business. I agreed to go to Ottawa to discuss the matter with him and with Dr. W. C. Clark, the highly influential Deputy Minister who would be my boss.

I had a long talk with Dr. Clark next day at luncheon, during the course of which I told him frankly that I had some reservations about serving under him because in the business circles I worked in he was considered to be extremely left-wing and socialist in his thinking. I can laugh now about this *naïveté* on my part in talking to one of the greatest civil servants Canada has ever had. Some twenty-five years later the same sort of things were being said about myself – again in the business circles I was accustomed to move about in.

Clark assured me he was not a socialist. I was impressed, however, with the progressiveness of his thinking and with his conviction that after the war a great deal should be done to alleviate the plight of the less fortunate in our society. I soon became a convert to this philosophy if I was not one already. Clark impressed me also with his firm belief that Canada must make a maximum effort in the war with Hitler. There was no question of his patriotism or of his dedication to the Allied cause. After this conversation, during which Clark had treated my questioning more than generously, I told Ilsley I would be honoured to serve in his department as a Special Assistant to the Deputy Minister.

Clifford Clark was the dominating genius of the department and, in fact, of wartime Ottawa. He was always interested in any new idea and generated more of them himself than the rest of us put together. Intellectually speaking, he was the most exciting man I have ever worked with. And his contributions in terms of proposals for social security legislation – family allowances, old age pensions, hospital insurance, and so on – have made a lasting impression on this country.

In the early 1950s, five of us in Toronto – Henry Borden, President of Brazilian Light and Power; Edgar Burton, President of Simpsons; Bill Harris of Harris & Partners; Jim Stewart, President of the Canadian Bank of Commerce; and myself – began what we hoped would become a practice of giving a formal dinner in Toronto once a year in honour of some public servant who we thought had made a major contribution to the development of Canada. Graham Towers of the Bank of Canada, Dick Hearn of Ontario Hydro, and W. A. Mackintosh, who had served in Ottawa, during the war were guests at successive dinners which most of the leading businessmen in Toronto and vicinity attended.

We were most anxious that Clifford Clark should be included in this number and I was despatched to Ottawa to discuss the matter with him. As I might have expected, Clark's reaction was quite automatic. He said that it had been his privilege to assist various ministers and prime ministers in the formulation and implementation of a variety of policies. He went on to say that as a civil servant he could not accept credit or other form of public recognition for his services. He thought civil servants should remain anonymous and that credit for successful policies should always be accorded the public's elected representatives – sentiments with which later on I was to wholeheartedly agree.

I pointed out to Clark that ours were private dinners to which no publicity was given. I said the idea was to give the business community an opportunity of thanking a few people who had rendered outstanding service to their country. I suggested that he think of the dinner as the businessmen's equivalent of the academics' honorary degree. Clark promised to think the matter over but I was not too hopeful that he would change his mind. Accordingly, I consulted his old friend, Bill Mackintosh, who by this time was back at Queen's University. Mackintosh remarked on Clark's strong feelings about the role of civil servants under our system of government and said he doubted if he would change his mind about the invitation unless he was pressed to do so by his minister. Douglas Abbott was then Minister of Finance and I talked things over with him. In his always generous and easy way, Abbott said that of course Clark should accept our invitation to the dinner and volunteered to urge him to do so. This he did and Clark agreed to come to Toronto immediately following a visit he was planning to Chicago. The dinner was arranged, and to the best of our ability we planned a great tribute to the man who, in the opinion of many of us, had in his own way contributed more than any other to the effort Canada had put forward in the war. But, tragically, Clark, who had been in poor health for some time, died suddenly just a few days before the dinner was to be held. He was sixty-three.

Mackintosh told me later that Clark had been very pleased and excited about being invited to a dinner by the business community which at one time had been so hostile to him and his ideas. He had spoken to Mackintosh several times about this and had spent many hours working on the speech he planned to make. I hope some day someone writes a complete biography of this extraordinary man.

Clark and Towers were a most impressive team which had great influence on successive governments. They were opposites in almost everything except that they shared a progressive view of things. Clark was hopeless at organization, planning ahead, and the delegation of authority. In the department, he often asked two or three men, all of whom were overworked, to take on some new assignment, each one thinking it was his sole responsibilty. Towers, as I have mentioned, was not only a very able central banker but also one of the best organizers I have ever come across. Clark was highly imaginative and continually bursting forth with new ideas. It was Towers' job to persuade him to discard those that were quite preposterous. Clark had a deep and abiding respect for the position of elected representatives of the people, especially ministers of the Crown to whom he was responsible. Towers always managed to keep under tight control any private adulation he may have felt for politicians. The personal interests and social habits of these two men were very different. Towers was always punctual; Clark, just the opposite. Often they seemed to irritate one another almost beyond endurance. But their deep respect for each other's abilities and talents never seriously wavered. As a team, there was no one who could touch them.

The second man in the Department of Finance when I joined it, not counting the minister himself, whom we all admired, was W.A. Mackintosh, Clark's old friend from Queen's University who had been persuaded to come to Ottawa soon after the war began. Bill Mackintosh was Canada's most respected economist. Moreover, he had a judicious disposition, had good judgement, and never got excited. He was, therefore, the ideal foil for Clark. Moreover, Mackintosh has always been a wonderful *raconteur* with a delicious sense of humour. Like me, he was labelled a Special Assistant to the Deputy Minister.

In addition to Clark, Mackintosh, and myself, there were two others on the policy side of things who should be mentioned. Robert Bryce, a brilliant graduate from the Universities of Toronto, Cambridge, and Harvard, who was always bubbling with ideas, and John Deutsch, later Principal of his old college, Queen's University. Some time later, Mitchell Sharp was to join the department. He left it after a few years to become Associate Deputy Minister of Trade and Commerce.

Clark had not given me a very clear idea before I joined the department of the work I would be called upon to do. He had talked vaguely about better liaison with the defence department and one or two other things but it was clear he had not thought much about it. From his point of view, there were endless things that needed doing, and a new body around the place might help to reduce the backlog.

Clark was away when I arrived in Ottawa to start work with the department. However, he had left me a long memorandum of instructions. He had gone to Washington for a series of discussions with the officials of the U.S. Treasury and required a great deal of information about the state of Canada's exchange reserves, balance of payments, external trade, details of wheat production, industrial capacity, liquid assets held by Canadians abroad, the budgetary position of the federal and provincial governments, what this might be like given an increase in defence expenditures, and a host of other questions. In those days, much of the information Clark was asking a brand-new member of his staff to obtain was simply not available, certainly not with any accuracy. It was only shortly before this that the Dominion Bureau of Statistics had published a first tentative attempt at depicting our balance-of-payments position. Fortunately, I had seen a copy of this publication. Otherwise, I might not have known even what the phrase "balance of payments" stood for.

Clark gave me twenty-four hours to provide him with the information he would need in Washington. As an afterthought, he noted that he had arranged for me to have an office and a secretary. It developed that the office had no telephone or buzzer system, and the secretary, a nice pleasant girl, had been doing bookkeeping work for so long that she had forgotten how to take shorthand and was a bit shaky with her typing. But I presumed that Clark had intended to be helpful.

I decided the only thing to do was to call on the Bank of Canada for assistance and proceeded to discuss the matter with Graham Towers and Donald Gordon. After expostulating about Clark's way of doing things and saying it would be quite impossible to get the information asked for in a week, let alone twenty-four hours, we all got down to business. Towers and Gordon supplied me with an office, telephone, secretary, and for practical purposes all the resources of the Bank of Canada. Twenty-four hours later, practically all the information had been collected, and I was about to telephone Clark in Washington when Donald Gordon burst into the room. He said I must remind Clark of our oaths of secrecy and that the conversation would be monitored.

When I got Clark on the line, his only interest was whether I had all the information he had asked for. I replied that, while I had it, I was doubtful of the accuracy of many of the statistics. This did not seem to trouble him any more than my warning that the call would be listened in on. Clark's reply to this intelligence was to instruct me to disguise my voice and to hurry up and give him the information. It took about half an hour to do this, and the job was not made easier by the fact that both Clark and I were talking out of the sides of our mouths like a couple of Chicago gangsters, presumably to confuse anyone who was listening to our conversation. Whoever was doing so must have gained a peculiar impression of the behaviour of two officials of His Majesty's Government in Canada.

Clark returned from Washington a few days before the federal-provincial conference on the Rowell-Sirois Commission's proposals. He told me enthusiastically that he expected this would be a highly significant event in the history of our country and invited me to sit in on the proceedings. I thanked him but declined the invitation on the grounds that I did not wish to waste the time. Clark had given me an immense amount of work to do and I expected the conference to be broken up by Mitch Hepburn before the second day was over. Clark was furious at my attitude and assured me the conference could not be allowed to fail.

But sure enough, on the second day, Hepburn made it clear he would have nothing to do with the federal government's proposals based on the Rowell-Sirois Report and the conference broke up in confusion. This left a shambles of the government's – or, more specifically, of the finance department's – plans for financing the war effort. To most people in Ottawa the plan had seemed so eminently sensible.

Clark, who was both depressed and angry, looked into my office briefly and suggested that, as I had been so smart in predicting the failure of the conference, I could take on the job of finding an alternative solution to the problem of financing the war effort. He left abruptly and I had no way of knowing if he were serious. I thought it best to assume he had been and immediately pushed all other work aside.

Two or three days later, I went to see Clark and said I thought there might be a solution to the problem; not one that would accomplish the social objectives of the Rowell-Sirois Commission, but it was at least a method of financing the wartime budgets. Clark, who was not a man to bear grudges as he might have done over my failure to attend the conference and who was always fascinated with any new idea, dropped what he was doing and asked me to explain in some detail what I had in mind.

My premises were that, as long as Hepburn was around, we should not expect co-operation from the provincial governments; that, however, a large majority of the people in English-speaking Canada was behind the federal government in the war effort and probably was prepared to accept some of the burden this implied; that if this public support was to be retained, the federal government must bounce back from its failure at the conference with tax proposals the provinces would have no option but to accept. I argued that the tax proposals should be confined simply to financing the war effort and not mixed up with social objectives no matter how overdue or desirable these might be. I suggested these social aims would have to be pursued after the war was over, although I acknowledged that a little something could be done to alleviate the financial difficulties of the poorer provinces in the plan I would put forward.

The plan itself was very simple. I suggested that the federal government should announce the taxes that it intended to impose, including the excess profits tax which already had been advocated. At the same time, the government should offer to enter into an agreement with any province that would give up its rights to levy taxes for the duration of the war. Provinces that agreed to do this would be paid a fixed amount each year based roughly on the amounts of their present tax revenues augmented somewhat in the case of the poorer provinces.

The federal government should make it clear that no province was being forced to enter an agreement. They were all free to go on levying their own taxes, but in that case they would not qualify for the fixed amounts to be paid by Ottawa. Moreover, the taxpayers in any province that failed to enter an agreement would be required to pay a total level of taxation that would not be bearable; the full tax rates to be levied by the federal government, plus the taxes imposed by a province that was unwilling to enter an agreement, would exceed one hundred per cent of taxable income in many cases. But I argued that would be the responsibility of the provincial government in question, not of Ottawa. It was my submission that a scheme along these lines would work and that every province would have to accept it if the federal government was firm enough. The situation would become chaotic, however, if the federal government were to get cold feet and start making special deals with individual provinces.

Clark, as was his custom, peppered me with questions, but I could see from his excitement that he thought this might be the answer to our problem. He asked Bill Mackintosh to join us and we went through the proposal with him again. Then we called on Mr. Ilsley, and after much discussion he agreed to lay the plan before the cabinet. A small cabinet committee was set up to go into it in detail, one of whose members was the Honourable P.J.A. Cardin of Sorel, an intelligent man of considerable toughness. I remember him saying when the proposal was explained to him, "Young man, I like your plan. It would be like playing poker with the provinces, but this time the federal government would have all the aces. I think a plan like this would work. But we in Ottawa must not waver. It will work but only if we remember that the strength is on our side."

That was the essence of the wartime tax agreements. The emphasis, all of it, was on the agreement angle. No mention was ever made of what might happen to any provincial government that did not go along; in other words, the alternative would in effect mean double taxation. It became my job to work out the details, and it took a year before all the provinces signed up. The last to do so was Ontario. Finally, Mitch Hepburn arrived in Ottawa to discuss the proposal, accompanied by half a dozen of his cabinet ministers and a dozen or so officials. Mr. Ilsley opened the meeting with me beside him. It took us half an hour or so to explain the proposal, laying great emphasis on the agreement angle. Mitch Hepburn, who was quick and intelligent and accustomed to use rather pungent language when he wished to shock people, listened carefully. He then walked around to me and whispered loud enough for Ilsley to overhear, in language designed to upset him, "Walter, does this mean you've got us by the — ?" I replied, also in a whisper, "Yes, Mitch, and we intend to keep on squeezing until you sign." Hepburn seemed to think this was funny. He laughed and said he would go back to the hotel as it would take his colleagues several days before the truth dawned upon them. This is more or less what happened but finally Ontario, after a good deal of expostulation, signed the agreement which was to last for the duration of the war.

When I had arrived in Ottawa to work for the Department of Finance, Clark asked me to establish a liaison or working arrangement with the Department of National Defence. In planning the financial measures that would be called for as a result of the war, it was important that we would have some vague idea of the probable build-up of the armed forces and the expenditures that would result.

I soon found that relations between the two departments, Finance and National Defence, were very poor. In fact, except for the ministers, members of the two departments were not on speaking terms. Faced with this situation, my first move was to visit the Department of National Defence in the hope that I would run into someone whom I knew. I proceeded to walk along the corridors looking at the names on the doors. The first name I recognized was that of Brigadier E.L.M. Burns who, fifteen years previously, had lectured on military engineering when I was at the Royal Military College in Kingston. I remembered Burns as a highly intelligent man who did not suffer fools gladly and sometimes gave the impression of being more sarcastic and cynical than he may have intended. I knocked on his door and walked into his office unannounced. Burns looked up from the work he was doing and said, "Hello, Gordon, what the hell are you doing here?"

I thought my best approach would be to provoke him, so I replied, "They tell me you are so badly organized at defence headquarters that not even an over-all 'appreciation of the situation' has been prepared." This phrase, much beloved in army circles, produced the reaction I had hoped for. Burns wanted to know what fool had said that. He reached into a drawer of his desk and produced a long and detailed memorandum of the department's best estimates of the war situation and how it might be expected to develop. The memorandum included suggestions respecting the desirable build-up of the Canadian forces, both in terms of numbers and in timing. This was exactly the kind of information the finance department needed. While I was not allowed to take a copy with me, as it was top secret, I was permitted to read it, which was all that was necessary at that preliminary stage.

After a good talk, Brigadier Burns took me around to meet the senior people in the department, during the course of which one of them asked me if anything could be done to expedite approval of a request for some $10 million of ammunition that was urgently needed for training purposes. I promised to look into it, and a full-dress meeting was called to discuss the matter a few days later under the chairmanship of Major-General Kenneth Stewart himself. This was impressive as Stewart was then Chief of the General Staff. He had with him at the meeting about a dozen assorted generals and colonels and one major who looked uncomfortably junior. I informed this galaxy of senior officers that, in checking the submission, officials of the Treasury Board – which at that time was a branch of the Department of Finance – had, horror of horrors, discovered an error in arithmetic. After two days' hard work, I was convinced that it would take weeks, if not longer, to straighten out this foul-up to the satisfaction of the bureaucracy. In the meantime I acknowledged that the training of certain regiments was being held up and proposed a somewhat unorthodox solution of the difficulty. I suggested that the original submission for ten million dollars' worth of ammunition should be forgotten; that, instead, the defence department should prepare a new submission for a new amount, say $9 million, making sure that this time the elementary arithmetic was accurate. I promised that, if they would give me the new submission before I left the building, I would have it approved by the Minister of Finance that afternoon. Mr. Ilsley agreed to this on my promise that, if he did so, relations between the defence and finance departments would be re-established on a cordial basis.

This was the time when the government was struggling with the first really big wartime budget. The amounts requested by the military were very large by any peacetime precedents. It was, of course, impossible to arrive at accurate estimates of what the Armed Services would, in fact, be able to spend, but the only minister who saw this clearly was Chubby Power, the Minister of National Defence for Air. I remember him telling Ilsley one evening that he would set his budget at any figure the Department of Finance might wish but that in practice he would enlist and train as many air crew and acquire as many aircraft as it was physically possible to do. He suggested the bookkeepers could tidy up after the war was over.

This kind of approach was highly disturbing to the orthodox. Moreover, when the final estimates were put together, accurate or inaccurate as they might turn out to be, the total proved most upsetting to the Prime Minister. Clark invited me to accompany him to a cabinet meeting at which the wartime budget was to be reviewed. It was my first experience before this august body, and my main impression was the reluctance of all the ministers to say anything in opposition to the Prime Minister, Mackenzie King. I was asked a question or two and soon found myself in the position of defending the budget proposals, much to the displeasure of the Prime Minister. In the end, he turned to Dr. Clark, who in a sense was the most respected man in Ottawa, and asked him whether in his opinion the proposed wartime budget was within the economic competence of the nation. Placed on the spot in this way, Clark did not hesitate for a moment. He replied, "Yes, Mr. Prime Minister, I think we can do it." That was that. The first big wartime budget was approved.

It was some time during 1941 that Dr. O.D. Skelton, Under Secretary of State for External Affairs and Mr. King's chief personal adviser, died of a heart attack. Skelton, also a Queen's man, was a great friend of both Clark's and Mackintosh's. Mr. King had persuaded him to go to Ottawa in the late 1920s to organize the Department of External Affairs, and the two men had always been very close in their relations. The immediate question on Skelton's death was who was going to succeed him, both as deputy head of the department and as Mr. King's most intimate adviser.

Hume Wrong was second in seniority to Dr. Skelton in the department. Mike Pearson was third but at the time was serving in London under Vincent Massey, the High Commissioner. It seemed unlikely that Mr. King would choose Wrong to take Dr. Skelton's place. And there may have been some question as to whether Mike, with his breezy cheerful manner, would be the best man to establish an intimate relationship with the lugubrious Prime Minister. Mr. King appointed Norman Robertson as Under Secretary in Skelton's place, and Pearson was ordered back to Ottawa to serve as Assistant Under Secretary under Robertson.

Everyone in Ottawa had a great deal of admiration for Norman Robertson who had made his mark as a brilliant man. He worked prodigiously hard all day and then sat up nearly all night reading everything and anything he could lay his hands on. However, Robertson was several years younger than Pearson and was junior to him in the service. Many people felt that Pearson was entitled to the top job, and in a small town like Ottawa the gossips had full play. In fact, for several weeks little seemed to be talked about except the allegedly raw deal Pearson had been served by Mr. King.

In the middle of all this, Mike returned to Ottawa and immediately accepted an invitation to speak to the Canadian Club about the bombing that was going on in London. The hall was packed and when Mike got up to speak he received a great ovation. He began by saying that, in the short time he had been home, he had heard stories about himself and his friend, Norman Robertson, and their relative claims to the job of Under Secretary. He added, "I think Norman was the right choice for the job. I shall be pleased and honoured to work under him. And I hope nothing more will be said by anyone on this subject." In those few sentences, Pearson showed everybody what a big and generous man he was.

During the summer of 1941, there was a great deal of discussion among officials in Ottawa about what could be done to contain the rising levels of prices and wages. It was felt that the Wartime Prices and Trade Board, under Hector McKinnon and Kenneth Taylor, was proceeding at too leisurely a pace and that more drastic action was needed in view of increasing dissatisfaction and complaints throughout the country. Those who felt this way included Clark and myself in the Department of Finance, and Towers, Donald Gordon, and James Coyne at the Bank of Canada. In addition, we enlisted the support of Arnold Heeney, the Clerk of the Privy Council and Secretary of the War Committee of the cabinet. Heeney, who had come to Ottawa originally in 1938 to serve as Mr. King's principal secretary, commanded the respect of everyone and in an inobtrusive manner produced cabinet minutes that were both concise and clear. These minutes were of great importance as, in effect, they became the directives to the various departments and agencies directly responsible for Canada's war effort.

Another intriguing character in the East Block at this time was Jack Pickersgill who had succeeded Heeney as private secretary to Mr. King. I encountered him in the corridor outside the Prime Minister's office one day simply dancing with delight. He said Mr. King had asked him to draft two speeches, the first coming down in favour of a ceiling on prices and wages, the second coming out against this proposition. Pickersgill had just left the Prime Minister who had complimented him on these drafts. In fact, Mr. King had said they were so good that he intended to use them both. I suggested that such a course might prove confusing to the public, to which Jack replied that this was what made it all so funny. However, he assured me that when the time came Mr. King would make one speech and that it would be in favour of the price-and-wage ceiling we had been advocating.

The plan that was being considered contemplated an immediate freeze of prices and wages on the understanding that the ceiling would be pierced whenever individual pressures became too strong. This was in marked contrast with the practice of the existing board which was tackling wages and prices on an industry-by-industry basis. Inevitably, by the time they finished with one industry, the situation in all of the others had got far out of line. The new approach was intended as a way of holding things until the board was able to deal with individual situations. However, this was not the policy that was finally adopted. Donald Gordon, who became Chairman of the Wartime Prices and Trade Board, favoured a much tighter system of control. Under his administration, wages and prices were frozen and every conceivable effort made to withstand pressures for adjustment. This policy worked for a time, but when the war ended it was impossible to hold back the pressures any longer. The whole machinery of the board had to be dismantled in a hurry, and very substantial increases in both prices and wages followed. Whether our original proposal of allowing prices and wages to increase gradually would have been preferable and whether it could have been made to work in practice are still matters of debate.

In view of my interest, Donald Gordon invited me to become a director of the Wartime Prices and Trade Board as the representative of the Department of Finance, and I served in this capacity until the spring of 1942. By that time, I was becoming increasingly incapacitated with the gout. Partly on this account and partly because much of the work I had been engaged on in the Department of Finance, including the completion of the tax-sharing agreements with the provinces, was coming to an end, it was decided I should return to Toronto. I did so and recruited a considerable staff for J.D. Woods and Gordon Limited, whose whole organization was then made available to the Wartime Prices and Trade Board on a nonprofit basis. For the next year or so, the Woods Gordon firm made a variety of investigations on the board's behalf.

Some time during the summer of 1944, the Department of Finance began to consider the kind of tax reductions that would be called for at the conclusion of the war. Taxes on corporations had been increased from sixteen per cent before the war to a minimum of forty per cent plus a one hundred per cent tax on "excess profits." Personal income taxes had been increased sharply and at that time were much higher than comparable taxes in the United States.

Clark contended that the greatest emphasis after the war should be on a reduction in corporation income taxes while others, myself included, felt that a major reduction in the rates of personal income tax was called for as well as the immediate discontinuance of the maximum rates under the Corporations Excess Profits Tax Act which did not produce much revenue. While I was no longer an official of the finance department, I nevertheless asked Clark if he would have any objection if I started a public debate on this whole subject. Clark, who was always a dedicated democrat and a firm believer in debate, replied that he thought this might be useful. I decided that the best way of going about this would be to begin by writing an article dealing with the subject for publication in a professional journal. The article, which was entitled "Post-War Taxation," was published in the December 1944 issue of *The Canadian Chartered Accountant*. The specific proposals I put forward were that:

(a) The maximum rates under the Corporations Excess Profits Tax Act should be abolished. This would reduce government revenues by an estimated $ 50 million

(b) The rate of corporation income tax should be reduced from 40 to 30%. This would have the effect of reducing government revenues by about $160 million

(c) Personal income taxes should be reduced dramatically with a consequent reduction in government revenues estimated at $350 million

These proposals would reduce government revenues by somewhat more than 20%. Based on the year 1944-45, the reduction in revenues would amount to about $560 million

This article received a great deal of attention in the public press. In addition, I wrote letters to the heads of all the large business and financial institutions in the country and to many other influential people enclosing copies of the article and asking for their views on whether the emphasis in post-war tax reduction should be on the personal or corporation income-tax rates. I received replies from several hundreds of my correspondents who overwhelmingly supported the thesis that the emphasis should be on a reduction in personal rates. This feeling was given considerable publicity, especially as many leading businessmen took up the issue and made speeches about it.

In the result, Clifford Clark and his officials in the Department of Finance modified their views, and when the time came placed the emphasis in post-war tax reductions on the personal rates. My campaign had been far more successful than I had ever dreamed.

There was a sequel to my work in the Department of Finance and the friends I had made there. In February 1946, Liz and I were spending the weekend with Alida and Craufurd Martin, two close friends, outside of Hamilton, when I received a telephone call from Ottawa. Clifford Clark was on the line and informed me that a Royal Commission was to be established to sort out some of the overlappings which had developed in the civil service, and at the same time to settle a scale of salaries for the administrative members of the service. He said one of the members of the commission would be Major General E. deB. Panet, an old friend of one of my uncles and a man I much admired. Another was to be a senior member of the British Civil Service. John Deutsch was to be the secretary. Clark went on to say that the Prime Minister would like me to serve as chairman. As Mr. King barely knew of my existence, I took this last remark with several grains of salt.

I explained to Clark that the firm was having a great deal of difficulty in reorganizing after the war and that personally I had taken on more work than I could handle. Under the circumstances I said that while I appreciated the compliment I was afraid I could not serve either as chairman or as a member of the commission. At this point Clark became noticeably distressed, and I began to suspect what had actually happened. I asked him if I was right in assuming that he had chosen a friendly ex-member of his department to set salaries, his own included, and then proceeded to have the Order-in-Council signed without thinking to inquire whether I could take on the appointment. In fairness to Clark, he was always extremely modest in his opinion, not only about what his own salary should be but about what it was appropriate to pay other senior members of the civil service. However, the rest of my interpretation was not far off the mark.

When Clark admitted this, I agreed to take on the job on the understanding that I would not be able to spend my full time on it, and that I would so contrive things as to complete the work within a relatively few months. This turned out to be possible because General Panet and Sir Thomas Gardiner, the senior British civil servant, spent their whole time on the work, with the result that we managed to complete our report by the end of June. In it, we pointed out the overlapping responsibilities of the Civil Service Commission and the Treasury Board, and submitted proposals for correcting what was the basic weakness in the control of the civil service. We also made recommendations respecting the salary scales of the senior civil servants.

Quite apart from its recommendations – very few of which, apart from the salary scales, were implemented – there were three things about the Royal Commission on Administrative Classifications in the Public Service which made it unique in its way. These were: first, the commission's report of some twenty-eight printed pages is one of the shortest Royal Commission reports on record; second, the commissioners spent approximately three months on their assignment, which again is probably the shortest amount of time spent by any Royal Commission on any assignment; and, third, the total cost of the commission amounted to $14,996.91, which yet again must have made it the cheapest or one of the cheapest of all Royal Commissions in the history of this country.

The principles, proposed by the Royal Commission on Administrative Classifications in the Public Service (only Clifford Clark could have dreamed up a name like that), as summarized above, were not very different from the much more exhaustive proposals made by Grant Glassco's Royal Commission on Government Organization some fifteen years later. The Glassco commission took two-and-one-half years to complete its work at a cost of $2,791,915.00. And most of its recommendations have been endorsed by successive governments and are in the process of being implemented. There must be a moral in this somewhere!

The submission of the report of this Royal Commission brought to an end the first phase of a long experience in Ottawa. For almost twenty years, I had been engaged either on investigations for successive federal governments or, during the war, in working with the Bank of Canada and the Department of Finance in the formulation and implementation of public policies. In the course of this experience and that gained as a professional practitioner dealing with government departments, I had acquired some knowledge of "the system" and of the personalities in the higher reaches of the civil service. I had worked closely with some of the senior officials and had acquired a high regard for them. I am thinking above all of Clifford Clark – but also of men like Graham Towers, Donald Gordon, Louis Rasminsky, Bill Mackintosh, Bob Bryce, Mike Pearson, Norman Robertson and Arnold Heeney. I was to continue to see all of these men in the years to come, and many of them have remained close friends. But from that time forward, my associations with Ottawa were to be somewhat different. In the future, my work there was to bring me more in contact with politicians and the political side of things than hitherto had been the case.

CHAPTER THREE

The St. Laurent
Government

Pearson's entry into politics; reorganization of the Department of National Defence; work for Mr. St. Laurent; Pearson under attack; invitation to join Mr. St. Laurent's government; a visit to the Far East.

I did not have anything to do with Louis St. Laurent during the war years although, like most people who were in Ottawa at the time, I gathered the impression that he was a very competent and able man. It was generally known that he had come to Ottawa as Minister of Justice and as leader of the federal Liberal Party in Quebec only to do a wartime job and out of a strong sense of duty. He made it clear to everyone that he intended to return to his law practice as soon as the war was over.

But it was inevitable that Mr. St. Laurent would be urged to stay on in Ottawa, and it was not long before rumours began to circulate that he would be the ideal man to succeed Mr. King as Prime Minister. This feeling was held by many people not only in Ottawa but throughout the country as well. I was one of those who felt this way, and on a visit to Ottawa in the fall of 1947 rather hesitatingly knocked on Mr. St. Laurent's office door in the Parliament Buildings and asked if he could spare me a few minutes. This he did with his usual graceful charm, and I remember telling him that as a relatively young man, in those days, from Ontario I felt it would be a wonderful thing for Canada if he, a French Canadian, were to become Prime Minister. He was non-committal, but I left with the feeling he could be persuaded to become a candidate.

This is what happened, and it became a foregone conclusion that when the leadership convention was called he would defeat his only two opponents, Jimmy Gardiner, the Minister of Agriculture, and Chubby Power. Probably there were some businessmen who thought the next leader should have been C. D. Howe, but I doubt whether he had any substantial support of this kind within the party. In any event, Howe did not become a candidate.

I received an invitation from my friend Duncan MacTavish, who was President of the National Liberal Federation at the time, to attend the convention as a guest. As I had such a strong feeling for Mr. St. Laurent and about the importance of his becoming Prime Minister, I decided to accept this invitation and set off for Ottawa. I did so with some misgiving, partly because at that time I did not wish to take any part in politics or even to be formally identified with a political party. I did not know the active members of the party and thought I might have rather a dull time on my own. But as I walked through the door of the Coliseum, I recognized the back of the man just ahead of me who, like me, was by himself. It was Bill Mackintosh, and we joined forces for the duration of the convention. We had an entertaining time commenting on the speeches and especially in telling each other how much more succinctly Mr. King could have made his several points.

I continued to see a good deal of Mike Pearson whenever we had a chance to get together. I had invited him, in January 1948, to be the guest of honour at the annual dinner of the Toronto Board of Trade of which I was the President. Later in that year, shortly after Mr. St. Laurent was elected leader of the Liberal Party but before he succeeded Mr. King as Prime Minister, Mike called to say something had turned up on which he wanted my advice. He made it clear that the matter was both urgent and highly confidential. He said he would be in Toronto the next day and suggested we have lunch together at the Old Mill where we were unlikely to be noticed.

After a stint as Ambassador to Washington, Pearson had succeeded Norman Robertson as Under Secretary, and Robertson had gone to London as High Commissioner. It was at this time that Mr. St. Laurent had become Secretary of State for External Affairs, and Pearson had established a very close relationship with him.

When we met for luncheon, Mike, who was then just over fifty, said that Mr. King had been intimating for some time that he thought he, Pearson, should consider entering politics, and had hinted that if he did so he might qualify some day for the top position. Pearson never trusted Mr. King and told me he would not serve under him. However, he said Mr. St. Laurent had now invited him to become Secretary of State for External Affairs when he, St. Laurent, became Prime Minister. Mike asked me what I thought he should do, pointing out he had no money to fall back on if he left the security of the civil service, and if later he or the Liberal Party were defeated. He said that he did not worry about that sort of thing himself, he could always go back to teaching if he had to, but that his wife, Maryon, was apprehensive.

Pearson also asked whether I thought he could be tough enough for a life in politics, pointing out that in his present occupation everyone seemed to like him; he had hosts of friends and, as far as he knew, no enemies. He was worried about how he might measure up in rougher circumstances. We had a long discussion, primarily about Mike's thoughts about the dangerous world situation and his hopes for NATO which both he and Mr. St. Laurent had been promoting hard in public speeches. I told him frankly that I doubted whether as a civil servant he could expect to get away much longer with making speeches advocating public policy as he had been doing on the NATO issue. I suggested that if he felt as strongly as he obviously did about this or other foreign policy issues then his proper course was to accept Mr. St. Laurent's offer and speak as a member of the government.

I said I did not know how he would react under the kind of pressures one must expect in public life. While his wit and charm and friendliness would be great assets in any occupation, only he could guess how he would get along under attack, an experience he had not so far encountered. We were good friends as this conversation witnessed, but our temperaments and experience were very different. That, I suppose, was why Pearson sought my opinion on what was for him a vitally important question.

The matter was settled very shortly after our luncheon meeting, with Mike keeping me posted on developments almost daily. He knew nothing about the elementary mechanics of politics, and I doubt if, at that time, Mr. St. Laurent knew much more than he did. But to Mr. King, the master in that field, the transferral of a popular and by this time quite well-known figure like Mike Pearson from the civil service to the House of Commons was a very simple matter. Mike called me one evening to say that Mr. King's idea was to appoint Tom Farquhar, the Member for Algoma East, to the Senate, and have Pearson elected there in a by-election. I do not believe that either of us knew where Algoma East was. Mike said it was somewhere in Northern Ontario. And both of us may have wondered whether an easily accessible urban seat might not have been more appropriate for this sophisticated diplomat. But Mr. King was quite definite. He said Algoma East was a safe Liberal seat; that Farquhar could get Pearson elected there and would do so as repayment for his senatorship; and that, once elected, Pearson would be able to hang onto the seat with a minimum of effort.

Accordingly Pearson was sworn in as Secretary of State for External Affairs on September 10, 1948, and shortly afterwards set off for Algoma East. It was not long before he began to tell us stories about what wonderful people live in that constituency, and how he was helping a young baseball player from there to get a chance in one of the major leagues, etc. He was going about the riding with Senator Farquhar or on his own, shaking hands and meeting people and obviously loving it. He was sometimes hard to get through to by telephone, and one weekend George McCullagh, the publisher of *The Globe and Mail*, tried to reach him from New York about something he thought important. McCullagh in desperation called me at "Seldom Seen," our farm near Schomberg, and in his usual colourful language proceeded to say what he thought of my friend, Mike Pearson, who was somewhere on Manitoulin Island and quite out of touch with the world and George McCullagh. McCullagh went on to give as his opinion that the wire fences in Manitoulin were used as telephone lines and that a moose or something equally large must have sat down on a fence somewhere and disrupted the service. I suggested, for the benefit of the twenty-one others on my party line, that it was more likely the wire fences in Manitoulin had been fused by McCullagh's choice of language but that I would see what could be done. I managed to catch Mike that evening while he was visiting with the customers in a poolroom at Little Current. He called McCullagh in New York and the world was saved – for that weekend anyway.

Pearson was elected in the by-election and retained the office of Secretary of State for External Affairs in Mr. St. Laurent's government for eight and a half years, during which time he became one of the world's best known and most respected public figures.

A general election was called in 1949, and one day early in the campaign when Mr. St. Laurent was in Toronto, he asked me to visit him at his hotel. Jack Pickersgill, who had stayed on as secretary to the new Prime Minister, was with him. Obviously it was he who had suggested that Mr. St. Laurent should see me. After a few preliminaries, the Prime Minister asked me if I would contest a Toronto riding and run in the election. He was very nice about it when I explained I could not accede to this request because of my position in, and my obligations to, my firm. But both of us were a bit embarrassed and slightly irritated with Jack for creating what was obviously a misunderstanding. Pickersgill, who always felt that politics was more enthralling than any other conceivable occupation, simply could not understand how anyone could possibly forgo a chance to run in an election. When, some years later, the chance came for him to do so himself, he did not hesitate.

Mike Pearson was in much demand as a speaker during the 1949 election campaign, not so much because people wanted to hear about foreign policy as because he was a "new face," had received a lot of publicity, and was always witty and good fun. He called me periodically during the campaign but respected my intention not to become identified with it myself in any way. On one occasion, he and his wife spent a night or two at "Seldom Seen" which is not far from Aurora where Mike was to attend a chicken barbecue and later speak at an evening meeting. It was a typically disorganized affair, with the chairman acting in a way that was bound to get him the sympathy of a country crowd. First, he introduced the people on the platform but overlooked several who were local dignitaries. The proceedings were stopped while this omission was pointed out and rectified. Then he could not find the flowers that were to be presented to an elderly spinster who had taught Mike at the Aurora Public School some forty years before. When the flowers were finally discovered, the chairman forgot the lady's name and inquired what it was in a whisper that everyone could hear. Finally, Mike saved the situation by capturing the flowers and presenting them to his old school-teacher with a resounding kiss. This produced great applause. As the farmer sitting behind me said to his neighbour, "Bet she ain't had many of them."

After the meeting, the local élite repaired to the house of an Aurora contractor where one could get a "shot" in the kitchen out of sight of any teetotallers who might be offended by the sight of politicians drinking alcohol. However, Pearson was soon seen sitting on the floor of the living room, drinking rye and ginger ale and entertaining everyone with his stories. The local reeve whispered to me: "He may talk 'way over the heads of ordinary people, but I think we can make something of this boy." He sounded like a boxing promoter who had discovered a promising youngster in some small gymnasium. Mike felt highly complimented as well as amused when I repeated this remark to him on the way home.

Prior to the 1949 election, I was called upon to undertake an assignment for Brooke Claxton, who had been appointed Minister of National Defence at the end of 1946. After the war, every effort had been made to demobilize the armed forces as quickly as possible. But late in 1948, Claxton was instructed to reorganize his department and to recruit and train the kind of force that might be needed for NATO in the light of the new threat from the Soviet Union. Claxton tackled the job with his usual vigour and energy. He was a close friend of mine and, while he was not as popular as Douglas Abbott, did not have C. D. Howe's great reputation in business circles, and lacked Mike Pearson's wit and charm, he was intellectually the strongest member of the government and had an infinite capacity for work.

Claxton explained his instructions to me and the reasons for them, and asked me to help him to reorganize the department. I thought it would be a mistake for me to do this, as it might be resented by members of the services if a civilian who had not been able to join the army during the war were called in to help reorganize the defence establishment. I suggested the names of one or two others for Brooke to consider in my place.

This did not seem to satisfy him, and at the end of our conversation it was agreed I would tackle the problems of reorganizing the civilian end of the department. Two weeks later, I reported that this would not work as the civilian and military sides of the department's work were so interwoven. Brooke commented that he had not expected it to work, and now would I please get on with the whole job, including the military side of things? He added that the matter was very urgent in view of the situation in Europe.

I found there was no resentment over my assignment. In fact, it was welcomed by the senior personnel in all three services, and I received full co-operation from them. They told me they were tied hand and foot by red tape and made it clear that if they were to have a chance of performing properly this would have to be cut through. As an example, a Major General in charge of one of the larger command posts was not allowed to authorize any expenditures in excess of twenty-five dollars without the specific approval of headquarters in Ottawa. A few years before, this same General, as a divisional commander in France, had authority to do things on his own initiative which involved expenditures of hundreds of thousands of dollars.

Another case which I used as an example in my report involved the various steps that had to be taken to secure approval of a maintenance project at Camp Borden for which the funds had been specifically provided in the Estimates. It required 116 days to get the contract awarded, and 152 days were spent on the paperwork involved – all this in connection with a project estimated to cost less than $7,000.

Obviously, a great deal of decentralization of authority and responsibility was needed. It was less obvious how the three services should best be organized. There were those, as far back as 1948, who argued in favour of a unified force. There were others who said this could not be accomplished quickly, even if it were thought to be desirable. Before reaching a conclusion, I decided to visit London, where I received great help from Norman Robertson, the Canadian High Commissioner, who was much respected by the senior civil servants in Britain. I gave Robertson a list of the people I wished to see, and he said my chances would depend entirely on Sir Edward Bridges who, during the war, had been Secretary of the War Committee of the cabinet and was then the senior Permanent Secretary to the Treasury and, as such, officially the head of the civil service.

Fortunately for me, Bridges became interested in my mission and arranged interviews for me with the people I was anxious to consult. I remember vividly a luncheon meeting at which Norman Robertson and I had an enlightening talk with Lord Tedder, a former history don at Oxford who had been deflected to the Air Force. Robertson had vouched for me beforehand so the conversation was frank and easy. I began by asking what would happen if the Russian Army suddenly started to march across Western Europe. The answer was there was nothing at all to stop them. Moreover, if they started any such move, they would be welcomed by the very large Communist parties in both Italy and France. Western Europe, like Eastern Europe, would then go Communist. Tedder said that of course the Russians might not know that any resistance would be minimal. Moreover, their casualties during the war had been staggering and they were not likely to be looking for new encounters. He added that if the NATO forces were built up quickly enough, and if the Marshall Plan was successful, everything might work out satisfactorily. But he left no doubt about the current danger.

I asked him what his reaction would be to the creation of a unified force in Canada under a single command. He said that this would probably be the solution sooner or later but that, in view of inter-service rivalries and the potential danger in Western Europe, it would be a mistake to try anything that could result in slowing down the rebuilding of our armed services.

I then asked him to define his position as Chairman of the Chiefs of Staff Committee. He played down its importance and implied he was just a member of the committee. He referred jokingly to Field Marshal Montgomery, the Chief of the General Staff, as not the kind of man who would take kindly to any suggestion that his position was subordinate to that of anyone else. I asked Lord Tedder whether in fact he as chairman was not often called in alone to see the Minister of Defence who, at that time, was the Right Honourable A. V. Alexander. Tedder said that usually all the Chiefs of Staff saw the minister together. Then he looked at his watch, smiled, and asked us to excuse him. He had an appointment to see the Prime Minister, alone, in fifteen minutes. I thanked him for making the point so subtly.

I saw various people in the United States also, including General Lyman L. Lemnitzer, then the head of the War College in Washington. Reaction in Washington to the idea of a unified force was very sceptical. For one thing, it was not believed that inter-service rivalries, if they were anything like those prevailing in the United States, could possibly be overcome. Moreover, it was suggested that in any foreseeable war involving Canada the Canadian forces would be expected to work and fight with their American and British allies. In these circumstances, it was the feeling that Canada's forces should be organized on much the same lines as the British and American.

I presented my report to Brooke Claxton shortly after returning from

Washington and London. Among other things, the importance of appointing a deputy minister who would be an *ex-officio* member of the Chiefs of Staff Committee and accepted as the equal of the service chiefs by all concerned was recommended. This meant finding a relatively young man who had done well and attained high rank in the war who was capable of integrating the civilian and military activities of the department and able to dispose of unbelievable amounts of red tape that had the department tied up in knots of frustrated indignation.

Claxton accepted my advice and the department was reorganized along the lines suggested. As Deputy Minister, he selected Bud Drury from the Department of External Affairs who, during the war, had become a Brigadier General. Lieutenant General Charles Foulkes was Chairman of the Chiefs of Staff Committee. Between Claxton, Foulkes, and Drury, Canada's armed forces and the Department of National Defence were reorganized and rebuilt in record time.

I saw Prime Minister St. Laurent on a number of occasions during the early 1950s and did a number of jobs for him. At the beginning of 1954, he asked me to revise and bring up to date the salaries of all the senior civil servants. This was not to be done as a Royal Commissioner, as was the case in 1946, but as a private individual giving personal advice to the Prime Minister. It meant, however, spending the best part of three months in Ottawa during which time I talked privately with every senior civil servant and reviewed with him the duties and responsibilities of his department or agency. For those three months, I seemed to be the most popular man in Ottawa.

On another occasion, late in 1954, Leslie Frost, the Premier of Ontario, asked if I would examine the then-existing, federal-provincial fiscal arrangements on behalf of himself and Mr. St. Laurent jointly. Mr. St. Laurent, who got along well with Mr. Frost, subscribed to this request, and with considerable misgiving I agreed to look into the matter for them. Before I got very far, however, I decided the arrangement would not work. I felt I should be responsible to the federal or to the Ontario government but not to both. I explained the matter to Mr. St. Laurent and Mr. Frost, and they agreed that I could not serve two masters. Leslie Frost added that if I could bring some new thinking to the Ottawa approach to the matter he would be quite satisfied. I then suggested to Mr. St. Laurent that it would be best if I were to work on behalf of Walter Harris, the Minister of Finance, rather than directly for the Prime Minister. This was arranged, and for several months a number of us from the Clarkson firm did our best to find a solution that would be acceptable both to the federal and to the provincial governments. I enjoyed working with Walter Harris, whom I like personally and for whom I have considerable respect. Having arrived at a formula which I hoped would be acceptable, I presented the conclusions to him and to Mr. St. Laurent. They seemed satisfied but some of their officials began to tinker with the plan put forward with, as I thought, no noticeable improvements.

Mike Pearson was proving to be an outstanding success as foreign minister. Everybody liked him and he was in great demand as a speaker, especially to non-partisan gatherings. His big test came in the fall of 1956 over the invasion of Egypt by British, French, and Israeli forces – the Suez crisis. An emergency session of the General Assembly of the United Nations was called on November 1. Two days later, it approved a suggestion by Pearson of an international police force to supervise a cease-fire. Not only was this Pearson's own idea, but it was his leadership and his negotiating skill that were required to get the necessary approval. Pearson's efforts and accomplishment were generally acknowledged and acclaimed throughout the world and resulted in his being awarded the Nobel Peace Prize in the following year. But he was violently attacked and never quite forgiven by the extreme pro-British element in Canada. In Ottawa, the Honourable W. Earl Rowe, acting leader of the opposition, said, "Let not the government believe it can any longer deceive the Canadian people by creating a fancy halo around the Secretary of State for External Affairs, as if he had already saved the world's peace and solved the Suez crisis." Howard Green, who was later to become Secretary of State for External Affairs in Mr. Diefenbaker's government, was even more bitter: "It is high time Canada had a government which will not knife Canada's best friends in the back." But despite such criticisms, this was the greatest personal triumph in Mike Pearson's long career in public life.

A few months after the resolution of the Suez crisis, a U.S. Senate committee revived old charges that Herbert Norman, the Canadian Ambassador in Cairo and an old friend of Pearson's, was a Communist. Pearson defended Norman in the House of Commons but the attacks continued. This was too much for Norman, a highly sensitive man, who committed suicide by jumping from the roof of his hotel in Cairo. This tragedy did not stop the attacks and Pearson continued to defend his friend even when his enemies – and he had made enemies over the Suez affair – used this to slander him.

I was reminded of our conversation at the Old Mill in 1948, when Mike had asked me if I thought he would be tough enough for a role in public life. He had proved himself tough enough over Suez. And I for one admired the way he had stood up for his friend Norman without regard for any damage this might do himself. It reminded me of his speech to the

Canadian Club in Ottawa in 1941 when Norman Robertson was chosen to be Under Secretary. I was to be reminded again of this sometimes unexpected strength in Pearson's complex character when he settled down after the calamitous defeat in the 1958 election to rebuild the Liberal Party.

Some important changes in the cabinet occurred before the 1953 election, at which time Mr. St. Laurent was seventy-one years old. He is said to have offered to step down in favour of Douglas Abbott if the latter would become Prime Minister. But Abbott did not have such ambitions and was well satisfied to be appointed to the Supreme Court of Canada. Lionel Chevrier became Chairman of the newly created St. Lawrence Seaway Authority, and Brooke Claxton was appointed Vice-President and the Canadian head of the Metropolitan Life Assurance Company for whom he had acted as solicitor before going into politics. Despite Abbott's popularity, it was generally recognized that the biggest loss to the government was Claxton who took with him his drive and toughness. He was a true liberal in all senses of the term and a firm and generous friend.

My relationships with Mr. St. Laurent had always been warm and friendly. One day in the late spring of 1954, he asked me to come and see him. I guessed what he might have in mind and decided to have a talk with Mike Pearson beforehand. He agreed that Mr. St. Laurent might be about to ask me to join the government, and he seemed to agree also with my reservations about doing so. The Liberals had been in power since 1935 and the government was showing signs of getting old and tired. I felt it was becoming increasingly cautious, increasingly disinclined to re-examine its own policies or to subscribe to new ones. Mr. St. Laurent was seventy-two, Mr. Howe was sixty-eight, and the departures of Abbott, Claxton, and Chevrier had been severe blows. I presumed it was hoped I might be able to fill one of these holes, at least to some extent, but as I pointed out to Pearson it would mean giving up a great deal. Ours was the largest professional firm in Canada, and my own practice was interesting and varied. I did not want to give this up for a junior position in a government that gave every appearance of being well set in its ways. But I did have the highest admiration for Mr. St. Laurent who I believed had done great things for Canada.

After a long discussion with Pearson, we agreed I should very seriously consider an offer to accept one of the senior portfolios, specifically finance or trade and commerce, but that I should decline anything else. Mike did not seem to think this would be in any way presumptuous on my part, only realistic. After all, he would not have joined the government himself more than five years before this except as foreign minister.

I went to see Mr. St. Laurent and, as expected, he invited me to join his government. He said they badly needed a minister from Toronto and that he personally would be very pleased if I would fill this vacancy. It was clear, and quite understandable, of course, that he did not have me in mind for one of the senior portfolios. I felt rather relieved about this, as it permitted me to decline his invitation without any doubts or reservations. Before doing so, I explained the kind of work I had been doing in the firm, my great interest in it, and my disinclination to give it up for an uncertain and possibly less interesting life in politics.

Mr. St. Laurent asked me to have a talk with Mr. Howe before finally making up my mind. I found Mr. Howe ready to receive me, and after a few preliminaries asked him what he liked about his experience in politics. He replied: "Where else could I get as big a job?" It was as simple as that. He could not seem to understand why I was hesitating. I tried to explain that I had a rather independent turn of mind, that I was my own boss more or less, and that I was uncertain what my position would be if I joined the government. I said, "If, for example, Mr. Howe, you were to bring a proposal to cabinet and as a new member I questioned it, what would your reaction be?" His reply was one of astonishment: "You'd do *what,* young man?" I had all the answer I required. Mr. Howe was not going to change, and neither was the government.

Nevertheless, it was with a real feeling of regret that I expressed my decision to Mr. St. Laurent. I could not help him or his government. It was too late for that. But I was unhappy about it nonetheless. Many years later, I tried to express in a letter to Renault St. Laurent the high respect in which I held his father:

> I have just finished reading Dale Thomson's book about your Father and cannot let the occasion pass without writing to some member of your family to say how I feel about it.
>
> While Thomson has done a workman-like job and obviously has great respect for your Father, I think he has failed to get across the tremendous impact which your Father made on so many people in this country and the inspiration he gave to us. Your Father was by far the ablest man I have known, or read about, in the public life of our country. I am not thinking only of his intelligence, of his objectivity and his business-like approach to the many problems he had to deal with, I am thinking also about the way he went about his work. It seemed to me that he was always dignified, was always well prepared and always gave the impression of being quietly confident about the views that he expressed. . . .

Being invited to join the government was heady stuff. While I had no second thoughts and no regrets about my refusal to accept, nevertheless I daresay that professional practice may have seemed a little tame in the weeks that followed. But this did not last long. In September 1954, Liz and I took off for Kyoto where I was to be the titular head of the Canadian delegation at a meeting of the Institute of Pacific Relations. Edgar McInnis, the very capable and experienced President of the Canadian Institute of International Affairs, was the real counsel to and spokesman for the Canadian group and in a considerable sense to the conference itself. Two other friends of ours, Blair Fraser, Ottawa correspondent for *Maclean's Magazine,* and Geoffrey Andrew of the University of British Columbia, were on the Canadian delegation and we saw a lot of them.

It was an interesting conference and we met a number of prominent Asians who were helpful and hospitable when we visited their countries in the weeks that followed: Hong Kong, Thailand, Cambodia, Ceylon, India. We were away for two months, the first time I had left the office for more than ten days at a stretch, except for stints in Ottawa and then I was always in touch by telephone. It was a new and fascinating experience, one that we had every intention of repeating.

On our return, I spoke to the Canadian Club of Toronto. I quoted what one of our travelling companions, Carroll Binder, a well-known American publicist and the editor of the *Minneapolis Tribune,* had to say about United States policy respecting Red China, of which he was highly critical. I went on to say: "All I can say is that, like Mr. Binder, I did not meet one person in the Far East who agreed with present United States policy. They all thought the present communist government would remain in power in China for a long time. And accordingly that present United States policy is wrong . . . The fact is – a sad fact if you will – that in the Far East at the present time, Americans are not popular and their policies are not trusted." That was in 1954.

CHAPTER FOUR

Two Public Inquiries

*The Royal Commission on Canada's Economic Prospects;
Committee on the Organization of Government in Ontario.*

For some time during the late 1940s and early 1950s, I had been worrying about the government's economic policies, and particularly the complacency with which Canadians were witnessing the sell-out of our resources and business enterprises to Americans and other enterprising foreigners. My concern about these matters increased following Mr. St. Laurent's invitation to me in 1954 to join his government and my refusal. Subconsciously, perhaps, I felt this might have been a chance for me to influence policy and opinion in this matter, though hardly in a cabinet which included C. D. Howe. In any event, early in 1955 I decided to try to start a debate about this question, as I had done ten years earlier over post-war tax policy. Accordingly, I drafted an article in which I raised questions respecting the validity of a number of our economic policies, including especially the question of selling control of our business enterprises to foreigners and the effect this could have upon Canada's independence. I concluded by advocating the creation of a Royal Commission to examine thoroughly the various issues that had been raised in the context of a forecast of the probable future growth of Canada's population and national output.

The article was to be published in the journal of the Canadian Institute of International Affairs, but before this happened it was agreed that I should ask Ken Taylor, the Deputy Minister of Finance, if this would be embarrassing to the department or to the Minister, the Honourable Walter Harris. I sent the draft article to Taylor, and after about three weeks had gone by without a reply called him on the telephone. He said he thought the suggestion of a thorough review of economic policies by a Royal Commission was a good one. He had talked it over with Mr. Harris who in turn had discussed it with the Prime Minister. He said I would be hearing from Mr. Harris.

Walter Harris called a few days later to ask if I would mind very much if the government took over my idea. He said he would like to put forward the proposal for a Royal Commission in his forthcoming budget speech but this would mean I would have to forgo the original plan of publishing the article. Naturally I agreed to this suggestion with alacrity. Instead of having to prod the government into taking action, they had been convinced by the draft article. My objective had been achieved with a minimum of effort, or so I thought.

In due course, Walter Harris made his budget speech and the proposal for a Royal Commission was well received. He then came to see me with a request from the Prime Minister that I should be the Chairman of the commission. I suggested that Graham Towers or Bill Mackintosh would be better qualified for this position but eventually agreed to take it on. The other commissioners were to be Omer Lussier of Quebec City, Dal Grauer of Vancouver, Andrew Stewart of Edmonton, and Ray Gushue of St. John's, Newfoundland.

Lussier was a forestry engineer, a Conservative in politics, but highly critical of Maurice Duplessis, the Premier of his province. Lussier was doubtful about his qualifications and thought of resigning from the commission within the first few weeks when he discovered what its scope would be. Fortunately he was persuaded not to do this. He is a highly intelligent man with a great deal of common sense and made a considerable contribution to the commission's work.

I had known Grauer for many years, first when he was a leftward-leaning professor at the University of Toronto and then as the somewhat rightwing President of the B. C. Electric Company. He held a doctorate in economics and had had a distinguished record in academic life and in business. Stewart and Gushue were respectively President of the University of Alberta and President of Memorial University in Newfoundland. They had known each other casually and Grauer and I were old friends. Apart from that, we were strangers to each other, coming as we did from different parts of the country and with different backgrounds. But we managed to get along together extremely well.

The Commission's terms of reference were purposely very broad:

To inquire into and report upon the long-term prospects of the Canadian economy, that is to say, upon the probable economic development of Canada and the problems to which such development appears likely to give rise, and without limiting the generality of the foregoing, to study and report upon:

    (a) developments in the supply of raw materials and energy sources;

    (b) the growth to be expected in the population of Canada and the changes in distribution;

    (c) prospects for growth and change in domestic and external markets for Canadian productions;

(d) trends in productivity and standards of living; and

(e) prospective requirements for industrial and social capital.

The first task was to find a secretary and director of research. I arranged to talk this over with Ken Taylor, Bob Bryce, John Deutsch, and perhaps one or two others. We all agreed it would be best to find a man from within the civil service. I said I wanted someone who was comparable to what each of them had been ten or fifteen years earlier in terms of energy and imagination. I added that it would be a great help if we could find a man who had some facility for writing clearly. Several names were suggested, but none of us felt any of them was quite good enough. I then asked what they would think of Douglas LePan, a man I did not know then except by reputation. LePan was in the diplomatic service, a poet and a writer who had mastered economics on the side. Everyone agreed he would be ideal if he could be persuaded to take the job.

LePan at that time was second in command at the Canadian Embassy in Washington, and I did not expect it would be easy to get him, even if he became interested in the undertaking. I went to see Mike Pearson about this, and more or less jokingly began by saying that when the government persuaded someone like myself to do a job for them, I thought the various departments should be prepared to help. Pearson agreed readily, no doubt thinking I had in mind finance and trade and commerce. When I said I would like to have LePan as director of research, I expected him to balk. Instead, he replied immediately that LePan would be the best possible choice and he would be glad to help me get him. After a short interval – during which LePan, as he told me later, had checked up on me as carefully as he could – he agreed to take the job and we got together to discuss it.

Altogether we spent five months planning the work in quite considerable detail and in recruiting staff. We settled on the main subjects to be covered, and decided on the various studies that should be undertaken for the commission, some by its own staff and some, we hoped, to be contributed by independent organizations. The scope of each of them was determined in advance and in considerable detail before the work was started. There were thirty-three of these studies, each of which was published separately.

In addition to the studies, the commission received some 330 separate briefs. While those submitting briefs were free to cover any points they wished, the commission wrote to most of them beforehand indicating the kind of information and opinions on which it wished to be enlightened. This added greatly to the value of the submissions and to the interest in the hearings.

The Commission recruited a research staff of twenty-four full-time and

61

fifteen part-time members, mostly from the universities. The senior members of this staff apart from Douglas LePan himself, now University Professor in the University of Toronto, were: John Davis, then a member of the staff of the Department of Trade and Commerce and later a cabinet minister; D. H. Fullerton, at that time with Harris & Partners of Toronto, now independent consultant and writer on economic issues; William C. Hood, at that time Professor of Economics at the University of Toronto, now associate Deputy Minister of Finance; and Simon Reisman, at that time a member of the staff of the Department of Finance, later to become the Deputy Minister of that department, and now an independent consultant.

The first few months spent in detail planning proved to be of great importance. Because of it everyone concerned with the work was made familiar with what the commission intended to cover, and conversely what it did not intend to do. It meant in effect that almost all the data collected and the opinions expressed in the briefs submitted at the public hearings fitted into some section of a great, predetermined blueprint. Without this detailed advance planning, it would have been quite impossible to complete the work within the self-imposed target dates which the commissioners set for themselves.

It was agreed at one of the first meetings that I would spend my full time on the work for a period of eighteen months, by which time we hoped to arrive at our conclusions. The other four commissioners agreed to meet from time to time to approve the scope of the inquiry, to attend the public hearings and later as often as necessary to hammer out the report.

The commissioners decided that in the public hearings, contrary to custom, they would ask the questions themselves and not use professional counsel. We believed that if the proceedings were kept on an informal basis in this way, and if the witnesses were not sworn, there would be more chance that the people appearing before us would speak their minds freely and without restraint. This proved to be the case, but it was hard work for Douglas LePan and the commissioners.

There was a great deal of public interest in the work of the commission and the hearings were well reported in the press. Some years earlier, the Paley Commission had attempted to forecast the future requirements of the United States for raw materials. But this was the first time that any country had attempted not only to estimate future requirements for materials but, as well, to forecast future developments on such an ambitious scale. Moreover, the public hearings of the commission provided a wonderful forum for people – or rather, for representatives of established organizations – to present their views on current topics and to suggest changes in established policies. A recurrent theme throughout the hearings was the concern felt about the acquisition by foreigners, mostly Americans, of Canadian resources and business enterprises, and the need to do something about this before it was too late. The commission heard more about this than any other single subject.

During the late summer of 1955, before we were ready to begin the public hearings, Douglas LePan and three of the commissioners, including myself, visited the Canadian Northwest. One evening in Aklavik, at the mouth of the Mackenzie River, a thousand miles north of Edmonton, we met with a large gathering of the inhabitants. Later the audience was divided into groups – whites, Indians, and Eskimos. I drew the Eskimos, and we had a good conversation with the help of one of them, a big handsome man dressed like the others in furs and caribou skins who acted as interpreter. I was afraid to ask his name for fear I would mispronounce it. But when I inquired what it was from one of the local officials, he suggested I should ask the man direct, assuring me I would have no difficulty with the pronunciation. I did so, and my new friend informed me that his name was Charles Gordon. I asked him if he knew where his father had come from. He replied that his father had been a sailor and had come from a certain town in Scotland. I told him this was the town my grandfather had come from and that in all probability we were cousins. This was greeted with great applause by all the Eskimos present who obviously had not needed the services of an interpreter.

The public hearings opened in St. John's, Newfoundland, on October 18, 1955, and with interruptions lasted until March of the following year. They were hard work as the Commissioners were scrupulous about studying every brief beforehand so that they could ask intelligent questions of the witnesses. One of the briefs was presented by the Communist Party of Canada. It was written in comparatively mild terms and obviously the strategy was to enlarge upon it during the usual question period. But the commission, also, had agreed upon its strategy beforehand. When I called for questions, my colleagues remained strangely silent. Accordingly, the proceedings were adjourned immediately and the witnesses before us lacked a forum and an opportunity for propaganda purposes. It had started to rain, and when one of them discovered this, he was heard to say, "That — Gordon has even fixed the weather for us."

The commission completed its work and agreed upon its conclusions within the eighteen months it had set for itself. It was apparent, however, that it would take some time to complete a full report. This being so, it was decided to summarize the commission's conclusions in a Preliminary Report which was dated December 3, 1956, and released to the public early in January 1957. The forecasts of population growth, of the increases in total output, and of per capita incomes, etc., opened people's eyes as to what Canada could become. And apart from everything else, these forecasts, and the publicity which had attended the commission's hearings, encouraged businessmen to think and plan ahead in a way few of them had ever done before.

Most of the commission's proposals were expressed in very general terms. Nevertheless, they provoked a great deal of attention and considerable controversy. C. D. Howe was furious. He had been away when it was decided to set up the commission and had always been opposed to the idea. Now he interpreted its findings as a criticism of policies for which he had been responsible, and to some extent this was quite true. Mr. St. Laurent was also publicly critical of the commission's report, which was unfortunate. If he and the Liberal Party had been able to accept the conclusions as a broad blueprint for the future, the defeat of the party in the forthcoming election might have been avoided. It was particularly unfortunate that the government was unwilling or unable to take immediate action on the commission's proposals for reversing the trend under which the control of so much of Canadian industry was being acquired by foreigners. A great opportunity to safeguard Canada's independence was allowed to slip by, and a few months later, in June 1957, the government went down to defeat.

The shrillest and most severe criticism of the commission came from the Maritime Provinces. The report drew attention to the lower living standards in that area. "What is required is a positive and comprehensive approach to the problem of the Atlantic region. With this as the objective, it is suggested that the people of Canada as a whole might be willing to assist the people of the Atlantic provinces in discovering, developing, and making the best use of resources in that area."

This broad generalization was supplemented by more detailed proposals, including the need for a comprehensive approach towards improving the transportation facilities of the area and the creation of a capital projects commission which, seven years later, was implemented as the Atlantic Development Fund. However, after the sentences quoted above, the report went on to say: "If it should turn out that there is not the necessary combination of resources in sufficient quantities to permit a substantial rise in living standards in the Atlantic region, generous assistance should be given to those people who might wish to move to other parts of Canada where there may be greater opportunities."

This sentence, taken out of context, was used to create a storm throughout the Maritimes. The commission's report was branded as "the second rape of the Acadians," who had been driven from the Maritimes in 1755. The commissioners, particularly the chairman, were blasted in the local papers, especially in the Fredericton *Daily Gleaner.* Angry letters were written to the papers by people who had not read the report denouncing the Royal Commissioners in particular and all Upper Canadians in general. The substance of the recommendations for improving conditions in the Atlantic provinces was lost sight of in a welter of furious indignation.

Not everyone reacted in this way, of course. Some people read the report before expressing an opinion on it. Among these were the editors of the Halifax *Chronicle-Herald,* who insisted that the commission's proposals were constructive and could be very helpful to the Maritimes. The amusing cartoon by Bob Chambers, which is reproduced here, appeared in the *Chronicle-Herald* at this time.

Report of the Royal Commission on Canada's Economic Prospects

I was curious how this criticism started and proceeded to make my own inquiries. At the request of some members of the Ottawa press corps, I had asked the government to give the press a chance to read the commission's report and prepare their stories in advance of its release. This is now regular practice and helps to ensure that important documents are accurately reported and presented to the public. But on this occasion the government refused to allow the practice and some of the newspapermen were angry. One of them, with the assistance of a member of the commission's staff, got hold of a copy of the report before the publication date. And his article was written in a way that inflamed the sensitivities of many people in the Maritimes. The damage was done, however, long before I found this out, and there was no way of undoing it. To this day, there are people in the Atlantic provinces who believe that the chairman of that Royal Commission would like to drag them and their children by the hair all the way to Upper Canada.

I returned to Toronto after the publication of the Preliminary Report, although I kept in touch with the work that was still unfinished. This included several of the studies and the preparation of the commission's Final Report which was being written by Douglas LePan. He became very ill in the spring of 1957, however, and it became necessary for me to return to Ottawa. It was soon clear that even if LePan lived – and there was considerable doubt about this for a time – he could not hope to write the whole report himself. This was a great blow not only to LePan, who had set his heart on doing this, but to all of us who recognized his brilliant mind and his unequalled talents as a writer. Fortunately, he had completed the first eight chapters which are beautifully written. They are very different in style and quality from the rest of the report, which had to be put together by myself and by some of the ex-members of the commission's staff who generously agreed to help out in the emergency.

The Final Report of the Commission was dated November 1957 but was not released to the public until April of the following year. It contained more than fifty proposals and suggestions. Many of these were reflected in the policies approved by the Rally of the Liberal Party held in January 1961 and influenced the thinking of the Liberal government that was elected in April 1963. In retrospect, it is surprising, as well as encouraging, to find how many of the Commission's suggestions have since been incorporated in legislation. The principal exception to this are the proposals respecting foreign investment. While the Commission did its best to bring the issue of Canada's economic independence before the public, successive governments have so far failed to deal with it effectively. The views of the Commissioners on this subject were prophetic:

Despite the tremendous contributions which foreign capital – and the management and technological skills and the access to markets that has come with it – has made and will continue to make to the development of our country, we do not believe Canadians will cease to be concerned about this matter unless something is done to make Canadian voices more strongly and effectively heard in some vitally important sectors of our economy in which non-residents exercise a large measure of control. In our view there are definite limits as to what should be done about this matter, and compulsion and discrimination should certainly not be countenanced. But to do nothing would be to acquiesce in seeing an increasing measure of control of the Canadian economy pass into the hands of non-residents and to run the risk that at some time in the future a disregard for Canadian aspirations will create demands for action of an extreme nature [*i.e.*, the nationalization of certain industries].

The Commission believed that the main objectives respecting foreign-capital investment in Canada should be:

First, to see a larger share of foreign capital invested in the form of bonds and mortgages, which do not involve control of large sectors of the economy; secondly, to see that the part of foreign investment which is invested in the resource and manufacturing industries is associated in some degree with Canadian capital and Canadian interests; and, thirdly, to ensure that control of the Canadian banks and other financial institutions is retained in Canada.

The following were suggested as desirable objectives for the operation of foreign-owned concerns operating in Canada:

(1) Wherever possible, such concerns should employ Canadians in senior management and technical positions, should retain Canadian engineering and other professional and service personnel, and should do their purchasing of supplies, materials and equipment in this country.

(2) They should publish their financial statements and make full disclosure of the results of their Canadian operations.

(3) They should include on their boards of directors a number of independent Canadians and they should sell an appreciable interest in their equity stock to Canadians. (We have in mind something of the order of 20% to 25%.)

The Commission pointed out that the granting of applications for mining rights, oil leases, and timber limits is the responsibility of the provinces under the Canadian constitution. With this in mind it was suggested that:

Provincial governments might well consider requiring foreign appli-
cants for such rights in future to incorporate under Canadian laws and
to take in Canadian partners. We suggest that the federal government
take similar action with respect to the Northwest Territories and the
Yukon.

I went to see Mr. St. Laurent in the early fall of 1956 at his summer place in
St. Patrick on the lower St. Lawrence. We spent a pleasant few hours talking about his plans for the coming session and the new legislation he was
thinking of introducing, including the creation of the Canada Council. At
the same meeting, I told him something of the conclusions reached by the
Royal Commission on Canada's Economic Prospects and our hope to present him with a Preliminary Report some time before Christmas. He
seemed interested and excited about the new ideas for policy which I
expounded but this new interest did not last for long after his return to
Ottawa. He was simply not in shape to defend the commission's proposals
against the criticisms of his colleagues in the cabinet and especially those of
C. D. Howe.

In addition to my conversation with Mr. St. Laurent in St. Patrick, I
had a private talk with Mike Pearson about the conclusions and suggestions contained in the Preliminary Report of the commission. He reassured
me by saying that he thought the changes and proposals contained in it
were desirable and that the report should serve a useful purpose. Neither of
us anticipated the extent of the criticism that was to come from Mr. Howe.

It is a natural characteristic of human nature to resist change or even
the thought of change. It is understandable, therefore, that in Canada it is
customary for reports of Royal Commissions to be received with blasts of
criticism. The reception of the two reports of the Royal Commission on
Canada's Economic Prospects were no exception. The Preliminary Report,
which was made public about six months before the June 1957 election,
was treated coldly by the Liberal government of Mr. St. Laurent. The
Final Report, which was released to the public shortly after the March
1958 election, received equally frigid treatment from the Conservative government of Mr. Diefenbaker.

However, it should be some comfort to Royal Commissioners to
remember that, if past experience is any guide, most of the proposals made
by Royal Commissions in Canada, no matter what their original reception
may have been, have usually been implemented sooner or later in one form
or another. It is significant that, in the years since the Final Report of the
Royal Commission on Canada's Economic Prospects was released, a great
many of its suggestions have found their place in legislation or have been
implemented at the administrative level.

It was a particular pleasure to have been associated so closely with Douglas LePan, an extremely intelligent and talented man. We worked long hours together, first on the detailed planning of the commission's work, including the thirty-three separate studies, then in preparing for the public hearings, and finally in pulling together the conclusions and proposals. In addition, we read most of the separate studies in draft form and frequently suggested changes to the authors prior to publication. All in all, I found it a stimulating experience.

Apart from any personal satisfaction in gaining some insight into new fields, I believe the work of the commission made a useful contribution to the development of our country. It made people think. It encouraged them, and especially businessmen, to look and plan ahead. And it presented some problems in a new perspective. One of the most important of these was the trend to absentee control over Canadian resources and Canadian business enterprises. Naturally I was disappointed that action to reverse this trend was not taken at the time. But at least after the Commission's reports Canadians could not say they had no warning of what was going on.

Shortly after the completion of the Final Report of the Royal Commission on Canada's Economic Prospects, the Honourable Leslie Frost, Conservative Premier of Ontario, invited me to undertake another public inquiry. Previous to this, I had helped Mr. Frost with a variety of matters, including one involving alleged scandals in the Department of Highways. The Woods Gordon and Clarkson Gordon firms were retained to look into the matter and at the same time to make proposals respecting the organization and procedures of the department. I had accepted this assignment with some misgiving because, in view of the public interest and concern, it seemed probable that the investigation would have an important influence on the survival or otherwise of the Frost government. We found that, while there had been a considerable amount of petty dishonesty on the part of departmental employees, there was no evidence to support charges of serious irregularities at the political level. At the same time, a thorough-going reorganization of the Department of Highways was recommended, including major changes in the way contracts were awarded. All these recommendations were accepted without question by the government, and, perhaps of equal importance, by the general public.

Then one day in the course of the 1958 election campaign, Frost telephoned to ask me to become chairman of a committee to review all aspects of the organization of government in Ontario. I was not at all anxious to do this, having only recently finished my job as Chairman of the Royal Commission on Canada's Economic Prospects. But Frost pressed me very hard. I pointed out to him that, while I was not taking an active part in the federal election campaign, I was a close friend of Mike Pearson's and would be embarrassed to take on anything while the campaign was in progress. Frost then said he would be glad to defer the announcement until some time after the election and asked me whom I would like to have serve with me on the committee. I replied that Bill Mackintosh would be my first choice, together with a lawyer who was familiar with the provincial governmental machinery. Mr. Frost replied, "Bill Mackintosh is fine. I have a high respect for him. But, Walter, must the lawyer be a Liberal, too?" After joking about this, we agreed that C. R. Magone, Q.C., the former Deputy Attorney General, would be an ideal appointment. It was also agreed that Jack Smith of Woods Gordon should be the secretary and, as such, responsible for much of the work.

The committee was formally set up by Order-in-Council, June 12, 1958, and was asked, in particular, to examine "into the relationship of the Provincial Boards and Commissions to the Government and the Legislature." In the course of our work, we interrogated all the Deputy ministers of departments and the chairmen of the various boards and commissions. I remember Judge Robb, the Chairman of the Liquor Licensing Board, appearing before us. He is a rather small man but full of confidence. In the course of our questioning about the work of his board, Bill Mackintosh asked what the policy was about granting banquet permits in dry areas. Judge Robb replied that licences in dry areas were granted only in the case of weddings. Mackintosh in his dry Scottish way then asked, "And why the discrimination against wakes?" Judge Robb had no reply. It was the only time he was discomfitted.

The committee's report, which was dated September 25, 1959, but not released until January 1960, found that boards and commissions occupy a useful and necessary place in modern government machinery. It pointed out that "properly conceived, these agencies are designed to fill gaps in the traditional departmental form of government organization." The departments, though continuing to handle the main responsibilities of government, are not equipped to administer some of the functions which such agencies perform.

Four principles were emphasized throughout the report: ministerial responsibility for the policies and operations of each department and each of the various boards and commissions; financial accountability to the Legislature for all expenditures; the importance of grouping related functions within a single organization; and the right of appeal from decisions of subordinate governmental agencies.

To my knowledge few if any of the Committee's proposals – unlike those of the Royal Commission on Canada's Economic Prospects – have, as yet, been implemented.

CHAPTER FIVE

Rebuilding
The Liberal Party

Leadership convention, January 1958; the 1958 election; the Liberal opposition; the Coyne affair; reorganizing the Liberal Party; my views on policy; the Kingston conference, September 1960; National Rally of the Liberal Party, January 1961; Keith Davey appointed National Organizer.

Louis St. Laurent was seventy-five at the time of the general election in June 1957. He was clearly too old for the job and the public sensed this. At the same time, they became captivated by the new Conservative leader, John Diefenbaker, and his blinding, if somewhat old-fashioned, form of oratory. The result was that the Liberal Party, after twenty-two years in office, was defeated, winning only 105 seats to the Conservatives' 112. While the Conservatives did not win an over-all majority, Mr. St. Laurent did not hesitate. He informed Mr. Diefenbaker that he would advise the Governor General to call on him to form a government. In the months that followed, until the Liberals held their leadership convention in January 1958, Mr. St. Laurent sat silently in his place in the House of Commons, looking tired and dejected. He had passed the stage where he could give any further leadership to his party.

Walter Harris, whom many people had expected to succeed Mr. St. Laurent as leader of the party and Prime Minister, was defeated in the June 1957 election, as were C. D. Howe and several other members of the cabinet. Among those who were left, only two remained who could be seriously considered as being capable of succeeding to Mr. St. Laurent's position: Mike Pearson and Paul Martin. Martin, who was first elected to the House of Commons in 1935, had always wanted to be Prime Minister. Pearson had certainly toyed with the idea, but now that the party was defeated he had no great desire to take on the long and arduous job of rebuilding that lay ahead. He had always been most interested in the international scene. And despite the fact that he had been a member of the cabinet for eight and a half years, he was strangely unfamiliar with House procedures and with the practical side of politics. Nor, it seemed, was he particularly concerned about domestic issues.

I believe that, if Pearson had been offered an important international position at this time, he would have taken it. It was pointed out to him, however, that it was through the Liberal Party that he had been able to attain the unique position he enjoyed in international circles and that, therefore, he had an obligation not to leave the party at this period of difficulty and decline. Pearson acknowledged this obligation and indicated that he would allow his name to be placed before the forthcoming leadership convention. At the same time, he made it clear that he was not seeking the job and would not make any strenuous efforts to obtain it. At about the time he was coming to this conclusion, it was announced that he had been awarded the Nobel Prize for Peace, the highest honour that could possibly be paid to a Canadian. This award, and all the favourable publicity which accompanied it, ensured that Pearson would be extremely hard to beat at the forthcoming leadership convention.

I helped to organize a large, non-partisan dinner sponsored by the Canadian Institute of International Affairs and the United Nations Association to welcome Pearson back from Oslo after he had received the Nobel Prize. Some difficulties were encountered in doing this, as political feelings were running very high with the prospects of a Liberal leadership convention in January 1958 and another general election to be called at any time. It was claimed, with some justification, that the dinner was intended to help Pearson win the leadership convention and, if he did so, to help him re-establish the fortunes of the Liberal Party. In these circumstances, it was not unnatural that the Conservatives should have considered invitations to attend the dinner with a somewhat jaundiced eye. Eventually, however, Mr. Diefenbaker agreed to name the Honourable J. M. Macdonnell, Minister without Portfolio, to represent the federal government at the dinner which was well attended and turned out to be a great success.

Nevertheless, by late December, I had become concerned by the stories I was hearing about Paul Martin putting on a great campaign. It looked as if the race might be very close indeed. I telephoned Mike Pearson about this four or five days before the convention began on January 14, 1958, and asked him what he was doing. He replied that he had not thought it would be necessary to do any campaigning and asked what I thought should be done. I told him I expected he would win the leadership anyway, but that if he did so by a narrow margin he would not have the authority he would need to rebuild the Liberal Party. I added that, while I was a complete neophyte in such matters, I would go to Ottawa immediately and would see him first thing next morning. It was in this way that I became a sort of self-appointed campaign manager for Mike Pearson at the 1958 convention. It was agreed that I should remain anonymous and should keep in the background. This objective was achieved largely, I suppose, because I had no experience with political conventions and knew absolutely nothing about the techniques that have been developed subsequently.

It is no exaggeration to say that at that time Pearson and I and his executive assistant, Mary Macdonald, were complete amateurs in politics. I found they had no money, no staff, and no campaign headquarters. The last of these requirements was rectified by taking a suite at the Chateau Laurier. The staff problem resolved itself in short order. Enthusiasts from all over the country began pouring into Ottawa, anxious to help Mike Pearson. One of them was an extremely energetic young man from Toronto named Keith Davey who soon demonstrated that he had great talents for political organization. We never did solve the money problem but managed to keep the total cost down to about $3,000 by the simple expedient of being anything but generous with our hospitality. It is alleged that at the next leadership convention of the Liberal Party in April 1968 some of the candidates spent over $300,000. It must have taken experts to do that!

The 1958 convention took a hectic three days and, in retrospect, it is easy to laugh about some of the near calamities. I remember running into Pearson at the exhibition grounds at Lansdowne Park in Ottawa and asking where he was going in such a hurry. He replied that he had promised to see some Alberta delegates who wished to cross-examine him about his views on farm policy. This made me nervous and I suggested that I should find out who these delegates were before he ventured to tell them what they should do about their operations. I discovered that more than a dozen Alberta delegates were waiting for him. All of them owned large ranches and all held university degrees, about half of them Ph.D.'s in Agricultural Economics. It seemed unlikely that there was much that Pearson could teach these people about farming. I informed them that he was on the way and would be with them in a few minutes. I then went back and told Mike about the kind of people who had asked to see him and suggested that, instead of volunteering his own views, if any, about western cattle raising, he should merely ask for their suggestions. This he did in his usual witty manner and by the time he was finished I have no doubt that all the Alberta delegates had decided he would be their choice for leader.

The result was a foregone conclusion. Pearson won by 1,074 votes to 305 for Martin. It was an impressive victory. I felt that our combined efforts in the four days before the voting had swung about 150 votes to

Pearson that might have gone the other way. In that case, his victory would have been somewhat less impressive. Another and perhaps even more important factor in his win was the decision of the Quebec caucus that they should support an English-speaking Protestant against Paul Martin on the grounds that Mr. St. Laurent, a French-Canadian Catholic, had been Prime Minister for nine years. If the tradition in the Liberal Party of switching alternatively from an English-speaking to a French-speaking leader was to be continued, it was the turn this time for an English-speaking Protestant to get the nod.

Pearson's first move as Leader of the Opposition was unfortunate. I had returned to Toronto immediately after the convention. Someone called me there to say that the Liberals were planning to move a vote of confidence in the government on Monday next. They had decided on the following resolution:

> That all the words after the word 'That' be struck out and the following substituted therefor:
> In view of the fact that, in the seven months His Excellency's advisers have been in office, Canada's total trade has ceased to expand, export markets have been threatened, and proposals for freer trade have been rebuffed;
> That investment has been discouraged and unemployment has risen drastically;
> That farmers and other primary producers have been disillusioned and discouraged;
> That relations with provincial governments have deteriorated into confusion;
> That the budget is no longer in balance, revenues are declining, expenditures are rising and parliament has been denied a national accounting;
> That there is growing confusion about defence and security;
> That day to day expedients have been substituted for firm and steady administration;
> And in view of the desirability, at this time, of having a government pledged to implement Liberal policies;
> His Excellency's advisers should, in the opinion of this house, submit their resignation forthwith.

I recall being unhappy about this resolution and thinking of telephoning Pearson about it. On reflection, however, I realized that I knew nothing about parliamentary practices and felt diffident about venturing an opinion in a field in which I was so ignorant. Pearson told me later that he also had had his doubts about the proposed resolution but that he was exhausted after getting practically no sleep for three or four nights and was not in a position to think clearly. He said that if I had called him it would have given him just enough encouragement to reconsider the matter. He added that if on any other occasion I ever had even the beginnings of a doubt about a proposed course of action he hoped I would not hesitate to let him know.

What happened was that Pearson made his first speech as Leader of the Opposition on Monday, January 20, and moved his resolution. This was just the opportunity that Diefenbaker was looking for. In a long and devastating speech on February 1 he called the resolution arrogance and tore Pearson and the Liberal Party apart. He then announced that Parliament would be dissolved and a general election held on March 31. Mike Pearson never quite recovered from the tongue-lashing Diefenbaker gave him on this occasion. He knew he was no match for Diefenbaker when it came to oratory, and for years afterwards he gave the impression in the House of Commons that he was secretly a bit afraid of his opponent.

Liz and I went to Ottawa to spend the evening of the election with the Pearsons. We had dinner in a room at the Chateau Laurier and all of us were nervous. Shortly after 7:00 P.M., the results from the Atlantic Provinces began to be announced. As soon as he saw the first returns, Mike said, "It's going to be a rout. Let's get down to Liberal headquarters and see if we can cheer them up." Somehow or other, he managed to keep smiling all that night despite the fact the Liberals had taken a devastating beating.

Among those defeated was Maurice Lamontagne in Quebec East, the riding that had been represented in Ottawa by Sir Wilfrid Laurier, Ernest Lapointe, and Louis St. Laurent. Lamontagne was a worthy successor to these three former giants, and if he had won in 1958, or even in 1962, when he was again defeated, he might conceivably have gone on to succeed Mike Pearson as Prime Minister. I have always had a great admiration for Maurice and we became close friends. And I have always believed in the Liberal Party's practice of switching from an English-speaking to a French-speaking leader and vice versa. It seemed to me that Maurice was one of the men who should be kept in mind when the time came.

I had helped raise some money for Maurice in the 1958 campaign and spoke to him several times on the telephone about his chances. He was a bitter enemy of Premier Duplessis and the Union Nationale and was under no illusions that Duplessis would like to see him beaten. I called Maurice after lunch on the day of the election to inquire how things were going. He replied that up to that time everything was going well. But, he added, if Duplessis decided to send in his goon squads and his swarms of illegal voters, the trucks would begin to roll by 4:00 P.M. He told me later his people spotted the first trucks at exactly four o'clock. This meant it was all over. Duplessis was out to beat Lamontagne and there would be no appeal.

Pearson hinted several times at the beginning of the campaign for the March 1958 election that he would like me to become a candidate in Toronto, mentioning the importance of obtaining a large Liberal representation from that area. I did not believe that in the current climate of opinion I could be elected, assuming I were successful in obtaining a Liberal nomination. I pointed out that, if I ran and lost, my potential usefulness to the Liberal Party would be finished. I offered, however, to help Pearson unofficially with some of his policy speeches on subjects that I was conversant with through the work of the Royal Commission on Canada's Economic Prospects. This I did do.

It would be difficult to exaggerate the magnitude of the Conservative Party's victory in the 1957 and 1958 elections – they were really two stages of the same operation – or, conversely, the overwhelming defeat of the Liberals. The Conservatives under John Diefenbaker won 208 seats on March 31, 1958, the largest number of members ever elected by any political party in Canada's history. The Liberals were reduced to forty-nine members, of whom more than one-half came from the Province of Quebec. Only four of them were especially effective in opposition, but these four – Pearson, Martin, Pickersgill, Chevrier – made up for all the others. With Maurice Lamontagne and Allan MacEachen to help them with research, these four front-benchers belaboured the government from the very beginning of its term in office and, despite their paucity in numbers, became a very effective opposition.

But the efforts of the opposition alone could not possibly be expected to defeat Mr. Diefenbaker and his massive majority. If this was to happen, several things would be necessary. First of all, Mr. Diefenbaker had to make mistakes and persist in making them. Second, the Liberal Party had to be reorganized from top to bottom. Third, the Liberal Party had to produce new ideas and new policies. Fourth, there had to be some new faces. And, of course, the Liberal opposition in Parliament had to continue to be effective. Even given all this, few people in April 1958 would have thought it possible for the Diefenbaker government to be defeated to all intents and purposes after a single term in office.

Pearson was sixty-one years of age and the prospects of him ever becoming Prime Minister were slim indeed. He had taken a tremendous beating, but despite this and despite the odds against him he showed great courage. With the help of Allan MacEachen and Mary Macdonald, he began to learn something of the rules of Parliament and to participate and soon to lead an effective opposition. With the help of Maurice Lamontagne, he began to master the various issues in the domestic field which hitherto had not been of great concern to him. He began to make the life of the government uncomfortable. He demonstrated by his persistence and hard work and also, of course, by his outward cheerfulness, that he was the effective Leader of the Opposition. I expect Pearson's victory in the 1963 election will be recalled as the greatest political come-back in Canadian history, perhaps as the greatest political achievement since Confederation. Within the short space of five years, he and the Liberal Party recovered from their devastating defeat and won victory from a government with 208 supporters in a House of 265. It is quite true that, basically, governments defeat themselves, and certainly the government of John Diefenbaker was no exception. But to win, the Liberals had to be able to present themselves as a credible alternative. This would not have been possible without the courage, hard work, and persistence of Mike Pearson.

The reasons for the Diefenbaker government's own mistakes were many and varied. Perhaps as important as any was the very size of their victory in 1958. Then there was Mr. Diefenbaker's own personality and experience, or lack of it. Basically, he was a one-man show. He had no ability to delegate. His government gave the impression of being disorganized, which it was, and that its members were uncertain about the course they were expected to pursue. Added to this was Mr. Diefenbaker's lack of knowledge and understanding of finance and economic matters. The country was in a period of recession during most of the time he was in office, but his government persisted in policies that would have been more appropriate, or at least a little less inappropriate, in periods of boom and of expansion.

Pearson was at his very best during the celebrated Coyne affair in 1961. James Coyne, the Governor of the Bank of Canada, had insisted upon pursuing a tight money policy during the previous several years. This policy, which tended to keep interest rates high and the Canadian dollar at a premium, aggravated the recession and certainly added to the amount of unemployment. Finally, the government decided to break with Coyne, and his resignation was demanded for the somewhat spurious reason that his pension had been increased by the Board of Directors of the Bank without the government's formal knowledge or approval. Coyne refused to resign on these grounds claiming this was a reflection on his honour and integrity. He put up a tremendous fight, claiming he should be given the opportunity of stating his side of the case. The government then introduced a bill declaring the position of the Governor of the Bank of Canada to be vacant – in other words, dismissing Coyne.

Pearson's job was to support Coyne in his claim to have his day in court without giving the impression that he believed Coyne's policies were right. He managed to do this with great success, but after a long and acrimonious debate, the bill was passed by the House of Commons. It then went to the Senate where the Liberals had a large majority. The Senators insisted that Coyne should be given an opportunity to appear before them. It was Pearson's rather delicate task to suggest to the Liberal Senators that, while they should give Coyne a chance to state his case in public, they should avoid any possible indication that they were in agreement with the policies that Coyne wished to defend. Anyone with less tact or less finesse than Pearson might easily have annoyed the Senators and produced a result that could have been very damaging to the Liberal Party. I spoke to Pearson on the telephone almost every day while the Coyne affair was in progress, and I well remember his difficulties and the skill he displayed in handling the Senators.

The Senate defeated the bill dismissing Coyne, whereupon Coyne resigned as Governor of the Bank of Canada, claiming his honour had been vindicated. He was succeeded by Louis Rasminsky, formerly a Deputy Governor, who is highly respected both in Canada and abroad. But the Coyne affair did not occur until the summer of 1961. Long before that came the necessity for a thorough reorganization of the Liberal Party. Pearson spoke to me about this in the early fall of 1959, when the report on the Organization of the Government in Ontario had been drafted and I had some time to spare. I agreed to talk to the people concerned, including my friend, Duncan MacTavish, and to look things over at the Liberal Party offices at 251 Cooper Street, Ottawa.

Duncan MacTavish, who at the time was both President and Treasurer of the Party, had suffered a severe heart attack and clearly was not able to undertake the tasks that lay ahead. He had served the party long and faithfully in good times and in bad, first under Mr. King, then under Mr. St. Laurent, and for the past two years under Pearson. It was hard for him to give up, but he agreed with me that there was no alternative. Pearson promised to make him a Senator, something MacTavish had always wanted, when the party returned to power, a contingency which at that time looked remote indeed. I was particularly delighted when, in 1963, Duncan MacTavish became the first Senator from Ontario to be appointed by the new Prime Minister, the Right Honourable L. B. Pearson.

In addition to MacTavish, I talked to many prominent Liberals, including all those connected with the party's organization. In the course of these conversations, I was able to assess not only what needed to be done in terms of organization, but also the general opinion about Pearson's leadership. I passed all this on to him in a letter dated November 5, 1959, which began as follows:

> Dear Mike:
>
> I enclose a memorandum on financial and organizational problems and some recommendations about what to do about them. As far as I could ascertain from the conversations I have had, everyone likes you, holds you in the highest respect and is fundamentally loyal to you. You have immense prestige and your power within the Party is more or less unlimited. You can make any decision you want to make without fear of opposition. In fact, the more decisions you make, the stronger you are likely to be. However, even some of your most ardent supporters have been influenced by the subtle propaganda that you have not the necessary toughness to be a successful Prime Minister or the necessary desire and decisiveness to do all the unpleasant things necessary to win the election. . . .

The "unpleasant things" included the appointment of a new National Organizer and the retirement of several old associates who could no longer make a useful contribution. Pearson agreed to these recommendations with considerable reluctance.

I reported that the bank was pressing the Liberal Federation to repay a loan of nearly $200,000, and that an essential first task would be to pay off this debt and get the finances of the party into proper shape. I undertook to help raise the $200,000, which was done mostly in Toronto, Montreal, Hamilton, Winnipeg, Calgary, and Vancouver. Like most people, I intensely dislike raising money. Nevertheless, this unpleasant job was begun in December and completed in the course of a trip to Western Canada which I made for this express purpose in January 1960.

Bruce Matthews took on the job of President of the Federation and became the official Treasurer as well. These were thankless tasks to assume when the fortunes of the party were at their lowest ebb, but Bruce accepted the challenge without a murmur. The Liberal Party is greatly indebted to him for having done so.

By the end of 1959 or the early part of 1960, I realized I was becoming identified with the Liberal Party in the minds of many people as a result of my various activities on Mike Pearson's behalf. This began to worry me as I had no desire to become involved in partisan politics – much as I liked and respected Pearson and wished to help him – if my views on public policy, developed in the course of the work of the Royal Commission on Canada's Economic Prospects, were to prove embarrassing or unacceptable to him or the Liberal Party. Accordingly, I made a number of speeches in 1960 which set forth my ideas in some detail. These were more in the form of short essays on specific policy questions, and in order to avoid the possibility of future misunderstandings, I wrote a number of letters to Pearson about them.

One of these was a long letter dated March 9, 1960, in which I outlined my position.* I told Mike I would like to do anything I could to help him become Prime Minister in the next two or two and a half years, though I expected this would depend more on Mr. Diefenbaker than on the preparations and actions of the Liberals.

> From a personal standpoint, I shall hope that the [Liberal] program will tend to be leftish, imaginative, reasonably clear-cut and that it will discard as many as possible of the old theories and beliefs that are no longer relevant. If it does not do these things, I doubt if the Liberal Party will regain power for some years to come despite the mistakes that Diefenbaker may make between now and the next election.

I said I would like to serve under Pearson as Minister of Finance, but that I had serious doubts about the task of getting myself and the Liberal Party elected, and also about the acceptability of my views on freer trade, integration with the United States, defence policy, and the need for a greater degree of direction and control of the economy by Ottawa.

I said I was against high tariffs but that I thought we would need more secondary industry if we were to "lick chronic unemployment," and that I did not think these objectives were necessarily incompatible. I went on to say that: "However, as I think you know, I would be very hesitant about a policy of all-out free trade – even on some regional basis like the North Atlantic area – unless I was more certain than I am now of where it would lead and the disruptions that would be involved. . . ." I expressed concern about the gradual economic and financial takeover by American capital, and said that if I were in public life, "I would wish to urge some modest steps to counteract what is presently going on in this direction. . . . I would prefer us to go in one direction or the other knowing what is happening and what we are trying to do about it. . . ." On the question of defence policy, I felt that "Canada should begin to take an independent line and should stop pouring money down the drain," an approach which admittedly might lead to a showdown with the Americans. I expressed particular concern "about the trade question and integration with the United States where I lack the instinctive convictions that most people of the Liberal persuasion seem to have. . . ." I concluded by saying I did not wish to say at that time whether I would run in the next election. Quite apart from the problem of getting elected, I was afraid I might find myself in disagree-

*See Appendix 1.

80

ment with Pearson or with the party on one or more of the policy issues mentioned.

I wrote to Pearson again on July 12, 1960, enclosing copies of three speeches on policy issues I had made in February, May, and June, and a draft of a fourth I was to make in August. I said:

> This material, plus the contents of the reports of the Royal Commission, covers practically everything on which I have any views that matter, or at least, that matter in the context of our discussions. In the last analysis, all this pretty well boils down to the points of policy raised in my letter to you of last March.
>
> I need not emphasize the importance of this whole subject to both of us. It is imperative that there should be no misunderstandings, and as I said on the telephone yesterday, I can easily go to Ottawa on Friday afternoon if you think a conversation would be useful. In any event, please call me when you have had a chance to look over this material.

Pearson telephoned me two days later, and the hand-written note I made of our conversation which appears on my copy of the letter of July 12 reads as follows:

> Mike called to say he had read the attached draft and the copies of the other 3 speeches that I sent him. He said he agreed *completely* with my ideas. He repeated this two or three times saying that this is exactly how he feels on these various issues with particular emphasis on the draft speech for Aug. 29. In the circumstances, he suggested there is no point in me going down to see him tomorrow evening.
>
> W.L.G. 8:00 P.M. 14/7/60

I knew, of course, that Pearson would always favour some kind of North Atlantic free trade area if this should ever become a practicable possibility. I had questioned this in my letter of March 9, but did not consider it to be a realistic proposition. Failing some kind of North Atlantic free trade area or Atlantic union, I was reassured that Pearson was opposed to any kind of merging of the Canadian and United States economies. I was against a continental approach, which I believed would lead to our political absorption by the United States. Pearson assured me that he agreed with this conclusion and I believed him.

Nothing could have been more explicit than Pearson's remarks to me on the telephone on July 14, as quoted above, and any doubts I may have had about possible differences of opinion about policies were resolved. Because of this, shortly afterwards I agreed to his request that I become Chairman of the Policy Committee at the rally of the Liberal Party to be held the following January. I knew quite well that, if I did so, I would be identified in the public's mind as an acknowledged member of the Liberal Party, and a prominent one at that. There could be no turning back in this regard, even though this would not necessarily commit me officially to run in the next election whenever it was called.

Some of the public speeches I made in 1960 attracted a good deal of attention in the press, partly because of all the publicity attached to the reports of the Royal Commission on Canada's Economic Prospects a few years before and my association with it, partly because it was unusual for a professional or businessman to speak out quite so forcefully on public issues, and partly because in these speeches I was clearly criticizing the policies of the Diefenbaker government and this, of course, made news.

In the speech to the Ontario Federation of Labour in Niagara Falls on February 13, 1960, I advocated an easier money policy and a reduction in the value of the Canadian dollar in order to stimulate the economy and reduce unemployment, which was very serious at the time. I was the first to propose devaluation, or certainly the first to do so unequivocally. As was to be expected, my proposal was reported in big headlines in the newspapers.

The sections of this speech – or rather this lecture, as it was too long for a speech (trade unionists are bears for punishment) – that attracted the most attention were those dealing with devaluation and with the economic independence issue. I suggested that the policy of the government should be "to reduce the present artifically high value of the Canadian dollar . . . and to modify the tight money policy. Such moves should stimulate our exports and reduce to some extent our imports, thus bringing our trade figures more nearly into balance." I referred to the benefits received from the Americans in developing our country, but then went on to say:

> The fact is, whether or not we are willing to admit it, Canada by degrees is losing a considerable measure both of her economic and her political independence. Our industries increasingly are becoming dominated by large companies, many of which are subsidiaries of American concerns; we are hearing more and more about the desirability of a "continental approach" to economic issues – frequently from the spokesmen of the companies in question; and our defence forces are dependent upon or integrated with those of the United States. Surely all this adds up to a very considerable loss of Canadian independence.

The speech of May 14, 1960, to the Canadian and American Mayors on "Inter-Governmental Financial Arrangements in Canada" in Chicago provided a chance to do some philosophizing on current trends:

> As a result of the process of industrialization, most people are a great deal better off in a material sense than they were a few decades ago. At

the same time the industrial system has reduced the economic independence of the individual – for example, he may find himself unemployed from time to time and he can expect to live for many years after he has retired from work. This encourages us to demand more and more from governments in the way of social and welfare services – unemployment measures, old age pensions, social security plans of various kinds. We have much more leisure time now and, accordingly, we need more recreational and cultural facilities. These various requirements and demands may create problems for our government representatives, yourselves included. But we, the public, seem to think that collectively we should be able to afford these things somehow or other. And, within reason, we are right . . . .

What I have been saying is simply this: That the process of industrialization has been and will continue to be the central dynamic force in our society. Four of its main effects have been to induce urban growth; to increase the demand for social facilities and services; to create an urgent need for expanded educational facilities; and to establish a seemingly endless need for more and better roads and highways. The problems that arise from these developments cannot be resolved by individuals or by the private sector of the economy. They must be met from the public sector or, in other words, by governments. You will have noticed that in each case it is local governments that must assume a major part of the responsibility, if not all of it . . . .

On re-reading my speech of June 6, 1960, to the Canadian Manufacturers Association, I am afraid some of my comments may have startled the more hoary prototypes of private enterprise, though not, I am sure, a majority of those present:

Now, these circumstances pose very special problems for Canadian industry and for Canadians as a whole. In some ways, this is accentuated by the fact that so much of our industry is controlled by non-residents of this country. Many of our industry spokesmen are the managers of subsidiaries of much larger American concerns. Understandably, they not infrequently seem to speak in an American rather than a Canadian idiom. And I suggest that often there is a real difference in the two.

For example, take the term "free enterprise." The people of this country have accepted the general principles of the welfare state – which is not exactly what most people have in mind when they talk about "free enterprise." Some of our biggest and best known concerns are publicly owned, and some of these are among our most successful undertakings. Furthermore, as I have said, a great many of our larger and more influential companies are controlled and managed by non-residents. In these circumstances, it is not surprising that the term "free enterprise" may have a slightly different connotation in Canada than it has in the United States. It would be more correct, perhaps, to describe Canada as having a "mixed-enterprise" economy rather than a free one.

If this is a correct assertion, as I believe it to be, it is understandable that many people in this country seem to be searching for a new and more satisfying set of values than is conjured by the single phrase "free enterprise." Speaking personally, I believe the profit motive is important, very important, but I do not believe it is the only motive that should be relied upon if our objective is to improve the level of human welfare for all Canadians – and to have something left over for those in less fortunate lands than ours. . . .

To my speech – or lecture – of August 29, 1960, to the National Federation of Canadian University Students in Vancouver,* I gave what at that time was a deliberately provocative title, "Whither Canada – Satellite or Independent Nation?" It attracted considerable attention and editorial comment. The following passages were noted in particular:

> While a case can be made for either of the courses I have mentioned – faster integration with the United States or the regaining of our independence – I submit that there is no excuse whatever for failing to face up to the dilemma in which we find ourselves today. To do nothing, to refuse to recognize the situation that confronts us or to admit its implications, will lead inevitably to our becoming a more or less helpless satellite of the United States. (The great majority of Canadians might never fully realize just when or how this happened.) Like many other people, I have thought a great deal about this issue. Having done so, I for one am prepared to say without any qualification that I hope Canadians will choose to regain a greater measure of economic independence than we now have. I believe we could be successful in this endeavour over the next decade or so if we really put our minds to it. . . .
>
> The United Nations and the NATO alliance are the cornerstones of Canadian foreign policy and should remain so. But, speaking personally, I feel less certain about NORAD and about the use of nuclear weapons that are not under Canadian control. Despite all the words – many of them contradictory – that have been uttered about the NORAD arrangement that was entered into so hurriedly and obviously without much serious consideration in the summer of 1957, it seems to boil down to the fact that Canada has contributed a few squadrons to

*See Appendix 2.

the American Air Force. . . . As I have suggested, if we really do wish Canada to retain her separate identity as an independent nation, we will have to re-examine our present defence and foreign policies and do something about stopping and then reversing the trend under which such a staggering number of our most dynamic industries have fallen into foreign hands.

It follows from what I have been saying that, in considering the pros and cons of any policy proposals, there are two tests above all others that should be kept very much in mind, *viz.*: Will the proposed policy result in more jobs and less unemployment? Will the proposed policy result in a further loss of Canadian independence, or the reverse?

I have quoted from these four speeches in 1960 because, taken as a whole, they expressed, as well as I was able to do so, my political and social philosophy which has not changed in its essentials. This might have been considered somewhat advanced or even radical in some circles at that time. Now, most people would be inclined to ask what was so new or different about the views I was putting forward.

Apart from clarifying my own thinking on these various matters, it was reassuring to know that Pearson shared the same viewpoints as I did. He may not have felt quite as strongly as I did about some points and from time to time he may have given in to pressures and said or done things with which I disagreed. But based on my close association with him over a long period of years, I believe that both in essentials and to a considerable extent in detail he agreed with the political philosophy and with the policies designed to implement it set forth in the speeches that I have quoted. If I had not believed this, I would not have participated so enthusiastically in the effort to make him Prime Minister.

I realized that I would have to be in a position of some authority if I were to influence public policy to the extent I felt to be important. The obvious post from which to accomplish this objective would be that of Minister of Finance, and I discussed this tentatively with Pearson on one or two occasions, as indeed I had done in talking to him prior to Mr. St. Laurent's invitation to me to join his government in 1954. I would be going into politics primarily because of my interest in promoting policies which I believed would benefit the average Canadian, and help Canada to retain her independence and, hence, her influence in the world. And while my principal concern was not with titles or position, I wanted to be reasonably sure of being able to accomplish these objectives. I went to considerable pains to ascertain that Pearson and I were in general agreement, both as to policies and in our political philosophy. It remained to be seen whether the Liberal Party, as such, would officially endorse the kind of policies we thought to be important.

Mike Pearson had always welcomed a discussion of new ideas. Following the Liberal Party's defeat in 1958, he suggested a conference be held of intellectuals and Liberal politicians at which all aspects of policy would be discussed. He felt it was essential to recapture the interest and support of the university fraternity and hoped to do so in this way. His first thought was to hold such a conference in the summer of 1959, but this proved to be too soon after the 1958 election; the climate was not yet right, and so it was decided to hold the conference one year later. Mitchell Sharp, who had resigned as Deputy Minister of Trade and Commerce over differences with the new Minister, the Honourable Gordon Churchill, and was then a Vice-President of Brazilian Light and Power, was invited to organize the conference. Sharp agreed to do this, and an enthusiastic group of about two hundred university professors, writers, and politicians, with a few labour leaders and businessmen for good measure, met in early September 1960 at Queen's University in Kingston for five days (and four nights) of freewheeling discussion.

The most controversial papers, and probably the best, were presented by Maurice Lamontagne on "Growth, Stability and the Problem of Unemployment" and Tom Kent on "Towards a Philosophy of Social Security." Both these papers attracted a considerable amount of attention in the press, both being described as "socialistic." Lamontagne was criticized for recommending a "prices review board." Tom Kent was attacked for suggesting that under certain conditions a tax on advertising might be one way of slowing down excessive activity in the economy if that should occur and, therefore, of containing inflation. Neither of these ideas was implemented when the Liberals came to power, but in September 1960 they indicated the direction of the thinking of the two most important members of Pearson's staff. Fortunately, he resisted immediate pressures that he should get rid of them.

From a political standpoint, the Kingston conference was a great success, for which Pearson was entitled to full credit. It was his idea and he insisted upon holding it despite the serious reservations of some of his colleagues. It showed the Liberal Party was alive, was not afraid to discuss new ideas and that many of the brighter academics were willing to participate in its deliberations.

As soon as the Kingston conference was over, we began to plan for the National Rally of the Liberal Party to be held in Ottawa, January 9-11, 1961, under the chairmanship of Paul Hellyer. As already noted, I had been appointed Chairman of the Policy Committee, with Maurice Sauvé as one of the regional vice-chairmen. Hellyer had suggested that all the policy discussions should be held in public and open to the press, something no political party had ever done before. This was an excellent idea and one that was to give us a maximum amount of publicity. But it called for a great deal of organizing and careful handling if approval of ill-considered or silly resolutions was to be avoided.

To begin with, we decided to break down the discussions under twenty-one policy headings and to appoint a chairman and a vice-chairman for each group or sub-committee. All resolutions sent in by provincial and constituency organizations, after being processed by the main policy committee, were referred to the chairman of one or other of these groups. In addition, they were supplied with "working papers" which gave the required background information and suggested tentatively the kind of conclusions to be drawn. The sub-committee chairmen were not under any compulsion to use these working papers but, in practice, they were pleased to have them. For the most part, these background papers, together with suggestions for the group chairmen respecting the kind of resolutions that might be desirable, were prepared by Tom Kent, Maurice Lamontagne, Robert Fowler, Maurice Sauvé, and myself, with a great deal of help from many others on specific subjects. It was an immense job for which Kent and Lamontagne, in particular, deserved much credit. Resolutions passed by the sub-committees were required to be considered and approved by the main policy committee before presentation to the plenary sessions of the rally. This was a check which we considered necessary and which worked out very well in practice.

The rally was a tremendous success. The attention given to it by the press and on the air provided the Liberal Party with millions of dollars of free publicity of a most valuable kind. Some eighteen hundred delegates, all of whom joined one or other of the twenty-one policy sub-committees, were given every opportunity to present their views and they did so with great vigour. And yet, because of the advance work on the working papers and the checks provided, the party produced a body of resolutions that were in the main consistent and non-contradictory in character. This does not mean that the delegates accepted without question all the suggestions that were presented to them. Many of them were improved or discarded and better ideas affirmed. It was a hectic three days, during which time I existed almost entirely on chocolate bars and whisky – there was no time for meals.

This is not the place to attempt to summarize all the resolutions that were passed. However, in view of the recurrent controversy over the Canadian independence issue, it may be worth while to quote part of the resolution that was approved under the heading "For a Strong and Independent Canada."

1. The most desirable way to counteract the tendency towards foreign control of our industry is to encourage greater Canadian participation in the ownership of Canadian enterprises and, thereby, make possible the most effective employment of both Canadian and foreign capital in the more intensive development of our national resources. It is, therefore, proposed that Canadian participation in ownership be encouraged by such measures as

  (a) taxation incentives;
  (b) the revision of the regulations governing the investment of pension, trust, insurance and other institutional funds;
  (c) a national program of information and education to reshape the attitude of Canadians to investment of savings.

2. In order to facilitate this development of Canadian ownership without disturbing unnecessarily the present enjoyment by Canadians of the benefits of foreign capital investment, foreign firms should be encouraged to foster Canadian participation by such measures as taxation allowances where Canadian ownership occurs, and the extension of the requirement that there be a majority of Canadians on the Board of Directors. . . .

4. Certain financial institutions such as the chartered banks, life insurance companies and trust companies must remain under Canadian majority ownership and control.

The ideas contained in this resolution were in tune with the suggestions made four years previously by the Royal Commission on Canada's Economic Prospects. They were in tune with the ideas which Pearson had agreed with in the summer of 1960, before I decided to commit myself to an active role in politics. It is true that this resolution ran counter to the accepted mythology of the Liberal Party of former days, as portrayed in the writings of Bruce Hutchison and others. But many of the policy resolutions approved at the rally in January 1961 broke with the former *laissez-faire* traditions of the party. This was just one of them. The changes were deliberately designed to bring the Liberal Party into line with the conditions that Canadians were faced with in the second half of the twentieth century.

The resolution on defence policy – which was approved in advance by Pearson – is important because of his later repudiation of it.

Canadian defence policy must be based on the fundamental truth that in the nuclear age, the only protection is the establishment and maintenance of a creative peace. . . . The main lines of Liberal policy will be:

1. Any extension of the possession of nuclear weapons under national control will greatly increase the danger of accidental outbreak of nuclear war and also the difficulty of achieving disarmament. Membership in the nuclear club therefore should not be extended beyond the four countries which now possess such weapons. The objective should be not the extension of ownership of such weapons but their abolition before they destroy the world.

Canada cannot deny nuclear weapons to other nations and at the same time arm her own forces with them. A new Liberal government therefore should not acquire, manufacture or use such weapons either under separate Canadian control or under joint U.S.-Canadian control.

2. Canada should continue to play an important part in the defence policy of NATO which seeks security through collective action. However, NATO's objectives and the means of achieving them should be reconsidered in the light of the conditions of today, rather than those of twelve years ago. . . .

3. Under a new Liberal government Canada will withdraw from NORAD insofar as its present interceptor role is concerned. Liberal policy would, however, provide for an appropriate Canadian contribution to continental defence in co-operation with the U.S.A. The Canadian role in such defence should be that of detection, identification and warning.

We would stop using our defence resources on interceptor fighter squadrons or on Bomarc missiles. For the U.S.A., with its vast resources and world responsibilities, these forms of defence may be necessary. There is no reason why Canada should participate in a role inappropriate to her circumstances.

A very heated debate took place over foreign policy, and specifically about the recognition of Red China. Delegates at the closing plenary session late on the last afternoon were not willing to approve the resolution presented to them and demanded another session of the sub-committee on foreign policy. This was agreed to, and it was decided that I should act as chairman during the discussion. About four hundred delegates attended, half of whom violently advocated the recognition of Red China without reservations and the other half as violently opposed doing anything of the kind.

It was a difficult meeting. Delegates were tired after three long days of discussion and debate. Strong language was used and tempers flared. During the course of this, my secretary came to the platform to inform me in a whisper that there was an urgent telephone call for me from Toronto. I replied that I could not possibly leave the meeting and gave her a message to relay to my caller.

After an hour or so, the debate quieted down to a point where I was able to suggest a compromise resolution, which Pearson had helpfully drafted for me in advance, to use in case of emergencies. Nobody liked the suggestion very much, but after some further argument it was approved reluctantly. I did not want four hundred delegates to go home depressed or angry, so I said there was something I wished to tell them in the strictest confidence before the meeting was adjourned.

I referred to my secretary's appearance and the urgent telephone call which I said happened to be from the head of a Red Chinese delegation in Canada to negotiate with the Department of Agriculture. These people had been in touch with me a week or two before, presumably because I had visited Peking in 1959 and they knew of me. (I had referred them to Ottawa and naturally had informed the authorities there about this.) I told the delegates that I had asked my secretary to give the Chinese representative the following message: "Mr. Gordon cannot speak on the telephone just now as he is closeted with a select group of fellow conspirators plotting the overthrow of the Canadian government." This story – it happened to be true – relieved the tension, and the meeting broke up with everyone in better humour.

In political terms, the rally was a tremendous success. Overnight the Liberal Party under Pearson became a credible alternative to the Diefenbaker government. The enthusiasm of those who attended the rally could not be hidden or played down. The Liberals had adopted bold new policies on many issues and seemed confident they could translate them into action. Of perhaps almost equal importance, many new people had become publicly identified with the Liberal Party.

The rally established the fact, if that were needed, that Pearson was the popular and undisputed leader of the Liberal Party. He had insisted that the rally should be held despite considerable opposition, and its success was a great personal triumph for him. From then on, it was not so much a question of whether the Liberals would ever be able to defeat the Diefenbaker government as when, in realistic terms, this hoped-for event might happen.

On a more personal note, what pleased and reassured me most was the fact that the Liberal Party in formal session had approved the kind of policies that I personally believed in and was prepared to fight for. From that time on, for all practical purposes, I was committed to the idea of seeking a seat in Parliament.

But despite the great success of the rally and the vast amount of publicity which attended it, there was no follow-up for a period of three months. No attempt was made to capitalize on the whole huge effort that went into it and the enthusiasm which it aroused. To this day, I do not know why Pearson gave, or seemed to give, the impression that he was dropping the whole thing like a hot potato.

Jim Scott, who had been appointed National Organizer about a year before the rally was held, fell into bad health about this time and was forced to resign. I had become increasingly impressed with the enthusiasm and drive of Keith Davey, President of the Toronto and Yorks Liberal Association, and recommended that he should be appointed National Organizer to succeed Scott. This was done in May 1961. Davey was just what the party needed. His optimism had no bounds, he knew or soon knew everyone in Canada who was connected with the party, he was popular with the press, and he seemed to have no objection to talking on the telephone to anyone at any hour of the day or night. His own enthusiasm was soon translated throughout the party apparatus. Keith and I worked very closely together through three national election campaigns, and in the process not only developed a considerable respect for each other but became firm friends. He was an invaluable member of the Pearson team.

CHAPTER SIX

The Election Campaign of June 1962

National Campaign Committee; my tour of southwestern Ontario; Troubled Canada; public-opinion surveys; candidates; directing the campaign; the results; the campaign in Davenport.

Planning for the 1962 election began in the spring of 1961. I became a member of what was known as the Leader's Advisory Committee and then Chairman of the Liberal Party's National Campaign Committee. Prior to that time I had been sitting in on the meetings of an informal group which became the nucleus of the Ontario Campaign Committee. This group met to begin with on Wednesday evenings in the Toronto Board of Trade Building. Later on, after the Ontario Campaign Committee was established, these meetings were shifted to my office on Wellington Street, where we would meet at noon over sandwiches and coffee.

The Chairman of what became the Ontario Campaign Committee was Dan Lang, who at that time was Treasurer of the Liberal Party in Ontario. Other members were Royce Frith, the President of the Ontario Liberal Party; Keith Davey, President of Toronto and Yorks (which later became the Toronto and District Liberal Association); and David Anderson, a Toronto lawyer and keen Liberal. Dick Stanbury, another Toronto lawyer who was active in the party, began to attend the meetings in late 1961 or early 1962; and David Greenspan, a long-time Liberal worker and organizer, also came from time to time. Bruce Powe, after he became chief organizer for the party in Ontario, sat in on the meetings.

Frith, Lang, Davey, Anderson, and Stanbury were old friends and had been involved in Liberal politics together for many years. Their first coup had been to get control of the Toronto organization, and more recently they had been successful in taking over the provincial organization and electing Frith president. They knew their stuff, but it seemed to me as an outsider that they spent too much time in wisecracking and did not quite appreciate how big a task it would be to dislodge Mr. Diefenbaker from power and put Mike Pearson in. However, my first objective was to get their confidence – they were all younger than I, and I was a neophyte in politics – so I did not volunteer many suggestions to begin with.

Both Frith and Lang were very popular in the party and knew people all over the province. Anderson, who came originally from Prince Edward Island, was not as well known but seemed quite willing to leave his law practice at the drop of a hat in order to visit any part of Ontario in a search for candidates. At that time, Davey concentrated most of his efforts in the Toronto area. This was essential because, if the party was to make a showing in Ontario, it was imperative to break the Tory grip on Metro Toronto. Bruce Powe, who came from Alberta, was handicapped to begin with by not knowing the party people in the province. But he overcame this and in an inobtrusive way and by dint of very hard work did a good job. I had been much impressed by Davey, who struck me as the most incisive member of the group. When he went to Ottawa as National Organizer, he agreed to remain a member of the Ontario Committee and continued to provide drive and decisiveness when this was needed.

The National Campaign Committee was a fairly loose body which operated in a somewhat different way in each province. In British Columbia, the chairman was Hugh Martin, an exuberant contractor who was as new to politics as I was. Hugh was a great enthusiast and a spectacular promoter, qualities that British Columbia Liberals badly needed at the time. His committee included John Nichol, later to become President of the National Liberal Federation, and Chairman of the National Campaign Committee in the 1968 election.

At that time, the Liberals in British Columbia always seemed to be fighting among themselves. Martin had run for the provincial presidency but lost to William Gilmour, a rather intense lawyer from the interior of the province. Gilmour claimed that because of his victory he should be the chairman for British Columbia of the National Campaign Committee. We explained that this did not follow and pointed to Ontario where Frith was the provincial president while Lang was chairman of the campaign committee. This did not convince Gilmour and he continued to be difficult. But we had the good sense to stick with Hugh Martin.

Earl Hastings, an oil-land man from Calgary, was the chairman in Alberta, and Joseph O'Sullivan, a Winnipeg lawyer, in Manitoba. The arrangement in Saskatchewan was different. Ross Thatcher, the leader of the Liberal Party in the province, insisted on being in complete control of everything and assured us he would deliver a good many seats when the federal election came if he were placed in charge. We had no alternative but to acquiesce in this arrangement.

The so-called "old guard" was still in charge of things in Quebec under Lionel Chevrier. Louis Gélinas, the treasurer, had great influence, two of his key organizers being Messrs. Perrault and François.

The chairman in New Brunswick was Charlie McElman, a skilled political practitioner and Premier Louis Robichaud's right-hand man. In Nova Scotia it was Irving Barrow, a Halifax chartered accountant. In Prince Edward Island the Liberal Party's fortunes were looked after by Alex Matheson, the ex-Premier and leader of the opposition, and in Newfoundland by Jack Pickersgill, with Joey Smallwood in the background.

The National Committee met from time to time, but in the main the various activities were watched over by Davey and myself. Among other things, we decided that every constituency in the country should be rated according to the chances of the Liberals winning it. This was based not only on past voting records but on the popularity of the candidate and all the up-to-date information we could obtain. This grading of constituencies according to priority helped the provincial campaign committees in allocating funds to the respective candidates and aided in the planning of visits by the leader of the party and other speakers.

Bruce Matthews was the National Treasurer. John Aird was in charge of fund raising in Ontario, and Louis Gélinas in Quebec. Gélinas, who was an excellent collector, felt that as he had been appointed by the leader of the party he was responsible only to him. His main concern was to finance the party in Quebec and provide funds for the three Maritime Provinces. Newfoundland seemed to be able to manage on its own. If there was anything left over, Gélinas was prepared to pay something towards the national campaign and the expenses of the national headquarters in Ottawa, but he was unwilling to give any commitment in advance. This was an unsatisfactory arrangement and we had many arguments about it. Things improved a bit in the 1963 campaign, and fell into place in 1965, by which time Aird had become National Treasurer and Jean Ostiguy had succeeded Gélinas in Montreal.

It was easy to work with John Aird. He made a careful estimate of what could be collected in Ontario and came extremely close to it. It was up to me to say how the total amount should be divided between the cost of the national campaign and the campaign in Ontario. With the help of Keith Davey and Paul Lafond at Liberal headquarters in Ottawa, and George Elliott from MacLaren Advertising we prepared a detailed budget of the cost of the national campaign including advertising, the cost of the leader's tour, and the expenses of the national office. We added to this the amounts to be sent to the Western provinces and the Northwest Territories. (The

Yukon was looked after by British Columbia.) From this total was deducted my best guess of what was likely to be forthcoming from Louis Gélinas towards the cost of the national campaign. The balance had to come from Aird. What was left would be available for Ontario to cover the cost of special advertising in that province, the expenses of the Ontario campaign headquarters, and the total amount that could be made available to the candidates. The actual amounts to be allocated between candidates was handled by Gordon Dryden, a difficult and time-consuming job.

Going at things in this manner – and there was no practical way of doing it differently – meant that candidates in Ontario, where we had the best chance of winning seats, received very much less money for their expenses than candidates in some other provinces. This was a reflection of the somewhat loose organization structure that had prevailed for many years and of the personalities involved. But I was not at all happy about it.

Alex Walton, a retired banker, agreed to take on the thankless job of collector in British Columbia, and did remarkably well in the 1962 and subsequent campaigns. In the course of this, he received much abuse, which he ignored. He just kept plugging away in the interests of the Liberal Party for which he earned our deepest gratitude.

In the spring of 1961, no one could tell when the next general election would be called, but all our planning was predicated on it being held in June 1962. Naturally there were rumours that it would be in the fall of 1961 or that it would be in March or May 1962. But we could not step up our work or slow it down with every rumour. I told Mike Pearson that we would plan for June. If it came earlier, we would not be ready, but we would do our best. We were lucky. The election took place on June 18, 1962.

By the spring of 1961, I detected a feeling in the Ontario group that I should get the feel of the situation in the field – and incidentally show what I could do when I was away from the quiet and security of my own office. I agreed to make a four-day trip through Southwestern Ontario to meet the local Liberals on the understanding that I would not be asked to make more than two speeches. The truth was I was nervous about speaking without a well-prepared text before me.

But once on the road, with Bruce Powe to help me, all that was forgotten. Everywhere we went, Liberals turned out to see the new face and I had to make two, three, or even four speeches each day. It was like a rehearsal for an election campaign, and I found that I enjoyed it. Of more importance, I detected an optimistic feeling among the Liberals I talked with, based on widespread dissatisfaction with Mr. Diefenbaker and his policies.

The tour began at Simcoe on June 5 with a speech to a noon meeting of the Rotary Club during which I suggested what the Minister of Finance should include in his budget, expected momentarily. I suggested that to begin with every effort should be made to restore confidence in financial and other circles. One step in this direction would be a clear and unequivocal statement that from now on the government would accept full responsibility for monetary policy which it had been blaming on the Bank of Canada. I argued for an easy money policy, lower interest rates, and a reduction in the artificially high exchange rate for the Canadian dollar. At the same time, I suggested that the government should announce its determination to reduce the huge annual deficits we had been incurring in our international transactions. I submitted that the government should establish a municipal loan fund and suggested a number of changes in the tax laws designed to stimulate business activity throughout the country.

The speech was deliberately provocative and, as expected, it received considerable publicity which, incidentally, helped to ensure the success of my tour through the rest of Southwestern Ontario. The opinions that I voiced throughout this trip represented the views of the Liberal Party as approved at the rally in January, and many of the proposals were included in the legislation presented to Parliament by the Liberal government some two years later.

After Simcoe, we visited Tillsonburg, St. Thomas, London, Ridgetown, Chatham, Leamington, and Windsor. In a speech to the Windsor Chamber of Commerce on June 8, three days after my Simcoe effort, I made some suggestions for stimulating the secondary manufacturing industries and in this way providing more jobs. This was of interest as conditions in Windsor were depressed at that time and there was a great deal of unemployment. Again, these suggestions were well reported in the press.

When I arrived in Windsor I was surprised to find Paul Martin there to meet me. I thought he would have been in Ottawa but I should have known better. He had not remained the Member for Essex East since 1935 without maintaining a firm grip on everything that happened in his suzerainty. I should not have expected to meet with the local Liberal associations without Paul being there to supervise. It turned out to be a dinner meeting of about two hundred party workers held in a roadhouse on the outskirts of Windsor. A dance band played all the time in the next room, separated only by a temporary partition. The noise was deafening; one could hardly hear oneself think, and speaking over the din was an ordeal – but not, of course, to Paul.

He introduced me in the most superlative terms. Paul is a born "ham," and his compliments were so exaggerated and so prolonged that after ten or fifteen minutes everyone was laughing. I had no choice but to abandon my prepared speech and talk about Paul in kind, always a good thing to do in Windsor. Compliments about Paul, no matter how embellished, were accepted as the gospel truth by the faithful in that area.

Paul had shaken everybody's hand before dinner, and as soon as the speeches were over we both went around the room and shook hands with everyone again. When we had finished, he told me we might as well leave as there was nothing more to be accomplished. As we stepped outside onto a kind of porch, Paul pointed rather dramatically to a dark corner. In an obvious reference to the prohibition era, he whispered, "I saw a man shot there one evening." I replied, "Paul, I hope it was not your finger on the trigger." His reaction made it clear that I had passed the test.

During the summer of 1961, I wrote *Troubled Canada*, subtitled "The Need for New Domestic Policies," which was published in December of that year. Frankly polemical in style, it was highly critical of the Diefenbaker government and its policies and advocated a broad spectrum of alternative policies based on the resolutions approved by the Liberal Party Rally in January 1961.

Among other things, the book was critical of the Diefenbaker government for failing to do anything about the increasing foreign control of Canadian industry. It suggested there were two main reasons for this failure. The first was "a fear that any move to reverse the present trend would provoke protests from those affected and from the United States authorities." The second reason was "that some professional economists, including many government officials, do not think the increasing foreign control of Canadian industry is actually or potentially a bad thing."

Troubled Canada proved to be a handy guide for many Liberal candidates in the election campaign that was soon to be upon them. And it was one of the reasons why in that campaign, and to a large extent in the 1963 campaign as well, nearly all Liberals seemed to be saying the same things and preaching the same doctrine from coast to coast.

In broad terms, planning for the 1962 election broke down into four parts: Strategy, candidates, publicity, and the already mentioned fund-raising. The strategy which eventually emerged was based on the policies approved at the National Rally in January 1961, and to some extent on surveys of public opinion. These surveys indicated the state of opinion on various issues, on what the various political parties stood for, the groups of people who traditionally supported the different parties, and the public's impressions of the characteristics of the several party leaders.

At first we tried out this relatively new technique of public opinion surveys, new as far as Canada was concerned at any rate, with the help of MacLaren Advertising. Prior to two by-elections in Ontario in 1960, some very elementary surveys were made, without the knowledge of the prospective candidates, to find out how each of them was thought of by the voting public. In Niagara Falls, for instance, the outstanding public choice was Judy LaMarsh, the only one of several prospective nominees who people believed could beat the Tory candidate. Some of the members of the Liberal establishment in Niagara had not felt that Judy would be the most appropriate candidate. However, when they were confronted with the results of the survey, everyone had to agree that she should be the one. Judy was successful in winning the nomination and, in due course, the by-election. I should add that I have not the slightest doubt she would have won the nomination anyway if she had made up her mind that this was what she wanted. However, it was probably better that she should do so with everyone's blessing.

The other survey showed that one of the prospective candidates, a popular trade unionist, had much the best chance of winning the by-election in Peterborough, a labour town. However, the man in question seemed to be *persona non grata* with the local Liberal establishment, which would not have him. He was passed over in favour of another candidate who, the survey indicated, would have little chance in an election. This proved to be the case and the Peterborough by-election was lost as a result.

All of us had, of course, read everything we could about John F. Kennedy's campaign in the 1960 presidential election and especially Theodore White's book, *The Making of the President: 1960.* We were, therefore, very much alive to and aware of the importance of public-opinion polls and surveys. Our difficulty was to get them made quickly and by experienced people. It was at about this time that Robert Winters mentioned that a friend of his, Sam Harris, the Treasurer of the Democratic Party in the State of New York, had suggested that we should use the services of Louis Harris (no relation), who had been in charge of all the survey work for the Kennedy campaign committee.

I met Lou Harris in this way, and was immediately impressed with him. He talked to Keith Davey, Tom Kent, and me on several occasions, and we determined that he was the man whose advice we had to have. He had a subsidiary company in Canada, or proceeded to establish one, and of course used Canadians for all the interviewing. The results were tabulated in Lou Harris' own office and, of greater importance, he interpreted them for us himself.

The surveys stressed that while the public was highly critical of the record of the Tory party, most people at that time were not nearly as critical of its leader, Mr. Diefenbaker. The erosion which occurred in the public's estimation of this man had just begun. In 1961, he was considered to be an honest, sincere, straight-forward man, an effective speaker, and a "clean-living, Christian gentleman." Moreover, the public felt the Liberals were too negative and too partisan in opposition.

Active Liberals, from Mike Pearson on down, found it almost impossible to believe these estimates of Mr. Diefenbaker or to accept the obvious conclusion to be drawn – that the proper strategy for the Liberal Party was to emphasize the positive aspects of the Liberal program in simple concrete terms, while attacking the Tory party for its weaknesses. It was clear that it would be a serious mistake to launch an assault on Mr. Diefenbaker personally. It was also clear that the Liberals should concentrate on a relatively few issues and explain what they would do about them. At the top of the list was the Liberal Party's program for dealing with the unemployment problem and promoting industrial growth.

The surveys indicated that the public did not have a clear impression of Mr. Pearson or what he stood for. Mike Pearson always made a tremendous impression before small groups and he commanded the affection and the loyalty of the members of the Liberal Party. His intelligence and cultured approach endeared him to his followers, but these were not reflected in a sharp, clear "image," insofar as the public was concerned. He had difficulty in projecting before large audiences, and he sometimes gave the impression that he was vacillating and indecisive. He seemed to lack the strong dominant qualities the public recognized in Mr. Diefenbaker. It was partly for this reason that we decided to place considerable emphasis upon the "Pearson team" in the 1962 and 1963 elections. An added factor was the need to demonstrate that, if the Liberals were elected, Pearson would have a lot of new and able people to choose from in forming his government.

The second part of the planning operation for the 1962 campaign was the selection of good candidates. It was extremely difficult to persuade first-class people to stand for election, partly because in 1960 and 1961 the chances of the Liberal Party doing reasonably well against the colossal majority of the Conservatives did not seem encouraging, and partly because the general standing of members of Parliament, not to mention the amount of their remuneration, was not high. I raised this latter question with Pearson in July 1961, and recommend that, if he became Prime Minister, members' indemnities and pensions should be increased, more secretarial and research assistance should be provided, members should be given passes to allow them to travel by air as well as by train, and, more generally, that a real effort should be made to upgrade the standing of M.P.'s. I recommended also that a firm promise be given to review the whole question of election expenses and the sources of funds to cover them. Pearson agreed to implement most of these proposals if he were elected, and I was authorized to inform prospective candidates to this effect. This made a considerable difference to our recruiting efforts.

In addition, it was clear that there would have to be examples of some new people who were prepared to stand if we wished to obtain good candidates throughout the country. A few of those who agreed to give the necessary lead included Captain David Groos, a popular ex-naval officer in Victoria; Jack Nicholson and Jack Davis in Vancouver; Jim Coutts, an extremely active Young Liberal in Alberta; Hazen Argue, late of the C.C.F. party in Saskatchewan; Fred Douglas, a popular United Church minister and Margaret Konantz in Winnipeg; Jack Lloyd, the Mayor of Halifax; Dr. John Stewart, formerly a professor at Columbia and then at St. Francis Xavier University at Antigonish in Nova Scotia; Sherwood Rideout, a prominent member of the Railway Brotherhoods, and Jean-Eudes Dubé in New Brunswick; Maurice Lamontagne, Maurice Sauvé, Bud Drury, and John Turner in Quebec. Bud Drury's decision to stand as a Liberal candidate in Montreal was particularly helpful.

In Ontario, some of the new candidates included Edgar Benson, a practising chartered accountant and Queen's University professor in Kingston; Lloyd Francis, an Ottawa controller and a prospective candidate in the next mayoralty contest against Charlotte Whitton; Lucien Lamoureux of Cornwall, who became the Liberal candidate in Stormont, and in due course went on to become perhaps the ablest Speaker in the history of the House of Commons; Larry Pennell, an extremely popular and able Brantford lawyer who was finally persuaded to run in Brant-Haldimand; and John Munro, a young alderman who became the Liberal candidate in Hamilton East. In addition to those mentioned, there were many other new and first-class Liberal candidates standing in Ontario, including: Herb Gray in Windsor; Eugene Whelan, a shrewd and humorous man from the Leamington area; Jim McNulty, a popular school teacher in St. Catharines; and Dr. Harry Harley of Oakville.

In Metropolitan Toronto, a number of new Liberal candidates soon began to make news. Mitchell Sharp, the former Deputy Minister of Trade and Commerce, was nominated in Eglinton to run against Donald Fleming, the Minister of Finance. Sharp put up a great battle and lost by only a small margin. Another contest which attracted wide attention was that of "Red" Kelly, the popular hockey player whom Keith Davey had persuaded to stand as the Liberal candidate in York West. Kelly is a fine man and created an excellent impression. Quite apart from that, he was the idol of all Maple Leaf hockey fans and became the most popular and most sought-after Liberal M.P. after the election.

Donald Macdonald, at thirty, was the youngest Liberal candidate in Toronto, running in Rosedale, then looked upon as an absolutely safe

Tory seat. Other new Liberal candidates in Toronto included Jim Walker in York Centre; Moe Moreau, a mining engineer in Scarborough; Ian Wahn, the head of his own large law firm, in St. Paul's; and myself in Davenport, about which I shall have more to say a little later.

I should also mention Ralph Cowan who ran in York Humber, and later became an embarrassment to the Liberal Party because of his bigoted views on French Canada which he expressed in forceful language at every available opportunity. Cowan had considerable ability, was a tireless worker and the possessor of an unpredictable sense of humour. One day in Parliament, he made a speech criticizing a bill which, as Minister of Finance, I was piloting through the House. When he finished, he came down and sat beside me in the front row and with a wide grin asked what else he could do for me. I replied, also with a smile, I hope, that I wished he would go straight to hell. This seemed to tickle Cowan who suggested that if all the ministers were to treat him in the same way it would be much better. From then on, I usually got along well with Ralph, which some of my colleagues in the cabinet found difficulty in understanding.

Not many of the new candidates I have mentioned had committed themselves by December 1961, and I was getting anxious, especially about Ontario where Liberals simply had to make an impressive showing if they were to get anywhere at all. At about this time, at a meeting of the Ontario Campaign Committee, Dan Lang asked me how I felt things were going and I said I was unhappy about the progress being made. He then asked if I felt there was anything more that he should be doing as chairman of the Ontario Committee. With this opening, I suggested that he should take two months' leave of absence from his law firm and scout Ontario for candidates. This he did with remarkable success.

The third element in our election planning was publicity. Pearson himself made the major contribution in this area, partly because he was very popular with the working members of the press and partly because, like all successful public figures, he had a flair for making news. In addition to Pearson, Keith Davey had made friends very quickly with the members of the Press Gallery in Ottawa, which was of great assistance to the Liberal Party. And this was augmented as the type of new candidates referred to previously were nominated and began to express their views on public issues.

The advertising and publicity proposals and suggested budgets were prepared by George Elliott of MacLaren's who had succeeded Al Scott and now worked directly with Keith Davey and myself. In addition, we set up a hard-working communications committee, which included in its membership Dick O'Hagan representing Pearson's office, and Maurice Sauvé who was thoroughly familiar with the formula which had helped Jean Lesage to win the Quebec election in 1960. The communications committee met frequently at Liberal headquarters in Ottawa, criticized George Elliott's proposals, and originated many new ideas.

Keith Davey and I developed an excellent working arrangement. Throughout the 1962 campaign I went to Ottawa once or twice a week. The rest of the time I spent campaigning in Davenport or in Ontario, with occasional visits to other parts of the country. Keith was in day-to-day – or rather minute-to-minute – charge in Ottawa. He was authorized to make decisions on the various matters that cropped up all the time, it being understood that if there were something of real importance, or something that involved a change in the campaign strategy that had previously been agreed upon, he would get in touch with me before making changes. I suppose that on the average, when I was not in Ottawa, we spoke to each other on the telephone three or four times a day throughout the campaign. It was a first-class arrangement and one that, in practice, worked most satisfactorily.

Many of the new candidates, myself included, were completely ignorant of the practical business of campaigning and of getting elected. In order to rectify this situation, Keith Davey, with the help of David Greenspan, organized a series of instruction courses which became known as campaign colleges. Groups of from twenty-five to fifty candidates and their campaign managers attended these courses which usually lasted from a Friday evening until the following Sunday afternoon. The subjects explained were the rudiments of politics; how to organize a riding; how to canvass; how to assess the Liberal Party's strengths and weaknesses in different areas; how best to use the news media at one's disposal; how to raise money; and how to use it most effectively. There is no doubt that these campaign colleges, which were started in Ontario but were later adapted for use in other provinces, were of a tremendous help to many Liberal candidates, and the information gained there assisted them to get elected. This was one of Davey's many contributions to the resurgence of the Liberal Party.

As Chairman of the National Campaign Committee, it was important for me not only to direct operations from the centre but also to work on my own campaign in Davenport and get around the country. The purpose in visiting other parts of Canada, including a good deal of Ontario, was to help to create news by explaining to the public what the Liberal Party stood for and, at the same time, to encourage the local candidates. In the six months prior to the date of the election, I made some twenty-five prepared speeches, quite apart from speaking off the cuff at many political gatherings, including those in my own riding and also on radio and television.

102

I remember arriving for a meeting at a small place near New Glasgow in December 1961, and meeting Dr. John Stewart who was to be our candidate in Antigonish-Guysborough. He said he had just obtained a copy of my book, *Troubled Canada,* and was looking forward to reading it. I knew, of course, that Stewart was a distinguished academic so I said, modestly I hope, that *Troubled Canada* was more of a political tract than a book. To this John replied, "In Nova Scotia, when we have to pay $3.50 for something, it's a book."

I was on good terms with Ross Thatcher in those days, mainly because I had agreed we would send him a little more election money from the central funds than he had expected. He had made me promise to speak at three nomination meetings in Saskatchewan, which I did, including Hazen Argue's in Assiniboia. It was quite an experience for someone who was completely new to politics. On March 20, I drove down to Assiniboia, which is about one hundred miles south of Regina, with Davy Steuart, one of the funniest men in active politics. We arrived about 11.30 A.M. to find the meeting in full swing. Steuart explained that the farmers had little to do in winter and would expect the meeting to continue until midnight, with time out for refueling at noon and again at about 6.00 P.M. When I came on to speak at about 9.30 P.M., I confessed to Steuart that I would only be good for about half an hour. He looked horrified, as in Saskatchewan that is considered as being just a warm-up, but volunteered to make a second speech himself if necessary.

After the meeting, two elderly ladies came up and complimented me upon my speech, which they said reminded them of Social Credit! They said they were members of the Social Credit Party and apparently had time on their hands that evening. After some suitable acknowledgement, I asked them if they understood what Social Credit stood for, and if so, would they explain it to me. But they were not to be trapped so easily. They replied, "We don't really understand what Social Credit is all about, but that is what makes it so intriguing."

After a long period of farewells, we set off at a late hour for, I thought, Regina. But it turned out we were headed for Moose Jaw to report to Ross Thatcher about the meeting. He did not seem to be too interested to hear that Hazen Argue had been nominated. He had expected that; in fact, he had so ordered. What really concerned him was the amount of money Steuart had raised from those attending the meeting. No political meeting was ever held in Saskatchewan after Thatcher became leader of the Liberal Party without a collection being taken. Finally, after much discussion, we were allowed to proceed on to Regina, and after a short sleep took off the next morning for two more nomination meetings before, exhausted, I caught the plane back to Toronto.

The results of the election of June 18, 1962, were as follows:

	June 1962	March 1958
Progressive Conservatives	116	208
Liberals	100	49
N.D.P.	19	8
Social Credit and others	30	0
	265	265

The Tories lost 92 seats and were far down in the percentage of the popular vote, from 53.7% in 1958 to 37.3%. The Liberals gained 51 seats and were a fraction ahead of the Tories in the popular vote. The Liberals increased their standing by 28 seats in Ontario, 11 in Quebec, 6 in the Maritimes, and 4 in British Columbia, but made practically no impression on the Prairies. Of the 18 seats in what used to be called "Tory Toronto," the Liberals won 12 and the N.D.P. 3; the Tories managed to hold on to only 3 seats. It was a tremendous victory for Mike Pearson, and no one expected that the new minority government of Mr. Diefenbaker would last for very long.

In the late summer or early fall of 1961, I had agreed tentatively to be a candidate if I could secure a nomination in Toronto. As Chairman of the National Campaign Committee, it had become evident that I must do this as an example. It was suggested that I should run in Davenport. Pearson had asked Andy Thompson to do what he could to get me elected in Toronto. Thompson had been an assistant to Mike Pearson during the 1958 campaign and afterwards had been elected to the provincial legislature in Dovercourt, whose boundaries at that time coincided almost exactly with those of the federal riding of Davenport.

There were a good many Liberals in Toronto who felt that, as a successful professional and businessman identified in the public mind with "Bay Street," I was not likely to be a winning candidate in a working class riding like Davenport. To overcome this difficulty, a petition was organized asking me to contest the nomination for Davenport in the next election. The petition was signed by some fifteen hundred people and naturally this in itself attracted a lot of favourable publicity. After this, there could be no question of my being treated as an interloper foisted upon the riding by a few interested members of the executive committee. In fact, when at some public meeting one of my opponents asked what right I had as a successful businessman to offer myself as a representative of the people of Davenport, the answer was very simple. I said that fifteen hundred people had signed a petition asking me to run there and then asked my opponent how many people had invited him to do so. When he did not answer I added that I was in fact a successful businessman; I did not dispute this; if I had been unsuccessful I would not have presumed to offer myself as a candidate. That seemed to end the argument.

Andy Thompson was, of course, a tremendous help in all this. As an Irishman, he has a warm disposition and a generous heart. And he had developed an organization in Dovercourt or Davenport – the two ridings being organized together – which would do anything for him, as later they were prepared to do for me. Andy helped me to get to know the storekeepers in the area and accompanied me on house-to-house canvassing tours. In addition, and of particular importance to me as Chairman of the National Campaign Committee, he introduced me to the leaders of the various ethnic groups and the editors of the ethnic newspapers, most of whom were friends of his. He was helped in this by his mother-in-law, Olga Riisna, an extremely intelligent woman who became one of my greatest supporters and for whom I developed a high and affectionate regard.

The nominating meeting in Davenport was held on Tuesday, January 23, 1962. Pearson was the speaker, and, as a result, the meeting was well attended by Liberals throughout Toronto. It attracted considerable attention in the press. My own campaigning in Davenport started shortly after my nomination and well before the election was called. Joe Grittani, who had directed many campaigns in the riding, agreed to be my campaign manager as a labour of love for the Liberal Party. He was a tremendous help to me, and I shall always be grateful to him. Andy Thompson spent a lot of time with me, and an effective if somewhat loose campaign organization was developed.

I was uncertain how I would get along at door-to-door canvassing, never having taken part in an election campaign before. However, once I overcame an initial nervousness, I enjoyed meeting a new and very different cross-section of people and learning something of their interests and their troubles. The main problem in the area at that time was unemployment, and many people had become almost desperate about it. I do not mean that they were starving, but they were unhappy about the fact they had no jobs. To some people, this was looked upon as a personal disgrace, something they should somehow or other be able to overcome. In some cases, and especially among the new Canadians, the wives were able to get jobs and were supporting the family, while the husbands were left at home to mind the house. This undermined their confidence and made them miserable and dejected.

To begin with, I called on most of the churches in the riding, and the priests in charge were very helpful in telling me about the difficulties their parishioners were up against. One of those I got to know was Father Gavard of St. Anthony's Catholic Church on Bloor Street. Several members of our campaign committee attended this church and informed me they thought that Father Gavard was a Conservative. I did not get this impression on my first meeting with him during the course of which he told me he had always been fascinated by politics and that he was a great admirer of President Jack Kennedy. I sent him a copy of *The Making of the President,* which he told me he read with the greatest interest. One day, when the campaign was well in progress, I noticed Father Gavard looking in the windows of our committee rooms. I greeted him and insisted that he come in and meet everyone who was working there, including those who were members of his parish. I remember introducing him facetiously as a new member of our campaign committee, knowing naturally that in his position he could not take sides publicly in politics.

Another big church in the area is St. Mary's of the Angels, which is run by the Basilian Fathers. As the parish is very largely Italian, the priests in charge were of Italian origin and spoke the language. They had been having a hard time because many of the Italian boys and younger men were without jobs in 1962 and had been getting into trouble. Understandably, their priests were inclined to be critical of the government for allowing these conditions to occur and to persist. At the same time, they were sympathetic to the Liberals who seemed determined to introduce policies designed to relieve the unemployment problem. I went back to see these Basilian priests on several occasions, but I remember one visit in particular which occurred some three and a half years later, during the 1965 campaign. By that time, the atmosphere was very different. Everyone seemed cheerful. They told me they had no more troubles because everyone was working, and working very hard. They made it clear they thought the credit for the change was due to the Liberal government and that I had had some hand in it. They assured me that they expected I would be re-elected, especially as they did not seem to think much of the chances of my Conservative opponent, Danny Iannuzzi, the publisher of the Italian newspaper who, despite his Italian name, is not a Catholic. The fact that I was not a Catholic either seemed not to matter. In fact, my friends, the priests, seemed quite happy to be photographed with me. With their approval, I used the photograph to advantage in my campaign.

There were, of course, many other churches in the riding. One of these, St. Anne's Anglican Church on Gladstone Avenue, is a Toronto landmark because it was decorated by members of the Group of Seven who painted murals on its ceiling. The priest in charge, the Reverend George Young, is quite a character who, I sometimes thought, would be a politician himself if, by so doing, he could help the poorer people in his community.

Douglas Morton had won Davenport for the Conservatives by defeating Paul Hellyer in the 1957 election, and again in 1958 by 4,245 votes. Joe Grittani insisted that Morton would be my principal opponent. He was right, although I thought that Bill Sefton, a senior executive of the United Steelworkers of America, the N.D.P. candidate, would be the man to beat. Sefton was a large good-looking man, and because of his connections with the Steelworkers was able to command a great deal of support from them. In fact, the riding seemed at times to be crawling with professional organizers borrowed from the Steelworkers. Moreover it was one of four Toronto ridings the N.D.P. had decided to concentrate their attentions on in the 1962 campaign. They felt, with some justification perhaps, that it was the kind of riding that, with heavy unemployment, they should win. However, they were too aggressive, and I suspect they frightened many people off.

I remember knocking on the door of a house in the south end of the riding just north of Queen Street, which had a large blown-up photograph of Sefton on the lawn between two heavy iron stakes. When the door was opened I said I was the Liberal candidate and, while I recognized that the occupants were supporters of the N.D.P., nevertheless if I was successful in winning the election, I would hope to represent everybody in the riding and so would like to meet them. The man who answered the door replied to this by saying, "Mr. Gordon, we're all for you. There are eight of us here and you can count on eight Liberal votes on June 18." I then asked about the sign. The reply was that the people who lived there felt it was easier to leave the sign alone than to raise difficulties and run the risk of getting hurt.

The results of the 1962 election in Davenport were as follows:

Bell, Raymond (Social Credit)	113
Clarke, Phyllis (Communist)	232
Gordon, Walter L. (Liberal)	9,101
Morton, M. Douglas (Progressive Conservative)	6,741
Sefton, Bill (N.D.P.)	5,177

I felt that my win with forty-two per cent of the vote was more than satisfactory.

CHAPTER SEVEN

The Election Campaign of April 1963

Difficulties of the Diefenbaker government; reversal of the Liberal Party's defence policy; fall of the Diefenbaker government; the Liberal Party's preparations; President Kennedy; the "Truth Squad"; the use of television; Sixty Days of Decision; the results; the campaign in Davenport; the first Pearson government.

The Canadian dollar had been under pressure both prior to and during the 1962 election campaign. In his budget speech on April 10, 1962, Donald Fleming, the Minister of Finance, had said: "The government has not hesitated, and will not hesitate in the future, to deploy a substantial volume of funds on one side of the market or the other in order to prevent sudden or erratic movement in our exchange rate." And a little later in the same speech, discussing Canada's relations with the International Monetary Fund, he had gone on to say: "Against such a background of general co-operation, the House will understand why the Fund, while naturally and properly retaining the ultimate objective of having Canada declare a fixed exchange rate, has not been disposed to press us into any hasty action which might prove to be premature and impossible to sustain."

Just three weeks later, on May 2, 1962, with the election campaign in full swing, the government was forced to accept a formal devaluation of the dollar and adopted a pegged rate of 92.5 cents in terms of the American dollar. This was a great humiliation for Fleming and indeed for the government as a whole. Naturally, the Liberals made the most of it throughout the remaining weeks of the campaign. My own position in the matter was a bit restricted, as I had been advocating devaluation for some time but not, of course, in the way it was brought about.

This is what I said in Owen Sound on May 31, 1962, in a speech on behalf of the Liberal candidate for Grey North:

Partly because of the government's tight-money policy, the Canadian dollar remained at a high premium all through 1957, 1958, 1959, 1960, and the first half of 1961. This was harmful to both our export and domestic manufacturing industries. Thus it added to the unemployment problem. Many of us said in those days that the dollar should be brought down to par or to a modest discount. Mr. Fleming replied at great length and on every occasion possible that this could not be done.

But a year ago, he changed his mind – or Mr. Diefenbaker changed it for him. Instead, however, of taking firm action and fixing the rate of exchange at par or at some appropriate discount, he proceeded to talk the dollar down in value. This caused considerable uncertainty and doubt.

Before long, the problem was to hold the value of the dollar up, not force it down. $400,000,000 was poured out of the Exchange Fund in the first four months of 1962 in a desperate attempt to do this. But these frantic efforts failed. In late April, it became apparent that we were faced with a financial crisis. Mr. Fleming was forced to go hat-in-hand to the International Monetary Fund for help. He was forced to devalue the Canadian dollar there and then. He was forced to agree to a fixed rate, something he said all along he would not do. . . .

Some other Liberals were less inhibited and claimed that devaluation meant the end of everything.

Immediately after the election, the Diefenbaker government accepted what came close to being an ultimatum from the Bank of Canada and, indirectly, from the International Monetary Fund. In order to avoid a further devaluation of its currency, Canada appealed once more to the International Monetary Fund for help. This had been granted in early May, but on condition that we would abandon the floating rate of exchange for the the Canadian dollar and comply with the I.M.F. rules and regulations in other respects. In June, the I.M.F. insisted on further conditions. In the result, Canada embarked upon a period of austerity, including the imposition of a restrictive monetary policy which would mean higher interest rates, the imposition of a surtax on imports, and substantial cuts in government expenditures.

I believed it was a serious mistake for Canada to have adopted a fixed exchange rate at the insistence of the I.M.F. I thought at the time it would be preferable to allow the Canadian dollar to find its own level even if it were to drop to eighty-five or even eighty cents for a short period rather than to accept direction from an international authority located in Washington. That authority might be influenced, at least to some extent, by points of view that would tend to reduce Canada's room for manoeuvre and independence. I called Mike Pearson as soon as I heard the news in June about the proposed austerity program and took the first plane to Ottawa to discuss the situation with him. But it was too late. Before I called him, the Governor of the Bank of Canada had persuaded Pearson to support the government in the course contemplated. I felt this had placed Canada in something of a strait-jacket.

The Conservatives, confronted with this financial crisis and demoralized by the election results, were in no mood to call Parliament any sooner than they had to. Mr. Diefenbaker announced the House would meet on September 27, more than three months after election day. This meant a somewhat frustrating summer, especially for the newly elected members. We sensed the government was on the skids and were anxious to have a chance to bring it down.

When the House did meet, I became the opposition's financial critic. I knew nothing about the rules or, in fact, about the practice of debating. But in order to establish my new position, I asked questions from time to time and made four or five speeches in the three months before the Christmas recess, much of which I was able to prepare carefully in advance. The first of these was a short speech on monetary policy on October 3. My second speech on October 22 was much longer. I reviewed the economic situation and presented the Liberal Party's program for recovery.

I came up against Mr. Diefenbaker only once in those first few months, which was fortunate for me. On November 29, 1962, he made a long statement about a report by the Glassco Commission and stated that Senator Wallace McCutcheon, Minister without Portfolio, would be responsible for its implementation. In replying to Mr. Diefenbaker's remarks on behalf of the official opposition, I made some reference to the fact that Glassco and I had been partners for over twenty years and that his son was married to my daughter. I then referred to Wally McCutcheon, who had been one of the active managers of the Argus Corporation, and to his new responsibility: "The Minister without Portfolio in his former capacities has had some experience along these lines, and if I was not afraid that you would think I was transgressing [the rules], Mr. Speaker, I would say that in these other spheres he has usually corrected things by effecting a change in the management." A roar of laughter greeted this remark because, naturally, everyone knew it was a reference to Mr. Diefenbaker. His expression showed he did not like it. He could not stand ridicule or being laughed at. The lesson was to stand me in good stead in the future.

This was not a good period for Mr. Diefenbaker. Two weeks before, when commenting on the Cuban crisis, which many people thought might provoke a nuclear war and thus the end of the world as we knew it, he had used language, perhaps unintentionally, that sounded as if he distrusted President Kennedy's statement that ballistic-missile sites were being installed in Cuba. It remained for Pearson a few days later to make it clear that Canada stood at the side of the United States in this matter, and would support the Americans against the Russians in any way we could.

Pearson was the strongest figure in this session of Parliament, and on December 17 he showed he was the first English-speaking politician to have some understanding of what was going on in the Province of Quebec. In the course of his speech that day, he said:

> To French-speaking Canadians, Confederation created a bilingual and bicultural nation. It protected their language and their culture throughout the whole of Canada. It meant partnership – not domination. French-speaking Canadians believed that this partnership meant equal opportunities for both the founding races to share in all phases of Canadian development.
>
> English-speaking Canadians agreed that the Confederation arrangement protected the rights of the French-Canadians in Quebec, in Parliament, and in federal courts. But most felt it did not go beyond those limits. This meant that, for all practical purposes, there would be an English-speaking Canada with a bilingual Quebec. The "French fact" was to be provincial only.
>
> This difference over the meaning of Confederation was obscured for many years after 1867 by other considerations. But it is the basic source of present misunderstandings and difficulties in the relations between the two races.

Towards the end of his speech, he made a proposal that eventually, after he became Prime Minister, was to take shape as the Royal Commission on Bilingualism and Biculturalism: "This means, I believe, that we have now reached the stage where we should seriously and collectively review the bicultural and bilingual situation in our country, our experiences in the teaching of English and French and in the relations existing generally between our two main racial groups."

This speech made a profound impact and greatly strengthened both Pearson's own position and that of the Liberal Party in Quebec. It was another example, perhaps, of how much he depended on his thoughtful and talented associate, Maurice Lamontagne. In a signed article in *Le Devoir*, André Laurendeau had this to say: "I cannot remember a single English-speaking statesman in Canada leading one of the traditional political parties who since the beginning of the twentieth century has been as explicit and as firm, nor who at the same time has formulated such a precise and such a broad proposal."

111

The three months in Parliament in the fall of 1962 was a good experience for the new members on the Liberal side. We learned something of the rules, we got to know each other, and we sensed it would not be long before Mike Pearson would be Prime Minister.

I was soon impressed by Judy LaMarsh, who had been first elected in a by-election in 1960 and re-elected in 1962. She was and is a cheerful, intelligent person with an earthy wit and independent mind. She had been a successful courtroom lawyer and was a source of strength in any debate she took a hand in. Judy was by all odds the best stump speaker in the party. With her low warm voice, her intuitive intelligence, and her ability to think quickly on her feet, she could establish a rapport with her audiences in no time flat. And she nearly always had something interesting and provocative to say.

I was impressed also with Donald Macdonald who, at thirty, was one of the youngest members of the Liberal caucus. He always spoke up forthrightly and with courage on the issues that concerned him, even when the leaders of the party were taking opposite positions. Others who soon began to make their presence felt included Bud Drury who, as an ex-Deputy Minister, knew much more about the system than the rest of us; Ben Benson, who everyone acknowledged was exceptionally able; Larry Pennell, also very able as well as being very popular; and Gene Whelan, a farmer politician with a delightful sense of humour reminiscent of Will Rogers. Apart from those of us who had been elected, the suggestions and contributions of Tom Kent and Maurice Lamontagne were quite invaluable.

The House adjourned on December 20 until January 21, 1963. In the interval, the Liberals were tremendously encouraged by a Gallup Poll published on January 9 which showed them with a fifteen-point lead over the Tories:

	January 9, 1963	June 18, 1962
Liberal	47%	37%
Progressive Conservative	32	37
N.D.P.	10	14
Socred	11	12
	100%	100%

It seemed clear from this poll not only that the Tories would lose, if an election were held at that time, but that the Liberals should be able to win an over-all majority.

And then, three days later at a meeting of the York-Scarborough Liberal Association on January 12, 1963, at the Canadiana Motor Hotel in Scarborough, Mike Pearson made a controversial speech about the use of nuclear weapons. He argued that, under the NATO and NORAD treaties, Canada was committed to use tactical nuclear warheads and that a Liberal government should and would honour these commitments. This speech was a highly important one and had considerable impact both on the public and on the Liberal Party.

Pearson asserted that the argument for or against nuclear weapons for Canada was a "political, not a moral one." Both in NATO and in continental defence, the Canadian government had accepted commitments for Canada in continental and collective defence which could only be carried out by Canadian forces if nuclear warheads were used. Canada should not, however, contribute to the strategic nuclear deterrent. Such retaliatory power should be left "almost entirely in the hands of the United States." He went on to say that the government should re-examine at once the whole basis of Canadian defence policy and, in particular, should discuss with the United States and with NATO "a role for Canada in continental and collective defence which would be more realistic and effective for Canada than the present one."

This was a carefully reasoned presentation and to many people it proved to be convincing. But those who did not agree with the conclusion failed to see what sense it would make to equip the Canadian forces with nuclear warheads if we intended almost immediately afterwards to discard them in favour of a role "which would be more realistic and effective for Canada," that is, a role which would not involve the use of nuclear weapons. It seemed to people who felt this way that once nuclear warheads were acquired by Canada it would be very hard indeed to get rid of them.

I expect that in taking the firm stand he did respecting the use of tactical nuclear warheads, Pearson was influenced by a number of considerations. Like most of us in the House of Commons, he had been profoundly affected by the Cuban crisis in October and by Mr. Diefenbaker's reluctance to state clearly whether Canada was prepared to back the American position. Then, as indicated in his statement, he was influenced by remarks made in Ottawa on January 4, 1963, by General Lauris Norstad, the retiring commander of the NATO forces, in which Norstad asserted that Canada was not living up to its commitments. Undoubtedly, Pearson had been impressed with Paul Hellyer's assessment of the role Canadian troops were playing in NATO after a visit he made with Judy LaMarsh to Europe in the fall. Hellyer was the Liberal Party's critic on defence matters. Pearson may also have been influenced by the views of some of the people he saw in New York on the weekend before he made his speech.

Mr. Diefenbaker seemed unable to make up his mind about the question of nuclear weapons, and this was the cause of much frustration, especially in the armed services. Many people believed it was time that some-one in authority – or someone who expected to be in authority – should indicate what he believed Canada's policy should be one way or the other, although whether Pearson's decision in this matter was the right one is open to considerable argument.

While these may have been some of the considerations that influenced Pearson in coming to his decision, he seemed to have overlooked the need to inform and convince his friends and colleagues in the party that a change in policy of this importance was imperative. After all, the Liberal rally just two years before, in January 1961, had come out strongly against the use of nuclear weapons. Pearson agreed with this at the time, and many of us had firm views on the subject. Some of us did not believe the leader of the party had the right, or should have the right, to reverse this policy uni-laterally.

Many of us were not convinced that there was or could be a realistic dividing line between tactical nuclear defensive weapons and strategic nuclear offensive weapons. Who is to say whether a weapon is essentially defensive or offensive in character? Moreover, I could not believe then, and do not believe now, that if nuclear weapons are ever used they can be restricted to short-range or so-called tactical weapons only. I suspect the other side would retaliate with everything it had at its disposal, in which case the world would be blown up long before the distinctions between tactical and strategic or defensive and offensive weapons could be settled to everyone's satisfaction. In these circumstances, I believed then and still believe now that the use, or possible use, of all nuclear weapons must be restricted, or that sooner or later the world as we know it will cease to exist. Therefore, it seemed to me at that time, and still does, that Canada should give an example by refusing to manufacture, control, or use nuclear arms of any kind. If that means qualifying our position under the NATO or NORAD treaties, we should do so.

As was to be expected, the Scarborough speech provoked a great deal of controversy. Pearson was acclaimed by some for being able to make up his mind and, in contrast with Mr. Diefenbaker, stating in unequivocal terms what the policy of a Liberal government would be. But in subse-quent speeches the policy seemed to go through some modifications.

On January 16, Pearson repeated the general tenor of his Scarborough speech, but stated more explicitly that a Liberal government would review existing agreements and would like them to be renegotiated. The key, he stated, was the commitment to arm the CF-104's, pointing out that changing the role of the air division would "take a little doing now." Still later, at a press conference on February 12, he indicated another shift in policy when he explained that his January 12 pledge for a full re-examination of defence policy did not necessarily mean seeking a purely conventional role, as it had been interpreted by many. "Maybe a conventional role would be best," he said, "but I don't know what the result would be." Meanwhile, Paul Hellyer publicly suggested that Mr. Pearson had been misinterpreted and stated that the "Liberals would not renegotiate defence agreements. We are going to live up to commitments until the equipment becomes obsolete in five years." *The Toronto Star* observed that "Mr. Pearson and his colleagues . . . are shifting the party's position on the issue to what appears to be a clear-cut policy in favour of nuclear arms. Whatever one may think about the party's pro-nuclear stand . . . it is clearer than the position Mr. Pearson enunciated last month."

On February 20, Pearson endorsed the stand taken by Hellyer and committed his future government to keep the existing nuclear weapons "as long as they are useful for defence." On February 23, in an address to the Quebec Liberal Federation, he stated:

> The Canadian government accepted years ago a defensive nuclear role and nuclear equipment to carry out that role. . . . So long as . . . we have [them], as long as they are not abandoned as obsolete, I believe we must accept the ammunition which alone makes them effective. . . . We Liberals . . . are against nuclear weapons. We are against all weapons. . . . But until weapons can be abolished . . . until we have a disarmament agreement, these weapons are necessary for the protection of peace.

It was said, in retrospect, that Pearson's stand on the use of nuclear weapons was responsible more than anything else for the defeat of the Diefenbaker government and the victory of the Liberals in the election which followed. Certainly, the stand taken by the leader of the Liberal Party on this issue was the subject of a great deal of discussion in the House of Commons that reassembled on January 21, and may well have helped to push Douglas Harkness into resigning as Minister of National Defence. This presaged the fall of the Diefenbaker government.

But the fact remains that defence policy was not by any means the main issue in the campaign which culminated in the election of April 8, 1963. And while according to our surveys early in the election campaign approximately three out of five people in Ontario and Quebec thought the Diefenbaker policy on nuclear arms was wrong, opinion at the end was about equally divided. Opinion in the West and in the Atlantic area may have been more critical, but if so, there were other considerations which would have offset this, especially in Western Canada where personal loyalties to Mr. Diefenbaker were strong. It is significant also that the Gallup Poll, which was published on January 9, 1963, showed the Liberals with a fifteen-point spread over the Tories, enough for an over-all majority. The results on April 8, 1963, gave the Liberals a spread of only nine points, quite a difference.

My own reaction to the Pearson speech at Scarborough on January 12 was one of considerable dejection. While I appreciated the case that he had made in reaching the decision, I was not convinced by it. And I was seriously disturbed to think that he would make a decision of this magnitude without consulting his closest friends and colleagues in the party. When I spoke to him about this, he told me he had been struggling with the problem for some time and had only made up his mind about it a few days before the Scarborough speech while on a visit to New York. He seemed to be genuinely sorry he had not spoken to some of us beforehand, and stressed his intention to have a thorough review made of Canada's defence policy if a Liberal government was elected, the clear implication being that we would forgo the use of nuclear weapons at that time. In the meantime, he felt we had made definite commitments and should live up to them.

Mike Pearson was my closest friend. I had spent three hard years doing everything I could to help him reorganize and rejuvenate the Liberal Party, to help him to become Prime Minister. I had run and been elected a Member of Parliament in 1962 and I was Chairman of the National Campaign Committee of the Liberal Party. I was committed personally by this time both to the Liberal party in general and to many of the Liberal candidates in particular. I decided, rightly or wrongly, that I could not – or rather, should not – drop out over this issue and comforted myself by thinking that, once we were elected, Canada's defence policy would be changed!

Jean Marchand and Pierre Elliott Trudeau, on the other hand, both of whom were expected to be candidates in the coming election, protested Pearson's new policy vigorously and refused to run. Trudeau was especially critical over this incident both of Pearson specifically and of the Liberal Party generally. Writing in the April issue of *Cité Libre*, he said:

> No importance was attached to the fact that such a policy [the acceptance of nuclear arms] had been repudiated by the party congress and banished from its program: nor to the fact that the chief had acted without consulting the national council of the Liberal Federation or its executive committee: nor to the fact that the leader had forgotten to discuss it with the parliamentary caucus or even with his principal advisers. The "Pope" had spoken: It was up to the faithful to believe.

Trudeau went on to document the long-standing official opposition of Mr. Pearson and the Liberal Party to nuclear arms and suggested that the switch was made under American pressure.

Fate had it that the final thrust came from the Pentagon and obliged Mr. Pearson to betray his party's platform as well as the ideal with which he had always identified himself. Power presented itself to Mr. Pearson; he had nothing to lose except honour. He lost it. And his whole party lost it with him.

Trudeau proceeded to urge all those concerned about Canadian independence to vote N.D.P. in the upcoming election, and concluded: "Governmental instability, the fragmentation of the opposition, the risk of 'losing one's vote'; these are minor dangers compared with the loss of integrity to which Mr. Pearson had led us."

One can only speculate on what a difference it might have made to Pearson personally and to the two Liberal governments he headed if Marchand and Trudeau had been with him from the start.

This incident raises the whole question of the right that the leader of a political party in or out of office should have to change important policy decisions on his own initiative. A Prime Minister, if he is supported by his cabinet and caucus – or, in other words, the government of the day – must be free to modify or alter established policies in the light of changed conditions, even if this means going counter to what was previously approved by the political party they represent. Ministers, including the Prime Minister, have a wider responsibility than just to carry out the directions and desires of their own particular party once they are in office. They must be accountable to the nation as a whole. A Prime Minister, however, is not likely to announce or to advocate a change in an important policy unless he is reasonably certain his colleagues will support him. Except in extraordinary circumstances, this means discussing things with them in advance. Any alternative to this procedure could lead to a dictatorship.

Presumably, no leader of a party in opposition would change course on an important policy issue unless he were reasonably certain that he would carry a large majority of his colleagues with him. But even then his freedom of action should be more restricted, if anything, than that of a Prime Minister as the head of a government. It was not practicable, of course, for Pearson to call another Liberal Party convention in January 1963, and request the delegates to reverse the defence policy they had approved just two years earlier, although ideally this is what should have been done. Failing that, he could at least have consulted the Liberal caucus before announcing the change he advocated. In a democratic system such as ours, I believe he should have done so.

By January 1963, it was clear that John Diefenbaker, who had already alienated thousands of Canadian voters, was losing ground both within his own party and within the cabinet itself. Since the summer of 1962, there had been speculation in the press that anti-Diefenbaker forces in the party and in the cabinet were marshalling to oust him as Prime Minister and party leader. When Parliament met on January 21, it was equally clear that it could not last long. There had been no budget, departmental estimates had not been passed, and only one supply motion had been approved. Revolt was stirring within the ranks of the Tories over Diefenbaker's indecision and the conflict over nuclear weapons policy. The beginning of the end came on February 3 at a stormy meeting at the Prime Minister's residence when several cabinet ministers openly indicated their displeasure. As a result, the Minister of Defence, Douglas Harkness, resigned on a matter of principle.

On Monday, February 4, when the House met, the Liberals immediately moved a motion of non-confidence, accusing the government of "lack of leadership, the breakdown of unity in the cabinet, and confusion and indecision in dealing with national and international problems." The fate of the Tory government was sealed when the Social Credit Party leader, Robert Thompson, also moved an amendment of non-confidence. The end came at 8.41 P.M. on Tuesday, February 5, when the government was defeated by 142 to 111. This was only the second time in Canadian history that a government had been overthrown by a vote in the House of Commons. Four days later, two more Tory ministers, George Hees and Pierre Sévigny, resigned; three others, Davie Fulton, Donald Fleming, and Ernest Halpenny, subsequently decided not to contest the forthcoming election.

The outcome of the June 1962 election and the difficulties confronting the Diefenbaker government at that time suggested it would not be long before another election – or the second instalment of the first one – would be upon us fairly soon. The National Campaign Committee of the Liberal party was kept in being, although some changes were made in its composition at the provincial level. We decided to make our plans on the assumption that the next election would be held at the end of March 1963. Again, we were fortunate in this choice of a target date. The election was held on April 8, 1963.

Earl Hastings dropped out as chairman in Alberta in favour of Jim Coutts who had run unsuccessfully in MacLeod in the June election. We had been unhappy about the way things had been handled by Ross Thatcher in Saskatchewan. Accordingly, it was decided to make a change there, and Otto Lang, Dean of Law at the University of Saskatchewan, was appointed provincial chairman. This annoyed Thatcher who made things as difficult for Lang as he was able to. In Nova Scotia, Allan MacEachen joined Irving Barrow as co-chairman, and a change was made in Prince Edward Island too. Bob Giguere had become chief organizer in the province of Quebec.

Liberals everywhere were cheerful and optimistic, and this was particularly true in Ontario. The National Campaign Committee was working well, and the whole organization under Keith Davey was in good shape and becoming more competent and professional all the time. Everyone was confident that, after the next round, the Liberals under Mike Pearson would be called upon to form the government. Even on the financial side the organization seemed to be working better. As in the past, Louis Gélinas proved to be an excellent fund-raiser and he became more co-operative in his relationships with Bruce Matthews, John Aird, and me.

On January 14, 1963, before Parliament reassembled after the Christmas break, we invited the leaders of the communications industry in Ontario to a formal dinner with Mike Pearson as the guest of honour. The purpose was to capitalize on the excellent press Pearson had been getting and to explain what his plans and policies would be if, as most people expected, he should be called upon to form a government in the near future.

The dinner which was very well attended was a great success. Pearson was in excellent form, both in his original remarks and in his answers to the questioning which continued for a considerable length of time. It was an auspicious beginning to the campaign which was to start officially three weeks later when Parliament dissolved.

We were able to field a number of excellent new candidates in the 1963 campaign. While, as previously noted, Jean Marchand and Pierre Trudeau had refused to run because of the position taken on nuclear warheads, Pearson had persuaded Guy Favreau to stand in Montreal. René Tremblay, the Deputy Minister of Trade and Industry in the Quebec government, became the Liberal candidate in Matapédia-Matane. Jean-Luc Pépin, Professor of Political Science at the University of Ottawa, became our candidate in Drummond-Arthabaska.

Favreau, a former Associate Deputy Minister of Justice, was a lovable, warm-hearted, gregarious man with an excellent legal mind. Unfortunately, he was not familiar with politics or with the key political personalities in Quebec. However, Pearson thought that he would soon overcome any handicaps of this nature and obviously had him in mind as a replacement for Lionel Chevrier as Quebec leader, and perhaps eventually as his own successor. Chevrier, who was born in Ontario and had always lived there until moving to Montreal in 1957, had not been accepted as the logical leader of the party in Quebec.

Two of the new candidates in Ontario who attracted considerable attention were Pauline Jewett and J.J. Greene. Pauline, a professor of political economy at Carleton University, returned to her native habitat at Brighton to run in Northumberland riding. Joe Greene, an Arnprior lawyer who had made quite an impression in 1958 when he ran for the leadership of the party in Ontario, became the Liberal candidate in Renfrew South. In addition, we had hoped that Walter Harris, the former Minister of Finance, would have another go, either in his old constituency of Grey-Bruce or somewhere else. But after much consideration, he decided not to do so.

In Manitoba, Margaret Konantz, who was engaged in a variety of community activities, became the Liberal candidate again in Winnipeg South and this time was successful. In Saskatchewan, Sidney Buckwold, the popular Mayor of Saskatoon, became a candidate. In Alberta, Keith Davey approached Harry Hays, the Mayor of Calgary, who eventually agreed to stand. He is a successful farmer and a world-famous cattle auctioneer who speaks bluntly and sometimes very fast. My first conversation with Harry, who later became a good friend as well as an impressive Minister of Agriculture, was on the telephone. I was called by a prominent Calgary Liberal who said they were trying to persuade the Mayor to run in Calgary South. He said they believed Hays could win the seat but that he was hesitating because he did not think the Liberal Party's farm policy, which included a two-price system for wheat, was any good. My Liberal friend said Hays was with him and asked if I would speak to him. Naturally I said yes and Hays came on the line. Harry said he did not like the Liberal farm policy and would have to say so if he were a candidate. Therefore he said he did not see how he could run. I replied I did not like the farm policy either; that I hoped he would run and then help us develop a better one. He agreed immediately.

Tom Kent, who had done so much in helping to develop the Liberal Party's program and was Pearson's speech writer, wished to run in the election, and Pearson agreed. It was not until well after the campaign was officially under way, however, that Tom felt free to leave Ottawa. He had been nominated in Burnaby-Coquitlam, which is on the outskirts of Vancouver, and his principal opponent was Tommy Douglas, the leader of the N.D.P. This contest attracted plenty of publicity, and while Tom did not win, he put on such a strong campaign that Douglas had to spend more time in his riding than, as the leader of his party, he might have wished to do.

The issues concerning the public were much the same in the April 1963 election as they had been in June 1962. Unemployment and the need to do something about it was the number one question, according to our surveys of public opinion. As usual, people were complaining about high prices. They wanted more to be done for older people in terms of pensions. There was more concern about foreign policy and the question of nuclear arms than there had been in 1962, but it was not nearly as important to the voters as questions of domestic policy.

Shortly after the campaign began, John F. Kennedy, the President of the United States, made some favourable comment about Pearson which Mr. Diefenbaker naturally pounced upon. Canadians as a whole were unhappy about our poor relations with the United States which had developed under Diefenbaker. But they would have resented any suggestion that Mike Pearson was the hand-picked candidate of Washington, and we were worried about what might happen if the incident was repeated. At about this time Lou Harris came in to see me about one of his surveys. He mentioned that quite frequently he saw the President who had a high regard for Mr. Pearson. Lou asked if there was anything the President could do to help. I replied somewhat brusquely that the best thing the President could do for Pearson was to keep quiet about Canada until the election campaign was over. I suggested that, as a professional politician, the President should know this. Harris promised to pass my message on and while I had no way of knowing whether he did so, we heard no more from Washington until after the election.

I learned what happened later, on a visit in September to attend the annual meetings of the International Monetary Fund and the World Bank. About twenty of us, including Louis Rasminsky, the Governor of the Bank of Canada, were invited to the White House to meet the President. We were gathered in small groups in a rough semi-circle, drinking martinis out of large goblets, when the President came in and started talking to each of the little groups in turn. I happened to be among the first of these, talking to the French Minister of Finance. When I was introduced, President Kennedy said he had heard of me from our mutual friend, Lou Harris. I asked him if Harris had delivered my message, and if so I said I hoped it had been expurgated. He laughed at this and said he received the unexpurgated version. He added that he should have realized that to say complimentary things about one of the contenders in an election campaign in another country could have just the opposite effect from what was intended. We then had quite a talk about the recent election in Canada, and how he thought his own chances looked for 1964. I found him gay and witty, with a fine sense of humour. Moreover, his knowledge of the international monetary situation was impressive.

When the party broke up, Rasminsky came rushing over to ask what the President and I had been discussing at such length and in such an animated fashion. I told him we were working on a scheme to reorganize the I.M.F. and had some new ideas on the subject of international liquidity. Rasminsky seemed a bit concerned until I broke down and admitted that we had really been talking politics, a subject in which central bankers profess to have little or no interest.

Election campaigns in Canada are very long and can become quite tedious not only to the general public, which does not become involved until the last week or so, but also to the party faithful. In an attempt to liven things up a bit, a number of gimmicks were suggested in the course of the 1963 campaign which I did not think would do any harm. One of these was planned in the hope that it would compel Mr. Diefenbaker to be more accurate in the statements he made from the public platform. Several of us in the opposition had been horrified by Mr. Diefenbaker's carelessness with the facts, or to use more partisan language, his continual distortion of the truth. He had a habit of leaving out important words or phrases in documents he quoted from in a way that gave a completely inaccurate impression of what had been said or written. For example, there had been a great deal of discussion and comment in the press and on the air about Pearson's speech on January 12, 1963, on the use of nuclear weapons. Mr. Diefenbaker misquoted so blatantly a release from Pearson's office on the subject that Pearson felt it necessary to raise the matter in the House on a question of privilege.

> Hon. L. B. Pearson (Leader of the Opposition): Mr. Speaker, I am raising a question of personal privilege arising out of a statement made by the Prime Minister in the house on Friday as reported in Hansard on page 3135. I have just had an opportunity of comparing that with the statement as it actually appeared in the press release issued by my office as to what I did say. The Prime Minister was quoting from a statement I made in Toronto on defence policy and he said:
>
>> I quote:
>> "Canada should contribute to the strategic nuclear deterrent." At the time, Mr. Speaker, I raised the question that this was a misquotation. I asked the Prime Minister if he would read again the paragraph from which he was supposed to be quoting. Since that time, Mr. Speaker, I have had a chance of reviewing the text released and from which the Prime Minister was quoting. The Prime Minister only omitted one word, Mr. Speaker, from the sentence in question, but it was an important word. He omitted the word "not." The statement I made read, "Canada should not contribute to the strategic nuclear deterrent."
>
> Right Hon. J. G. Diefenbaker (Prime Minister): The document I had before me was as I read it. I say to the hon. gentleman that if the document was incorrect, that is the one I sent to Hansard. In the face of his explanation, as always may I say that I accept it. . . .
>
> Hon. L. B. Pearson (Leader of the Opposition): Mr. Speaker, in view of the fact that on Friday the Prime Minister quoted from a document which was a report of a statement I had made, and in view of the

fact that the report he quoted differed in a vital respect from all other reports issued by my office, would the Prime Minister table now or tomorrow the document in question from which he was quoting so that it may be identified and, if necessary, corrected?

When the election campaign got under way, it was suggested that a "Truth Squad" should attend all Mr. Diefenbaker's meetings and immediately afterwards issue a statement correcting any misstatements he might make. The object, of course, was to remind the public that many of Mr. Diefenbaker's pronouncements should not be taken literally. With Pearson's approval, Judy LaMarsh was asked to become a one-woman Truth Squad, and with some reluctance she agreed to do so. She attended two or three of Mr. Diefenbaker's meetings early in the campaign and afterwards drew attention to his misstatements. But we underestimated Mr. Diefenbaker who, in his day, had no equal as a campaigner. From the platform, he pointed to Judy in the audience and accused the Liberals of arrogance, of deliberately setting out to smear him, and of casting doubts on the integrity of Canada's Prime Minister. With this ploy he won the sympathy of the press and of the public, who became highly critical of the Liberal strategy. The Truth Squad had to be abandoned and both Judy and Keith Davey were castigated for it. This was quite unfair to them. While it was not my idea, I had approved it in my capacity as National Campaign Chairman and so, for that matter, had Pearson himself. But while the issue of the Truth Squad attracted a lot of attention early on in the campaign, I do not believe it had any bearing on the outcome. If anything, it probably left an impression on the public mind that some people, and certainly the Liberals, had doubts about the veracity of some of Mr. Diefenbaker's statements.

What we should have done was to have had one or two people follow Mr. Diefenbaker, with no fuss or fanfare, to make notes of his inaccurate statements. If these had been published towards the end of the campaign, it would probably have made more impression on the public. But that is hindsight.

We were very conscious of the importance of television throughout the 1963 campaign and of Pearson's difficulty with the medium. He was at his very best with small groups where his ready wit and easy humour, together with his quick intelligence, always made a great impression. He could charm the birds out of the trees, as the saying goes, but for some reason he seemed to freeze up or to become a bit pontifical when exposed to either a television camera or a large audience. He then seemed unnatural in his manner and was handicapped by a high voice, a slight lisp, and a peculiar habit in his enunciation, which he seemed unable to break, of placing the emphasis in the wrong places.

Without any noticeable success, we tried to persuade Pearson of the importance of being rested and relaxed before he appeared on television during the campaign, even if this meant cutting out other activities. And in the prepared programs for free-time television, every effort was made to depict him in conversation with one or two other people whose job it was to ask questions and keep him interested. Most of these programs were prepared and filmed by Robert Crone of Toronto, assisted by his wife, Vi. Both of them were great admirers of Mr. Pearson and he liked working with them.

Bob would put a program together designed to capture and retain the attention of the viewers. It might include some shots of Pearson speaking at a big rally and then show him politicking in a small town or village, usually concluding with a close-up often filmed in the Crone studios, making a short statement on some aspect of Liberal policy. Alternatively, the whole program might consist of a discussion of a particular subject, such as old age pensions, by Pearson and two or three others in his livingroom.

When one of these "canned" programs was nearly completed, Keith Davey and I would review it very carefully with the Crones. This part of our job was always given top priority in view of the importance of the medium. If we had doubts about a program or any part of it, we would insist it be discarded, even when there was practically no time left before a deadline in which to prepare a replacement. Frequently, this meant that Bob Crone would have to work for twenty-four or even forty-eight hours at a stretch. But he agreed with Davey and me that it was better not to put a program on at all than to approve one in which Pearson appeared indecisive, or looked distraught and overtired. In fact, we never missed a deadline, thanks primarily to Crone, but we came very close to doing so many times.

David Anderson did a fine job in organizing a series of open-line television shows in various parts of Ontario in the 1963 election. Some senior member of the party, Mitchell Sharp or Paul Hellyer or myself, for example, would appear with two or three local candidates and answer telephone questions from the viewers. I remember appearing on one such program in Hamilton with Joe Macaluso and Jim Custeau. One viewer asked Macaluso whether, as an Italian Canadian and a Roman Catholic, he thought he had any chance of being elected in Hamilton West. I held my breath as Joe, who is dark and good-looking and makes an excellent impression on TV, answered very quietly that he believed Canadians were prepared to judge people on the basis of what they are themselves and not on where their parents or their grandparents came from. He said he did not think a man's religion had anything to do with whether he would or would not make a good M.P. And he added that, based on his experience in civic elections – he was a Hamilton alderman – he thought the voters could be trusted to make up their minds about who was best able to serve them. It was low-key and most effective. Another viewer asked Custeau, our candidate in Hamilton South, what he thought about the high cost of drugs. He replied to my horror that, as a practising druggist, he felt drug prices were too low and proceeded to enlarge upon this opinion at some length. He was not elected.

David Greenspan and Gordon Edick did wonderful work in Ontario during the 1963 election in organizing the various rallies at which Mike Pearson appeared and making certain they were attended by large crowds. This involved everything from bringing bus loads of the faithful from neighbouring points to seeing that the speaker's lectern was of the right height. David and Gordon became the acknowledged experts in this field and staged successful rallies in London, Orillia, and Kingston.

The biggest show of all, which again was organized by Gordon Edick, was the final wind-up of the campaign. This took place at Maple Leaf Gardens in Toronto with an overflow meeting at Massey Hall. The police estimated that fifty thousand tried to get into the Gardens, but no one should think this was quite spontaneous. I have discovered since that Edick distributed tickets for one million reserved seats free of charge!

But despite the fact that the Diefenbaker government had been torn apart by resignations and internal dissension, despite the fact that it had been defeated in the House, despite the fact the Liberals were united, confident, and better organized than they were in the 1962 election, and despite the fact that in January the opinion polls had showed the Liberals should win the election handily, things did not go as well as we had hoped. By early March, our campaign seemed to have bogged down and Pearson to have run out of steam. He had got off the mark too soon and was obviously tired. The low point was a poorly attended rally in Quebec City on Sunday, March 17. There were so many speakers and they spoke so long that the broadcast time was over before Pearson was even called to the microphone.

Jean Lesage, who had served with Pearson in Ottawa in Mr. St. Laurent's government, failed to help until late in the campaign. It is tempting to speculate that if he had come out for Pearson earlier, it might have made the difference of the four additional seats needed for an over-all majority.

Mr. Diefenbaker, despite all his difficulties, had managed to mount a much more vigorous campaign than anyone would have believed possible a few weeks before. Quite frankly, we were worried. Something drastic was needed to sharpen up the Liberals' campaign during the last two weeks before election day or we would lose the great opportunity we had been hoping and working for during the previous five years.

In mid-March, Keith Davey, Royce Frith, and Dan Lang met in my office in Toronto to discuss what could be done. Somehow or other the campaign had to be made to come alive again during the last two weeks. And we felt we must convince the public that we knew what had to be done and how we planned to go about it if we were elected to form the government on April 8. To be successful, this had to be presented in simple terms and with conviction. We decided – it was Keith's suggestion – to recommend that in the last two weeks Pearson should stress in specific and unqualified language what a Liberal government would plan to do about domestic issues in its first one hundred days in office. We listed ten topics to be dealt with in ten separate short speeches during the last two weeks of the campaign, all encompassed in the theme of "one hundred days of decision."

I got in touch with Mike who was in the Maritimes and arranged to meet him in Halifax on Thursday, March 21. When I arrived at the Nova Scotian Hotel, I was pounced upon by some of the newsmen on the tour who were sympathetic to Pearson and to the Liberal cause. They said the campaign was very sour and something simply had to be done to put new life into it. I told them not to worry. I then went up to see the Pearsons in their suite. Both of them looked tired and dispirited. Mike was fed up with campaigning, and I had some difficulty in persuading him that a new approach was imperative for the next and last two weeks if he was not to be defeated. I said that even if the present trend were checked and then reversed, he could no longer hope for a clear majority. This was a bitter blow to him after working so hard for five years on the reorganization of the Liberal Party, and I doubt if he believed me. He had been so sure the election was in the bag. But after a while, I began to get him interested in the proposal I had come to Halifax to make. He said he was inclined to agree in principle but that the concept of "one hundred days of decision" would have to be changed: People would mix it up with the "one hundred days" that preceded Napoleon's defeat at Waterloo!

I argued that not too many Canadians had even heard of the Battle of Waterloo, and very few would know of the hundred days that preceded it. I suggested that some people might remember the hundred days that followed Franklin D. Roosevelt's inauguration as President of the United States, but if they did this would be a good and not a bad analogy. Pearson, however, as an old history professor, was adamant. Moreover, he had been looking forward to talking more about foreign policy and defence in the final two weeks, and was reluctant to concentrate on domestic issues in which he was less interested. I showed him the latest opinion surveys which indicated that unemployment and the need to do something about it was the issue that the public was most concerned about. Foreign policy and the question of nuclear arms were far down the list of issues in terms of the public's interest.

In the end, Mike agreed to our proposal except for the "one hundred days of decision." He accepted the theme but insisted the time period be changed. He called me after I had returned to Toronto to say he had decided to make it "sixty days of decision," a major reduction in the time in which we were committing ourselves to act on a variety of issues. We were all to regret this when soon afterwards Pearson was called upon to form a Liberal government.

Both Mike and Maryon Pearson seemed cheered up and more confident again by the time I left Halifax. For this alone my trip had been worth while. But I was not at all sure Mike would stick to the program that had been agreed to. He was very tired and beginning to show his age. And the uncertainties about the outcome of the election, which he had thought was so surely in his grasp, were making him irritable and nervous.

The next week was a tense one for those who were directing the campaign, but the "sixty days of decision" theme went over well with the press, and Mike made a number of good speeches on successive days which produced favourable publicity. He did depart from the theme once or twice and he was less specific in his policy statements than we could have wished, but on the whole he was much more effective during the last two weeks of the campaign than he had been earlier.

Pearson was planning to spend the last weekend of the campaign resting at a private house on Vancouver Island. Keith and I decided I should visit him again, mainly to give him encouragement, but also to stress the importance of sticking to the theme we had agreed upon. I flew to Vancouver and then by helicopter to the house on Vancouver Island where the Pearsons were staying. Again, I found an atmosphere of depression, but for a different reason. Pearson was ill with a heavy cold and laryngitis and was running a high fever. It seemed unlikely that he would be able to continue the campaign. He was in bed with nurses in attendance who had strict orders from the doctor that no one was to see him. However, when he heard I was in the house, he insisted on talking to me. I reported that in the previous week he had managed to put new life in the campaign with the "sixty days of decision" theme. I urged him to continue with this theme if he were able to campaign at all during the final week. I told him I felt better about the prospects than I had done in Halifax the week before, but urged him not to count upon an over-all majority. I said I thought we would win between 125 and 135 seats, but that my own guess was it would be closer to the lower than to the higher number. Pearson said that while he was very tired and was feeling awful, he would go through with his program for the last week if it killed him. He seemed very determined about this, and I left feeling he had been encouraged and cheered up.

The results of the election of April 8, 1963, are shown in the following table with the comparable figures for 1958 and 1962:

	April 1963	June 1962	March 1958
Progressive Conservative	95	116	208
Liberal	129	100	49
N.D.P.	17	19	8
Other	24	30	0
	265	265	265

In the five years since the great Diefenbaker victory in 1958, his party's standing in Parliament had been reduced by more than one-half, and its popular vote from 53.7% to 32.9%. The Liberals under Pearson's often-inspired leadership had come back from their devastating defeat in 1958, when they were left with only 49 members, to a position with 129 members and the certainty of forming the next government. This was a truly remarkable victory for Mike Pearson who, people were saying a short five years before would never make a politician. He succeeded where most men would have given up because of his many talents, including his courage and determination, his inner strength and sense of humour, his intelligence and ability to keep cool in periods of crisis, and because of his charm and persuasiveness in getting new men and women to help him. But not even this could have made success possible in such a short time if Mr. Diefenbaker had not made so many blunders; he should be credited with an assist in the great Liberal win.

We were especially pleased about the success of the Liberals in Ontario and the Atlantic region; no longer could we be labelled as primarily the party of Quebec. At the same time, we were disappointed at our failure to make any real impression on the Prairies. Nevertheless, it was a great victory for Mike Pearson and the Liberal Party.

My own campaign in Davenport was considerably easier than my first venture there in June 1962. Doug Morton, who won the seat in 1957 and 1958, and who had turned out to be my principal opponent in 1962, was persuaded to run in another riding. Bill Sefton, the previous N.D.P. candidate, had died. Their successors were handicapped by having less money to spend on organization. Once again, Joe Grittani agreed to act as my campaign manager, and we were assisted by large numbers of volunteer workers from all over the city. I had to give priority to my responsibilities as Chairman of the National Campaign Committee, but nevertheless was able to spend a good deal of time campaigning in Davenport. There were the usual entertaining incidents.

I remember walking along Dundas Street one cold afternoon in March and stopping to speak to a pleasant-looking man who was staring at the window of a local grocery store. He greeted me in a very friendly fashion and then said he was only sorry that I was not going to meet his rabbit. He went on to say that his rabbit had a very estimable character and they were very fond of one another. He explained that the rabbit lived very well in his small garden in the summertime, but was having a rather hard time of it these cold March days. Then with another look at the grocery store window, my friend asked if I would feel like staking his rabbit to a lettuce leaf. I was entranced with this imaginative tale, and said I would love to stake the rabbit to a lettuce leaf if it were not for the election laws and the fact that, if I were seen giving money to or for the rabbit, the transaction might be misinterpreted. However, I agreed the rabbit's needs must be looked after and suggested that, if my new-found friend would stay by the grocery store for a few minutes after I had left the scene, perhaps someone might come along who would be able to take care of things. We parted with mutual expressions of esteem and my best wishes for the rabbit who, my friend assured me, would have voted for me if only his name had been included on the voters' list.

The results of the election in Davenport were as follows:

Vic Cathers, N.D.P.	4,347
Walter L. Gordon, Liberal	11,023
Pauline Miles, Progressive Conservative	4,520
Roland Ring, Social Credit	245

What we liked best of all was that we won every single poll, after making allowances for those who voted in the advance poll ahead of time.

But quite apart from the result in Davenport, I was well satisfied with the efforts made on behalf of Mike Pearson and the Liberal Party during the previous three and a half years. The party had been pulled together and reorganized. We had developed and then codified a broad spectrum of new policies which the party had accepted and then proceeded to advocate with a united voice. The only exception was the change in defence policy which, fortunately, had not proved to be a major issue in the election. We had conducted two election campaigns, in 1962 and again in 1963, with considerable success considering what we were up against. We knew what we planned to do and looked forward to the months and years ahead with considerable confidence.

While the Liberals did not win an over-all majority on April 8, 1963, it was clear, with 129 members to 95 for the Conservatives, that Pearson would be called upon to form the government. His first task was to decide upon the cabinet. While I was visiting the Pearsons one afternoon in mid-April at Stornoway House, the residence of the Leader of the Opposition, Pearson spoke to me about a few of his proposed appointments and asked rather casually if I would like to take on the organization and development of the new Department of Industry. This surprised me as I had had so much to do with the new policies of the Liberal Party and was expecting to be in a position to see that many of them were implemented. I questioned my ability to do this if I became the minister in charge of a new department, even though it was a department from which we hoped great things. I was mindful of Pearson's advice to me about joining Mr. St. Laurent's government in 1954. On that occasion he thought I should not accept the invitation unless I was to be Minister of Finance or even Minister of Trade and Commerce, then a much more important post than it was to be in the Pearson government.

Accordingly, I replied to the suggestion by saying that I had always assumed I would be Minister of Finance if the Liberals were called upon to form a government. This was agreed to without further comment. But the fact that Pearson had suggested the other portfolio raised a small doubt in my mind respecting his views about his new government, and the extent of his personal commitment to the policies we had fought for.

Pearson told me he had decided to appoint Paul Hellyer Minister of National Defence. I thought my brother-in-law, Bud Drury, a one-time Deputy Minister of the department with a distinguished war record, should have been appointed to Defence, particularly if we were going to reverse our policy again and forgo the use of nuclear weapons as had been decided at the Liberal rally in January 1961. After all, it was Hellyer who had urged Pearson to take the line he did about defence policy in January 1963, and he was not likely to want to change things. But I was not asked for my opinion.

Pearson told me of his other decisions, or most of them, and it was evident that those who had been with him in the House in opposition from 1958 to 1962 and the ex-civil servants who had been elected were to be prominent in the new government.* Cabinet-making is no easy task, especially in Canada and it is, of course, the Prime Minister's sole prerogative to choose the people he wants to work with. In practical terms, he must do

*See Appendix 12.

this from among the members of his party who have been elected. His cabinet should be balanced in terms of regional representation and also, but perhaps less importantly nowadays, in terms of religious beliefs, and preferably it should include members of both sexes. In addition to these considerations, a Prime Minister must take into account the question of past loyalties, the following which respective claimants have within the party, seniority and so on. Nevertheless, the over-all impression of the first Pearson government was that the "old guard," who were not whole-heartedly in sympathy with the party's new policies, many of whom had not contributed very much to the electoral victory, were to predominate. In a way, it was a triumph for seniority over the new spirit that had been created in the Liberal Party.

There was no clearly stated policy as to what ministers should do respecting their previous business connections and investments in order to ensure their complete objectivity and independence. Everyone surrendered any corporate directorships he happened to hold. In addition, because my job as Minister of Finance was a particularly sensitive one, I resigned from the Board of Governors of the University of Toronto and from certain charitable organizations that conceivably might appeal to the government for funds or favours. I severed completely all connections with my two professional firms – Clarkson, Gordon & Co. and Woods, Gordon & Co. – and I transferred all my investments to a trustee. Under the trust deed, I was not entitled to be informed how my assets were invested while I remained a member of the government.

The principal member of the new Prime Minister's personal staff was Tom Kent, whose title was changed from time to time but whose job was policy and speech writing. Tom, at one time a member of the staff of the London *Economist* and a former editor of *The Winnipeg Free Press,* had been working closely with Mike Pearson for the previous two or three years. He had assisted greatly in preparing the Liberal Party program which was approved at the rally in January 1961, and in the preparation of policy and strategy papers in the 1962 and 1963 election campaigns. In addition, he had helped Pearson in writing speeches and statements for the press. While they sometimes rubbed each other the wrong way, Kent's contribution to the Liberal cause had been immense, and he had become almost indispensable to Pearson. Naturally enough Tom, with his exceptional ability and easy access to the Prime Minister at any hour of the day or night, had great influence on issues of broad policy and those relating to party politics. On matters having to do with the routine of government, he worked closely with Gordon Robertson, the Clerk of the Privy Council. Pearson's practice was to see both of them together first thing each morning. In addition, he often saw Tom throughout the day whenever something turned up that needed special or immediate attention.

Mary Macdonald, who had been with Pearson for many years, was his Executive Assistant, and he relied on her for advice and encouragement more than he let on. She was devoted to him and resented bitterly any criticism of him that appeared in the press or anywhere else. Mary is intelligent and intuitive, with a great interest in parliamentary and political manoeuvring and political personalities. She was always intensely loyal to Pearson, but sometimes advice which is subjective and influenced by passionate likes and dislikes can lead to trouble, and occasionally it did. Dick O'Hagan, formerly of MacLaren's, was Press Secretary, Annette Perron was the Prime Minister's Personal Secretary, and Jim Coutts of Alberta became Appointments Secretary.

These were all good people, and all of them were intensely loyal to the Prime Minister. Unfortunately their duties and responsibilities tended to overlap and were not as clearly defined as I may have indicated. And as Pearson did not wish to place any one of them in charge, there was a good deal of friction and frustration in his office from time to time.

There was a similar lack of clarity and decision respecting the purely political aspects of the party's affairs, including its finances. I had had a great deal to do with party organization for the previous several years and particularly since being appointed National Campaign Chairman in the summer of 1961. But now the National Campaign Committee was dismantled and something of a vacuum was left. Bruce Matthews, the President of the National Liberal Federation, lived in Toronto and only came to Ottawa occasionally. Keith Davey was National Organizer and John Aird became National Treasurer in 1964. All three of them reported directly to the Prime Minister but found it difficult to see him. There was no one for key party people throughout the country to speak to and get decisions from, or to make recommendations to about appointments. As a result, the excellent organization we had developed with so much work and trouble began to deteriorate.

Pearson, with all his fine qualities and talents, had little sense of organization and no ability to delegate responsibility. He much preferred to do everything himself which, of course, was quite impossible. I suppose the same thing can be said of many political leaders; certainly it was true of Mr. Diefenbaker. Keith Davey continued to come to me for help, and if I felt his difficulties were sufficiently serious, I would sometimes intercede on his behalf. But this was not an adequate solution to what was basically a weakness in our organization structure.

My own personal staff included Brian Land, a friend of Keith Davey's and a senior librarian at the University of Toronto who became my Executive Assistant. Brian has a delightful sense of humour as well as a great deal of common sense. He was soon on excellent terms with everyone in Ottawa, despite the fact he did not engage in gossiping or in leaking stories to the press. Nancy Burpee, who was working in Nigeria at the time of the election, bought her way out of her contract to become my Private Secretary. Barbara Hunter became Associate Private Secretary a year later and stayed on with me as secretary, both while I was a private member in 1966 and later when I rejoined the government. Muriel Mersey was the fourth senior member of my staff and did a marvellous job in handling the numerous and varied problems of constituents. She was a tremendous help to Barbara during the year I was a private member, and rejoined my staff as a Special Assistant when I re-entered the cabinet in 1967.

It was a small staff compared with those of other ministers, but most effective. Of equal importance, everyone was always cheerful no matter what the circumstances. This made a good impression, as did our firm rule that all incoming letters must be acknowledged without delay. I am convinced I had the ablest and most effective personal staff of any minister during my time in Ottawa.

Brian returned to the University of Toronto in 1964 to head a new School of Library Science, and Alan Donnelly of the Canadian Press succeeded him. Later on, when I rejoined the government in 1967, David Smith, the President of the National Federation of Young Liberals, became my Executive Assistant. Nancy Burpee, on my advice, accepted an invitation to become Director of Admissions of the Graduate School at the University of Toronto in the fall of 1965. She was a lively, intelligent, and very helpful member of the staff during the two and a half years we worked together. On one occasion, when I was being subjected to considerable criticism, she is reputed to have replied to a long-distance call from an irate businessman who said he wished to come and shoot me: "You will just have to stand in line and take your turn like everybody else." While I question the truth of this story, it is an indication of why we had a cheerful office.

CHAPTER EIGHT

The 1963 Budget

First session of the Pearson government; the budget.

The House met on May 16, 1963, and it was soon apparent that the bitterness, the irritations, and the irascibilities of the previous Parliament had been carried forward to the new one, with Diefenbaker and Pickersgill and sometimes Pearson contributing as much as anyone to the sharp exchanges. The Speaker gave considerable leeway to Mr. Diefenbaker as the ex-Prime Minister, and Diefenbaker took advantage of this to flout the rules day after day. There was no time limit on the question period and the ministry was peppered with question after question every day. It was clear the opposition was going to do its best to prevent the government from getting any more of its program passed within the "sixty days of decision," which had been talked about so much in the last two weeks of the election campaign, than could be helped.

The debate on the Speech from the Throne took up the full eight days allowed for under the rules, with considerable emphasis being given to defence policy and the use of nuclear warheads. Time was spent on necessary supply and appropriation bills and a modest beginning on the Estimates. Seven days were devoted to debating a motion to set up a defence committee which, in ordinary circumstances, might have been expected to go through without comment. Allan MacEachen managed to announce the government's program, or part of it, for dealing with unemployment, including the novel idea of paying a $500 bonus for winter-built houses. He did this in the form of a statement about labour conditions on Motions. The Economic Council of Canada Act received first reading, and debates were initiated on resolutions to establish a Department of Industry and the Municipal Development and Loan Fund.

But that was about all of any substance that was accomplished prior to the introduction of the government's first budget on June 13. This gave the opposition parties the opportunity they had been looking for and they pounded away at me week after week. They complained about the propriety of bringing in a number of consultants to help in the preparation of the budget, and at great length about many of the budget proposals themselves.

On August 2, 1963, seven weeks after the budget was introduced, the House adjourned until September 30. Despite the combined efforts of the opposition parties, the government had been able to get through some important legislation in the two and one-half months since it met on May 16. Major amendments to the Atlantic Development Board Act created a $100 million capital fund to be administered by the Board and used to finance projects in the Atlantic region for which satisfactory financing arrangements were not otherwise available. The Department of Industry Act established a new department, whose primary responsibility was to foster the efficient development of the Canadian manufacturing industry. The Economic Council of Canada Act established a body which would initiate research projects on all aspects of Canadian economic development, make policy recommendations to the government, and publish an annual review, studies, and reports. The Municipal Development and Loan Fund Act established a $400 million fund to be administered by a board and used to finance municipal capital projects, thereby increasing employment in the construction industry. Amendments were put through which increased the remuneration of Members of Parliament. It is also noteworthy that a motion to establish the Canada Development Corporation, "a measure to increase Canadian participation in industries and undertakings," was approved on June 20, but the bill did not come up for debate during that session of Parliament.

Quite apart from the bills that were passed, the government did manage to announce in one way or another what it intended to do about the various matters it had committed itself to decide during the first "sixty days of decision." This was pointed out by Maurice Lamontagne on June 25, in the course of a speech on the budget.

> The measures proposed by the Minister of National Revenue represent a new effort to improve our housing policy. The program set forth by the Minister of Labour will reduce technological and seasonal unemployment and considerably improve our vocational training system throughout the country.
>
> The new twelve-mile limit will be of great advantage to our Canadian fishermen.
>
> But it is perhaps from the new agencies proposed by the government that more long-term results should especially be expected. I refer to the economic council, the department of industry with its area development agency, the Atlantic development board, with its $100 million fund, the municipal development and loan board, the develop-

135

ment corporation and the appointment of two ministers who will be in a better position than ever to deal with the quite different problems of western and eastern agriculture. In this way, the government wishes to introduce economic planning in our country, a planning which would not only point to the objects to be attained and the means required to achieve them, but which would also promote and foster development through proper credit, financing and grant policies. Such a planning is urgently required. The government is ready to introduce it as soon as parliament gives its agreement.

Those are the main items ... of the sixty-day economic program. ...

There were a number of other matters that took place during the summer of 1963 which should be mentioned. Before Parliament assembled on May 16, Pearson had visited Prime Minister Harold Macmillan in London and President Kennedy at Hyannisport on Cape Cod and had been very well received. During the summer, the Prime Minister announced the creation of the Royal Commission on Bilingualism and Biculturalism, and Judy LaMarsh outlined the first version of the Canada Pension Plan. Paul Martin worked out a new agreement with the Province of British Columbia respecting the development of the Columbia River, and just before the adjournment of Parliament on August 2, Allan MacEachen announced that a trusteeship would be created to administer the affairs of five Maritime unions in an attempt to eliminate violence on the Great Lakes.

When the new Parliament assembled on May 16, 1963, the Liberals were feeling cocky following their election victory. The members of the opposition parties, on the other hand, were angry and bitter and seemed determined to frustrate the government by every means at their disposal. No mercy was shown to anyone on the government side, and the atmosphere was thoroughly unpleasant.

The first budget of the new Liberal government, which was presented under these conditions, attracted unprecedented criticism. It is still sometimes referred to in the press as "the fiasco of Walter Gordon's first budget." While this may be true insofar as the commotion raised about the circumstances of its preparation is concerned, it is not true when applied to most of the substance of the budget proposals and their effectiveness.

Ever since the fall of 1962, it had seemed probable that there would be another election soon and that the Liberals would win it. I expected to be the Minister of Finance in a new Liberal government, and for several months had been thinking about the kind of policies that should be put forward in the first budget. In fact, many of my ideas were set forth in *Troubled Canada* which had been published in December 1961. In other words, I was not approaching the task of preparing the new government's first budget cold. I knew in broad terms the kind of policies we wished to promulgate. It remained to work them out in detail.

A few hours before the first Pearson cabinet was sworn in on April 22, 1963, I ran into Bob Bryce on the street. He had been Clerk of the Privy Council and Secretary to the Cabinet under Mr. St. Laurent and throughout the Diefenbaker years. Bryce and I were old friends and we had a pleasant chat. I told him that, from all I had heard, a major reorganization would be needed at the Department of Finance; that I expected to be the minister; and that I had asked Pearson to appoint Bryce Deputy Minister if he were willing to take on the job. Bryce told me that he had always hoped to return to Finance as Deputy Minister and that he would be delighted to do so if the Prime Minister so requested. My recollection is that I had settled this with the Prime Minister some time between the date of the election, April 8, and the date when the government was formed, April 22.

After being sworn in, I repaired to the Confederation Building where George Nowlan, the former Minister of Finance, was awaiting me. This was a pleasant gesture on Nowlan's part, a man who was always generous and big-hearted. He introduced me to the senior members of the staff, nearly all of whom I knew, and then departed.

I thought it would be unfair to Kenneth Taylor, the Deputy Minister, to start on a false note, especially as he is a man whom I had known and liked for over thirty years. Accordingly, I told him frankly of the decision to make changes at the department and to appoint Bryce as Deputy Minister. Taylor was polite about this, but naturally was unhappy and upset.

I then saw Wynne Plumptre, the senior Assistant Deputy Minister, whom I had known since school days. He volunteered the information that the department was in a mess, that the assistant deputies went their own separate ways, and that there was no co-ordination or direction of their activities. He implied that he assumed a new Deputy Minister would be appointed and that he naturally hoped he would be considered for the post. I told him immediately that Bryce was to be appointed. Plumptre replied that Bryce was the most respected member of the civil service and that in his view this was a wise and proper choice. He readily accepted the decision in a most generous way. I then had talks with the other three Assistant Deputy Ministers – Claude Isbister, Simon Reisman, and G. G. E. Steele, who was Secretary of the Treasury Board – during the course of which it became clear to me that the department badly needed to be pulled together.

A day or two later, the Prime Minister told me that, while we had promised a budget within sixty days, he thought it would be impossible to release Bryce from the Privy Council office until some time in July and that, therefore, I would have to get along as best I could without him. I said this would be very awkward, particularly as I had informed Ken Taylor of the decision to replace him, but Pearson was firm about not being able to get along without Bryce for at least two months.

Budget-making in these circumstances became extremely difficult. A budget had not been presented for two years. Ken Taylor's nose was a bit out of joint about the plan to appoint Bryce as Deputy Minister, and the rest of the staff, while willing enough, needed new direction. It was understandable, also, that the sense of urgency which I felt, having just finished a successful election campaign and before that a highly critical session in the House of Commons, was not shared by all the civil servants in the department.

To get around this difficulty, I had called in David Stanley of Wood Gundy (who had travelled with Pearson during the election campaign, was thoroughly familiar with the Liberal Party platform, and had helped to write some of the leader's speeches); Geoff Conway, then at Harvard, who had helped with the preparation of some of the planks in the Liberal platform; Martin O'Connell, of Harris and Partners, who had rendered similar assistance; and Rod Anderson of Clarkson, Gordon and Co., who would provide figures, I hoped, for the preparation and presentation of the financial statements. All these men took the oath of secrecy and, having done so, I felt they were in exactly the same category as dollar-a-year men who have helped governments both during the war and subsequently. I had been one myself and, as such, had helped with the preparation of two budgets in the 1940s.

There was a bit of conflict between one or more of these newcomers and the regular staff at the department. Moreover, some of the new ideas that were proposed (and eventually incorporated in the budget) were opposed by the officials who expressed their criticisms to me both singly and as a group. They were quite frank in doing this, which I appreciated. Some of them were especially critical of measures designed to encourage foreign owners of Canadian corporations to accept Canadian partners, the argument being that this would cause difficulties for us in Washington and, quite possibly, retaliation.

I said that as far as I was concerned the budget should deal with a variety of objectives (some of which might appear to be contradictory in purely economic terms). In particular, I felt the budget should do four things.

First and foremost, it should include measures to stimulate the economy and provide more jobs. I thought it especially important to do things which would promote activity in the depressed areas of the country. This did not provoke any disagreement in principle.

Second, the budget should raise more revenues so that the

government's finances would be brought under reasonable control within twenty-four months. I argued that it was much better to do this in the first year in which the government was elected than to try to do it later. All of the officials were in favour of raising additional revenues and I asked them for suggestions. They recommended, among other things, that the exemption of the sales tax from building materials and from production materials should be rescinded. I had some reservations about rescinding the exemption, insofar as production materials were concerned, but the officials pressed me hard to face up to this. It was not until long afterwards that I discovered that this latter measure had been discussed on a previous occasion, and that certain officials in the Department of National Revenue (not the top ones) had prepared a memorandum which anticipated practically all the difficulties that this measure later encountered in the House.

Third, I believed the budget should include measures to encourage Canadian subsidiaries of foreign concerns to sell more of their shares to Canadians. Most of the officials were opposed to this for the reasons previously noted.

Fourth and finally, I insisted that there should be amendments designed to block some of the existing loopholes in the tax laws. I stated that, as a professional accountant who was fully aware of these loopholes, I could not bring in a budget that did not make some attempt to stop current abuses. As I recall, there was a mixed reaction to this on the part of the officials.

After very strenuous efforts, we produced a series of budget proposals dealing with my four objectives and a budget speech. The speech itself was much criticized by the officials, and Plumptre volunteered to take another crack at it. He writes very well and I was grateful to him for this. However, the draft that I received did not reflect all the points of view I wished to make, and with Stanley's help we produced an alternative which, after much editing and polishing, I felt portrayed my understanding of the Liberal government's philosophy and policy.

I went over the budget with the Prime Minister several times, and very carefully. He expressed great delight with it and said he felt it would put the Liberal Party on the map. The budget was my responsibility, of course, but it was reassuring to know the Prime Minister was so pleased with it. I asked him if he would like me to show it to Tom Kent, his personal adviser on policy matters, and whether I could properly do this under the general principle of budget secrecy. He instructed me not to do so.

At some stage during the discussions with the Prime Minister, I said that Rasminsky was opposed to parts of the budget for fear they would annoy the Americans. He did not wish us to do this because of his experiences the previous year over the exchange devaluation. I said I felt that the

Prime Minister should hear these reservations from Rasminsky himself rather than have them retailed through me. Accordingly, Pearson and I had lunch at the Bank of Canada, at which meeting Rasminsky voiced his strong objections to the proposals designed to encourage foreign-owned subsidiaries in Canada to sell some of their shares to Canadians. He was particularly critical of the proposed differential in the withholding tax. At the same time Rasminsky strongly endorsed the proposals for raising additional revenues including in particular rescinding the exemptions from the sales tax.

After the luncheon, the Prime Minister and I walked back from the bank building to our respective offices. We discussed Rasminsky's reservations, and Pearson said he did not take them seriously and that I should not give way on the withholding tax differential. I asked him whether it would not be wise to discuss the budget proposals with a committee of cabinet, including Lamontagne and Sharp in particular, in view of the fact that it introduced so many new features. Pearson replied that, if we brought in a group of cabinet ministers, they would all want to make changes, and he did not think this was desirable. He repeated that in his view it was a first-class budget which should really establish the position of the party. Therefore the budget proposals were not discussed in cabinet until either the morning of their presentation to the House or perhaps the day before. No one voiced any serious reservations about any of the proposals although quite obviously they had no real chance to study them.

I remember asking Pearson several times for his views about the speech itself, and in particular whether he felt that any sentences were too partisan. He replied that he thought it was very mild and not to change it. Despite this, a number of references were ultimately deleted which I felt to be more critical than might be called for in a budget speech.

Nevertheless, I was accused of making a partisan speech. This was probably inevitable, given the circumstances of the time. The Conservatives had just been defeated in a highly charged election in which two of the main issues had been their inability to cope with the high level of unemployment and their financial mismanagement of the national finances. Our people were feeling their oats, as the saying goes, and were anxious to cheer whenever they got a chance. It is quite true that the speech included some digs, but reading it again several years later it does not seem to be nearly so partisan as was alleged at the time, both by the opposition and by some sections of the press.

The budget was delivered on Thursday evening, June 13, well within the sixty days following the formation of the government, in accordance with our promise. The economic philosophy of the new Liberal government, which emphasized the importance of reducing unemployment, was expressed in the following terms:

Our rate of growth over the past six years as a whole has been quite inadequate. We have had a falling rate of new investment. We have had chronic deficits in our international balance of payments. And most important, we have had chronic unemployment.

All of these problems are interrelated; if we can cure one, we shall relieve the others. For example, our international balance of payments deficit on current account has averaged almost $1.2 billion annually in the past six years. This has meant that we have been importing goods and services which we should have produced at home, and that we have failed to find export markets for goods which we should have sold abroad. If this situation had been corrected, the increased production in Canada might well have meant not less than 150,000 more jobs and our unemployment problem would have been reduced accordingly.

The added investment needed to provide this increased production and employment, and the increased production and employment itself, would all have produced higher government revenues. This would have been reflected in reduced budgetary deficits.

I could go on to describe our difficulties and what we propose to do about them strictly in terms of economics. But perhaps hon. members will forgive me if I speak in more human terms tonight, and about the human tragedies that inevitably result when economic conditions are unsatisfactory and our national affairs mismanaged.

The grim experiences of continuing unemployment are to be found in nearly every part of Canada, in nearly every constituency. Most members of this house know of men and women and of whole families whose lives have been warped and whose futures impaired by long periods when they were looking for non-existent jobs.

My own riding of Toronto Davenport is a high unemployment area. Many of the people who live there came to Canada quite recently, and they are not fully familiar with either the language or the customs of their new community. They face frustrating disadvantages in their battle for a decent life. Similar conditions I suggest prevail in most other constituencies across the country.

The prevalence of unemployment is a wrong that must be righted. Any Canadian, young or old, who wants a job must be able to find one. Any Canadian must be able by his work and his savings to make his own direct contribution to the well-being of his family, his community and his country. This is a basic tenet of Liberal philosophy. It is an aim which we are dedicated to achieve.

It is the view of this government that unemployment is the most serious domestic problem facing Canada today. I shall review briefly the steps which we are taking to combat it.

The measures advanced or to be advanced for relieving unemployment were then described. A new Department of Industry to promote more employment opportunities in the manufacturing industries, and especially in the automobile industry; an Area Development Agency to encourage new investment in areas of slow growth; the provision of a substantial capital fund to be used by the Atlantic Development Board; loans to be advanced by the Municipal Development and Loan Board; tax incentives to promote new capital investment in the private sector; increased winter works in designated areas; encouragement of house construction in the winter months, as already announced by the Minister of Labour, etc.

The Speech went on to discuss the recurrent deficits on current account in our balance of payments and the government's views about budgetary deficits. It continued:

> I have discussed in frank terms, Mr. Speaker, our unemployment problem, the problem of the deficits in our balance of international payments, and the problem of our federal budgetary deficits.
>
> In seeking solutions to these problems our salvation does not lie in isolationism; it does not lie in withdrawing unto ourselves and ignoring the currents of progress and change around us. Let us remember that we are a great trading nation dependent on our relationships with our friends throughout the world. We must not at the first storm signals of economic danger simply throw up a ramshackle tariff against imported goods and imported ideas and imported obligations and seek to bury our heads in the sand. That way lies stagnation.
>
> The way of the future, the way of prosperity, the way of national pride, involves the fullest participation in the world around us in an economic sense as in every other sense. It involves expanding our trade in conjunction with our friends. It does not involve isolating ourselves from the trend toward international co-operation and freer interchange of goods and services. Rather it involves participating to the fullest in these new movements and moulding them to our best advantage.
>
> These are the views, the broad economic philosophy if you will, of this Liberal government. It is our purpose to see these views are translated into action.

In later years, *The Winnipeg Free Press* and other papers in the F.P. Publications chain, made a practice of referring to me as a protectionist and isolationist. The above paragraphs do not support such allegations.

After discussing the question of foreign control of Canadian industry, the speech went on to say:

> It may be useful for me to outline the view of this government as to how

harmonious relations with foreign investors here can best be preserved.

We believe that industry in Canada, wherever it is controlled, should operate with due regard to the over-all interest of Canadians and the Canadian economy. This means that Canadian raw materials should be processed to the greatest possible extent in Canada, in order to provide employment to Canadians and contribute to prosperity in this country. It means that export markets should be sought actively wherever they may be found, and should not be limited out of regard for the interests of parent or associated companies abroad. It means that industry here should make a conscious effort to purchase its raw materials, components and supplies from Canadian sources whenever these sources are competitive.

It means that industry should employ Canadian service firms wherever possible. I am thinking of Canadian engineers, architects, and other professional people, Canadian insurance and advertising firms, and Canadian consultants of all types.

It means that industry should exert itself to expand in Canada all the industrial functions which can efficiently be carried on here; and I am thinking particularly of increased basic industrial research and design. It means that industry should seek to provide the fullest opportunity for Canadian employees at all levels, including managerial, scientific and technical personnel.

Above all, I am convinced that a growing partnership between Canadians and investors from abroad is the best way of strengthening the harmonious relations with foreign capital which it is our object to preserve. Foreign investors can further the growth of this partnership by selling minority interests in their enterprises to Canadians; and by electing a number of independent Canadian directors to represent these interests.

I suggest that a 25 per cent equity interest is in most cases appropriate to ensure that a Canadian point of view is always available when company policy decisions are arrived at. A smaller percentage would probably not be sufficient for this purpose. A larger percentage would be neither necessary nor in many cases practicable. In fact, even a 25 per cent interest in most new or existing enterprises is not something that could be realized overnight. It is an objective to be worked toward over a period of years, although I hope this period can be a relatively short one.

The budget contained a great many proposals for stimulating employment, for plugging loopholes in the law (some of them of a most blatant kind), for dealing with the problems of foreign investment, and for raising revenues: new manufacturing and processing enterprises located in designated areas of slower growth to be granted an exemption from income tax for three years; such enterprises to be entitled to write off new machinery and equipment in as little as two years; any taxpayers to be entitled to write off the cost of new buildings in designated areas of slow growth in as little as five years; manufacturing and processing industries anywhere in Canada to be allowed to deduct depreciation of new assets acquired within the next 24 months at a rate of 50% per annum – this privilege to be restricted to Canadian residents and to companies having a minimum of 25% Canadian ownership; excesses of expense account living to be disallowed; full capital cost allowances on expensive automobiles to be disallowed; amendments to the Income Tax Act to discourage dividend stripping; exemption from withholding tax on interest on new issues of Canadian bonds and debentures sold to non-resident banks, companies or trusts which are free of income tax in their country of residence; the withholding tax on dividends payable to non-residents to be increased to 20% or reduced to 10% depending on the degree of ownership by Canadians of the companies in question; a 30% sales tax on takeover of Canadian companies by non-residents; withdrawal of the exemption from sales tax on building materials and also for production materials and equipment; advance in the dates on which corporations should be required to pay their income taxes.

This was a lot of ground for any government to cover within two months of its formation and, quite frankly, I was well pleased with it. But because it was so comprehensive, the budget was bound to attract a lot of criticism. It is no exaggeration to say it did so!

Some economists said the proposals were contradictory; they included incentives to encourage expansion while, at the same time, raised taxes which could be expected to have the opposite effect. This was true, of course, but as I have implied we had more than one objective. We wished to stimulate expansion and provide more jobs. At the same time, we were anxious to get the government's finances under control after six years of deficits.

Some members of the business community objected to the measures designed to plug existing loopholes in the tax laws and especially the proposed crack-down on expense accounts. The house builders' lobby, one of the best organized in the nation, put on a vociferous campaign against the proposal to rescind the sales tax exemption on building materials. They are still doing so.

Businessmen generally were opposed – and I think rightly so – to the proposed rescinding of the sales tax exemption on production materials and equipment. The financial community was extremely critical of the proposed 30% takeover tax on sales of Canadian companies to non-residents. And the U. S. State Department and its representative in Ottawa, Walton Butterworth, the U. S. Ambassador, directed a jaundiced eye on all the measures designed to modify the effects of foreign control of Canadian companies, which were described as being both discriminatory and retroactive. There was a lot of talk about the unfairness of "changing the rules of the game" after it has begun, something that every government in the world does in some degree almost continually.

Initial press reactions to the budget, while not wildly enthusiastic, nevertheless recognized its objectives. *The Globe and Mail, The Winnipeg Free Press* and *The Toronto Star* editorialized as follows on June 14:

BUILDERS DISLIKE MATERIALS TAX
EXPENSE ACCOUNT CURBS HAILED

Calling on Canadians to face the hard facts of life, Finance Minister Walter Gordon last night proposed measures to expand Canadian investment, production and employment and to halt the growing foreign ownership of domestic resources. . . .

Finance Minister Walter Gordon must expect his first Budget to be measured against the boasts he made before being elected. . . . His Budget is not bold and expansionist: it is essentially restrictive. The stick is much in evidence but the carrot is lacking.

There should be no quarrel with the objectives that Mr. Gordon declared in his Budget speech. . . .

The Globe and Mail

STRONG MEDICINE FOR THE ECONOMY

Mr. Walter Gordon's first budget sets at least one Canadian precedent. Never before in our history has the finance minister of a minority government so resolutely set aside considerations of immediate popularity in order to administer strong medicine to an ailing economy. . . .

The Winnipeg Free Press

The average Canadian tax-payer will find little of direct personal benefit in Finance Minister Walter Gordon's first federal budget.

But the long-term impact on the nation's economy should be substantial. For Mr. Gordon has moved deliberately toward three major objectives which must be met before Canada can enjoy a durable prosperity.

The first and most important of course is high employment. . . . The second is the recovery of Canadian control of our economy. . . . The third is a balanced budget. . . .

In all, the budget won't have Canadians dancing in the streets. But it does provide assurance that purpose and direction have been restored in the handling of the nation's economic affairs.

The Toronto Star

In retrospect, I believe the substantive proposals contained in the budget of June 13, 1963, were sound. The main proposals for stimulating the economy and thus providing more jobs, for plugging blatant loopholes in the tax laws, and for bringing the national finances under control were remarkably successful.

However, the failure to obtain public acceptance of these various measures and, more particularly, of the proposals for dealing with the foreign control issue was unfortunate, to say the least. This was due in part to my limited experience in Parliament and in part to the timidity of a new government which had the support of only a minority of the members. As a result, we embarked upon a series of revisions and retreats which did great damage, both to me personally and to the government as a whole.

The first shot was fired on Friday morning, June 14, by Douglas Fisher, the Member for Port Arthur, who on the Orders of the Day asked whether any outside consultants from Toronto had assisted in the preparation of the budget. Nearly four weeks earlier, on May 18, this had been reported in *The Financial Post* in an article headed "New Breed of $1-a-Year Men Helping Liberals Make Plans." The author, Clive Baxter, had mentioned all the consultants by name. There was nothing secret about their presence in Ottawa. Despite the fact that it was generally known that outsiders had been brought in to help with the budget, a big issue was made of this in the weeks to come.

In reply to Fisher's inquiry, I said that everyone who assisted in the preparation of the budget had taken the oath of secrecy and that I accepted full responsibility for the budget. However, I did not give a direct answer to Fisher's question. This led to further probing questions and aroused suspicions. After thinking the matter over, I decided to make a full statement later in the afternoon. In doing this, I gave the the names of Messrs. Stanley, O'Connell, and Conway, and concluded my statement in the following terms:

> I regret my hesitancy this morning to reveal the names of the three individuals I have mentioned. This hesitation stemmed from my feeling that the budget is the product of the work of a great number of department officials and I did not think it fair to single out individuals for certain attention.
>
> Mr. Churchill: That was not the reason.
>
> Mr. Gordon: Since these three gentlemen had all taken the necessary oaths it did not seem to me that there could be any special question about their status. However, it now seems desirable that their

names should be made public and certainly I have no reason to make any mystery of them. In doing this I wish to express my personal thanks to these gentlemen, along with all the other people who have assisted me so greatly since I became Minister of Finance. I hope they will be able to continue to help me in the future. I should like to reiterate that I accept full responsibility for the budget and for the secrecy maintained in the course of its preparation. Subject to this principle of ministerial responsibility, it will be the policy of this government to continue to seek specialized advice and assistance from experienced people in all walks of life and all occupations whenever this may be in the public interest.

When the House met next at 2.30 P.M., Monday, June 17, the Honourable D. S. Harkness, M. P. for Calgary North, added to the suspicions about the secrecy of the budget preparation by rising on a question of privilege. He stated:

On Friday morning, June 14, there was delivered to a Calgary law office at 9.30 A.M., by the first morning mail delivery, a memorandum entitled "Proposed Changes in Canadian Taxes." The memorandum summarizes the budget, has a budget resolutions index, and attached to it are appendices containing the budget resolutions. The whole runs to twenty-five pages and is under a covering letter from Clarkson, Gordon and Company of Toronto. The envelope containing this material is metered, and the meter stamp bears the date of June 14.

The question which arises is how this material could have been prepared, multigraphed and delivered by ordinary mail to a Calgary office by 9.30 A.M. on Friday morning. It may be possible that this analysis of the budget could have been prepared, the material mimeographed and the whole dispatched to Calgary, and I presume to every other city in Canada, and then delivered within the times I have given. However, it seems somewhat improbable. . . .

I replied immediately as follows:

I am hardly in a position to speak on this matter without looking into it, mainly because I am no longer a member of Clarkson, Gordon and Company. I do know that for many, many years that firm, as well as many other firms in all parts of Canada, including all the banks and various other institutions, have received copies of the budget speech after it has been delivered in this House from the offices of the Bank of Canada in their area. I know that this particular firm, Clarkson, Gordon and Company, have in the past made a point of summarizing the main points in the budget that night and issuing them that night or the following morning at an early hour. Apart from that, I am not in a position to say anything about this matter until I make inquiries.

I was, of course, fully aware of the dangers posed by the implications of Harkness' question of privilege, and immediately telephoned Jack Wilson who had succeeded me as senior partner of Clarkson, Gordon & Co. I asked him to send me by wire a complete description of what had happened. He did so, and later in the day I was able to read it to the House. It explained in detail how the budget summary was prepared on the evening it was delivered and how it was sent to Calgary in time for distribution on the following morning.

While the explanations of the points raised by Fisher on the Friday after the budget presentation, and by Harkness on the following Monday, were quite specific, nevertheless the seeds of suspicion had been sown. This made it harder to withstand the subsequent attacks on the substance of the budget proposals.

On the same day as Harkness spoke on his question of privilege, Mr. Diefenbaker moved to adjourn the House to debate the question of outside assistance in the preparation of the budget. There was considerable discussion and the Speaker ruled the motion out of order. His ruling was appealed and a formal vote taken, which upheld the Speaker. The following are examples of the editorial comments:

> It is sadly true to form for the House of Commons to get far more excited about the Finance Minister getting expert outside help in the preparation of the budget than in the budget itself. That document is full of tough meat and will need long chewing and digestion. The House shrinks from such hard work. It prefers the much easier task of denouncing Mr. Gordon for getting studies and analyses made by three bright young men with training for the job.
>
> *The Montreal Star,* June 18, 1963

> The important thing . . . is not who is privy to Government secrets, but to insure that the secret information is not put to any improper use. In the case of Mr. Gordon's advisers, there is no suggestion of impropriety and the criticism is irresponsible.
>
> *The Globe and Mail,* June 17, 1963

> The fact that the three persons he used as consultants had been sworn to secrecy does not make any the less the fact that they continued to receive their salaries from their outside firms while serving him briefly as Minister; that they saw even the final drafts of the budget; that their services to Mr. Gordon were kept from the House until the questions

were asked; and that Mr. Gordon did not answer these questions at once but only after some delay. . . .

The Montreal Gazette, June 17, 1963

Every day in the House from then on, I was subjected to searching questions about the way the budget was prepared, about the outside consultants who had been brought in, and about some of the proposed changes and other measures.

There was an immediate outcry in financial circles over the proposed thirty per cent takeover tax which involved some technical difficulties for the stock exchanges. The President of the Toronto Stock Exchange, General Howard Graham, and some of his officials came to see me. After studying the problem, General Graham informed me that while they did not like the proposed measure the technical difficulties could be worked out satisfactorily. Eric Kierans, the President of the Montreal Stock Exchange, struck an entirely different attitude. He arrived to see me late Tuesday afternoon, June 18, with eight or nine members of his committee, all of whom were prominent members of Montreal Stock Exchange houses. Kierans handed me a letter criticizing the budget and particularly the proposed takeover tax couched in highly intemperate language. He then proceeded to harangue me in my own office and practically incited the stock brokers present to sell the market short when it opened the following morning. He admitted that his letter to me had been given to the press before he came to Ottawa, so the fat was in the fire.

It seemed clear that if nothing were done there would be a very serious break in the stock market despite the fact the officials of the Toronto Stock Exchange had by this time let me know that they could work out the technical difficulties. I thought this over during the evening and the following morning informed the Prime Minister that I felt there was no alternative but to withdraw the proposed tax "because of administrative difficulties."

I remember telling Pearson that I would resign if he would like me to do so. I was taking quite a beating and, understandably, he asked me how I was feeling and if I had enough confidence to carry on. I assured him that I had, and later when he was asked if I had offered to resign he replied in the negative. I mentioned this to him subsequently and said that, in view of his statement, I also would say, if asked, that I had not offered to resign as I had not done so in a formal way or in writing. He agreed with this. My difficulties were not lessened when Richard O'Hagan, the Prime Minister's Press Secretary, decided to poll the members of the Press Gallery on whether Pearson should call for my resignation. Naturally word of this was relayed to me very quickly.

When the House met on Wednesday afternoon, June 19, I made a statement to the effect that the much criticized takeover tax would be withdrawn:

> Hon. Walter L. Gordon (Minister of Finance): Mr. Speaker, certain administrative difficulties have arisen respecting the immediate application of the proposed 30 per cent tax on takeovers, announced in the budget speech on June 13. One of the difficulties is in connection with new financing now under way for the expansion of existing businesses. This cannot be allowed to lapse or be deferred until detailed regulations have been formulated.
>
> It may take a little time to work out satisfactorily the difficulties referred to. Pending a solution, the government proposes to withdraw paragraph 11 of the budget resolution respecting the Excise Tax Act.
>
> Since the budget was delivered I have had a number of conversations about this matter with people familiar with the administrative side of the securities business, including the presidents of the Toronto and Montreal stock exchanges, and a senior officer of the investment dealers' association of Canada. I have also heard by telegram from the president of the Vancouver stock exchange. Most of the people I have talked with have pointed out the administrative difficulties I have referred to, but are anxious to find a solution that will be consistent with the government's statement of disapproval of takeovers of Canadian concerns by non-residents.
>
> This attitude is not shared by the president of the Montreal stock exchange. In a letter to me dated June 18 he states that "a non-resident takeover convers great benefits on the Canadian economy." Either before or just after an interview with me yesterday, and without informing me of his intention to take such action, the president of the Montreal stock exchange handed copies of his letter to members of the press. The letter is intemperate and irresponsible in tone and content.
>
> Some hon. Members: Oh, oh.
>
> Mr. Gordon: It is a strange communication coming as it does from a man who holds the position of president of an important Canadian stock exchange. I want to make it clear that this government disagrees completely with the interpretation of the national interest expressed by the president of the Montreal stock exchange. Our attitude to the desirability of maintaining and increasing Canadian ownership of Canadian assets was clearly set out in the budget speech. It remains unchanged.

As was to be expected, this action unleashed further attacks and questions in the House and another barrage of newspaper headlines calling for my resignation. The following are examples of the editorial comment:

> Looking at the Budget and at the efforts of Mr. Gordon and Mr. Garland to clarify it, we begin to feel that the only realistic method by

which the Government might go about recapturing confidence would be to withdraw the whole thing and start over again. . . .

Those who know Mr. Gordon's background well and admire his ability may feel that he has made a number of unfortunate mistakes in the past few days but with experience he could prove to be a distinguished minister. This we would not dispute but we do submit that the country cannot afford the luxury of his gaining that experience.

The Globe and Mail, June 26, 1963

Perhaps Mr. Gordon can perform useful service in some other capacity or department, but he has unquestionably disqualified himself for his present portfolio. His continuance in office will not only jeopardize the future of the Government as a whole but could also upset the present delicate balance of power in Parliament, and the nation can afford neither. No individual, no matter how highly valued by his colleagues or well qualified to hold his portfolio, is that important.

The Winnipeg Free Press, June 22, 1963

It has become obvious that haste and parliamentary inexperience have played far too great a part in the framing, presentation, and defence of the Budget. The Government has got itself into a fine mess from which it can fully extricate itself only by frank and full admission that the Budget is off the rails.

The Montreal Star, as quoted in *The Ottawa Journal,* June 26, 1963

When twenty or thirty members of the opposition kept yelling at me at the same time, I was reminded of an incident many years before when in a boxing match my jaw was broken in two places. I thought on that occasion my best course was to continue to appear as calm and confident as possible and to hope for a chance to catch my opponent with his guard down. The same kind of assessment of my position seemed appropriate at this period of the budget debate.

Mitchell Sharp made an effective speech during the budget debate, pointing out that at the time of the conversion loan of 1958, the Diefenbaker government had informed some two hundred investment dealers in confidence of its intentions in advance of any public announcement. All of them respected this confidence, despite the fact they could have made very large sums by taking advantage of it. If this was a reasonable thing for the government to do in 1958, Sharp asked, why was it considered unreasonable to bring in outside help in preparing a budget in 1963? Maurice Lamontagne, who also spoke, paid me some pleasant compliments.

The Prime Minister had agreed to let me choose my own parliamentary assistant for the Department of Finance. I had no difficulty in picking Edgar J. Benson from Kingston, a chartered accountant and Queen's professor. Ben is intelligent and a very hard worker who never seems to lose his cool. He was a tremendous help while he was with me in Finance. But it was not very long before he entered the cabinet in his own right. Five years later, he, in turn, would become the Minister of Finance. Ben was another Liberal member who made an excellent speech in the budget debate, which began as follows:

> Mr. E. J. Benson (Parliamentary Secretary to the Minister of Finance): Mr. Speaker, having listened to debates in this house over the past years it is with some diffidence that I rise to make my modest contribution to this budget debate. It has disturbed me, Mr. Speaker, that over the past four days, culminating in a vote last evening, the content, the economic aims and implications of the budget speech delivered on June 13, 1963, received very little attention. Instead we have witnessed a deliberate diversionary action which, through implication, attempted to destroy the character of persons who could not defend themselves in this chamber. I deplore this kind of debate.
>
> An hon. Member: Who started it?
>
> Mr. Benson: Today I should like to discuss some of the aims and implications of the budget recently presented. . . .

The budget was approved in principle by a vote of 119 to 74 on Wednesday, June 26, but my trials were by no means over. Members of the government had become increasingly disturbed by the attacks on me, both in the House and in the press, and by the activities of the housebuilders' lobby. I was urged in cabinet to make some further concessions to meet some of the objections, especially to the sales tax on building materials.

On July 1, at a meeting with several ministers, including Garland, Lamontagne and Sharp, Garland suggested that I should modify the withdrawal of sales tax exemption on building materials so that it would come in in stages on three different dates, as recommended by the House Builders' Association. Sharp urged me to stand firm. Shortly afterwards, however, the whole cabinet assembled at Harrington Lake, where the Prime Minister was recovering from an operation to remove a cyst from his neck, to discuss the situation. I urged everyone to stand firm and to let the storm blow itself out. But this time only Harry Hays, Judy LaMarsh, and Maurice Lamontagne backed me up. I felt I had the choice of resigning or agreeing to amend the original resolution so that the exemption from sales tax on building materials would be withdrawn in stages.

As I had no intention of resigning, I decided to succumb to this pressure from the cabinet and bring in new resolutions to the Income Tax Act and the Excise Tax Act. This I did on Monday, July 8. I announced a number of changes but by far the most important was to bring in the sales tax on building materials in stages. Another change was to permit companies to qualify as having "a degree of Canadian ownership" if twenty-five per cent of their stock was made available for purchase by Canadians, even though Canadians might not have actually acquired the shares in question. As was to be expected, I was accused of introducing a new budget and ridiculed accordingly. It was a humiliating experience.

The newspaper reaction to these important changes in the budget was anything but complimentary:

> We regret that Finance Minister Walter Gordon has bowed to political pressure in making drastic new revisions in the federal budget. In doing so, Mr. Gordon has made a substantial retreat in his attempt to work toward a balanced budget. And he also appears to have made a withdrawal in his efforts to prevent growing U.S. control of Canada's economy. Both objectives remain, but we can expect little progress toward them this year as a result of the watered down proposals announced by Mr. Gordon last night in the House of Commons.
>
> *The Toronto Star*, July 9, 1963

BUDGET RETREAT COULD END GORDON'S CAREER

> A second major retreat last night from the budget he brought down in the House of Commons with such strident partisanship only twenty-five days ago raised fresh doubts about the political future of Finance Minister Walter Gordon. . . .
>
> In April he came to office with an outstanding reputation as a leading consultant to both business and governments. As a minister of finance, he is discredited today in the eyes of the business community, his colleagues in the Cabinet, the rank and file of the Liberal Party and the civil service. Not even his long and close friendship with Prime Minister Lester Pearson may be sufficient to overcome these impediments. . . . In some quarters it is suggested that the Minister will take on a new stature by his statement last night, the reasoning being that it takes a big man to admit such a big mistake. But in politics, things frequently do not work that way. . . .
>
> *The Globe and Mail*, July 9, 1963

George Nowlan, former finance minister, said Monday night Napoleon's retreat from Moscow "did not go so far or so fast" as Finance Minister Gordon's budget retreat.

"The whole budget should have been withdrawn," he said. "To all intents and purposes it has been withdrawn through staggered dates and alleviating the burdens imposed June 13. Of all the irregular procedures that this House has been subjected to since Confederation, this is the worst."

"Is this the final version?" Opposition Leader Diefenbaker interjected at one point. There was opposition laughter at Mr. Gordon's use of the word "clarification" and jeers and cries of "shame, shame" and "chicken" at other points in his statement. . . .

The Winnipeg Free Press, July 9, 1963

The uproar over the budget, and the changes which have had to be made in it, may have one good effect. They may compel Parliament and the public to take a good look at the whole budget-making process as it is carried on in Canada.

This country has inherited from Britain the tradition that a budget is a thing of mystery. It is prepared in the tightest secrecy by the minister of finance and a few advisers with elaborate precautions to prevent premature disclosure, and then sprung on Parliament. It immediately becomes a party issue, with the government trying to get it through the House of Commons unchanged while the Opposition attacks every detail that is at all controversial. Under these circumstances, it requires a major upheaval – such as occurred in the present case – to make any substantial change possible.

Toronto Star, July 10, 1963

This was not the end of the budget controversy. There were innumerable difficulties and complaints about the withdrawal of the exemption of sales tax on production materials. As stated earlier, nearly all these difficulties had been foreseen by some officials of the Department of National Revenue.

The housebuilders' lobby was well organized and was especially vociferous about the withdrawal of sales tax exemption on building materials. The lobby quietened down a bit after the decision to introduce this measure in stages but they have never ceased their objections.

By the time the House adjourned on August 2 the budget itself had been approved, and also the amendments to the Customs Tariff Act and the Excise Tax Act. The amendments to the Income Tax Act, which had not been debated in any great detail, were held over until the fall. The debate on this last of the budget bills was recommenced on October 16, and while there were many interruptions while other business was attended to it was not disposed of finally until December 5.*

---

*This may seem a long time to take to deal with one budget and its amending bills, but Randolph Churchill, in the second volume of his biography of Sir Winston Churchill, writes that it took seventy parliamentary days and 554 divisions to get the finance bill (that is, the budget) through the British House when Lloyd George was Chancellor of the Exchequer in 1909. Randolph Churchill quotes Lloyd George on the subject of cabinet approval: "Asquith was a much stronger Prime Minister than most people imagined. If he said he'd back you up he would see you through." Asquith asked Lloyd George to explain his budget proposals, and after he had done so, observed: "The Chancellor has given us a very cogent account of his proposals. I think they are of such importance that every member of the Cabinet should say how he feels about them." Apparently everyone

In retrospect, I am confident that no member of the House of Commons seriously believed that I or any of the outside consultants who assisted in the preparation of the 1963 budget conspired to leak its secrets to our business associates or ex-associates. But it was considered to be "good politics" for the opposition to insinuate that this might have been the case. It was an effective way of bringing discredit on a new minority government early in its first session at a time when partisan feelings were intense and tempers high.

Quite apart from this aspect of the matter, there are some lessons to be gained from this experience. The first is that the old established tradition – according to which budgets are prepared by the Department of Finance, without consultation or discussion with other officials or outside experts, and without informing the cabinet of what is going to be proposed until a few hours before presentation to the House – is out of date and should be changed. If, for example, we had been able to resolve the administrative difficulties respecting the thirty per cent takeover tax with officials of the Toronto Stock Exchange before the budget was presented, a lot of our difficulties would have been avoided.

Similarly, while I believe it is important under our system for governments to have the right to announce changes in the rates of any existing tax on budget night or at other times, to become effective immediately, I believe it would be better to hear representations respecting other proposed amendments to existing tax legislation before they are presented to Parliament as firm government policy. If it had been possible to do this at the time of the 1963 budget, some of the difficulties encountered in connection with rescinding the sales tax exemptions, for example, might have been avoided. Important changes in our taxing statutes can have such wide repercussions throughout the whole economy nowadays that they should not be decided for all intents and purposes by a relatively few people in the Department of Finance without public discussion and debate.

There is also the question of "budget secrecy" and the absolute responsibility of the Minister of Finance for any leaks that might occur, intentionally or by misadventure, through the action of any member of his department (or any other department, including the printing bureau). For example, Wynne Plumptre told me long afterwards that he took his draft of the 1963 budget speech home with him the night before he presented it to me. He had planned to read it through again before delivering it the next morning. But it was his birthday and his wife had arranged for them to go

spoke against them, whereupon Asquith said: "We have had a very fair and frank expression of opinion from every member of the Cabinet and it seems to me the weight of the argument rests with the Chancellor." Things were somewhat different in the Canadian cabinet in 1963!

out to visit friends. So Wynne locked the draft speech in his briefcase which he hid in a cupboard. On his return later in the evening, he found his house had been broken into. The burglars had found his briefcase and broken the lock. The draft budget speech was strewn about the floor but still intact.

More sophisticated thieves might have realized that some enterprising reporter could have been a good market for this prize. If that had happened and inspired stories had been published about what might be expected to be included in the budget to be presented in the following week, as the responsible minister I would have had to resign from the government immediately. This might have saved me from some subsequent headaches, but I am not at all sure it would have made much sense.

A postscript. On March 11, 1966, I was a head table guest at a dinner of the Institute of Chartered Accountants of Ontario at which Eric Kierans, who had given up the presidency of the Montreal Stock Exchange to become a minister in the Quebec government of Jean Lesage, was the speaker. His views had changed on a number of questions, including the need to ensure Canada's economic independence. Quite recently he had attacked the American government for imposing guidelines of behaviour for Canadian subsidiaries of U.S. parent companies. He made an excellent speech, which I could well agree with. When it was over he said to me, "Walter, we are coming closer together all the time." To which I was able to reply, "Yes, Eric, but I have not changed my position in the slightest."

CHAPTER NINE

Some Negotiations with Washington

U.S. interest-equalization tax; Canada's balance of payments; two opinions on what is happening to Canada; the Canada – United States Automotive agreement; the Heeney-Merchant report.

While the budget controversy was still raging, on Thursday morning, July 18, I had a call from the American Embassy to say that a representative of the U.S. Treasury was coming to Ottawa to see me and would like to call at my office at exactly twelve noon. He was not entitled to deliver his message to me until that time. This sounded a bit mysterious and coming as it did from the office of the American Ambassador, Walton Butterworth, it may have created a mild undercurrent of irritation. This was because Butterworth, unlike his two able and charming predecessors, Douglas Stuart and Livingstone Merchant, was in the eyes of many people in Ottawa almost a prototype for the "ugly-American" type of United States diplomat.

In any event, it so happened that I had undertaken to see James Stillman Rockefeller of the National City Bank of New York that morning, and I could not very well put him off. Accordingly, I asked Wynne Plumptre, the senior Assistant Deputy Minister of Finance, if he would be kind enough to look after the representative of the U.S. Treasury when he arrived at the office and take him to the Rideau Club for a drink. I promised to meet them for lunch by one o'clock at the latest. I arrived at the club at about ten minutes to one to find Plumptre, J. R. Beattie of the Bank of Canada, Mervyn Trued, an Assistant Secretary of the Treasury, and Francis Linville of the American Embassy in Ottawa. Trued had already informed Plumptre and Beattie of the reason for his visit.

Soon after my arrival in the crowded lounge of the Rideau Club, Trued handed me a communication from the Honourable Douglas Dillon, the

U.S. Secretary of the Treasury, and suggested in view of its importance I might like to read it immediately. Trued was nice enough about this but obviously serious. Accordingly, I opened the letter and proceeded to read it. Having done so I realized how serious the matter was. The President of the United States was proposing to Congress an interest equalization tax which would substantially increase the cost of borrowing in the United States by all foreign countries, including Canada. I expected it would mean a run on the Canadian dollar which, if not checked, would cause a devaluation of the currency, a second devaluation within a period of fourteen months. This would mean a financial crisis of major proportions. It would be a long time before faith and confidence in the Canadian dollar could be re-established.

I asked Plumptre and Beattie to look after Mr. Trued and Mr. Linville at luncheon and asked them all to excuse me as it would be necessary for me to return to my office immediately and prepare a statement for the opening of the House at 2.30 P.M. The statement, which I made at the opening of the day's session, concluded with these words:

> Now, Mr. Speaker, quite clearly the measures proposed by the President of the United States will have wide repercussions in each of the twenty-two countries I have mentioned. These repercussions, if the President's proposals are approved by Congress, may well have an important effect upon Canada's balance of payments and upon the Canadian economy as a whole. It would be unwise for me to say more than this, however, until there has been time to give careful study and consideration to all the implications of the President's proposals.

All of us in the Department of Finance and at the Bank of Canada fully realized the significance of the President's message. If there were any doubts about this, the reactions in Canadian markets later that day and the next were enough to show what was about to happen; that is, another devaluation of the Canadian currency, for which the United States would have been directly responsible.

I called Douglas Dillon on the telephone and gave him some indication of our concern. I asked him if he would be able to receive someone from Canada to discuss the matter some time on the Saturday afternoon or evening. Dillon agreed to this and Louis Rasminsky, Wynne Plumptre, and Ed Ritchie of the Department of External Affairs left for Washington. I did not go myself because I thought this would attract too much attention to the seriousness we attached to the President's message.

However, I was on the telephone almost continuously with Plumptre and Rasminsky in Washington, and also with Dillon. It was not until the Sunday afternoon, however, that Mr. Dillon became convinced of what was likely to happen in Canada if some relieving action by the United States was not approved and announced almost immediately. After much discussion it was decided that the only way out of the difficulty would be to exempt Canada completely from the proposed interest equalization tax. This left two things to be done. First, the drafting of a statement to be issued simultaneously in both Washington and Ottawa, and second, obtaining President Kennedy's approval both of the action to be taken and of the wording of the statement. We convinced Mr. Dillon that both these things would have to be done before the opening of the markets on Monday morning. Somehow he managed to get in touch with the President and obtain his approval. The statement which was issued in Washington and Ottawa on the Sunday evening, July 21, indicated that Canada would be exempted from the proposed tax and included the following paragraph:

> The Canadian authorities stated that it would not be the desire or intention of Canada to increase her foreign-exchange reserves through the proceeds of borrowings in the United States, and it is the hope and expectation of both governments that by maintaining close consultation it will prove possible in practice to have an unlimited exemption for Canada without adverse effect on the United States.

The Prime Minister made a statement about this whole matter when the House met on Monday, July 22, the closing paragraph of which read as follows:

> From Canada's point of view the objective must be a further substantial reduction of our current account deficit in the balance of payments. This government has made clear on numerous occasions that the correction of our balance of payments position, with its favourable effects on employment, is a central objective of our economic policies.

While the immediate emergency was over, thanks to the prompt action on the part of the Canadian government and its officials, and the co-operation of Douglas Dillon and President Kennedy, nevertheless we had been given another sharp reminder of Canada's dependency upon the United States. If these two senior American officials had not wished to be co-operative, or if Douglas Dillon had been unwilling to give up his plans for the weekend, Canada by the Monday morning would have been in the midst of a major financial crisis. Almost certainly this would have led to another devaluation of the currency.

This crisis had been avoided, but at a price. As was stated in the communiqué, it was not Canada's intention to build up her exchange reserves through the proceeds of borrowings in the United States. Later this was interpreted by our American friends to mean that under no circumstances would Canada increase her reserves above their present levels. This caused us considerable embarrassment in the management of our exchange reserves and placed another limitation upon the flexibility and freedom of Canadian monetary policy.

Soon after the House adjourned on August 2, I went to Washington to meet Douglas Dillon and thank him for his help during the crisis over the Interest Equalization Tax. I found him to be a pleasant, straight-forward man with a considerable understanding of and sympathy for the Canadian position. He had been a successful investment banker before beginning his distinguished career in public service under President Eisenhower, but had been surprised by the reaction in Canadian financial markets to the announcement of the interest equalization tax proposal. Charles Ritchie, the Canadian Ambassador to the United States at the time, had gone with me to call on Mr. Dillon. At the end of our visit, Dillon said that George Ball, the Under Secretary of State, had heard I would be in town and had sent a message asking me to call on him when I got through with Mr. Dillon.

I had met George Ball on several occasions, when the Democrats and Liberals were out of office, at meetings of the Bilderberg Group. This was a group of European and North American politicians, businessmen, and academics which met periodically under the chairmanship of Prince Bernhard of The Netherlands. The name of the group was taken from the town in Holland where the first meeting had taken place.

Ball and I were on a first-name basis and I was, therefore, somewhat startled when, almost immediately after Ritchie and I arrived in his office, he began a tirade in which he criticized Canada and the Canadian government in general and me and my June 13 budget in particular. His tone was heated, his choice of language gaudy, and his facts inaccurate. But this did not seem to trouble him in the least. By the time he first stopped to draw breath, some twenty minutes later, I had decided to reply in the same vein. I made it clear that he had no right to speak to a member of the Canadian government in the way he had done, and pointed out, moreover, that he did not seem to know what he was talking about.

I proceeded to point out the facts about Canada's balance of payments position. I referred to the very heavy deficits we had been running on current account in our balance of payments with the United States and the fact that, while a considerable part of this deficit had to be covered by imports of capital from the United States, a significant part was met by the surplus we earned on our current account transactions with other countries. I pointed out that, to this extent – and it was a significant extent – we were assisting the United States in their balance of payments difficulties. I explained to Ball that if we reduced our borrowings in the United States, as he seemed to think we should do, then inevitably we would have to reduce the deficit we were running on current account with the United States. He could not have it both ways. I suggested that he should understand his facts before proceeding to lecture Canadian officials another time.

I also gave Ball some of the statistics of the extent of non-resident, mostly American, control of individual Canadian industries and said that it was only because of the magnitude of this foreign control that Canadians were disturbed about what had been happening. George agreed at once that he had not understood the problem and thanked me for explaining the situation to him. When we left his office we were on good terms again.

That evening, at a small dinner to which Douglas Dillon had been kind enough to invite me at his house, Ball turned up, I think quite unexpectedly. After dinner, he made a short speech in which he said he had come to the dinner to thank me for the way in which I had explained the Canadian situation to him that morning. He said he had learned more from me about Canada in half an hour than he had ever known before. Ritchie remarked to me afterwards that he felt this was quite a triumph and he hoped I would come to Washington more frequently. He added that the scene that morning in George Ball's office was something new in his experience of international relations.

The first meeting of the Joint Canada–United States Committee on Trade and Economic Affairs since the election of the Pearson government took place in Washington on September 20-21, 1963. The Canadian delegation consisted of Paul Martin, Secretary of State for External Affairs; Mitchell Sharp, Minister of Trade and Commerce; Bud Drury, Minister of Industry; Harry Hays, Minister of Agriculture; Louis Rasminsky, the Governor of the Bank of Canada; Charles Ritchie, Canadian Ambassador in Washington; and myself, as Minister of Finance. As I recall it, the United States was represented by Dean Rusk, Secretary of State; Douglas Dillon, Secretary of the Treasury; George Ball, Under Secretary of State; Orville Freeman, Secretary of Agriculture; Luther Hodges, Secretary of Commerce; John Kelly, Assistant Secretary of the Interior; Walter Heller, Chairman of the President's Council of Economic Advisers; Christian Herter, Special Representative for Trade Negotiations; Frank Coffin, Deputy Administrator of the Agency for Economic Development; and Walton Butterworth, U.S. Ambassador to Canada.

We arrived in Washington late Thursday afternoon, September 19, and soon afterwards attended a reception. When I arrived, I found a large group gathered around George Ball and Louis Rasminsky, who were engaged in an altercation about the balance of payments problems of Canada and the United States. Ball, who evidently had forgotten all about my conversation with him in August, was saying that Canada was being anything but helpful in these matters. Someone suggested that I might like to give Rasminsky a hand in the argument, but I resisted this temptation. Rasminsky was quite able to handle George Ball by himself, and seemed to enjoy doing so.

After the formalities were dispensed with at the meeting of the Joint Committee, which began on the Friday morning, I proceeded to outline the Canadian position on the balance of payments issue. I pointed out that during the previous four years Canada's deficit on current account with the United States had amounted to $5,800 million. This was covered to the extent of $280 million by our surplus on current with other countries; to the extent of $320 million by capital inflows from such other countries; and to the extent of $640 million by Canada's gold production available for export. Part of these receipts were used to augment Canada's exchange reserves, but $1,000 million was used to help finance our current-account deficit with the United States. This left a balance of $4,800 million to be covered by capital inflows from that country.

I emphasized that while it might appear at first glance that we had embarrassed the United States by importing $4,800 million of capital from that country in the four-year period, mostly borrowed in the New York market, in fact we had contributed approximately $1,000 million to the American balance of payments position. If we discontinued all capital imports into Canada from the United States, necessarily we would have to bring our current account deficit with the United States more nearly into balance. This would mean either stepping up our exports to the United States or reducing our imports from that country.

I added that the Canadian government was disturbed about Canada's current account deficit and also about the extent to which the imports of capital from the United States for direct investment were leading to an ever-increasing control of Canadian industry by Americans. However, I stressed that strictly in terms of the American balance of payments problem, we had been a help to them in the past rather than the opposite. While this proposition was put carefully and in some detail, I was not at all convinced that my points were being appreciated by the members of the American delegation.

At the end of the first day's meeting, Dean Rusk, the chairman of the American delegation, stressed that nothing should be said to the press about the nature of our discussions until the conclusion of the meeting on Saturday, when a communiqué would be issued. This was agreed to, but immediately after the meeting Luther Hodges, the Secretary of Commerce, gave the press a highly coloured version of what had taken place throughout the day. He was particularly incensed about Canada's insistence that a greater proportion of the North American production of automobiles and components should take place in Canada. Understandably the Canadians were annoyed that Mr. Hodges should have spoken to the press after we had all agreed not to do so, but perhaps we should have realized that that sort of thing happens all the time in Washington.

Before the next meeting began on the Saturday morning, Harry Hays asked me how I felt things had gone the previous day. I told him that I had been disappointed and felt I had not succeeded in getting the Canadian story across about the balance of payments situation. Harry replied that he had watched the Americans carefully as I made my presentation. He said that in his view our story had got across to some of them, and he urged me to find some pretext for doing it all over again that morning. He argued that if they were given the story a second time it might begin to stick. Accordingly, shortly after the Saturday session began, I found an excuse to repeat my dissertation of the previous day. This time, thanks to Harry, I did feel that the Canadian position was more clearly understood by our American opposite numbers.

The next meeting of the Joint Committee was held in Ottawa towards the end of April 1964. Again there was considerable discussion of the proposed automobile agreement. Douglas Dillon, who by this time had a clear understanding of Canada's balance of payments position, was very helpful. After the meeting he consented to go on a television program with me. In the course of it, he agreed that Canada had a balance of payments problem; that it was important for Canada to reduce the deficit on current account with other countries; and that to do this Canada would have to reduce its current account deficit with the United States. He explained that this could be done either by increasing Canada's exports to the United States or by reducing its imports from that country. He said that everyone agreed that the first of these alternatives was preferable. He then said that if we were going to step up our exports to the United States, this would require an increase in our exports of manufactured goods, and he agreed that the most logical place to begin was to step up our exports of automobiles or automobile components. This statement by the U.S. Secretary of the Treasury was of the greatest importance.

Just prior to the meeting of the Joint Committee in Ottawa, George Ball had made a speech at a meeting of the American Assembly in Harriman, New York, in which he had belaboured Canada for borrowing so extensively in the United States and thus embarrassing the United States in its balance of payments difficulties. Ball arrived in Canada for the meeting of the Joint Committee to find himself criticized in bold headlines in most Canadian newspapers for the accusations he had made in his American Assembly speech. He seemed quite surprised by this reception.

That evening, there was a dinner at the Country Club for the visiting Americans. Pearson had spent the day at Harrington Lake and arrived looking well and sunburned and in wonderful form. In welcoming our American visitors, the Prime Minister paid special attention to George Ball. He said he was reminded of a particularly gruesome murder which took place on Hampstead Heath while Pearson was serving in the Canadian High Commissioner's office in London. The constable, in giving his evidence, had stated that he found the victim, a young lady, decapitated and dismembered, but that she "hadn't been interfered with." Mike then turned to Ball and said with a wide grin, "Now, George, you can decapitate and dismember us if you will, but you must not 'interfere' with us." Judging from the laughter it was evident that everyone present, including George, had got the Prime Minister's message.

But George Ball is irrepressible, as anyone who has read his book, *The Discipline of Power,* published in 1968, will testify. In this book the man whom many believed would have become Secretary of State if Hubert Humphrey had won the presidency in November 1968 described how he believes the affairs of the world should be arranged, given the fact that the United States is by far the most powerful nation in it. His views about Canada's future in this scheme of things are expressed as follows:

> Canada, I have long believed, is fighting a rearguard action against the inevitable. Living next to our nation, with a population ten times as large as theirs and a gross national product fourteen times as great, the Canadians recognize their need for United States capital; but at the same time they are determined to maintain their economic and political independence. Their position is understandable, and the desire to maintain their national integrity is a worthy objective. But the Canadians pay heavily for it and, over the years, I do not believe they will succeed in reconciling the intrinsic contradiction of their position. I wonder, for example, if the Canadian people will be prepared indefinitely to accept, for the psychic satisfaction of maintaining a separate national and political identity, a per capita income less than three-fourths of ours. The struggle is bound to be a difficult one – and I suspect, over the years, a losing one. Meanwhile there is danger that the efforts of successive Canadian governments to prevent United States economic domination will drive them toward increasingly restrictive nationalistic measures that are good neither for Canada nor for the health of the whole trading world.
>
> Thus, while I can understand the motivating assumptions of the Canadian position, I cannot predict a long life expectancy for her present policies. The great land mass to the south exerts an enormous gravitational attraction while at the same time tending to repel, and even

without the divisive element of a second culture in Quebec, the resultant strains and pressures are hard to endure. Sooner or later, commercial imperatives will bring about free movement of all goods back and forth across our long border; and when that occurs, or even before it does, it will become unmistakably clear that countries with economies so inextricably intertwined must also have free movement of the other vital factors of production – capital, services and labour. The result will inevitably be substantial economic integration, which will require for its full realization a progressively expanding area of common political decision.*

This new effort in diplomacy or, if you will, this re-emphasis of George Ball's forthright opinions, attracted a somewhat annoyed, but at the same time mildly amused, reaction in Canada. But George Ball's views about our future should be taken very seriously. From the reports which I received while I was in government from the Canadian officials who had occasion to visit Washington quite frequently, I became convinced that at least the more junior people in the State and Treasury Departments held decidedly imperialistic views about Canada. We should be grateful to George Ball for having given public expression to them. Those Canadians who do not wish to see their country absorbed by the quiet but nonetheless insidious form of colonialism now in vogue in Washington will do well to take Mr. Ball's opinions at their face value and then plan to counteract them.

Incidentally, some of the assertions contained in the passage quoted are open to serious question. For example, there is no justification for implying, as George Ball does, that the average *per capita* income of Canadians would necessarily improve merely because the economies of the two countries were integrated. There is a lot more to it than that.

Mr. Ball is not the only recent author to predict the integration or absorption of Canada by the United States. In discussing the takeover of Canadian business and Canadian resources by Americans in *The American Empire*, which was published in 1968, Amaury de Riencourt writes:

But any practical steps to halt the trend or reverse it would lead to such a drastic fall in the Canadian standard of living that they could never be tolerated.

The violent reaction to Canadian Finance Minister Walter Gordon's mild attempt to do so in 1963 illustrates the stark impossibility of resisting this wholesale takeover: "So devastatingly hostile was the reaction that the effect on the government in the interval was almost traumatic," states an expert on Canadian affairs. What is clear is that

*Copyright © 1968 by George Ball.

165

an increasingly large proportion of Canadian businessmen are merely employees of American companies headquartered in New York, Detroit, or Chicago. And these American companies, parents of Canadian subsidiaries, owe their first allegiance to American, not Canadian, legislation and interests. As a result, no Canadian subsidiary dares contravene the United States' antitrust laws or the Trading with the Enemy Act. Inevitably, unobtrusively, American legislation applies in Canada in an extraterritorial way. It is also obvious that if the international market for goods produced on both sides of the border were to shrink substantially, American companies would probably not hesitate to close down their operations in Canada so as to maintain full production in the United States.

Those who believe that there is no threat to Canadian independence point to the fact that the United States was developed out of British capital in the nineteenth century. But that capital was in the form of redeemable bonds, whereas United States investments in Canada are in the form of outright ownership of subsidiaries. American investments, again, are controlling investments, providing not only the financial resources but the technical skills, the managerial know-how, the research and development, and the overall business policy. Furthermore, not only are a majority of the large Canadian corporations American-owned but they also happen to be in the most dynamic sectors of the economy....

That is what one international observer believes is happening to Canada.

A major economic objective of the Pearson government was to reduce the deficit in our current account transactions with the United States. In order to achieve this, we felt we must reduce the difference between our imports from and exports to the United States of automobiles and parts. In 1964, Canada's share of the total production of automobiles and parts in North America was four per cent, whereas our consumption was seven per cent. The government believed that Canada's share of the total production should be increased over a period of years until it more nearly coincided with our share of the total consumption. Even Douglas Dillon had admitted the desirability of this in a television broadcast.

Attempts to develop a satisfactory scheme to stimulate Canadian production of automotive vehicles and parts date back to the report of the 1961 Royal Commission on the Auto Trade, chaired by Professor Vincent W. Bladen of the University of Toronto. In 1962, when George Nowlan was Minister of Finance, the Canadian automotive manufacturers suggested to the government that customs duties on the importation of automatic transmissions into Canada be remitted in order to assist them to overcome a major production problem. The government countered with a proposal, initiated by Simon Reisman and Arthur Annis, two senior officials in the Department of Finance, acceding to the industry's request provided the companies concerned would agree to increase exports on a dollar-for-dollar basis. For every dollar of imports of automatic transmissions, on which duty was remitted to the manufacturers, the companies would have to undertake to increase exports by an equal amount. The companies accepted the plan, and although American officials were uneasy about it there were no protests from the United States government. This was the arrangement in effect when the Liberal government took office in April 1963.

For the year 1962, Canadian imports of automotive vehicles and parts had amounted to $642 million, while exports were only $62 million. The resulting deficit of $580 million accounted for more than two-thirds of Canada's $848 million unfavourable trade balance in that year. Clearly some further development of export incentives was necessary to help close the gap. In the late summer of 1963, Bud Drury, the Minister of Industry, announced details of a new automotive export incentive scheme which linked tariff rebates to export performance. Under the terms of the plan, Canadian automotive companies were to be permitted for a period of three years to import automotive parts duty free to the extent that each company increased its Canadian manufactured exports over the 1961-1962 base period. Drury predicted that the plan, which he described as "expansionist but not protective," would increase the exports of Canadian auto parts by as much as $200 million a year and create a large number of new jobs in the automobile industry.

This time there was a strong reaction from the United States. The new plan was the subject of considerable discussion at the meeting of the Joint Canada–United States Committee on Trade and Economic Affairs in September of 1963, and was opposed by Luther Hodges, the U.S. Secretary of Commerce, in strenuous terms.

On September 26, 1963, an editorial titled "Canadian Protectionism" appeared in *The New York Times* attacking the Canadian plan. "Canada . . . our biggest customer has delivered the latest setback to the Administration's hopes of liberalizing barriers to international commerce. . . . Recourse to protectionism, whatever the guise, will not profit Canada." The editorial admonished Canada for trying to improve its competitive position: "Over the long run, its labour force will gain more employment and its industry greater utilization by competing in areas where Canada possesses economic advantages. The attempt to protect and build the Canadian automobile industry at the expense of the United States is not in this category."

Meanwhile, the Big Three automobile companies, General Motors, Ford and Chrysler, were reported to be anxiously lobbying Washington to help kill the scheme. In October, Luther Hodges stated that if automobile manufacturers in Canada (that is, the subsidiaries of General Motors, Ford, and Chrysler) did not like the legislation, they "ought to get up on their hind legs and say so." Hodges told the press that he had put up "a damned good case" against the Canadian plan (at the meeting of the Joint Committee) and let it be known that if the Canadian government were presumptuous enough to disregard his views, the United States might have to take retaliatory action. Retaliation came under the provisions of a seldom-invoked American law which requires the automatic imposition of countervailing duties on imports to the United States which receive a "bounty" in the country of origin. According to the American interpretation, the Canadian automotive products export incentive scheme amounted to a bounty and was, therefore, unacceptable.

In the light of this opposition to the Canadian scheme, discussions began between officials of the two governments towards the formulation of a formal trade agreement on automotive vehicles and parts. It was not until December 11, 1964, however, that we were able to announce that the Canada–United States Automotive Agreement had been concluded under the terms of which Canada agreed to permit free entry of autos and auto parts from the United States and other countries conditional upon a considerable increase in production by Canadian manufacturers. In return, the United States indicated that it would seek congressional approval for the abolition of existing tariffs on the importation of automobiles and automotive parts from Canada. From the Canadian standpoint, the new agreement was multilateral and conditional, but from the viewpoint of the United States it was bilateral and unconditional. This meant that the United States had to obtain a waiver under the terms of the General Agreement on Tariffs and Trade (GATT).

The automobile industry in Canada, as well as in the United States, was and is dominated by three companies, General Motors, Ford, and Chrysler. Among them, these companies account for about ninety-five per cent of the production of cars on both sides of the border. In other words, the structure of the industry in North America is monopolistic or, to be more exact, oligopolistic.

In these circumstances the Canadian government felt it necessary not only to enter into an agreement with the U.S. government but also with each of the automobile manufacturers. Under these industry agreements, each Canadian manufacturer undertook:

(i)   To raise the value of their vehicle output between 1965 and 1968 by at least the same proportionate amount as the increase in the value of their sales in Canada;

(ii) To increase the output of the Canadian auto and parts industries over the same period by a further one-third of the 1964 level in addition to normal growth; and

(iii) To maintain the level of Canadian content at not less than current levels.

Under the agreement, the American automobile companies may import, free of duty, finished vehicles or components for vehicles from their Canadian subsidiaries, from Canadian parts manufacturers, or from foreign-owned automobile manufacturers located in Canada, provided they fulfil certain requirements designed to prevent overseas auto manufacturers from gaining duty-free access to the American market through Canada. For parts or components, imported as such and not assembled into completed cars, at least fifty per cent of the aggregate value must be North American content. The same applies to the chassis of completed cars. For parts or components, other than chassis, imported as constituents of completed cars, at least forty per cent of the aggregate value must be North American content up to January 1, 1968, and fifty per cent after that date.

The Automotive Trade Agreement was a tremendously important achievement for the Pearson government. It meant a considerable capital investment in Canada to facilitate the greater volume of production here that was called for. It meant the creation of thousands of new jobs and it relieved our balance-of-payments difficulties. It is true that it accepted the rationalization of the automobile industry on a continental basis. I did not like this in principle, but as three companies dominated the industry on both sides of the border, this acceptance merely acknowledged the existing fact. It is not a pattern that should be adopted for other industries.

As a result of the agreement, the long-term trend in the United States for the disappearance of independently owned parts manufacturers, or their acquisition by the Big Three automobile manufacturers, was speeded up in Canada. This was most regrettable, but in the long run it seemed inevitable in any event. Short of expropriating the Big Three automobile manufacturers in Canada, or of the federal government exerting some form of detailed direction of their operations, neither of which alternative was thought to be practical, there was no other way of achieving the government's objectives except, of course, by increasing the "Canadian content" requirement which would have been considered protectionist in its application. On balance, it was a good deal for Canada as the statistics on the accompanying table demonstrate.

In the four-year period, the value of the total production in Canada increased enormously. Despite this, the imbalance in our exports and

	1964	1968	Increase
Number of vehicles manufactured	670,000	1,177,000	507,000
Total value of factory shipments	$2,300,000,000	$4,000,000,000	$1,700,000,000
Number of employees in the industry	71,000	90,000	19,000
Value of exports to the United States	$99,000,000	$2,400,000,000	$2,301,000,000
Value of imports from the United States	$716,000,000	$2,900,000,000	$2,184,000,000
Difference between value of imports and exports from and to the United States	$617,000,000	$500,000,000	$117,000,000
Canadian share of North American production	4%	6%	2%
Canadian share of North American consumption	7%	8%	1%

imports of automobiles and parts to and from the United States was reduced by $117 million with a corresponding impact on Canada's deficit on current account with the United States. If nothing had been done, the difference between the value of imports and exports from and to the United States, which amounted to $617 million in 1964, would most certainly have increased considerably as the output of the automobile industry increased. As things have worked out, however, this difference was reduced to $500 million in 1968 and was reduced still further in 1969, but this favourable result has since been reversed.

The agreement was much less advantageous to the United States, and it has been asked why the government of that country, which opposed the 1963 Canadian scheme, was persuaded to approve it. It is probable that the United States went along partly because the American parent companies of the Canadian automobile manufacturers saw advantages in rationalizing production in co-operation with their Canadian subsidiaries and pressured Washington to conclude the agreement. Perhaps the American government went along partly because George Ball, the Under Secretary of State, believed that, if such an agreement were concluded, it would bind together in a formal way the industry in the United States and Canada, a move in the direction of greater integration of the two economies in keeping with his own economic philosophy. Probably the United States went along partly because there were other important issues between our two countries, and Washington was not anxious to provoke further disagreements or misunderstandings.

Another reason why this pact was accepted in Washington was the demonstrated determination of the Canadian government to do something, unilaterally if necessary, to reduce the trade imbalance in auto vehicles and parts with the United States. The senior Canadian negotiator reported back to me one remark he made to his American counterpart after a particularly difficult session. He told them: "Listen, we have a pretty tough so-and-so as Minister of Finance who won't hesitate to go ahead with measures to shape consumer demand in Canada unless we get some results." By this he meant reducing automotive imports into Canada by unilateral action and requiring a drastic cut in the number of models produced in Canada if necessary.

The Automotive Agreement was signed by Prime Minister Pearson and President Lyndon B. Johnson on January 16, 1965. It came into effect in Canada shortly afterwards through an Order-in-Council made under the provisions of the Customs Tariff Act. It was approved by the House of Commons on May 6, 1965. The agreement was submitted to the United States Congress on March 20, 1965, but was held up for months before the necessary approval was obtained. It so happened that I was able to do something which helped to expedite this approval.

At about this time – March 31, 1965 – Douglas Dillon retired as Secretary of the Treasury and was succeeded by Henry H. Fowler, a former Under Secretary and a Washington lawyer. Soon after taking office, Mr. Fowler made a proposal for an international conference to reform the monetary system. He did this without much prior consultation with the Group of Ten countries which had been considering the matter of international monetary reform for several years. This made the Ten, or some of them, angry and not disposed to be co-operative. These ten countries, made up of the world's most industrialized nations, believed that the complex problems of world liquidity would have no chance of being solved at an international meeting attended by a large number of underdeveloped nations without prior agreement among themselves. But having made his proposal public, which was received so coolly by the Group of Ten, Fowler's problem was to extricate himself without further alienating the Ten, on the one hand, and without antagonizing the countries not members of the Group of Ten which welcomed the idea of an international conference, on the other.

It seemed to me to be in everyone's best interest to help the new U.S. Secretary of the Treasury out of an awkward situation. Accordingly, on July 30, I had a talk with him in Washington concerning his dilemma. After consulting the top officials in the Department of Finance and the Bank of Canada, I wrote to Fowler on September 7, 1965, proposing that advance discussions concerning an international conference take place first among the deputies of the Group of Ten in consultation with the International Monetary Fund, following which the discussions should be broadened in the executive board of I.M.F. in order to include other countries. The advantage of this proposal was that the membership of the executive board included representatives of many countries other than the Group of Ten, and there would be no need to seek agreement about which countries should be selected to participate in the preparatory committee.

In order to carry out this proposal, it would be necessary to convince the underdeveloped nations in private conversations that the most likely way to secure the agreement of the Group of Ten was to use the I.M.F. for such discussions. At the same time, the Europeans had to be persuaded that the board of the Fund was a better forum from their point of view for preparatory discussions than any alternative the underdeveloped nations were likely to press for. In this way, the Fund could be presented privately to both sides as a workable compromise. In my letter to Fowler, I offered Canadian support for such a procedural arrangement.

In his reply, Fowler concurred with my views about the need to work through the Group of Ten as a first step and through the Fund as a second step. We met again in Washington on September 26 just before the annual meeting of the International Monetary Fund. As a result of our discussions, and thanks to the persuasiveness of Louis Rasminsky, the proposal was accepted as a basis for compromise by both sides, and Fowler was able to resolve his dilemma without loss of face. Following the meetings, Fowler said to me: "Walter, you did me a great favour and now I owe you one. What can I do for you?" My reply was: "Get the automotive agreement passed through Congress."

Fowler agreed to go to work on this immediately. He mentioned that within the last two days the President had also spoken to him in the same vein. Fowler was well liked by the Congressmen and had a lot of influence with them. They listened to his representations and soon afterwards gave their approval to the agreement. It was signed into law by the President on October 22, 1965.

In January 1964, Prime Minister Pearson and President Johnson jointly requested two diplomats, Arnold Heeney, twice a highly successful Canadian Ambassador to Washington, and Livingstone Merchant, twice U.S. Ambassador to Ottawa, "to study the practicability and desirability of working out acceptable principles which would make it easier to avoid divergencies in economic and other policies of the two countries." Messrs. Heeney and Merchant selected a dozen "cases" which had been the cause of recent friction between the two countries and asked senior officials of both governments who had been involved in them to review the facts and to suggest how they might have been more satisfactorily handled. The areas selected included the American interest equalization tax in conjunction with the Canadian withholding tax, trade with Cuba, the labour dispute on the Great Lakes, the extraterritorial implications of domestic legislation, and nuclear weapons. The two sets of studies were considered by the authors in the preparation of their report, *Principles for Partnership*, which was described as "a dialogue between friends" and was published on July 12, 1965.

The report contained several specific recommendations. These included the removal by the United States of regulations affecting export trade by American branches and subsidiaries in Canada, the establishment of a joint committee of deputies to back up the existing Joint Ministerial Committee on Trade and Economic Affairs; closer co-operation and coordination in the production and distribution of energy; the broadening of the functions of the International Joint Commission; the more effective utilization of the Permanent Joint Board on Defence; and closer co-operation in financial relationships. The authors also discussed principles for "timely and sufficient consultation in candour and good faith at whatever level of government is appropriate." They found the evidence "overwhelmingly in favour of a specific regime of consultation." On the one hand, Canadian authorities "must have confidence that the practice of quiet diplomacy is not only neighbourly and convenient to the United States but that it is in fact more effective than the alternative of raising a row and being unpleasant in public." On the other hand, United States authorities "must be satisfied that . . . Canada will have sympathetic regard for the world-wide preoccupations and responsibilities of the United States." It was both "important and reasonable" for Canadian authorities to have "careful regard" for U.S. preoccupations and responsibilities. In the absence of "special Canadian interests or obligations," it was best to avoid as far as possible public disagreement "especially upon critical issues." The report acknowledged that the Canadian government could not be expected to concur "automatically and uniformly" since it could not "renounce its right to independent decisions and judgement in the vast external realm." Note was also made that the United States should take into account Canada's special obligations and relationships with Britain, the Commonwealth, and France.

President Johnson described the Heeney-Merchant report as "a serious and constructive contribution to still better relations between Canada and the United States." Prime Minister Pearson expressed the hope that it would receive "especially careful and serious study by both governments and people." He was careful to point out, however, that although he had always believed in quiet diplomacy, "We must always reserve the right to make a statement publicly when we feel it is right to do so."

The initial newspaper reaction to the report was critical. Charles Lynch in *The Ottawa Citizen* thought that Heeney had been "conned . . . into signing a report recommending that the Canadian government should keep a civil tongue in its head when commenting on United States foreign policy. Alvin Hamilton, a prominent Tory front-bencher, proclaimed that he had lost confidence in Arnold Heeney, and called the report's recommendations a "diplomatic sell-out" to the United States which would make Canada the "lap-dog" of the United States in foreign affairs. Although denied by Heeney as "gross misconstruction," the report's recommendations were interpreted by some as proposing silence by Canada on American policies in return for special economic considerations. The report was defended by Bruce Hutchison in the F.P. Publications chain, and later comments in such periodicals as *Maclean's Magazine* and *The Financial Times* were more balanced.

While I did not make any public comment or criticism of the report, I felt, privately, that if its recommendations were put into practice Canada would be tied more tightly than ever to the United States and that it would become increasingly difficult for us to take an independent stand on policy. We are more likely to get attention in Washington – and eventually to be more respected there – if we state our position on important policy issues clearly and publicly.

CHAPTER TEN

The Trials of
Minority Government

Friends and associates; a meeting with the N.D.P.; financial legislation; a speech in New York; federal-provincial conferences in 1963; federal-provincial conference in Quebec City, March 31, 1964; poor morale within the government; opting-out legislation; the Canada Student Loans Act; the flag debate; a visit to Japan; the Rivard case; the furniture affair; the Dupuis incident.

The second session of the first Pearson government began on February 18, 1964, and was to continue until April 3, 1965. It was a frustrating session for the Liberals despite the improvement in economic conditions and the reduction in unemployment. The efforts which the opposition parties had made during the first session to disrupt and delay the proceedings were continued with long question periods every day and innumerable questions of privilege and appeals from the Speaker's rulings. Tempers were short and ministers, in particular, became tired and discouraged. It was not a successful session for the Liberal government, despite the fact that a lot was accomplished.

I continued to see a good deal of my friend, Mike Pearson, and also of Bud Drury, my brother-in-law. (His wife and my wife are sisters.) The other ministers I felt closest to in the first Pearson government were Maurice Lamontagne, Ben Benson, Harry Hays, Larry Pennell, Judy LaMarsh, Allan MacEachen, and Guy Favreau. Maurice Lamontagne had been a friend from his days as a professor at Laval when he was an outspoken adversary of Premier Duplessis. He is intelligent, an idea man, a fine companion, and a man of courage and integrity. He was of tremendous help to Pearson when he served as his assistant during the five years of opposition from 1958 to 1963.

Ben Benson had been a great help during the year he had worked with me as Parliamentary Secretary. Naturally I was sorry to lose him, but I was among those who had been strongly urging his promotion to the cabinet, which he most certainly deserved. Ben is intelligent, sound in judgement, and he never seems to get excited. He was popular with the caucus and was the obvious choice in the spring of 1968 to become Minister of Finance in Pierre Elliott Trudeau's cabinet.

Larry Pennell, one of the most popular Members of Parliament, succeeded Benson as Parliamentary Secretary in the Department of Finance. He was especially helpful in getting financial legislation through the House. He, in turn, was elevated to the cabinet in July 1965 as Solicitor General.

Harry Hays is very shrewd and was proceeding to make a great success of his job as Minister of Agriculture. He did not like wasting time in the House and was frequently away on government business, which annoyed the opposition. But they soon found out that Harry is not a man to be trifled with. Alvin Hamilton, who was Minister of Agriculture in the Diefenbaker government, made a long speech on October 14, 1963, attacking Harry for his alleged shortcomings which he documented with a great assortment of figures and statistics. Hays, obviously angry, jumped to his feet as soon as Alvin had finished and made a most effective and obviously unrehearsed reply. He accused Hamilton of talking a "lot of junk," and devastated Alvin's careful documentation with the remark that "statistics are for losers." He challenged Hamilton to meet him at the Experimental Farm for a personal contest in milking and implied that he doubted if Alvin, who was an ex-school teacher, not a farmer, would even know which side of the cow to work from. Unfortunately, Harry was in hospital throughout the whole of the 1965 election campaign and, in consequence was defeated by a very small margin. He firmly believed that Canadian farmers were entitled to higher prices for their products and that ever-increasing subsidies were not the answer. I agreed with him.

Judy LaMarsh has a warm and generous nature and supports her friends. Moreover, she is intelligent, quick-witted, and can hold her own in any company. Unfortunately, Pearson did not seem to understand or appreciate her volatile disposition and therefore failed to take full advantage of her undoubted talents. Allan MacEachen is a talented and progressive-minded man who could be very effective in debate, and sometimes, if he felt strongly, could make a case in cabinet with considerable force. Guy Favreau had a great capacity for friendship and a wonderfully generous disposition, but he became engulfed by circumstances and in fields in which he had little or no experience. Undoubtedly, the troubles he got into contributed to his early death in 1967, when he was only fifty years of age. This was the greatest of the several tragedies of the Pearson administration.

These seven – Lamontagne, Benson, Pennell, Hayes, Judy LaMarsh, MacEachen, Favreau – and I usually agreed on most policy issues and consequently we had considerable influence in cabinet. As a rule, the Prime Minister, who was instinctively progressive in his approach, agreed with us – or we agreed with him, whichever way one likes to put it.

There were others in addition to the ones that I have mentioned who were good fun and entertaining. Jack Pickersgill is highly intelligent and always full of quips. On one occasion, after a long discussion of all the conceivable pros and cons respecting some rather unimportant item of policy had been threshed to death, one of our more deliberate colleagues rather ponderously proceeded to review the subject all over again. Jack, who was sitting beside me, whispered that he felt the man in question was probably one of the most valuable members of the cabinet. "He always manages to remind us how long it takes the average man to grasp an elementary idea." By nature, Pickersgill is more conservatively inclined than I am, but he is a fighter and a prolific producer of ideas. Paul Martin has a good sense of humour and considerable ability; at times his circumlocutory style could be very amusing. I liked him but he had difficulty in making up his mind on hard issues; he usually seemed to seek a mild and non-controversial solution which, in the long run, weakened his position.

Paul Hellyer is a strange, serious, energetic man. He seemed to keep to himself a lot and appeared to be even more frustrated than the rest of us by the way government business was conducted. I never got to know him well. Mitchell Sharp is articulate and can be persuasive in the way he presents a case. He had been a civil servant for many years before entering politics, and a deputy minister to C. D. Howe. He and a number of others gave the impression of never fully accepting the new policies and philosophy the Liberal Party had approved in January 1961 and this led to some disagreements.

I had known Maurice Sauvé since the days of the Royal Commission on Canada's Economic Prospects. He is a strong man and able, but sometimes in his anxiety to get ahead he offended others in the cabinet and caucus. Lucien Cardin, Hédard Robichaud, and Jack Nicholson were competent ministers whom I liked and respected. Cardin has considerable strength and courage, but did not like the sordid side of politics and I am sure is glad to be out of it. Eddie Robichaud is doing well in the Senate, and Jack Nicholson, who has succeeded in a wide variety of occupations, made an excellent Lieutenant-Governor of British Columbia. René Tremblay, a pleasant, cheerful man, died of a heart attack in 1968 at the age of forty-five. He left a charming wife and four small children. It was a great tragedy.

Lucien Lamoureux was a friend for whom I developed an increasing admiration, first as Deputy Speaker then as Speaker of the House. He has a marvellous sense of humour and both he and his wife are charming hosts on all occasions.

One very old friend of mine was Senator Duncan MacTavish. He was a highly successful Ottawa lawyer and a former president and a former national treasurer of the Liberal Party. But I had known him long before that. Whenever I was having trouble in Parliament, as I was in the summer of 1963, I would call MacTavish. He would pick me up and we would have lunch together at his house in Rockcliffe. He was a great host and a wonderful *raconteur* and we had many laughs together. Ottawa has never been the same for me since he was killed in an automobile accident on November 16, 1963.

Naturally enough, there was considerable speculation when the Liberals were first elected about the possibility of the new minority government making a working arrangement with one of the smaller groups in the House. It was in this connection during the fall of 1963 that Keith Davey came to see me to say that he and Douglas Fisher of the N.D.P., whom he had known since college days, had had an off-the-cuff talk to see if there would be any possibility of the Liberals and the N.D.P. agreeing to some kind of formula for working together. He said Fisher seemed to be receptive and thought a few representatives of each party should meet to talk things over. I consulted Pearson about this, and while he did not expect anything would come of it, he thought we should explore the subject. It was agreed that we would meet quite informally in my apartment on a Sunday afternoon. Mike Pearson, Allan MacEachen, Keith Davey, and I were to represent the Liberals, and Tommy Douglas, Douglas Fisher and David Lewis the N.D.P. It transpired that neither Pearson nor MacEachen was able to come at the last moment. Pearson called my apartment to explain his absence to Tommy Douglas and apologize for it. However, his failure to appear may have raised suspicions in the minds of the visiting N.D.P.'ers. Tommy Douglas said very little, and David Lewis made it clear he would oppose any kind of working arrangement with the Liberals. Pearson, with his authority as Prime Minister and his talent for negotiation, just might have been able to produce a plan that would have appealed to them, but Davey and I were not able to make much progress. It was a friendly meeting, but nothing came of it.

My second budget was presented on March 16, 1964. It proposed very few changes but at the Prime Minister's request I had had to agree to reduce the highest rate of withholding tax from twenty per cent to fifteen per cent. This removed one of the incentives for Canadian subsidiary companies to make shares available to Canadians, and in my opinion the removal was a mistake. But Pearson wished to meet the complaints of the U.S. State Department and some sections of the Canadian business community.

While the budget forecast a deficit of $455 million for the year 1964-65, the actual deficit for that year turned out to be only $39 million. In practical terms, the national finances were rapidly being brought under control.

At the time I was presenting the budget for the year 1964-65, I was also beginning to consider what the budgetary position was going to be a year hence. In particular, I was concerned about mounting expenditures, and wrote a long memorandum to the Prime Minister about this on March 30, 1964, which concluded as follows:

> But if we are faced a year from now with boom conditions (we may, of course, be faced with the exact opposite) I would hate to see us forced to increase taxes. Therefore I suggest the safe and sensible thing to do is to see how much we can reduce expenditures if we have to. If you agree in principle, I think we should begin the preparation now. In doing this, I shall need your full support and that of our colleagues.

At the same time, according to my notes, I talked to Pearson about a number of proposals in connection with financial legislation which the Department of Finance was working on, or which were under consideration, namely:

(a) Revision of the Insurance Companies Act. We had in mind easing the existing restrictions on investment in common stocks; and preventing the control of federally incorporated life companies from being sold to foreigners.

(b) Revision of the Bank Act. This would be a major undertaking which we could not hope to complete in 1964. Again, I mentioned that we intended to prevent the control of Canadian banks from being sold to foreigners.

(c) Revision of the Bank of Canada Act. The main objective was to make it crystal clear that the government, rather than the Governor of the Bank, must take responsibility for monetary policy.

(d) Proposed legislation *re* magazines. The purpose was to assist domestic publications to survive.

(e) Legislation respecting the ownership of newspapers, again with the objective of preventing their acquisition by foreigners.

(f) The Canada Development Corporation. This proposal had been referred to in the 1963 budget and in the Throne Speech.

(g) Important changes in the Income Tax Act, the Sales Tax Act, and withdrawal from the estate tax field in favour of the provinces.

It will be seen that we were working on plans to safeguard the control of certain key institutions from falling into foreign hands. Pearson was fully in accord with this objective and so, I believe, were most members of the cabinet.

During 1963 and 1964, I took every opportunity to explain the facts of Canada's balance of payments situation to both American and Canadian audiences. And also the Canadian government's concern about the extent to which the control of Canadian industry and resources was falling into foreign hands. To my surprise, I usually received a more sympathetic reception from American audiences than I sometimes did from those at home. Certainly this was true in the case of a speech to the New York Economic Club in April 1964. It was a big meeting, attended by the leading bankers and businessmen in New York. It is the custom at the conclusion of such meetings for someone designated in advance to ask the speaker one or two highly provocative questions which he is expected to answer extemporaneously. One question addressed to me was worded something like this: "Mr. Gordon, we know you and your government would like to see some changes in the present trend towards increasing control of Canadian industry by Americans. But supposing we didn't like what you proposed to do about it and decided to move in the military. What could you do?"

I replied that quite obviously there would be nothing we could do to stop the U. S. Marines from moving in. But I reminded the audience of what had happened to the English after absorbing Scotland in 1603. The Scots had retaliated in a different way. They had merely moved to London and taken over all the important jobs in banking, in business, in education, and in politics. I mentioned that both the then Prime Minister of Britain (Sir Alec Douglas-Home) and his predecessor (Harold Macmillan) were Scotsmen, and so were the Governor of the Bank of England and the heads of all the principal commercial banks at that time. I said if that was what my New York friends wanted, we were ready. We would take over all the top jobs in the United States before they realized what had happened. This seemed to amuse the audience.

The first federal-provincial conference under the chairmanship of the new Prime Minister was held July 26-27, 1963. The two major topics for discussion were the Municipal Development and Loan Fund and the proposed Canada Pension Plan. In speaking on the Municipal Loan Fund bill in the House on June 11, I had given the assurance that loans would be extended only with the "express approval" of the provinces and that assistance would "be given in ways which fully observe both the spirit and letter of the constitution." Nevertheless, on July 11, Premier Jean Lesage of Quebec wrote to the Prime Minister stating, "I am sure I am expressing the unanimous feeling of the members of the Quebec Legislative Assembly when I say that they consider as a breach of your promise fully to respect provincial rights in your management of the affairs of this country the fact of proceeding unilaterally to establish a municipal loan fund." On July 19, Premier John Robarts of Ontario released a letter to the Prime Minister in which he argued that Ontario municipalities would benefit more if the province got an increased share of the tax dollar than by the proposed Municipal Loan Fund.

During the July conference, provincial opposition to the Municipal Development and Loan Fund bill was finally overcome only by agreeing that the amount involved ($400 million) would be divided among the provinces according to population and that no funds would be allocated to any municipality without the approval of the provincial authorities concerned. Although the latter point was reasonable, the division of the fund according to provincial population made something of a mockery of this important legislation to relieve unemployment. It seemed pointless to allot about five per cent of the fund to Saskatchewan, for example, where there was little unemployment, and only four per cent to Nova Scotia where unemployment was very high.

Little progress was made at the July conference towards resolving provincial opposition to the proposed Canada Pension Plan. Jean Lesage took the occasion to announce that Quebec planned to establish its own pension scheme, not only to protect provincial rights but also to secure funds to finance provincial economic development. Further discussions on the pension plan were postponed.

The main topic at the federal-provincial conference of November 26-29 was fiscal relations. My own views had been stated in my June 13th budget speech when I pointed out that the federal government had a special responsibility in the matter of ensuring adequate production and employment throughout the country. "Fiscal policy is an important means of achieving this objective. Most people will agree . . . that if the federal government were to give up a major part of its present revenue sources, even in exchange for compensating expenditure adjustments, its ability to exert an influence through fiscal policy over the level of economic activity in Canada would be weakened." Nevertheless, it was clear to all of us that the provinces required some measure of financial assistance.

The Liberal government had proposed that equalization payments should be based on the *per capita* revenues of the two highest provinces, rather than the average or the highest, with revenue from natural resources partially taken into account. One evening while the conference was in session, the Prime Minister stated that he wished to increase the amount of the proposed tax concessions by about another $30 million or so, in order to increase the revenues of the provinces by a total of some $87 million per annum. He said he thought the best way of doing this would be to grant the provinces seventy-five per cent instead of the current fifty per cent of the revenues from inheritance taxes. This proposal was made without any prior discussion with me or any of the officials of the Department of Finance, and I protested vigorously. I pointed out that if this were done more or less on the spur of the moment, and without proper consideration, the federal government would find itself in an awkward position if and when it wished to amend the Inheritance Tax Act, since the provinces would then be able to claim a majority (seventy-five per cent) interest in the revenues derived from it. But Pearson was anxious to appease the provincial premiers and the change was agreed to against my strong advice. The new proposal was announced after a dinner for the premiers on November 28. In itself, Pearson's action was relatively unimportant, but it indicated the kind of trouble governments can make for themselves when the ordinary lines of cabinet responsibility and departmental communication are disregarded.

Speaking in the House on December 2, the Prime Minister asserted that the main achievement of the conference had been setting the direction towards co-operative federalism. He justified the use of the two richest provinces for the equalization calculation not because it saved the government much money, as compared with using the single richest province, but because it provided a different distribution and greater "certainty and stability." He also supported the modified use of natural resource revenue as well as the change in the percentage of succession duties granted the provinces as designed primarily to meet the needs of those provinces which do not benefit at all from equalization. Although neither "perfect nor final," he believed it represented a large step towards full equalization and helped meet pressing provincial fiscal needs.

A vitally important federal-provincial conference was held in Quebec City from March 31 to April 2, 1964, in an atmosphere of strain and tension. Extensive security measures were enforced in the light of threats by Separatists to disrupt the proceedings. There were demonstrations, and members of the Lesage government were obviously nervous, but there was no actual violence.

The federal government proposals put forward by the Prime Minister were received almost with contempt by Premier Lesage and his associates, who seemed to feel the federal authorities had no real understanding of what was going on in Quebec or of the determination of Quebeckers, their government included, to be *maîtres chez nous.* There was a serious disagreement over the proposed Canada Pension Plan, which was to be a "pay-as-you-go" plan and not a funded plan. The Quebec government stated its intention to proceed with its own pension plan which would be fully funded. This meant collecting far more in pension contributions in the first decade or so than the amounts that would be paid out in pension benefits. The difference would provide the provincial government with badly needed capital funds for investment purposes. There were disagreements over the federal government's proposals to pay family allowances to young people of sixteen and seventeen who remained in school and to provide guaranteed bank loans for university students. And apart from everything else, there was an angry demand that the federal government should make more tax revenues available to the provinces. At the press briefing following the conclusion of the conference, Lesage rather ostentatiously managed

REPRINTED WITH PERMISSION THE TORONTO STAR

"Maître chez nous."

not to sit beside Pearson, and instead proceeded to give the press and the television viewers his own interpretation of what had gone on. To say the conference was hardly a success would be the understatement of the year.

In an attempt to improve relationships with individual members of the Lesage government, I asked René Lévesque, an important Liberal minister and the man responsible for Hydro-Québec, to have lunch or dinner with me the next time he came to Ottawa. I remember his contemptuous reply: "I can see no advantage in that. And, anyway, I never go to Ottawa if I can possibly avoid it." Not a convincing instance of Gallic charm and politesse.

We returned to Ottawa on Thursday, April 2, thoroughly discouraged and feeling that Canada might well be on the point of splitting up. But over the next three days, Tom Kent worked out a new approach which he submitted to the Prime Minister on Monday morning, April 7. Tom and Gordon

REPRINTED WITH PERMISSION THE TORONTO STAR

Federal Provincial Conference, Quebec City, March 31, 1964

Robertson had had some discussion about the proposed Canada Pension Plan with Jean Lesage in Quebec City in August of the previous year. They knew that Lesage favoured a "funded" plan, and they had done some preliminary work on a new Canada Pension Plan along such lines. With this background Kent proposed that:

(a) A fundamental change would be made in the Canada Pension Plan if Quebec would agree to alter its plan in some particulars so that the two plans would be almost the same. The federal scheme would become a funded plan as in the case of the Quebec plan. The other provinces could participate in the federal plan or set up their own. If they decided to join the federal plan, the amounts accumulated from contributions in their respective provinces would be made available to them for investment.

(b) As a *quid pro quo,* Quebec would support a constitutional amendment which would permit survivorship benefits to be included under the Canada Pension Plan.

(c) Substantially larger amounts of tax revenues would be made available to the provinces in the next two fiscal years. At the federal-provincial conference in November 1963, the federal government had agreed to increase the provincial share of tax revenues by some $87 million per annum beginning with the fiscal year 1964-65, despite the fact that the existing tax-sharing arrangement did not expire until March 31, 1967. At the conference in Quebec, it had been agreed to set up a Tax Structure Committee consisting of the Ministers of Finance or Provincial Treasurers of the federal government and the provinces to review the financial needs and responsibilities of the several governments and the division of the various tax fields between them. But obviously this would take time, and the provinces wanted to know what was going to be done about their need for more revenues in the meantime. It was now proposed that additional amounts should be made available to them in the last two years of the current tax-sharing arrangement over and above the $87 million that had been agreed to in November 1963.

(d) The Quebec government had its own plan of family allowances for sixteen and seventeen-year-olds. Because of this, the extended federal allowances would not be paid to Quebec residents. Instead, an equivalent amount would be paid to the Quebec government.

(e) A similar formula would be made available to any provinces – that is, Quebec – which wished to rely on its own student loan program.

Tom Kent's proposals were approved by the Prime Minister, and Tom set off for Quebec to find out whether they would be acceptable to the Quebec authorities. Maurice Sauvé, who had been keeping in touch with Claude Morin, the Quebec Deputy Minister of Federal-Provincial Affairs, went with him. Lesage was in the process of preparing his budget in which he proposed to impose a substantial increase in taxes and to blame the difficulties in which Quebec found itself on Ottawa's intransigence. However, he liked Tom's proposals and agreed to put off his budget for a short time in the hope they might be implemented.

Tom Kent and Maurice Sauvé returned to Ottawa well pleased with their reception in Quebec. They submitted the proposals at a meeting at Sussex Drive on the evening of Wednesday, April 9, which Favreau, Lamontagne, MacEachen, and I attended. The Prime Minister asked me whether, as Minister of Finance, I could accept the changes. I replied that I would like to think about the proposals overnight and would be in touch with him early next morning. But I said that while the proposals would be a bit messy – we would have somewhat different systems in different provinces – my immediate reaction was that this would be a small price to pay if it were necessary to keep Quebec within Confederation.

Pearson was at his best when a solution to a problem had to be found in the midst of a crisis. He did not get excited and he seemed to work effectively when there was a lot of tension. This was one of those occasions. We had failed badly in Quebec. Now, at the last moment, Tom Kent had come up with a formula that might retrieve the situation, at least to some extent. Pearson was prepared to accept the new formula and not worry too much about any new problems it might give rise to.

I spent most of the night considering the proposals, including the political considerations and the drubbing we could expect to receive from the opposition in the House of Commons. But next morning, after a talk with Bob Bryce, I told the Prime Minister I thought we should give the plan a try.

Claude Morin and Claude Castonguay, who had done a lot of work on the Quebec Pension Plan, came to Ottawa on Saturday, April 11, to work out some of the detailed changes with Tom Kent, Joe Willard, the able Deputy Minister of Welfare, and Don Thorson of the Department of Justice who was responsible for the drafting. Maurice Sauvé sat in on the discussion. It took another week, however, before everything was finally settled and Pearson was able to advise the provincial premiers of the changes advocated.

I had urged Pearson to take John Robarts, the Premier of Ontario, into his confidence while the discussions with the Quebec people were going on. I knew that Robarts, who had left the Quebec meeting as discouraged as the rest of us, would do anything within his power to save Confederation. Those were the stakes we seemed to be playing for.

Revamping the original Canada Pension Plan almost completely was a complicated business and obviously it had to be done quickly. But unfortunately it became an undertaking of the Prime Minister's office, and Judy LaMarsh, the responsible minister, was not kept fully informed of the reasons that made the changes necessary or, indeed, of all that was going on. Naturally, Judy resented this. If Pearson had taken the trouble to explain things to her fully, and then had asked her to back him up in the changes he believed to be necessary, I am sure she would have done so with the utmost loyalty. As it was, she felt ignored and hurt and reacted accordingly.

The same thing was to happen again in 1967 when Judy, as Secretary of State, was responsible for the C.B.C. Pearson assumed personal responsibility for the reorganization of that institution and for the selection of the top management to succeed Alphonse Ouimet, who wished to resign. Again, Judy was to be bypassed and, again, she resented this keenly, especially as Pearson, with all the other things he had to do, allowed the C.B.C. situation to drift month after month without finding a solution.

There is no doubt, however, about the value of Tom Kent's contribution – first, in finding a way out of the *débâcle* at the Quebec conference and, second, in working out the details with Joe Willard of what was really an entirely new Canada Pension Plan. He was under great pressure and became increasingly exasperated, however, with the Prime Minister's method of working. Shortly before Pearson was to leave for London for a meeting of Commonwealth Prime Ministers, Tom made some suggestions for improving the way things were organized in the Prime Minister's office. When nothing was done about this, he wrote to Pearson submitting his resignation. Tom told me about this and so did the Prime Minister. Pearson acknowledged Tom's great abilities and asked me to try to work out some arrangement under which his services could be retained, but in a somewhat different way and not in the Prime Minister's own office.

Morale both in the cabinet and in caucus was very low at this period, that is, the summer of 1964. We thought we might be defeated in the House at any time. Pearson, with the help of his personal staff, was trying to do far too much himself and had little time for his key ministers. Moreover, his habit of changing policies and programs after they were first announced gave the impression of indecision and a lack of confidence which played into the hands of the opposition. He was under tremendous pressure as a result of which he was often testy and irritable. He and Diefenbaker let few days go by without scrapping and taking digs at one

187

another. The press was beginning to refer to them as the "two aging gladiators," much to Pearson's indignation.

I decided to take advantage of Pearson's request to find a suitable spot for Tom Kent to point out some of the reasons for the government's current malaise. I did so in a long memorandum dated July 16, 1964, which dealt with many of the problems that were bothering us. I began by reminding the Prime Minister that we had been confronted with a most difficult parliamentary session. The continual harrying, the clever disruptions of the work of the House, and the unforgivable personal attacks had made many of us wonder why we stayed in Ottawa at all. As a result, all of us had become tired, discouraged, frustrated, overwrought, and overly critical of everyone, ourselves included. I assured the Prime Minister that his personal position within the party was very strong. "But if you want to make the most of it, we shall have to stop changing our minds and qualifying our decisions . . . This in my opinion is your and our Achilles' heel. It makes the government look weak and indecisive at a time when the country is calling for strong leadership."

I observed that in recent months Pearson had become increasingly dependent on Tom Kent "because of his brilliance, his resourcefulness, his imagination, and the fact that he was always there." But, in the process, the regular lines of communication between the Prime Minister and his principal ministers and their departments had become blurred and responsibilities had become uncertain. This had been bad for morale and had led to mistakes that could have been avoided if the full resources of cabinet ministers and of the civil service had been engaged in the normal way. I advised him not to try to replace Tom Kent by someone in his own office who would "cross departmental lines and assume on occasion the prerogatives of a sort of Deputy Prime Minister." An alternative might be to appoint a first-class man from within the civil service to take charge of his office, to be responsible for dealing with the daily crises that might arise, but not for the development of policy on issues of major importance.

In my memorandum I observed that, because of his training and experience, Pearson was inclined to try to do too many things himself and, as a result, to spend too little time with his key ministers. This, more than anything else, had led to many of our troubles. Unless a fair proportion of time was spent with his principal ministers, I cautioned Pearson, he could not expect them to feel they were important members of his team. The lack of team spirit had led and could continue to lead to trouble. I advised him to hold regular, short meetings with the ministers he depended upon most as a sort of inner cabinet, and to require these ministers to make more of the decisions and accept a greater share of responsibility. He should also find someone to relieve him of much of the work in connection with party organization, since necessary decisions were not being made.

I believed that Pearson should begin to think about where the Liberal Party was going in terms of the next election. The first thing to consider was the most desirable date for an election from our point of view, assuming the decision rested with us. Since the flag debate was now under way, it was clear it should be disposed of before an election. In addition, the pension plan should be passed by Parliament and the Canada Development Corporation established. Any important cabinet changes should be made well in advance of an election.

In concluding my memorandum, I expressed the hope that the Prime Minister would ask Tom Kent to take on the study of economic interrelationships of the different sections of the country, which he had announced in the House was to be done. I suggested that Kent might produce a lengthy paper on this within six to nine months which would argue the imperative necessity of a united Canada and state what the aims and objectives of a united Canada should be. I did not think a formal academic approach to this question was realistic or that it could be finished in time to do much good. But the above proposal would, I believed, meet the commitment Pearson had given in connection with such a study, would resolve the problem about Tom Kent, and at the same time could produce some of the long-term answers we had been seeking.

Nothing came of these proposals. By the time Pearson returned from England he had forgiven Tom Kent who continued in his old position in the Prime Minister's office. Relationships between Pearson and the members of his cabinet were not changed. Guy Favreau was not relieved of his responsibilities as House Leader, as I had urged, for another four or five months. And the flag debate, which had begun in June, went on and on.

The legislation allowing provinces to contract out of joint federal-provincial programs and assume sole responsibility for them with financial compensation was one of the most significant developments of "co-operative federalism." Under the pressure of Quebec demands, opting out was discussed at the federal-provincial conference in November 1963, where it was unofficially approved in principle. In the budget speech on March 16, 1964, I stated that the federal government was prepared to transfer to the provinces "full financial responsibility for some of these established shared-cost programs of a continuing nature and to make suitable fiscal adjustments either in a larger share of the direct tax field or by changes in, or by supplements to, the equalization payments. . . ."

At the tense federal-provincial conference from March 31 to April 2 in Quebec City, several premiers expressed their reservations about opting out. Premier Robarts, for example, raised the question of the implications of "contracting out" for federal representation. However, the secret post-conference negotiations between Quebec and Ottawa were based largely on the principle of opting out, and the settlement featured a doubling of the annual increase in tax abatement. In addition, it provided financial compensation for non-participation in the student loan plan and the extension of family allowances. During May and June, Quebec and Ottawa, in a series of meetings, worked out the details of a contracting-out formula, including the number of programs at stake, and the operation and timing of the transition period. In September 1964, the Prime Minister announced that opting-out legislation was being prepared, but the bill was not introduced in Parliament until December 18, the last day of the session. Among its provisions, the bill stated that any province wishing to contract out of a joint plan must guarantee that it would not alter the program during a transition period of from two to five years. Once this transition period was over, the province would be free to do what it wanted with the additional revenue it had received from Ottawa – to continue the service in its existing form, introduce modifications, or even abolish the program and use the money in other ways. A three-stage operation was outlined in the bill:

1. From January 1, 1965, Ottawa would free the personal income tax field by an amount equal to the total expenditures of the federal government during the last year for the financing of joint programs which a province wished to leave.
2. During the transition period, equalization payments to the provinces would be added to, or subtracted from, depending on whether the fiscal equivalent granted was more or less than the actual expenditures of a province in administering the program.
3. At the end of the transition period, a final fiscal equivalence would be determined and the province or provinces in question would then be free to handle the program as they wished without further recourse to Ottawa.

The province of Quebec announced its intention to assume sole responsibility for the administration of such programs as hospital insurance, old-age assistance, aid to the blind and invalids, unemployment insurance, student aid and public hygiene. In return, it would receive an additional twenty per cent of the income tax field, bringing the provincial share to forty-four per cent.

When the House reassembled in 1965, it was evident that the opting-out legislation would precipitate bitter opposition and a split within the Conservative Party. Erik Nielsen spoke for the Diefenbaker "One Canada" wing of the party in a long manifesto claiming that the Liberal policies, particularly opting out, were leading to a special status for Quebec and thus to the dismemberment of the country. On March 5, the press reported that Léon Balcer, Paul Martineau, and others favourable to the legislation were being issued an ultimatum to conform or get out. The Tory caucus continued to meet daily and on March 10 decided that members would be free to speak or vote as they pleased. But on March 17, when I moved second reading, Mr. Diefenbaker conspicuously left the chamber. It was obvious, however, that the bill had the support of the other parties, and on March 30, 1965, a Conservative amendment (shelving it for further consideration) was defeated 109 to 69 and the bill passed on division.

On July 13, 1964, I introduced the Canada Student Loans Bill in Parliament. It provided for individual loans of up to $1,000 a year to full-time, post-secondary students. Loans would be made to students with satisfactory scholastic standing who were Canadian citizens or who had resided in Canada for a year and planned to stay. The government would pay the interest while the borrower was a student and for six months afterwards; after this time, the student would take over repayment himself of both interest and principal in from five to ten years. The loans were guaranteed by the government in case of default and insured against death, and they could not exceed $5,000 for any one student. The maximum yearly limit for loans ($40 million for the year 1964-65) was apportioned among the provinces according to the proportion of the national total of eighteen to twenty-four-year-olds. For non-participating provinces, an equivalent compensation would be calculated on the basis of the cash cost to the federal government of operating the plan in participating provinces.

There was every expectation to begin with that the bill would be approved relatively quickly. There was a general consensus on the need for aid to higher education. Furthermore, the provinces had all been previously consulted. Student loans had been discussed at the federal-provincial conference in Quebec a few months before, and although Quebec had opposed the plan as a violation of provincial autonomy and, in fact, had threatened to take it to the courts, Lesage later saw fit to opt out rather than oppose the bill on principle. On July 20, he announced that Quebec intended to opt out of the federal plan and continue to administer its own loan plan which had been in operation for several years. In the Quebec Legislative Assembly, Opposition Leader Daniel Johnson charged that the loan plan, like the extension of family allowances, represented an inexcusable excursion into provincial jurisdiction, and he criticized the Lesage government severely for not taking stronger measures. Lesage summed up his position: "If I claim respect for the autonomy of Quebec in the name of Quebec, I do not have the right to go and tell the other provinces what they should do."

Nevertheless, the bill met bitter opposition in the House of Commons from the Créditistes and French-speaking Progressive Conservatives who attacked the constitutionality of the bill, arguing that it was an invasion of provincial rights over education. Several argued that it also infringed the Quebec Civil Code by permitting persons under twenty-one to obtain bank loans.

As debate dragged on, feelings began to run strongly against the "delaying" tactics of the Quebec M.P.'s who were referred to by some sections of the English-speaking press as the "wrecking crew." Many people felt it unfair for Quebec members to hold up a measure desired by the other nine provinces and which would not apply in their province. Under the pressure of public opinion and the fact that if not passed soon the necessary machinery would not be in operation for the coming school year, the eight-day debate finally concluded on July 24 and the Canada Student Loans Act passed 137 to 14. (The fourteen opponents consisted of six Progressive Conservatives and eight Créditistes.)

It was proposed in Pearson's original resolution that the Canadian flag should consist of three red maple leaves enjoined on a single stem on a field of white with two blue bars on either side. This design was the Prime Minister's personal choice and, after he was discovered trying it out at Harrington Lake, it became known as the Pearson Pennant.

The flag debate began on June 15, but there had been endless questioning about the issue for several months before that. It continued for week after week and became much more acrimonious than even the budget debate of the previous year. It was not until September 10 that the Prime Minister was able to announce that the party leaders had agreed to refer the question of the design of the Canadian flag to a committee of the House. But the question of what would happen when the committee submitted its report, especially if it were not unanimous, was left unsettled. The committee did not report until November 30, 1964. The recommendation for the new Canadian flag, of quite a different design from the one originally proposed, was finally approved at 2.15 A.M. on December 15.

Liz and I set off for Tokyo in early September, thankful to leave the frustrations of Ottawa and the bickering of the House of Commons. I attended a three-day joint ministerial meeting with our Japanese opposite numbers, at which Paul Martin and the Japanese Foreign Minister acted as joint chairmen. We were entertained extensively and most generously, and at the conclusion of the meeting the Prime Minister of Japan, the late Hayato Ikeda, came out of hospital to preside at a luncheon in honour of the Canadian delegation. It was a lavish affair, and we were all relaxed and enjoying ourselves, especially Paul Martin who was relieved the meeting had gone off well. When the meal was over, the Prime Minister made a serious speech for half an hour or so on trade, finance, and economics. But as he spoke in Japanese, it was necessary at the conclusion of his remarks for an interpreter to repeat the whole thing over again in English. I remember smiling to myself about how Paul was going to handle these subjects in his reply, especially as neither of us appeared to have followed the Prime Minister's speech too closely. But I had underestimated Paul's dead-pan sense of humour. After thanking the Prime Minister for his hospitality, Paul stated, without a single muscle twitching to give himself away, that the Canadian delegation had met before the luncheon and decided that the Canadian Minister of Finance would reply to the Prime Minister's important speech. He then sat down leaving me no option but to rise and do the best I could do in the unexpected circumstances. In the presence of the Japanese Prime Minister and all his principal colleagues, I could not very well accuse my colleague, the Canadian Secretary of State for External Affairs, of being a practical joker.

Liz and I stayed on in Tokyo for another few days to attend the annual meetings of the International Monetary Fund and the World Bank. I made a speech on the somewhat technical subject of international liquidity, but this time it was most carefully prepared and polished in advance, with the help of a contingent of senior civil servants and central bankers. Delivering it was not as much fun as the occasion at the Prime Minister's luncheon, but I felt a good deal more confident about its content.

Guy Favreau was under especially heavy pressure from the time the House reassembled in September 1964. Pressure came in connection with the Harold Banks case and a variety of other matters, including a formula for repatriating the Constitution. Banks, the former head of the Seafarers International Union, had skipped bail and disappeared. He was found by Robert Reguly, a *Toronto Star* reporter, living comfortably on the New York waterfront at the international union's expense.

Then on November 23, Tommy Douglas asked a question about Lucien Rivard and Charles Groleaux, who were being held in Bordeaux jail and whom the United States was seeking to have extradited to face charges of dope smuggling. Douglas asked whether any complaints had come to the Minister of Justice that persons in high positions in Ottawa had tried to bring influence to bear on Pierre Lamontagne, a Montreal lawyer and no relation of Maurice Lamontagne, who was acting for the American government, urging him not to oppose a motion to grant these men bail. He also asked whether Favreau had ordered an investigation, which he understood he had done, what the results of the investigation were, and whether any charges had been laid. Favreau said he would deal with the matter when his Estimates came before the House later in the day.

When that time came, Erik Nielsen, the Progressive Conservative Member for the Yukon, presented a lengthy case against Favreau in connection with the Rivard affair. It was alleged that Raymond Denis, Executive Assistant to René Tremblay, the Minister of Citizenship and Immigration, had offered a bribe to Pierre Lamontagne, the counsel for the American government, if he would not oppose the granting of bail to Rivard. Moreover, it was alleged that both André Letendre, Favreau's chief Executive Assistant, and Guy Lord, a former assistant to Favreau, had also brought pressure on Lamontagne in the form of telephone calls. Favreau was asked why no charges had been laid. He replied that he had reviewed the report on these various matters by the R.C.M.P. but had concluded – and the Commissioner of the R.C.M.P. had agreed with him – that there was not sufficient evidence to justify criminal charges. He was asked why he had taken it upon himself to make this decision, instead of referring the matter to the "law officers of the Crown," that is, the officials in his department. He replied that he felt there was not sufficient evidence for a conviction and that he was prepared to rely on his own professional judgement in such a matter. It was a long and acrimonious discussion over an afternoon and evening, towards the end of which Guy became noticeably excited and upset.

When the House met the next day on Tuesday, November 24, Guy Rouleau rose on a question of privilege to say that he had resigned as Parliamentary Secretary to the Prime Minister because he had made representations in the case of Rivard. He also stated he had not informed the Prime Minister about this until that morning. After Rouleau's announcement, Favreau stated that the government had decided that a judicial inquiry under Chief Justice Frédéric Dorion should be held to look into the matter and cited the proposed terms of reference. In the course of a prolonged and angry question period, in which it was claimed the proposed terms of reference were inadequate, the Prime Minister was asked whether he had any prior knowledge of the case:

Hon. D. S. Harkness (Calgary North): Mr. Speaker, I should like to direct a question to the Prime Minister in order to clear up what appears to me to be an ambiguity, as I am sure it appears to other hon. members, consequent upon some of the answers given to questions today. Was the Prime Minister informed by the Minister of Justice of any of the circumstances of this case, which is now going to be investigated, prior to those circumstances being brought out in this house yesterday?

Mr. Pearson: I think the Minister of Justice has dealt with this matter, Mr. Speaker.

Some hon. Members: Oh, Oh.

Mr. Harkness: Mr. Speaker, the reason I asked the question is that it appeared from questions and answers that the Prime Minister had not been informed about his parliamentary secretary. It was not clear whether he had been informed about any of the other circumstances, and my question is this. Was he informed by the Minister of Justice in regard to any of the other circumstances of this case prior to those circumstances being brought to the attention of this house yesterday?

Mr. Pearson: I was informed by the Minister of Justice of some of the circumstances shortly before his estimates came before the house. He told me this matter would be before the house during the consideration of his estimates. He told me the facts of the matter. My parliamentary secretary, who has just resigned, has already indicated in his statement that he had not informed me of this matter until this morning.

Mr. Harkness: Mr. Speaker, the Prime Minister's answer touched upon the ambiguity I mentioned, which was the reason for my question. When the Prime Minister said he was informed before the minister's estimates were put before the house, does he mean he was informed yesterday or a week ago? When was he informed?

Mr. Pearson: Mr. Speaker, I think I was informed on the day before his estimates were brought before the house. . . .

These replies placed Favreau clearly on the spot. After what Pearson had said, Favreau could not very well claim that he had told the Prime Minister something about the case some months before. He had not done this in a formal way but rather in the course of a more or less casual conversation on an airplane in which he and Pearson and some others were returning from a meeting. In these circumstances it was not unnatural that Pearson should have forgotten about it. But as Pearson did not correct the impression he had given in answering Harkness' question, he left himself open to the accusation that he had misled the House. And he left Favreau to defend himself against charges that not only had he failed to bring proceedings against government officials who were alleged to have offered bribes and to have brought influence to bear on behalf of an accused dope smuggler but, moreover, that he had failed to inform the Prime Minister of any of the circumstances.

During the same question period on November 24, René Tremblay was asked about the resignation of Raymond Denis as his Executive Assistant. Tremblay stated that, at the time of his resignation, Denis had informed him of the charges against him. He had denied the charges but Tremblay accepted his resignation nevertheless. He was asked if he had informed the Prime Minister and replied, "I did not feel that I had to advise the Prime Minister that my assistant had decided to resign and leave my office." What he did not say, and could not say in the circumstances, was that he had advised Favreau about Denis and that Favreau was to inform the Prime Minister.

The whole matter was discussed again in an increasingly angry atmosphere during the course of the next two days, both on the Orders of the Day and during further discussion of the Justice department's estimates. Naturally, the subject was played up in the press and on the air, and a speculative article appeared in *The Globe and Mail* suggesting that the Ontario members of the Liberal caucus were urging Pearson to discipline Favreau and Tremblay. At the same time, it was being suggested that Pearson was being let down by his Quebec ministers. Such suggestions were, of course, extremely dangerous from the standpoint of unity within the Liberal Party and, indeed, within the nation. They were particularly unfortunate coming as they did on top of the bitterness precipitated by the flag debate.

The morale of the government and of the caucus was at a low ebb and, in these circumstances, I decided to enter the debate in defence of the two ministers concerned. I was influenced in this decision both by the need to refute the suggestion that the Ontario members were critical of two Quebec Ministers, Favreau and Tremblay, and by my friendship for Guy Favreau, a wonderful, overworked man who was taking a bad beating in the House day after day. After scribbling a few notes I rose to speak on Thursday, November 26, following a long and typical speech by Mr. Diefenbaker. I was interrupted continually but managed to make a number of points. The first was that the revised terms of reference would allow the commissioner every scope not only to determine whether there were grounds for taking criminal proceedings against Denis and others but also to examine the question of alleged improprieties. The second point was the necessity of finding out how a report of the Royal Canadian Mounted Police marked "Top Secret" had got into the hands of Erik Nielsen and members of the press. The third point was that having referred the whole matter to the commission of inquiry, it was not proper for Members of Parliament or members of the press to prejudge the guilt or innocence of the people involved. This was the kind of thing that was indulged in by U. S. Senator Joseph McCarthy in the early 1950s. As an example, I referred to the question asked by Erik Nielsen of the Minister of Citizenship and Immigration: "Likewise the Minister of Citizenship and Immigration should rise and tell the committee what he knows. I challenge him to rise now and tell the house where he was when the bribe was offered." I suggested, "If ever there was an attempt to prove guilt by alleged association, that was it." I ended my speech as follows:

> In conclusion, Mr. Chairman, I wish to say a word about the way this matter has been used, deliberately or otherwise, in Parliament and in some sections of the press to undermine the unity of this country.
>
> Some hon. Members: Oh, oh.
>
> Mr. Nugent: Are you going to bring the flag in too?
>
> Mr. Gordon: We should not pay too much attention to speculative articles, but some members will have seen one this morning suggesting that the Prime Minister may be asked by a group of Ontario members to discipline two principal members in this government, not because they are guilty but in the interests of political expediency. Now, most of us who have known the Prime Minister of this country for many years know – and I say this categorically – that he is not the kind of man who would consider that kind of action for one moment. As a member of Parliament from Ontario I consider it a privilege and an honour to have as colleagues two ministers like the Minister of Justice and the Minister of Citizenship and Immigration. We need more men like them in public life. I have no doubt about their complete honesty, integrity, and courage. I have no doubt that they are here, like some other hon. members, not because they prefer this kind of life to something else but because they think it is their duty to do what they can in the interest of their country.
>
> Mr. MacInnis: Would the minister permit a question?
>
> Some hon. Members: Sit down.
>
> Mr. Gordon: They have the complete support, Mr. Chairman, of all of us who know them, particularly – and I want to emphasize this – of all the members from Ontario. There is no foundation for the kind of speculative articles to which I have referred. I can only say, Mr. Chairman, that if a man like my hon. friend the Minister of Justice were ever forced to resign for the kind of political reasons suggested I for one would not be happy to remain in this house.

Andrew Brewin of the N.D.P. who followed me was highly critical of what I had said and he described it as pitiable. Certainly my speech was not particularly profound. Nevertheless, it helped to encourage the Liberals, including Guy Favreau and René Tremblay. And when on the following day, a Friday, the terms of reference for the inquiry were extended, the steam went out of the debate.

At the end of December, Guy wrote me a long letter, which I shall quote in part, as it indicates why he had so many friends:

Dear Walter:

I would not want to let the last day of this year pass, without sending you at least a brief note of gratitude and appreciation.

I shall never forget your friendly words of comfort and your constant encouragement during the trying days of the end of November. I shall never forget either how you dared rise in the House in my defence, at the very moment when so many were speechless and I myself was performing so badly.

You know how I feel about true friends at moments like these. I shall not elaborate, except to say most sincerely "thank you!" . . .

Guy was quite certain he would be exonerated completely when Chief Justice Dorion presented his report. But some of us were not so sure. The whole matter boiled up again in early March when Rivard escaped from jail. He was not recaptured until July 16, 1965.

At first, it was expected that Chief Justice Dorion would submit his report in two or three months at the most, but his investigation dragged on and was given plenty of publicity. It was not until the evening of June 28, on Pearson's return from a Commonwealth Prime Ministers' Conference in London, that the Dorion report was delivered. Cabinet was called for 11:00 A.M. the next morning to consider it. Favreau, who had read the report earlier, was not present. As soon as we heard the findings – that, in the opinion of the Chief Justice, there was a *prima-facie* case against Denis, that Favreau should have submitted the case to the legal advisers in the department, that Rouleau had tried to use his influence to secure bail for Rivard, etc. – it was clear that Guy would have to resign as Minister of Justice and that his political career was probably finished. I left cabinet to go to see him and express my sorrow and my sympathy. He was in Jack Pickersgill's office away from prying newsmen. He was upset but courageous as always. I stayed with him for about half an hour, and it was only as I was leaving that he told me of Jack's suggestion that, while he should resign as Minister of Justice, he should remain a member of the cabinet. I had some private reservations about this but it did not seem the proper time to voice them. My personal opinion was that he might be better off to get out of politics – he was not likely to recover in any complete way from this disaster – and return to the practice of law. Perhaps I should have said so.

In a statement to the House that day, June 29, after tabling the Dorion report, Pearson announced Guy's resignation as Minister of Justice but said he would continue as a member of the cabinet. In due course, he was appointed President of the Privy Council. McIlraith took over Public Works and Cardin became Minister of Justice. Tremblay, who had been completely exonerated by the Commissioner, was to continue as Postmaster General.

The next day, June 30, prior to adjournment, Gordon Churchill raised the question of Pearson having misled the House the previous November when he failed to recall that Favreau had said something to him about the Rivard affair in the course of a plane trip in September. Pearson had set the record straight about this in a letter to Chief Justice Dorion dated December 14, 1964, but had not said anything in the House. In the light of Pearson's letter to the Chief Justice, a motion had been made on December 17 that the matter be placed before the Commons Committee on Privileges and Elections. The Speaker had ruled the motion out of order and had been upheld 122 to 105. But, in effect, nearly half the members at that time presumably felt that either the Prime Minister had misled the House or, at the least, the whole matter should be thoroughly examined. Now, in June, Churchill revived the matter. He referred to Pearson's appearance on television the previous evening in the course of which he had said, "We must deal with the sinister and growing involvement of crime in politics." Churchill continued:

> Why did he not deal with it in September of 1964 when the name of Rivard came up and when he discovered later, after his memory had assisted him, that some of the people very close to him were involved with this man? We have had a whole galaxy of people of the underworld mixed up in this case. This, Sir, is one of the most critical situations that has faced any government of this country. It is a very critical situation for Canada. I think it is deplorable that we have reached the stage in this country that we have to have a judicial inquiry which comes up with findings that international crime has infiltrated into high circles of the Government.
>
> The man who can take action is the Prime Minister, but he is not a man of action. He will just shift and sway and, as I have said on more than one occasion, make statements in the House on which I am not able to place complete reliance . . .

It is probable we would have heard more about Pearson's lapse of memory if the House had not adjourned that night. I was afraid the matter would be reopened when Parliament reassembled on September 27 and that the Prime Minister would be formally accused of misleading the House in answering Harkness' question on November 24, 1964. But the election intervened.

To return to the situation in the House in December 1964, when the

Dorion inquiry was announced. This inquiry took the pressure off Guy Favreau at the time. But the government was to take a further buffeting before the Christmas adjournment. On November 30, Donald MacInnis (P.C., Glace Bay) placed on the Commons order paper a question regarding the involvement of unnamed ministers in the bankruptcy of Futurama Galleries, a Montreal furniture store owned by Max and Adolph Sefkind, which had been examined in the course of the Quebec government's investigation into bankruptcy frauds. This unusual question sent reporters exploring, and when they approached Maurice Lamontagne, he decided to put an end to the rumours by explaining how his name had come to be among Futurama Galleries' outstanding debts at the time of bankruptcy.

On December 8, the "furniture story" appeared in the press. It stated that Maurice Lamontagne and René Tremblay had obtained furniture from the Sefkinds without making down payments or subsequently paying for it. There were rumours and suggestions that in some way the Sefkinds had obtained orders or favourable treatment from the government. Tremblay probably added to this rumour by informing the press that there was no connection between his furniture purchases and the fact that in 1961, when he had been a deputy minister in Quebec, he had authorized a loan to another Sefkind enterprise. The two ministers were severely criticized, and the furniture scandal, coming as it did on top of the Rivard affair, became a major issue.

On December 18, 1964, a motion was made to adjourn the House to discuss the matter. In the course of the debate, both ministers explained what had happened. In the spring of 1962, Maurice, who was not a member of Parliament at that time and who earned only a modest income, bought some furniture on credit. In December 1963, when he was a member of the cabinet, he bought some more. The next month, after the Sefkinds had gone bankrupt, Maurice received a statement of what he owed from the Bank of Montreal and proceeded to pay his debt in instalments. Maurice stated that the Minister of Public Works had informed him that neither the Sefkind brothers nor any of their companies had made any attempt to sell anything to the government since April 1963, when the Liberals had come to power.

René Tremblay stated he had ordered some furniture from one of the Sefkind companies in the summer of 1963. The first delivery was made on November 15, 1963, and additional deliveries on November 28, December 19 and January 10, 1964, but the full order was not completed. On February 19, the Bank of Montreal advised that the furniture company had gone bankrupt. Six days later, Tremblay sent the bank a cheque for $3,341.69. On March 2, he sent a second cheque for $240.21 – after making some adjustments as some of the furniture ordered had still not been deliv-

Royal Commission on Canada's Economic Prospects, 1955.
Left to right: A. E. (Dal) Grauer, Omer Lussier, Douglas
LePan, Walter L. Gordon, Ray Gushue, Andrew Stuart.

At Keno Hill, Yukon with the Royal Commission.

Left to right: Lester B. Pearson, Edgar MacInnis,
Louis St. Laurent, Walter L. Gordon, A.D.P. Heeney.

With Louis St. Laurent in Quebec City, 1947.

The author's favourite photo. Two days' fishing on the
Bonaventure River in Quebec, July 1952.

The official photograph for the 1962 campaign.

The Founders of the Committee for an Independent Canada.
Left to right: Abraham Rotstein, Peter Newman, Walter
L. Gordon.

With Keith Davey, January 27, 1976.

With Beland Honderich, January 27, 1976.

ered by then. Tremblay's case was very simple. He had not paid earlier because his order had not been completed. Those of us who know Maurice Lamontagne well could fully understand his position also. He is a most honourable man but he had no money, or very little. It never occurred to him to borrow what he needed to pay his bill. He just let the matter drift.

But this was the sort of thing the public could understand. Most people buy furniture on time and are required to make down payments at the time of purchase. The public was suspicious of two ministers who were not required to make down payments with their orders. And the fact that these were two more ministers from Quebec did not help matters. We were to hear a great deal about the so-called "furniture scandal" from then until the next election.

The Christmas break did not provide any respite from rumours of further improprieties. Yvon Dupuis had been promoted to the cabinet in the previous February 1964, as Minister without Portfolio. Shortly afterwards, Eric Kierans, the Minister of Revenue in the Quebec government, told Premier Jean Lesage that he suspected Dupuis of having accepted $10,000 in 1961 to facilitate the obtaining of a licence for a new racetrack in his home riding. Lesage informed Pearson of this accusation at that time, but Pearson took no action. By December 1964, however, the situation had become very different. Lesage realized that in light of the Rivard affair another discovery of "corruption" might bring the Pearson government down before the much desired opting out legislation was passed. He warned Pearson that the Dupuis case was more or less common knowledge and that the Union Nationale was certain to use it as ammunition when the Quebec legislature convened on January 21. Lesage urged Pearson to get rid of Dupuis before public charges were made. Pearson then gave Dupuis two weeks to produce evidence in his defence, after which he called on the R.C.M.P. to investigate. Their preliminary report was unfavourable and on January 17, 1965, Pearson asked Dupuis to resign from the cabinet. Dupuis refused, claiming that he was being framed by his provincial enemies. Late on January 22, however, it was announced by the Prime Minister's office that Dupuis was no longer a member of the government. In March, he was formally charged on three counts of influence-peddling, found guilty, and fined $5,000 or a year in jail. He appealed the sentence and was acquitted on April 16, 1968.

Two other incidents which indicated the mood or tone of that session were the Minaudo and Asselin cases. On November 30, Mr. Diefenbaker alluded to shady government dealings in the case of Onofrio Minaudo, a criminal convicted of murder and armed robbery who had entered Canada illegally and was deported by the government only after a delay of several years. However, as the previous Conservative government shared the blame for the delay, the opposition did not dwell on this case for very long.

The other incident involved Eddie Asselin, a Liberal M.P. who had been elected in 1962. He had been accused by a provincial board of inquiry of having made an "unlawful and unconscionable" profit in 1961 at the expense of the Protestant School Board of Montreal. This matter was given a lot of publicity and it was suggested that Asselin should resign from Parliament. The case was brought up in the Montreal courts and Asselin was cleared. Nevertheless, he gave up his seat on July 22, 1965, and did not run in the election which soon followed.

What with one thing and another, 1964 had been a depressing year for the Pearson government. The mood of its ministers was not made easier when we read in the press that various pundits were in favour of a continuation of minority government, as so much had been accomplished despite – or perhaps because of – the government's lack of a majority. Some of us felt, on the contrary, that we were performing under intolerable conditions, and that the sooner some party was given a clear mandate by the public and a majority in Parliament the better it would be for everyone.

CHAPTER ELEVEN

Financial Legislation in 1965

The 1965 budget; legislation dealing with magazines and newspapers; revision of the Bank Act; control of Canadian banks; the Mercantile Bank of Canada; the Canada Development Corporation; future tax arrangements with the provinces; control of expenditures; accomplishments of the first Pearson government.

When the House reassembled on February 16, 1965, the Prime Minister announced some changes in the Old Age Security Act based on the hearings of a Joint Committee of the House and Senate on Pensions. He stated that the age at which the flat-rate pension of seventy-five dollars a month would become payable was to be reduced by one year at a time over a five-year period. By 1970, everyone would be entitled to the seventy-five dollars a month at age sixty-five. The debate on the Canada Pension Plan was resumed, and the bill was finally passed on March 29, 1965. Despite the many changes that were made to the original proposal, this was one of the greatest achievements of the Pearson government.

My own responsibilities in the legislative field, in the short third session of the first Pearson government which began on April 5, 1965, were quite heavy. There was the budget, a controversial bill dealing with magazines and newspapers, the decennial revision of the Bank Act, amendments to the Bank of Canada Act, and the Canada Development Corporation.

I had begun work on the budget during the previous fall and, in particular, had been considering a cut in personal income taxes. This was designed in part to give relief to the middle-income group of managers and professional men in an attempt to stop the brain drain to the United States. I had talked to the Prime Minister about this in late November or early December and again in February. Since I was planning a tax cut, it meant that any significant programs which might be presented to cabinet for discussion would have to be resisted. Writing to the Prime Minister on February 9, 1965, about a possible tax cut, I said:

> As you know, I feel strongly that this is the right course for us to follow. First of all, I believe we must show that, as a government, we are able to say no from time to time and to resist some of the more obvious pressures. But apart from this, we have allowed public expectation of a tax cut to increase in recent weeks and months without throwing cold water on the general idea as I did a year ago. You may have noticed in the paper this morning a reference to the report of the Canadian Tax Foundation which refers to the growing expectations of a tax cut and which suggested that the recent review of the Economic Council of Canada was being interpreted as endorsing this policy.

I had hoped for an early budget, but the second session did not prorogue until April 2. While the new session began on April 5, it was followed by an Easter recess and the budget was not presented until April 26. It was a wonderful occasion for a Minister of Finance, especially one who had been criticized as severely as I had been less than two years before. Our policies had been proved successful, the Canadian economy was in excellent shape, and the prospects for the future were encouraging. I expressed this in the following words:

> When this government first came into office we stated a number of economic objectives. Our first goal was a high level of employment for Canadians and the reduction of unemployment. The second was a high and sustainable level of economic growth. Third, we wanted a better regional balance in both employment and growth. We also wished to bring into closer balance our trade and other current international transactions. To realize these objectives, we recognized that our industry, especially our manufacturing industry, would have to become more vigorous and competitive. We expected that as unemployment was reduced and these other objectives achieved, we would also be able to move toward a balanced budget. Moreover, we sought over the long term to improve the degree of participation by Canadians in the ownership and direction of businesses operating within our borders and using our resources.
>
> We may all take pride in the extent to which these goals have been achieved. . . .

I was also able to announce a dramatic improvement in the federal government's finances. The 1962-63 fiscal year produced a budgetary deficit of $692 million. This had been reduced to an estimated $83 million for the fiscal year just ended. (The actual deficit for the year turned out to be only $39 million.)

Partly as a result of the policies introduced in 1963, the Canadian economy in the following two years had expanded faster and unemployment had been reduced further than in the United States. In the United States in 1964, the total output of the economy increased by 6.6 per cent, whereas in Canada the increase was one-third as much again. In 1964, unemployment in the United States was reduced by seven per cent. The rate of reduction in Canada was almost twice that figure. The Canadian economy was in a very healthy state. Unemployment was at its lowest level since 1957. The output of goods and services was at record heights and was still rising. Prices were reasonably stable. Our international competitive position remained strong. The capacity of our industry was being used more fully. Business confidence was reflected in the highest level of capital investment we had ever had. All areas of the country, almost all types of industry and agriculture and most groups in the community were sharing in this advance.

The proposals put forward in the budget speech included:

(a) The creation of the Canada Development Corporation.
(b) Legislation to deal with the magazine problem and preserving Canadian ownership and control of Canadian newspapers.
(c) A ten per cent reduction of the basic tax payable under the personal income tax law, subject to a maximum reduction of $600. This represented a tax cut of $265 million a year, the largest tax reduction in twelve years.

The budget contemplated a deficit for the year 1965-66 of $300 million. In fact, the deficit for that year amounted to only $39 million, the same figure as for 1964-65. The nation's finances had been brought under firm control.

The legislation respecting the ownership and control of magazines and newspapers proposed that the cost of advertising primarily directed to a Canadian market in a non-Canadian owned periodical or newspaper should be disallowed as a deduction from taxable income. We had been struggling with this problem ever since April 1963 when the Pearson government was formed, but had had great difficulty in arriving at a solution. Some Canadian newspaper publishers were concerned that control of the press might be lost to Canadians, and had been urging the government to take preventive action. At the same time, pressure was brought to bear on the Prime Minister not to do anything that would interfere with *Time* or upset its proprietor, Henry Luce, and for a while it seemed probable that nothing would be done. Apart from other considerations, the passage of the automotive agreement through the U.S. Congress had run into difficulties, and it was felt the agreement might not be approved if a full-scale row developed with Mr. Luce. But eventually a proposal was put forward which provided restrictions on advertising placed in foreign-owned magazines with the exception of *Time* and *Reader's Digest,* on the grounds they were now being published and printed in Canada, and in Canadian newspapers subsequently acquired by foreigners. Two small newspapers then owned by non-residents were exempted.

I was quite aware of the power and influence of Mr. Luce and of the difficulties being encountered in getting the U.S. Congress to approve the automobile deal. I was aware also of rumours that *La Presse,* by far the largest French-language daily in the province of Quebec, might be sold to European interests sympathetic to the Separatist cause, and of another rumour that the proprietor of *The Globe and Mail* was considering the sale of his newspaper to American interests. In these circumstances, I thought it wise to support the compromise proposal, even though it meant exempting *Time* and *Reader's Digest.*

While the proposal came from the Prime Minister, it was up to me to present it to Parliament, as it involved amendments to the Income Tax Act and, therefore, was a budget item. The proposal to exempt *Time* was attacked strenuously in the House, and the Liberal caucus in particular was highly critical of it. Fortunately, I had always made a practice of being frank with caucus about any legislation I was responsible for sponsoring. I followed the same course of taking members of caucus into my confidence on this occasion and explaining the whole situation to them. I said I did not like the *Time* exemption any more than they did, but this was the price we had to pay to get approval of the automotive agreement, and at the same time to make sure that the two important newspapers referred to would not be sold to foreigners. I asked caucus to support me in a thoroughly unpalatable task, and the members agreed to do so.

Quite apart from the criticism over the exemption of *Time* and *Reader's Digest,* the government as a whole, and myself in particular, were subjected to heavy attack by a majority of Canadian newspaper proprietors over what they asserted was a threat to the freedom of the press. Some of the more courageous working newsmen pointed out that the government's proposals did not interfere in any way whatever with the freedom to print and publish anything – news, opinions, or ideas. All it did was to restrict the market available to Canadian newspaper proprietors who might wish to dispose of their properties to the highest bidder, irrespective of who might be the buyer. Max Bell's F.P. Publications chain and Howard Webster's *Globe and Mail* were particularly virulent in their attacks. *The Winnipeg Free Press,* in an article on June 19, 1965, printed my picture with those of

Adolf Hitler, Joseph Stalin, Fidel Castro, King George III, Benito Mussolini, and Juan Peron, all of whom, it was claimed, had interfered with the freedom of the press. The comparison was obvious, even if a little silly. I was a bit miffed, however, at being likened to George III, who was insane for many years.

I wondered sometimes what the editors of these newspapers would have said had the government done nothing while *La Presse* was acquired by foreign supporters of the Separatists in Quebec, and *The Globe and Mail* by American interests which perhaps might hold that hydrogen bombs should be used in Vietnam and that Canada should be forced to participate in that conflict.

Nearly two years later, on February 21, 1967, I stopped off in Winnipeg on the way home from a trip to Calgary and addressed large audiences at United College (now the University of Winnipeg), the University of Manitoba, and the Vincent Massey High School. It was clear from the question periods that a great many of the younger people in Manitoba shared my opinions on the independence issue. As might have been expected, *The Winnipeg Free Press,* while their reporters attended the meetings, practically ignored my visit, despite the large crowds and the obvious interest of the students. This was particularly annoying to Tom Axworthy who had had a lot to do with the arrangements. I tried to console him by pointing out that, thanks to the legislation passed in 1965, at least foreigners could not be in a position to engage in such selective reporting.

Not all the publishers or proprietors were opposed to what the government intended doing. St. Clair Balfour, the President of the Southam Company, and Beland Honderich of *The Toronto Star,* agreed with the government that something needed to be done. In a letter I wrote to the Prime Minister about this on May 14, 1965, I mentioned a conversation I had had with Balfour following the representations made in Pearson's office by the Canadian Daily Newspaper Publishers Association. Balfour reported that the delegation felt that they had been very well received, and that Basil Dean, the publisher of *The Edmonton Journal,* a Southam paper, had been convinced by the government's arguments and had written an article over his own signature to this effect. Balfour said that, following the meeting, the President of the Association, Richard Graybiel, believed that the government would drop the whole thing, but Dean's conclusion was that, after consideration, the Prime Minister would say why the government intended to proceed with the legislation and would then proceed to do so. He said the reference to the possibility of *La Presse* being acquired by European interests made a deep impression and that this would help to soften the opposition of many of the newspapers.

Nevertheless, Balfour said we should expect another round of opposition as the publishers felt this might be useful background if, in the future, any government should consider imposing sanctions on the press through the medium of tax legislation. Balfour told me quite frankly that one of the reasons for the strength of the opposition was the references made at the publishers' meeting to certain paragraphs in Tom Kent's paper at the Kingston conference. He volunteered that these had been taken out of context and that few of those present had read the paper. He made it clear where the inspiration for this line of criticism came from.

My impression, after a long talk with Balfour, was that most of the publishers would not prolong their opposition, although most of them would run another round of editorials. This might not be true for the Thomson interests which, as Balfour said, were frantic that this action on the part of the government might make it difficult for them "to own everything everywhere in the world." Balfour thought their opposition, as expressed at the meeting, was so exaggerated that it had backfired.

There was little trouble or controversy over the amendments to the Bank of Canada Act, which made clear that it was the government, and not the Governor of the Bank, that must be responsible for monetary policy.

The revisions to the Bank Act, however, were another story. The decennial revision of the Bank Act is always a major undertaking for any government and any Minister of Finance. On this occasion, the whole matter had been preceded by an intensive study conducted by the Royal Commission on Banking and Finance, established by the former Diefenbaker government, under the chairmanship of Dana Porter, then Chief Justice of Ontario.

A great many of the recommendations of the Royal Commission were incorporated in the revisions of the Bank Act which were presented to Parliament, but there were some important ones which were not. These included a recommendation to lift the six per cent ceiling on the rates of interest which the banks might charge and a proposal that the federal government's banking legislation be extended to cover the "near banks," including the trust and loan companies, etc.

One of the main themes of the Commission's report was the desirability of encouraging more competition in the banking business and, it was argued, this could best be accomplished by removing the restriction on the interest rates the banks were entitled to charge their customers. This provision had been in the Bank Act since Confederation and was intended to protect the public from excessive charges. It seemed to be the view of the commission, however, that interest rates would come down if the ceiling were removed. Having been a customer of various banks for many years, I could not help feeling this conclusion was naïve. Incidentally, in the United States, while there is no ceiling on the rate of interest the banks there may charge, there is a ceiling on the rates they may pay for deposits, which has much the same effect.

I was very much in favour of encouraging more competition in the banking business because, as I pointed out some time later in my book *A Choice for Canada,* seventy per cent of all deposits in Canada in 1964 were with the eight chartered banks and almost fifty per cent with the big three – the Royal, the Commerce, and the Montreal.

It seemed to me that these eight banking institutions, and certainly the three biggest, were essentially oligopolies. Moreover, their growth is dependent in large measure on government policy respecting increases in the money supply. For these reasons I was inclined to the view that the government should continue to retain some measure of control over the operations of the commercial banks, including the rates of interest they might charge their customers.

I believed the trust companies were the most practical source to look to insofar as competition with the Canadian chartered banks was concerned. Their business had been growing at a relatively faster rate, although from a much smaller base, than had the business of the banks in recent years. This was pointed out by the bankers, naturally enough, who claimed it was quite unfair that they should be restricted on the rates of interest they could charge while such restrictions did not apply to the trust companies. The trust companies at the end of 1964 still had only ten per cent of the total deposits compared with seventy per cent in the case of the banks. It seemed to me their relative advantage in respect to the rates of interest they could charge might well be continued at least for the next ten years.

After long consideration and much soul searching, and after careful consultation with the cabinet, it was decided not to lift the ceiling on the rates of interest the banks could charge. However, when I introduced the revised Bank Act in the House on May 6, 1965, I left a loophole for myself to reconsider this matter if conditions changed.

> Mr. Gordon: As long as the general level of interest rates remains reasonably close to current levels, the exceptions being made in the case of mortgage loans and the customary service charges on personal loan plans should allow the banks to adopt somewhat more flexible interest rate policies on both loans and deposits. If, however, at some future time there should be a general rise in world interest rates which would make these proposals unworkable, then the Government would reconsider the six per cent limit.

The decision of the government to retain the interest ceiling was warmly applauded on all sides of the House but, naturally, was objected to most strongly by the banking fraternity, and I was severely criticized by them for it.

As I have indicated, the Royal Commission on Banking and Finance recommended that in the revision of the Bank Act the "near banks" should be embraced under federal legislation and thus become subject to federal supervision. Nothing was said in the commission's report, however, as to how such action could be justified under the Constitution. Under the British North America Act, "banking" is designated as coming within the federal authority. There is no definition of the word "banking," however, and I could find no support either from the law officers of the Crown – that is, the Department of Justice – or from outside counsel whom I consulted privately, which would have justified the federal government assuming the proposed powers of supervision over the so-called "near banks." Moreover, the government concluded that any attempt to arbitrarily usurp such

REPRINTED WITH PERMISSION THE TORONTO STAR

powers would automatically provoke a major controversy with the provinces which was the last thing we wished for at that time. Accordingly, this recommendation of the Royal Commission was not accepted.

The proposed revisions to the Bank Act which I brought forward included provisions designed to prevent control of Canadian banks from falling into foreign hands. It was provided that not more than twenty-five per cent of the shares of any Canadian bank could be held by non-residents, and that no single person or associated group, resident or non-resident, could hold more than ten per cent of the shares of any bank. These provisions were similar to those that had been introduced in September 1964 in the amendments to the Insurance Companies Act and the Trust and Loan Companies Act and approved during the previous session of Parliament.

When these amendments to the Insurance Companies Act and the Trust and Loan Companies Act were introduced on September 23, 1964, it was stated that similar provisions would be included in the Bank Act and made retroactive to that date. Shortly afterwards, David Rockefeller of the Chase Manhattan Bank came to see me in Ottawa. He was to have dinner with the Prime Minister, but came to my apartment for a drink and a talk ahead of time. I had met David Rockefeller on several occasions and knew of the close friendship between his father, the late John D. Rockefeller Jr., and the late W. L. Mackenzie King. They are said to have communicated with each other not less than once a week over a long period of years. No important decision was ever made in the Rockefeller family without first consulting Mr. King. It was more or less automatic, therefore, that David Rockefeller, not knowing what to do with his life after graduating from Harvard, should turn to Mr. King for advice and counsel. Mr. King invited him to come to Ottawa. Rockefeller was met at the station at about 8:00 A.M. and driven directly to Laurier House. This was at a time when Canada was fully engaged in the Second World War. Nevertheless, the Canadian Prime Minister found time to devote the whole day to the problems of his young friend.

Mr. King reminded Rockefeller of his own early career when, after graduating from the University of Toronto, he had proceeded to Harvard and after that to the London School of Economics and the University of Chicago. He advised Rockefeller to attend the London School and then to study for a Ph.D. degree in economics at Chicago, a university in which the Rockefeller family was keenly interested. Mr. King suggested that Rockefeller should then proceed to interest himself in the family bank, the Chase Manhattan. After giving this advice, Mr. King personally escorted David Rockefeller to the station in the late afternoon, by which time the course of his future life had been settled. He studied at the London School of Economics, obtained a Ph.D. degree in economics at Chicago, and at the time of our conversation in Ottawa was Vice-President and well on the way to becoming President of the family bank.

Rockefeller reminded me that the Chase and the First National City Bank of New York were rivals; that Citibank had bought control of the Mercantile Bank of Canada; and that, if Citibank were coming into Canada, then it was important to him that the Chase should also be represented here. Rockefeller said that he had decided the best way for the Chase to accomplish this objective would be for it to acquire effective control of the Toronto-Dominion Bank, the fifth-largest of the Canadian chartered banks, which of course had offices all across the country. I pointed out that under the proposed legislation his bank would be entitled to acquire a ten per cent interest in the Toronto-Dominion Bank. He replied that this was not enough for his purposes; that he had concluded that anything less than a twenty per cent interest would not give the Chase effective control over the management of the Toronto-Dominion Bank. He asked, therefore, if the Canadian government would not reconsider its decision in order that the Chase Manhattan might proceed with its objective.

I explained to Mr. Rockefeller that this was the very thing the proposed legislation was intended to prevent. This did not seem to satisfy him, however, as he raised the matter again that evening at dinner with Pearson. The Prime Minister spoke to me about this the next day, or shortly afterwards. When I explained the situation, Pearson agreed with me that we would be in difficulties if we allowed the Chase Manhattan to acquire control of the Toronto-Dominion Bank. If that occurred, it would be almost inevitable that the other large banking institutions in the United States would follow suit. They would proceed to purchase control of other Canadian banks. And if this happened, it would not be long before Canada would lose control over the banking institutions in this country.

In the course of our conversation, David Rockefeller had referred to the acquisition of the shares of the Mercantile Bank of Canada, previously owned by Dutch interests, by Citibank. David Rockefeller's cousin, James Stillman Rockefeller, the President of Citibank, and Robert P. MacFadden, a Vice-President of that institution, had come to see me in July 1963 about their proposed purchase of the shares of the Mercantile Bank. Prior to seeing me, Mr. MacFadden had had some conversations with Louis Rasminsky of the Bank of Canada, of which I had been advised.

Before seeing Rockefeller and MacFadden, I had had a talk with Bob Bryce, the Deputy Minister of Finance, and Clayton Elderkin, the Inspector General of Banks, and had asked them to be present at the meeting. I had said that immediately afterwards I would like them to prepare a

212

memorandum of what transpired. This was done by Elderkin who, after checking it with Bryce, and getting his approval, submitted his memorandum to me. The memorandum, which is dated July 18, 1963, is a long and complete record of the discussion that took place that morning.*

Mr. Rockefeller said during the meeting that National City Bank had made an arrangement with the shareholders of Mercantile to acquire the shares of the latter bank, but that no firm commitment had been made. He said his people considered that Canada was one of the more important countries in the financial world, that they would like to participate in its growth, and that he had asked for this interview to obtain the viewpoint of the government with respect to the proposed purchase. In reply, I said that I was glad to have the opportunity of expressing the views of the government regarding the proposed transaction. I said it was highly unlikely that a charter would be granted by Parliament for a bank that was to be non-resident controlled. Not only would the government not be in favour of such action, but both of the minor parties had expressed opposition to an extension of foreign control in financial institutions. I emphasized that the situation in 1963 was different from that in 1953, when the Mercantile Bank received its charter. Since that time, the Royal Commission on Canada's Economic Prospects had recommended that control of Canadian chartered banks should be in the hands of Canadians and had suggested that "appropriate action be taken to prevent control passing to non-residents." I also referred to the matter of relations between the Bank of Canada and the chartered banks, which Messrs. Rockefeller and MacFadden had discussed with Louis Rasminsky, the Governor of the Bank. Problems might arise in carrying out monetary policy if a foreign-controlled bank was prevented from co-operating because of laws or regulations in the country of its parent.

In response to a question, Mr. Rockefeller was told by Elderkin that it was the practice to revise the Bank Act every ten years and that the Act was each bank's only charter; it would be possible to stop a bank carrying on business when the revised Act came into force if its charter were not continued thereby. I pointed out that, while I myself might not have volunteered this information, no doubt Messrs. Rockefeller and MacFadden were quite aware of it. Mr. Rockefeller recalled that the licences of Canadian banks to do business in New York State came up for renewal annually.

I said that it would normally be unfair to apply retroactively any legislative restrictions on control of banks by non-residents, but since the National City people were now aware of the government's views about the possibility of their acquiring the shares of the Mercantile, the government

*See Appendix 3.

would not consider that they would be entitled to exemption from any legislation in respect of foreign ownership that might be enacted in the future. In conclusion, I said that, if the National City proceeded with its plan, it might tend to encourage restrictive legislation and advised Messrs. Rockefeller and MacFadden not to proceed with their proposed action. Mr. Rockefeller then said, "In other words, if we do so, it will be at our own peril." I replied that I would not have volunteered this expression, but I thought Mr. Rockefeller had sized up the situation correctly.

It will be seen that James S. Rockefeller stated that, while his bank had made arrangements with the Dutch interests to purchase the shares of the Mercantile Bank, no firm commitments had been entered into pending their ascertainment of the views of the Canadian government in the matter. I made it clear to Mr. Rockefeller that the Canadian government would not look favourably upon such a transaction. I also said that as he was now informed of the government's views, Citibank would not be entitled to exemption from any legislation respecting foreign ownership that might be enacted in the future.

Following the meeting in my office in July 1963, and despite the warnings given as recorded in Elderkin's memorandum, Citibank purchased the shares of the Mercantile Bank of Canada. In a sense this was a direct challenge to the Canadian government which the government was not prepared to let go by unnoticed.

It was decided that in the revision of the Bank Act, the charter of the Mercantile Bank should be renewed. However, a provision was included which was designed to restrict the bank's future growth as long as Citibank retained more than a ten per cent interest in it. When this became known, officials of Citibank immediately brought pressure to bear upon me to change the government's proposals. Officers of several of the Canadian chartered banks called me to urge that nothing should be done to thwart the objectives of Citibank in any way. I suspected that this was not out of any deep affection for Citibank, but rather from fear that the officials of that bank might retaliate by urging the appropriate authorities in the United States to restrict the activities of Canadian banks in that country.

It so happened that I was in Washington on the day after the provisions of the revised Bank Act were announced. I was surprised when two high officials of the American government raised this matter with me on behalf of Citibank. They ceased to protest, however, when I explained that Mr. James S. Rockefeller and his colleages had gone ahead with their transaction despite the warnings they had been given. But this was not the end of the matter. The question of the restrictions to be placed upon the future activities of the Mercantile Bank of Canada blew up into a major row in the early months of 1967. (This is described in Chapter Fourteen.)

The resolution to set up the Canada Development Corporation was introduced on May 3 but the legislation was not reached before the House adjourned on June 30. The plan envisaged by the government was explained in some detail in a speech I made to the Canadian Institute of Actuaries on September 20, extracts from which follow:

> I would now like to turn to the goals of the Corporation in putting these equity funds to work. Let me summarize these for you briefly.
>
> First, the Corporation should actively participate in major expansion projects of large existing enterprises as well as in the initiation of new projects.
>
> Second, the Corporation should stand ready to purchase a controlling or substantial minority interest in existing Canadian enterprises which might otherwise be sold to non-residents. There have been many instances where the owners of large family businesses found it necessary or desirable to sell out and, in any event, turned to foreign concerns because there was not a ready market closer to home.
>
> Third, the Corporation could, where suitable opportunities occur, acquire Canadian businesses or resources now owned by non-residents, and provide an additional source of funds where non-resident owners of large enterprises in Canada want to bring in substantial Canadian participation. . . .
>
> It will be apparent from what I said earlier about the CDC operating in the private sector independently of government influence, that these objectives may be realized only by applying sound commercial and business-like criteria in the management of the CDC's affairs.
>
> Considering these objectives, and appreciating their full import, it is clear that the CDC will have an important role to play in Canada's future development. To be successful, however, it will have to be capable of operating on a large scale, and it will require top flight management. . . .
>
> I might add that the management and board of the CDC would probably not, as a matter of course, participate directly in the management of all the enterprises in which they acquire investments. I would, however, expect them to take a much more active interest in the corporate policies of the companies in which the CDC invests than is the case with, for instance, our insurance companies and mutual funds. As I indicated earlier, the CDC should invest its funds only in projects that can be expected to yield a satisfactory return commensurate with the risks involved. . . .

Once the House adjourned on June 30, I was able to spend more time with

Al Johnson, Assistant Deputy Minister of Finance, who had been doing a great deal of preliminary work in connection with the Tax Structure Committee of the federal and provincial governments. Johnson and I saw eye to eye on most things, and it was not long before we had come to some tentative conclusions respecting joint programs and future tax arrangements with the provinces. We concluded that while the principle of equalization should be continued, a new formula should be worked out which would make it more equitable. Equalization, after all, is simply a means of transferring tax revenues from the wealthy to the less wealthy provinces, something we should be prepared to do in Canada.

In its election manifestos in 1962 and 1963, the Liberal Party had agreed to withdraw from established shared-cost programs in the welfare field if the provinces so desired, in which case appropriate tax resources would be made available to them. Obviously this would create a messy situation if some provinces decided one way and some provinces another, as they were entitled to do under the opting out legislation passed earlier that year. In these circumstances, Johnson and I concluded that at the appropriate time the federal government unilaterally should inform all the provinces of its intention to withdraw from shared programs in the social-security field that had become well established. This would include hospital insurance, old age and unemployment assistance, and disabled and blind persons' allowances. At the same time, the federal government should reduce its taxes in order to permit the provinces to increase their tax revenues so as to pay for the continuance of the programs in question.

We considered it important that the federal government should not weaken its ability to influence the rate of growth of the economy and, therefore, that it should retain its right to initiate capital spending programs in such other fields as the Trans-Canada Highway project, either on its own account or jointly with the provinces.

Having agreed among ourselves on this tentative approach, the staff of the department was in a position to tackle the formidable task of working out the details.

During the late summer of 1965, I had time to do some preliminary thinking about the next budget, the budget for the year 1966-67. I was worried about the preliminary expenditure submissions of the various departments for that year. It was clear that these preliminary requests would have to be cut back sharply if we were to avoid some major difficulties in financing the government's programs. Accordingly, in early September I asked George Davidson, the Secretary of the Treasury Board, to prepare detailed figures showing how the preliminary expenditure estimates for the year 1966-67 could be cut back by $200 million, by $400 million, or by $600

216

million, as the case might be. Davidson promised to have this ready early in November. At the same time, he stated that in his opinion cuts of $600 million were not realistic. But ministers of finance have to do a lot of trading. I thought if I urged cuts of $600 million, I might have a better chance of getting $400 million. And I hoped and expected that would be sufficient.

As things turned out, the House was not to meet again. A general election was called on September 8 to be held on November 8, 1965, and Parliament was dissolved. It had been a stormy Parliament of three sessions. But despite its many difficulties, the first Pearson government had to its credit an extraordinary record of accomplishment during the two-and-one-half years it was in office.

Mike Pearson's greatest personal achievement was his early understanding of what was happening in Quebec. This may have been due in large measure to the advice and warnings he received from Maurice Lamontagne. But it was Pearson who was perceptive enough to accept this advice and to act upon it. It was Pearson who established the Royal Commission on Bilingualism and Biculturalism. Without a Prime Minister in Ottawa who was willing to negotiate and to make concessions, the Quebec situation might well have got completely out of hand.

On the economic front, the expansionary measures introduced soon after the Pearson government took office stimulated business activity, following the slowdown at the end of 1962, and reduced the rate of unemployment more effectively and more quickly than most people would have believed possible. Among other things, an important agreement was negotiated with the United States, as a result of which the production of automobiles and parts in Canada had been greatly increased, thousands of new jobs had been created, and the imbalance in our transactions with the United States on current account had been reduced. The first Pearson government brought the national finances under firm control following many years of deficits and was able to introduce a substantial reduction in personal income taxes.

A great deal was accomplished in the area of social legislation. The Canada Pension Plan was implemented; Old Age Security pensions were increased from sixty-five dollars to seventy-five dollars a month and were to become available in a few years from age sixty-five instead of seventy; a national labour code was established with $1.25 an hour minimum wage in all federal jurisdictions; family allowances were extended to sixteen and seventeen-year-olds who remained in school; and the Student Loan Act was brought into existence. It remained for the Canada Assistance Act and Medicare to be passed by the next Parliament for Canada to have a respectable social-security base – a major achievement of the Pearson government. Pearson himself is entitled to take personal credit for the agreement on a new Canadian flag, after a long and bitter debate in Parliament. This symbol of the New Canada will be a lasting tribute to his memory.

A major non-political redistribution of political boundaries was introduced. In addition, some study and research were done on the subject of controlling election expenditures. Real political democracy will not be realized in Canada until the question of political contributions is faced up to, and the influence of the contributors – trade unions as well as business corporations – is reduced.

Legislation was introduced to ensure that control of the chartered banks, federally incorporated trust and loan companies, and Canadian newspapers will remain in Canadian hands. This was of great importance. Little else was done, however, to reverse the trend towards ever-increasing foreign domination of the Canadian economy.

Finally, major changes were proposed in the bill to revise the Bank Act, which was introduced but not passed during the third session of the first Pearson government.

Much of the credit for these achievements must go to Pearson. He was sixty-six years old when he became Prime Minister in April 1963, and it was inevitable that he should begin to show his age. Yet he was the leading character for the two-and-one-half years of his first government, quite apart from his position of Prime Minister. Like everyone, Pearson had his shortcomings. He had never been a good administrator, and he had little sense of the importance of clear lines of authority and of the need for delegating responsibility. Of more importance to a politician, he was never able to impress or gain the affection of the general public the way he had with his friends and associates in the Liberal Party. The public was put off by his habit of thinking out loud and of retreating and changing his position in the face of opposition.

But judged by the achievements of the first Pearson government, his record at the time of dissolution in September 1965 was an impressive one. Had it been possible for him to retire at that time, as I believe he would have liked, there could have been little criticism of his performance as party leader and Prime Minister. He had done far more than any fair-minded person could have hoped for. But from a practical standpoint, there was no one to whom he could have turned over the leadership of the party in 1965. And so he had no option but to face another election campaign and another term of office. This was not a pleasant prospect for a man who, for several years, had been continually under strain. After all, he must have been just as tired and just as weary, if not more so, as any of his colleagues.

CHAPTER TWELVE

The Election Campaign of November 1965

Timing of the election; the campaign; the results; the campaign in Davenport; my resignation.

Nineteen hundred and sixty-four had been an unhappy year for the Liberal government. There was the disastrous federal-provincial conference at Quebec at the beginning of April and the changed policies that had followed, of necessity improvised and put together very quickly. There was the long-drawn-out and emotionally charged debate over the flag issue. There was the prolonged discussion of the Canada Pension Plan and the many changes to it which were received with derision by the opposition. In November, there was Guy Favreau's serious discomfiture over the Rivard matter, including the involvement of the Prime Minister's Parliamentary Secretary and certain ministerial assistants. And finally, there was the "furniture affair" and the alleged implications in it of Maurice Lamontagne and René Tremblay.

Everyone was tired and discouraged and existence in Ottawa was anything but pleasant. Moreover, there could be no certainty as to how long the government would last. Every week or so – almost every day it seemed – we thought we might be beaten. Life as a member of a minority government is a most uncertain business.

While my own position had improved greatly insofar as the public and the House of Commons were concerned, sections of the business and financial communities were opposed to some of the policies I had put forward and continued to complain both about the policies in question and about me personally. Probably because of this my relations with Pearson were not as easy or as intimate as they had been. I felt disenchanted with the way things were going and was debating whether or not when the time came for Parliament to be dissolved I should seek re-election. I could see little point in continuing as a Member of Parliament if I was unlikely to accomplish the things we had all set out to do. High on my list were steps to regain a greater measure of control over Canadian resources and Canadian business enterprises.

But in the fall of 1964, Pearson began to think about the possibility of an early election and spoke to me about directing the campaign once more. He also suggested that I take another portfolio. He mentioned External Affairs and I said I just might be interested in taking on that department at some future date, provided we were prepared to take a more independent line *vis-à-vis* the United States, especially over the Vietnam question, and provided we changed our defence policy. But we did not discuss this seriously. I told him I had been thinking of not running again but that if I did so, I would like to stay on in the finance department for another two years at least, in order to complete the work in hand. Apart from the revision of the Bank Act, this included settling the tax arrangements with the provinces, establishing the Canada Development Corporation, new proposals to reverse the trend towards foreign domination of the economy, and possibly a new tax act, depending upon the date of completion of the report of the Carter Commission and the nature of its proposals.

With my position in the cabinet settled, I got down to the hard-slugging job of organizing for an election. The political side of things in a party sense had been neglected since the Liberals formed the government in April 1963. But with the help of Keith Davey, we proceeded to get things back in shape. After the House adjourned for the Christmas recess, I wrote a long memorandum to Pearson which was dated December 30, 1964, that shows the state of our thinking about an election at that time.*

I began by citing the pros and cons for calling an election. Among the pros, I mentioned that "we could not survive another year like 1964"; that we could win an election then (according to an opinion poll we had just received); that we might lose support if we waited until Mr. Diefenbaker retired; and that we should strike while economic conditions were favourable. Among the reasons for not calling an election were the fact the public did not want one and that another national campaign was undoubtedly the last thing Pearson himself would wish to contemplate. On balance, I suggested an election should be held in June or September 1965, if the opinion polls continued to indicate that we could win.

I then went on to indicate the kind of legislative program and the kind of preliminary organization that might be called for if the decision was in favour of an election. These matters included the question of a budget and the Canada Development Corporation, and a major cabinet reorganization.

*See Appendix 4.

Very few of my proposals were implemented. I had suggested, for example, that Pearson should persuade Mitchell Sharp to run in Winnipeg and try to organize support for the Liberals in the prairie provinces where he was popular. If he was successful, he would have a political base to work from and hence have some claim one day to succeed Pearson as Prime Minister. Pearson told me he spoke to Sharp about this but that Mitchell was reluctant to leave Eglinton, the riding he had won in 1963. I was disappointed with this decision which I considered was a serious political mistake. But Mike said that Mitchell was quite definite about it.

The House reassembled on February 16, 1965, and we encountered the same kind of frustrations we had experienced throughout 1964. Pearson hesitated about making a decision respecting the election, pending receipt of Chief Justice Dorion's report. Naturally, we did not wish to have this delivered and published in the middle of a campaign. While Pearson, Davey, and I continued to talk about the coming election and I continued to write him letters and reminders on the subject, nothing was decided. The Dorion report was not submitted until June 28, following which Guy Favreau resigned as Minister of Justice. The National Campaign Committee had met four days before, and on June 30 I wrote to the Prime Minister urging him to call an election for September 27 or October 4, despite the fact this would have meant enumerating in the month of August. In my letter, I stated that the question of an election depended to an extent on the public reaction to the action taken as a result of the Dorion report, including whatever changes the Prime Minister made in the cabinet. There were six reasons in particular for favouring an election:

First, subject to the public reaction respecting the Dorion report, everyone thought "we could win an election quite handily." The conclusions of the various Provincial Chairmen added up to 155 seats as a minimum. Most of them thought we would win considerably more. In the past, I had been on the cautious side in these matters but I thought Pearson "could safely count on 155 seats if the public is satisfied we have moved decisively in the Dorion matter."

Second, the federal Liberal Party executive, the National Campaign Committee, and almost every member of the cabinet (except Drury and MacNaught) were in favour of an early election, and a big majority of the Liberal caucus was in agreement. If there were not one, everyone would feel let down and it would be extremely difficult to get them up again. Apart from the fact that everyone believed we could get an overall majority, people thought "we would be foolish not to have an election while Diefenbaker is still around." His value to us (in a negative sense) was acknowledged everywhere at that time.

221

Third, if we did not have an election soon, we would become the captives of the opposition because of redistribution. Theoretically, the redistribution scheme could be passed by Parliament by March 1966. However, most people seemed to think there would be delays and that the new system would not be in operation before the end of 1966. No one would want an election in the first half of 1967, Centennial Year. Most people reasoned from this that, if we did not have an election in 1965, we would not have one (failing a defeat in Parliament) for more than two years. Once the opposition parties realized this, they would be able to make our lives extremely difficult.

Fourth, it was desirable that we should strengthen the position of the federal government *vis-à-vis* the provinces. This could be accomplished automatically by a resounding victory at the polls, especially if this included clear endorsation by the Province of Quebec. If our position were not strengthened, I hated to think what would happen in the Tax Structure Committee, for example.

Fifth, economic conditions were excellent. But people were beginning to worry about the situation in Britain and elsewhere and the repercussions this might have on Canada.

Sixth, there was also the question of the Carter Commission Report which was expected momentarily. I was afraid it might seriously upset the business community. I said, "It is not something I would like to try to handle as a minority government."

The main argument against an early election was that most of the redistribution maps had been published, and therefore it was felt by some that we should wait until redistribution was in effect before going to the country. Some people felt quite strongly about this, although I suspected they had not thought through the implications of waiting as long as two more years.

"My own opinion is that we should have an election at the earliest possible date, possibly as soon as Monday, September 27, or Monday, October 4." Either of these dates would have meant a short campaign, which was desirable, since it could not really get under way until after Labour Day. If public reaction to the action taken on the Dorion report were favourable, I said I would like to see an election announced before the federal-provincial conference met on July 19 or, alternatively, before the end of July.

As far as the public was concerned, there were two strong reasons which would justify calling an early election. The first was the need for vindication of the action taken on the Dorion Report. The second was a request for a mandate to implement the program outlined in the Speech from the Throne. "A combination of these two subjects should justify any government in asking for a renewal of public confidence – or, if you like, make it desirable to do so."

In my letter, I expressed reservations about using federal-provincial relations as an excuse for an election. If this were done, we would run the risk of an election being fought between the federal government and the provinces. "Ideally," I wrote, "I would prefer you to call the election before, rather than after, what may be a somewhat strenuous federal-provincial conference."

My letter concluded: "A number of people feel we missed the boat by not having an election in June. However, the thoughtful ones agree that there was an argument for waiting until the Dorion report was in, and your judgement in doing so has now been confirmed. In any event, I believe we have a second chance – and that if an election is called some time next month, we can still get the kind of majority we need to face whatever may lie ahead. My own strong opinion is to call an election without delay."

I felt there were two compelling reasons above all others for calling an election in the early fall, apart from the general weariness of the government and the desirability of a new mandate. First, if we did not we would be prevented from doing so until the fall of 1967, some two years later. If we left things any longer, we should have to wait for the redistribution of the electoral boundaries and, after providing for accidents and delays, this was not likely to be completed and the new constituencies organized before the end of 1966. No one would want an election in the first half of 1967 when we would be beginning to celebrate the one hundredth anniversary of Confederation. This would mean that no election could be held until the fall of 1967. But the only defence of a minority government is the threat of dissolution. If this threat were effectively removed, we would be at the mercy of the opposition for a full two years, something no minority government in its senses would wish to contemplate.

There was a second reason that was not mentioned in my letter. I was very much afraid that, if the House reassembled on September 27, the points made by Gordon Churchill in his speech on June 30, which questioned the veracity of the Prime Minister, would be raised again. I thought the Prime Minister would be accused once more of misleading the House in his answer to Harkness' question on November 24, 1964, respecting his prior knowledge of the Rivard affair. I was fearful that if this issue was skilfully handled by the opposition, Pearson could be destroyed and, with him, the Liberal government.

But despite all the arguments, Pearson could not make up his mind. He hated the thought of another gruelling election campaign against Mr. Diefenbaker. Moreover, he was listening increasingly to the views of his contemporaries in the business world who knew little about the political considerations but who, nevertheless, were strongly opposed to an election. Despite this, by mid-August, Pearson gave me the clear impression that he intended to call an election in the fall.

In the latter part of August, Pearson made a trip to Western Canada where he was enthusiastically received. In speeches to Liberal Party gatherings, he came very close to saying there would be a fall election, and by the time he returned to Ottawa most people assumed that this was so. But Pearson was exhausted by his trip and again began to have doubts about calling an election, and perhaps about whether he had sufficient strength to go through with a campaign. Tom Kent, Keith Davey, and I met with him on the evening of August 30 to discuss the latest survey made by Oliver Quayle, which showed that in early August the Liberals had a thirteen-point lead over the Tories compared with only a nine-point spread at the time of the last election in April 1963.

According to the survey, we should have been able to win an additional ten to twenty seats, say fifteen, mostly in Quebec. These would be at the expense of the Créditistes and the Tories. The Tories would probably have lost seats to the Socreds in the West. The issues that most people were concerned about were still the bread-and-butter questions. In order of priority, they were: the high and rising cost of living; unemployment; taxes and spending; prosperity and industrial growth; Medicare; and education. There was no great interest in the federal-provincial relations issue as far as the mass of the people were concerned.

In a memorandum summarizing the survey, I indicated the survey results meant that in the campaign we should stress what we had done – prosperity, pensions, the flag, etc. We should appeal for a strong federal government to build a new Canada. We should request a mandate to proceed with such programs as Medicare. I stated that it would be a mistake to emphasize the Quebec problem, "not because we do not consider it the number-one domestic issue but because people in English-speaking Canada do not like being reminded of it." Also, every time we mentioned the "two founding races," we offended unnecessarily the one-quarter of the population that belongs to neither of them. I believed it critical that we – most importantly Pearson himself – "must not be defensive." We should *not* react to Diefenbaker or to the charges he would make against us. The proper strategy would be to leave him strictly alone. It would be especially important not to reply to his taunts and charges about immorality in politics.

With this kind of campaign, I felt, we should make nearly as many gains in English-speaking Canada as in Quebec – for a total of, say, from 150 to 155 seats. Our guess was that a different campaign stressing the Quebec issue would result in a loss of seats in English-speaking Canada. How many, it would be hard to say. We might stand to lose as many as we could expect to pick up in Quebec and end up about where we were before, but with a different geographical distribution. (This, in fact, is about what happened.)

The next morning, August 31, I spent about one-and-one-half hours with the Prime Minister at Sussex Drive. He was tired, undecided (so I thought), and depressed. We discussed the pros and cons of the election question at length. I reminded Mike that, while we had been friends for years, I was quite aware of the fact that I had been irritating him of late – we often seemed to be at cross purposes. This seemed to me inevitable, given our respective jobs and responsibilities and the pressures we had been working under. I said I accepted the situation as just that, but added that, as I had told him before, I would be happy to drop out altogether if he would like me to.

Mike replied that he would like to make some major changes in the cabinet again next spring (presumably after an election). I said I knew he was pressed by some people in business circles to get me out of finance, and repeated I would be glad to get out altogether if this would help him. I said that in reality as Minister of Finance I was the second man in the government and if I were going to stay on I would not be prepared to move to another portfolio at this time. I explained that I might be interested in External Affairs some day but that if I went there too soon some would think it implied I was being groomed to succeed Pearson. I said that this was not my ambition.

When I left Sussex Drive, I felt Pearson was weakening on the election question – that he really did not want to face it, but that he hesitated to say so to me. On the surface, he implied he was going ahead with the election. Late that afternoon, Paul Martin called me in an agitated state. We had dinner together and he told me that Mike had changed his mind and was not going to call an election. Pearson had said that according to the Quayle survey we would be beaten if we went ahead. Paul felt this reversal would be very hard to justify to those who were expecting an early election.

I called Pearson after dinner and asked to see him that night or next morning before cabinet. We settled for nine o'clock the next morning. When I got to his office, I found his staff was in a state of gloom – the election was off, they said. I told Pearson of my conversation with Paul Martin who had got the wrong impression from him about our chances which I reviewed with him again. We were thirteen percentage points ahead of the Tories, according to the Quayle survey. We should win an over-all majority. I predicted that we would do so. He said he would resign if we did not and that I would have to go with him. I said I would do so, but assured him that if we did not mismanage the campaign we should win. I asked him, in putting the question to the cabinet, not to give a wrong impression about the latest poll as he must have done to Paul. He agreed. When I left, he was in a quite different frame of mind and I felt the election would go forward.

When Pearson met with his Ministers at 10.15 A.M. or 10.30 A.M. that morning, August 31, he was cheerful and seemed confident. He put the question of the election to them quite fairly; if anything, he gave the impression he wanted to go ahead. He asked everyone's opinion, starting with Paul Martin. Martin asked if he could speak last, as did Jack Pickersgill. Pearson agreed to this, adding that of those absent Harry Hays was all for an election and that Arthur Laing had called to say he had changed his mind and was now for it. My recollection is that all the other ministers were present. All said they favoured an immediate election except for Watson MacNaught, who was strongly opposed and who gave the impression that he knew he would be beaten personally (which he was); Maurice Sauvé, who was opposed unless certain new and able people from Quebec were willing to stand now but not later (that is, Marchand, Pelletier, and Trudeau); Paul Hellyer, who said he did not have all the facts that we did but that in his opinion we would not do as well in Toronto as before; and Paul Martin, who despite some pressing refused to give an opinion even after asking to speak last. Some member of the cabinet must have leaked the views of individual members to Peter Newman, who was remarkably accurate in his column the next day.

Eventually, Pearson said he would make his decision by the following Tuesday (after Labour Day) but it seemed clear – or reasonably clear – he would go along with the views expressed by the great majority of ministers.

In my notes of this meeting, I made the following entry: "I am more responsible than anyone for the decision – one Mike did not want to make. If we do not get a majority I will have to offer my resignation from the government – whether Mike does so or not."

After my conversation with Pearson on August 31, I assumed it was understood that I would continue to carry on as Minister of Finance until the job I had set out to do there was completed. I would not have stood for re-election if there had been any doubts in my mind on this score. And as already stated, I had no reservations about the way things were going in the finance department at that time.

It was announced on September 8 that Parliament had been dissolved and that a general election would be held on November 8. Jean Marchand, who in the 1963 campaign had refused to run because of Pearson's unilateral decision about nuclear warheads, agreed to be a candidate on this occasion, if seats could be found for Gérard Pelletier and Pierre Elliott Trudeau as well as for himself. There were elements in the party in Quebec who opposed this, but Pearson was firm about it, and all three – Marchand, Pelletier, and Trudeau – became candidates. I was delighted, as this new blood was needed from Quebec and, in addition, it indicated that the strength of the more progressive elements in the party would be enhanced after the election.

However, just when I was thinking what a coup this was for Mike, he telephoned to say that Robert Winters was considering going after the nomination in York West, the seat previously held by "Red" Kelly. I protested that Bob, much as I liked him personally, with his conservative outlook and his association with "Big Business," would not help us in the Toronto area where our main opposition would come from the N.D.P. I said it would be assumed that Bob would be in the cabinet, which would mean four cabinet ministers from Toronto. Apart from everything else, this would retard the opportunities for men like Donald Macdonald, David Hahn, and other excellent M.P.'s from the Metro area. Moreover, I suggested that coming after Marchand, Pelletier, and Trudeau, Bob's addition to the Liberal team would be confusing to the public who were uncertain enough as it was about what the party stood for.

After thinking the matter over, I called Mike back again to say I thought it was unfair to Bob to encourage him to return to politics. I assumed he would be doing so only if he and his friends believed he was the man to succeed Pearson as leader when the time came. But I pointed out the Liberal Party was now very different from the one when Bob had been C.D. Howe's protégé in Ottawa. I suspected that he did not fully appreciate this and that if he were elected he would be an unhappy man with little chance of realizing his ambitions. Mike replied that it was all settled, that Bob was going to run.

The campaign got off to a bad start, thanks to Jean Lesage who insisted on proceeding with a prearranged speaking tour of Western Canada despite the federal election. I urged Pearson to persuade Lesage to defer this trip in everybody's interests, his own included. Pearson told me later that he had tried to do this but that Lesage would not hear of it. He proceeded out West, ostensibly to explain and get support for the aspirations of Quebec and the objectives of his government. But his trip was a disaster. He gave the impression of being arrogant, he refused to answer questions, and he engaged in controversies with the press and with members of his audiences. The headlines were very damaging. The result was to foster the anti-Quebec feelings which had been stirred up by the activities of the Separatists and accentuated by the Rivard and furniture affairs. Not only did Lesage's trip spoil our chances of picking up a few seats on the Prairies, but it hurt us badly in some parts of Ontario and other sections of English-speaking Canada.

In a memorandum to Pearson of August 31, summarizing the contents of the latest Quayle survey, I had warned that a campaign stressing the Quebec issue would lose us seats in English-speaking Canada. This is exactly what happened, as a result of the speaking tour of Jean Lesage and, later, the skilful campaign waged by Mr. Diefenbaker.

A Quayle survey taken early in October showed that the Liberals had lost considerable ground since August but that we could still win a majority if we waged a good campaign. I reported this to Mike in a memorandum dated October 18, 1965: The Quayle sampling took place between September 29 and October 7, that is about two weeks before Pearson had begun campaigning. It showed that, as of that date, we could win a small majority. The N.D.P. percentage was up. This was mainly due to gains in Quebec and in Toronto, but it did not look as if they would gain seats over all. The spread between us and the Tories had narrowed since August. We had dropped in Quebec, where it did not matter, and in the Maritimes, where it did. The spread in over-all terms was just about the same as it was in the previous election, but the distribution between regions had changed. We had maintained a fourteen-point spread in Ontario between August and September – it was twelve per cent at the time of the last election – and we were thirty points ahead of both the Tories and the Créditistes in Quebec.

As I interpreted the statistics, it indicated that we would lose some seats in the Maritimes; win a lot of seats in Quebec; hold our own or perhaps pick up three or four seats in Ontario; not count on anything on the Prairies; hold our own or possibly do a little better in British Columbia.

We could improve this picture and gain a respectable majority if we campaigned all out on *our* issues in the last three weeks. The main things going for us were: prosperity and the fact that we were the government. Some people would ask themselves: Why take a chance on change? The main things going for the Tories were, first, the allegations about scandals and, second, some of their proposed programs.

I advised Pearson that on no account should he talk about Diefenbaker or the scandals, nor should he ever mention either subject in any derogatory sense. We should talk continually about prosperity, the fact that people must have jobs, about Canada and Canada's position in the world, and about the need for a strong majority government in Ottawa. I urged the Prime Minister to have one speech with a few variations, and to keep on repeating it. The memorandum recommended that all candidates should be urged to campaign positively, and never to react to the opposition's issues; to hammer home the prosperity issue; and to pose the choice: "The continuation of prosperity under the Liberals *or* a return to a Diefenbaker government."

At the same time, I sent a campaign letter to all our candidates. The letter stated that the campaign was going well, taking the country as a whole, and that our strategy was being proven right. It went on to report that Mr. Diefenbaker was making a few yards with his allegations about wrongdoing, but he was beginning to exaggerate and therefore was becoming less credible. Obviously he was "desperately anxious to embroil the Prime Minister and other prominent Liberals into making counterattacks or defensive statements." Mr. Pearson had no intention of playing Diefenbaker's game in this way. It was Mitchell Sharp's responsibility – on behalf of the Liberal Party – to reply to Diefenbaker when he made "unusually wild or misleading statements." The rest of us were to leave this sort of thing to Mitchell. The letter concluded with advice to candidates that they not be afraid to keep on saying: "In Canada, Liberal times mean good times." It also suggested that they could, in good conscience, point out that the smaller parties – the N.D.P. and the Socreds – had no chance of either forming a government or becoming the official opposition. "A vote for them, in effect, is a vote for Diefenbaker."

But Mr. Diefenbaker single-handedly staged a vigorous and effective campaign in which he played up to the anti-Quebec sentiments in English-speaking Canada. He amused his audiences by repeating all the French names that had been in the news in recent months – Rivard . . . Denis . . . Lamontagne . . . Tremblay . . . Rouleau . . . Dupuis . . . Favreau . . . and so on – and implied that the Liberal government was mixed up with dope smugglers and enmeshed in bribery and general corruption.

Before Pearson himself began to campaign, Keith Davey and I started to give a daily press briefing at Liberal headquarters on Cooper Street, Ottawa. The main purpose was to let Liberals across the country know we were in business and also to keep the press happy by giving them something to write about no matter how unimportant. At one of these meetings, a reporter asked me to comment on a speech by Senator Wallace McCutcheon the night before in which he had criticized Liberal policies in general and me in particular in no uncertain terms. I answered that, if Wally McCutcheon really had such strong feelings, he should give up his Senate seat and run against me in Davenport. I challenged him to do so. The next day, McCutcheon replied: "If all the people who disagree with Walter Gordon were to run against him in Davenport, there would be more candidates than voters." There is no doubt he scored on the exchange.

We discontinued these press briefings once Pearson began his campaigning. I did not see as much of him as I had done in the two previous campaigns. But one day I did accompany him on a long trip through southwestern Ontario which went particularly well. That evening, in the course of a speech in Wallaceburg, he announced that I would be continuing as Minister of Finance in the new government. I paid little attention to the Prime Minister's actual remarks because, as I thought, all that had been settled before the campaign began. However, his announcement was played up by the press, and it upset Robert Winters.

Winters called on Pearson the next day at the Constellation Hotel near Malton where Mike was staying. They had an angry altercation about my role in the next government. Apparently, Pearson had promised to appoint Bob Minister to Trade and Commerce which to Bob might have meant that he could become a second C.D. Howe. Bob might have assumed that Mitchell Sharp would move from Trade and Commerce to become Minister of Finance. All I know is that Mike and Bob ended up shouting at each other, forgetting perhaps that there are Liberals everywhere, including employees in hotels. It was a matter of hours before I heard all about the argument.

Pearson was determined to fight this election on his own, and he discouraged his colleagues from participating on any important scale. He seemed anxious to disprove the public's assessment of him as a vacillating politician, as reported objectively, but unhappily, by all the opinion surveys. He was not successful. He could not bring himself to be specific about future policies and gave the impression of being indecisive. The public was confused.

Pearson did show that Davey and I were wrong on at least one point. We had urged him not to reply to what Diefenbaker was saying about the Rivard and furniture affairs. But Pearson insisted upon doing so late in the campaign on a national television program. He appeared on the program looking angry and indignant; it was his best TV performance in the campaign, and quite effective.

But again, later in the campaign, he made an unfortunate reply to a question while campaigning one morning in the East End of Toronto. He was asked what he would do if he failed to win an over-all majority. Without thinking, he said he would call another election. This answer was recorded on tape. He flew to Vancouver that afternoon and upon arrival there was asked to enlarge upon what he had said that morning. He denied having said he would call another election if the Liberals did not obtain a majority. This reply was also recorded. The two tapes were then played back to back all over Canada, with the suggestion that the word of the Prime Minister could not be trusted.

We had planned to stage a major rally at the Yorkdale Plaza in Toronto during the last few days of the campaign. Gordon Edick and David Greenspan, our two experts in this field, were in charge of the arrangements and a crowd of twenty-five thousand turned up. Gordon had checked everything just before the meeting, but when Pearson appeared to speak, it was discovered that the public-address system had gone dead. After considerable confusion, Pearson tried to address the crowd through a loud hailer, but this was not successful. It was simply impossible for him to make his speech. Understandably, this was upsetting to the Prime Minister, but the crowd was enthusiastic and good-natured and did not seem to mind. I was moving around quite a bit, and at one point at the back of the hall, I overheard this conversation between two middle-aged ladies:

First lady: "This is the most exciting political meeting I have ever been to. Such a tremendous crowd and we have seen everybody so well and so clearly."

Second lady: "Yes, and we have not had to listen to any political speeches!"

I believed right up to the end of the campaign that we would win by a small margin and that at long last Pearson would become Prime Minister with a majority behind him. We had started the campaign with 129 seats, which meant we only needed to add another four for an over-all majority. But we failed to do this, principally I think because of: Lesage's Western trip which was very damaging from our standpoint; Diefenbaker's skilful anti-French-Canadian campaign; and Pearson's inability to be specific about policies. More than anything else, we failed to keep to our own issues. Instead, a great deal of attention was paid to the question of Quebec and the difficulties of some of the government's French-speaking ministers. This was fatal for the Liberals.

The results of the election of November 8, 1965, are shown in the accompanying table, with the comparable figures for 1962 and 1963.

	November 1965	April 1963	June 1962
Progressive Conservatives	97	95	116
Liberals	131	129	100
N.D.P.	21	17	19
Other	16	24	30
Total	265	265	265

We had won two more seats than we had before, but our popular vote had fallen from 41.9% to 40.2%. It was a sorry outcome to an election we should have won, which we certainly would have won if it had been held earlier.

My own campaign in Davenport in the 1965 election was highly successful. There had been rumours that some wealthy Winnipegers were collecting a fund of $50,000 to beat me. As one would expect, this story helped me considerably. To underline things, we decided to spend as little money as possible on my campaign. In fact, our expenditures were less than half what they had been in 1962. Joe Grittani had decided he should not take an active part in party politics following his appointment to the Board of Broadcast Governors. Accordingly, Lex Thomson, the President of the Association, took over from Joe as campaign manager and did an excellent job. The other members of the executive at that time were John Stroz, Percy Pike, Marie Guthrie, Cathy O'Neill, Kay Kelly, Brian Land, Jerry Bilak, Emma McLaughlin, Olga Riisna, Peter Bosa, Horst Bolik, Al McConachie, Bruno Vatri, and Vic Artuso. All of them and scores of others worked their heads off. Again, we won every poll and almost sixty per cent of the votes cast.

Abraham, Nelson W. (N.D.P.)	2,918
Gordon, Walter L. (Liberal)	9,887
Iannuzzi, Dan (P.C.)	3,907
Kashtan, William (Communist)	225

I called Mike on election night, Monday, November 8, and reminded him of my undertaking to resign if we did not get an over-all majority. He sounded tired, dispirited, and thoroughly exasperated by the fact we had failed to win our majority. He said it would be he and not I who would be doing the resigning, and that he intended to do this right away. I said I would talk to him about this when I arrived in Ottawa the next day or on Wednesday. I did not see him on Tuesday. Pearson met with members of the cabinet on Wednesday. While he said something about resigning, everyone urged him to stay on which, quite properly, he immediately agreed to do.

In the course of the discussion, I said I had advocated the election more strongly than anyone else and felt I should bear a large share of the responsibility. Someone remarked that, with only two or three exceptions, we had all been in favour of the election. Someone else said we could have won it if it had been held in June or July or in September, that we had put it off too long. And, of course, while the results were disappointing, we were in a much stronger position after the election than we would have been if it had not been held.

I had lunch with Pearson the next day at Sussex Drive. I found him flushed and irritable. He started right in to say there would have to be some major changes in the cabinet. From the way he spoke, I interpreted this to mean he wished to raise the question of the finance portfolio once again, despite what had been said about this both before the campaign began and publicly in the course of it. I replied that he did not need to worry about me. I had said I would resign if we did not get an over-all majority and was prepared to go through with my undertaking. I had my letter of resignation with me. I handed it to him and he put it in his pocket with a nervous gesture without reading it. I said I would like him to read it so he pulled it out and did so.

Pearson appeared to be unhappy about the ending of our political partnership but did not seem to realize that as well it would mean the culmination of our long personal friendship. He asked me in a casual kind of way, because he knew what my reply would be, if I would accept another portfolio. He then asked if I would like to go to Washington as ambassador. I reminded him that he had offered me the Washington post on two occasions before I had entered politics. I said I still had no interest in such an appointment. He then told me that Keith Davey would have to go immediately and that he wanted to get rid of Tom Kent as soon as possible. In addition, he said that Lamontagne and Tremblay would have to leave the cabinet. I was left to wonder how he would get along without these men – Lamontagne, Kent, and Davey – who had helped him so loyally through numerous crises and vicissitudes.

Some of my friends in the Liberal Party, including Keith Davey, thought I should not have submitted my resignation; that I should have carried on as Minister of Finance as if nothing had happened. They believed Pearson would have given in, as he often did when he was confronted with strong opposition to his wishes. He might have done so. But I had said I would submit my resignation if we did not win an over-all majority and I would never have felt comfortable if I had failed to do so. The next move was up to Pearson. He chose to accept it.

In December, after returning from a trip to Europe, I began to hear rumours about the reason Pearson had been so anxious to get me off the scene so quickly, but it was not until well into January 1966 that I began to believe them. During the course of a conversation with him on the morning of January 15, I raised the question of the stories I had been hearing about his undertakings to members of the financial community, before and during the election campaign, that I was to give up the finance portfolio. Pearson conceded that he had implied this to certain influential individuals who, of course, would have retailed the story to their friends.

CHAPTER THIRTEEN

A Choice
for Canada

Changes in the Bank Act; the Spencer case; the Munsinger affair; A Choice for Canada; thoughts about Mr. Pearson's successor; speaking tour; the Liberal Party conference, October 1966; speech to Toronto Advertising and Sales Club.

For some time I had been having considerable difficulty with the cervical vertebrae in my neck, which produced muscle spasms, headaches, and severe pain. This had bothered me throughout the 1965 election campaign. I had hoped it would clear up by the time Liz and I returned from the trip we made to Europe immediately following my resignation from the cabinet, but there did not seem to be much improvement.

Quite apart from this physical discomfort, I felt trapped and frustrated by the position I found myself in. I had no wish to continue as a private member of Parliament, with little or nothing to say about policy matters or about the affairs and objectives of the Liberal Party. But I had just been elected by a large majority, in part because the voters in Davenport expected me to continue as Minister of Finance pledged to carry out certain policies, policies which my successor, Mitchell Sharp, was not in sympathy with.

I was naturally unhappy about the change in my relationship with Mike Pearson who had been so close a friend for many years. And, of course, I was discouraged by my inability to persuade the public, and especially the business community, of the need to safeguard Canada's independence. This was one of the main reasons why I had gone into politics in the first place.

However, by the beginning of the year 1966, I had concluded that I must remain a Member of Parliament for a time at least. It would have been misunderstood if I had given up my seat immediately. As I would have a great deal of spare time on my hands, I decided to write a book primarily about the independence issue but touching as well on some other policy questions. This I proceeded to do, mostly at "Seldom Seen" near Schomberg, lying on my back to ease the pain in my neck and using a board to write on.

After the session started, I usually spent about three days each week in Ottawa. It seemed senseless to be there for more than this because, as a recent member of the cabinet and ex-Minister of Finance, it was inappropriate for me to become a member of any of the parliamentary committees or to participate in the debates. Moreover, I felt that too much advice or advocacy on my part would be resented by some of my ex-colleagues.

Soon after my return to Canada early in December, I had called Mitchell Sharp to congratulate him on his impending appointment as Minister of Finance. I said there were a number of matters on which I would be glad to fill him in. I had in mind the discussion I had had with George Davidson, the Secretary of the Treasury Board, about keeping the next year's expenditures down to reasonable levels, and also some views about the revisions to the Bank Act which would have to be re-introduced when Parliament assembled. Sharp was busy at the time but said he would call me. He did not do so, and early in January rumours began to circulate that he was contemplating some major changes in the revised Bank Act which I had introduced in the House in May 1965, changes that would be looked upon as a great boon to the commercial banks. At a meeting of the Liberal caucus, Sharp had given some indication of this but had implied that the changes were ones that I had had in mind. I thought this had given our members an inaccurate impression and, accordingly, wrote to him on January 5, 1966.

In my letter I said I thought that the press interpretations of what Sharp had said in a speech to the Canadian Club of Toronto regarding the Bank Act went further than was perhaps justified by the words he had used. However, because of those interpretations, and because of his necessarily guarded reply in caucus to a query about the Bank Act, I thought I should write to him about it. Mitchell had mentioned in caucus that I had planned to propose some new amendments to the revised Bank Act. This was correct, but while the proposed amendments were lengthy, they did not amount to much in substance. I told Sharp that, although Rasminsky and Elderkin would have liked me to propose the complete lifting of the ceiling on interest rates, I could not recommend this. However, I had left myself a loophole when I introduced the bill. At that time I said the question of the interest ceiling might have to be reopened if there were a world-wide rise in interest rates and this, of course, had happened. I had asked Bob Bryce to try to find a formula for tying the ceiling to some simple measuring stick or statistic and thus introduce some element of flexibility. My own choice was to let the ceiling fluctuate with changes in the bank rate. While this would not be welcomed by the Bank of Canada because there would be objections to changes in the bank rate from time to time, I believed it had some merit. I, for one, could support a change of this kind.

In my letter I told Mitchell that I would not be able to support a complete removal of the ceiling as recommended by the Porter Commission. Quite apart from everything else, such a move would be a complete reversal of the government's policy as announced eight months before. My letter continued: "You may not have anything like this in mind, but just in case you have, I thought it worth while suggesting it might be useful for us to have a talk about it well in advance."

Sharp did not reply to my letter but I had sent a copy of it to the Prime Minister who asked me to discuss it with him on January 15, at which time he agreed the subject should be aired in caucus. This was done on January 26, 1966. I began my remarks to the caucus by saying that I did not intend to abuse my position by asking difficult questions of my former cabinet colleagues. I did, however, want to say something about the conclusions the Liberal Party should draw from the November 1965 election results. I thought we had been "very lucky" in the last election, having gained two more seats despite a drop in the percentage of the popular vote. But we should not count on being able to do it again. I believed that the government's decisions about the Bank Act would be very important insofar as public opinion was concerned. In my remarks I said, "The kites that have been flying suggest the government is planning to lift the interest ceiling." Certainly the financial community thought so, and bank stocks had been going up. I suggested that, in economic terms, this would be the wrong decision. It would mean interest rates would go up across the country, especially in the outlying areas. In political terms, I thought that lifting the interest ceiling would be equally unwise. I urged the government not to make a hasty decision before hearing the views of a committee of the caucus, which I believed should be set up for the purpose.

I had strong support for these views in the caucus, especially from Maurice Lamontagne. I did not advocate a rigid adherence to the ceiling on interest rates but felt there should be some check on what the commercial bankers might be tempted to do if left entirely to themselves. I had suggested one possible formula in my letter to Mitchell Sharp of January 5. But he was not inclined to compromise, and no committee of caucus was established to study the matter. Sharp introduced legislation to eliminate the interest ceiling altogether, and on July 7, 1966, he managed to get the resolution approved in the House by a vote of 86 to 59. By arrangement, Maurice and I were not present when the vote was taken.

The new Parliament met on January 18, 1966, and the next day a question was addressed to Lucien Cardin, the Minister of Justice, as to whether surveillance was being continued on a "Mr. Spencer," recently dismissed by the Post Office Department. Cardin replied in the affirmative.

From then on, the Spencer affair became a major issue, with Cardin and the government being accused of denying Spencer his ordinary rights as a citizen. On January 31, Cardin made a full statement respecting the dismissal of George Victor Spencer from the Post Office Department, which he concluded as follows:

> I want to emphasize that the investigation in this case was handled in the same way as other security investigations were handled prior to the time this government took office in 1963. If this case proves anything, it proves the effectiveness of Royal Canadian Mounted Police counter-intelligence. I am satisfied that our security operations are in good hands, and I have seen nothing to suggest there are valid grounds for objecting to the manner in which these operations are being conducted.

This did not end the matter. Members of the opposition continued to argue that Spencer had been improperly dismissed, denied his pension rights, etc., and pressed for a judicial inquiry into the whole affair. Cardin stated that he did not feel it would be either necessary or useful to initiate such an inquiry. But Pearson, who was obviously concerned as to whether Spencer had been fairly dealt with, agreed to consider the suggestion. This added to the pressure on Cardin who was attacked with increasing violence by Mr. Diefenbaker, Erik Neilsen, and others. Although I have no evidence to support this, I believe that Cardin convinced the Prime Minister there should not be a judicial inquiry. In any event, on February 23, in the course of a debate on the Justice Department Estimates, Pearson said: "I wish to confirm the view which has been given by the Minister of Justice that an enquiry into this matter is not necessary and would not be useful."

The opposition continued to hammer away, however, and on Friday, March 4, when the Estimates of the Department of Justice came up again, Mr. Diefenbaker attacked Cardin without mercy. Cardin, when he was a member of the opposition some years before, had made a highly critical speech about Mr. Diefenbaker which had not been forgotten or forgiven. It was suggested that Diefenbaker was now out to destroy him. But Cardin has a great deal of spirit, and *Hansard* records that he gave as good as he received. It was during this rather fierce debate on March 4, 1966, that Cardin made the first public reference to the Gerda Munsinger affair which, incidentally, he called "the Monseignor case."

> Mr. Cardin: Whether or not hon. members opposite agree with it, I have made my case. I am convinced of the correctness of the decision I

have made and there is not one person in the house who is going to make me say I am wrong when I know I am right.

I am willing to listen to hon. members on all sides of the house who bring forward criticisms and constructive advice on the difficult problems concerning the administration of security matters. But a while ago the right hon. gentleman [Mr. Diefenbaker] was accusing us of hiding the truth, of hiding evidence from the committee. Well, I can tell the right hon. gentleman that of all the members of the House of Commons he – I repeat, he – is the very last person in the house who can afford to give advice on the handling of security cases in Canada.

Some hon. Members: Hear, hear.

Mr. Cardin: And I am not kidding.

Some hon. Members: Hear, hear.

Mr. Diefenbaker: And again applause from the Prime Minister. I want that on the record.

Mr. Cardin: I understand the right hon. gentleman said he wants that on the record. Would he want me to go on and give more?

Some hon. Members: Go on. He wants it.

Mr. Cardin: Very well.

Some hon. Members: Hear, hear.

Mr. Cardin: I want the right hon. gentleman to tell the house about his participation in the Monseignor case when he was prime minister of the country.

Both Larry Pennell and Jean Marchand spoke on March 4 and in accordance with the cabinet's decision confirmed that there would not be a public inquiry into the Spencer case. However, shortly after they had spoken, the Prime Minister entered the debate. Spencer had by then requested an inquiry into the manner of his dismissal from the civil service, and Pearson now agreed that there should be one, despite what Cardin, Pennell, and Marchand had said. The Prime Minister announced that he would telephone Spencer personally and offered to let David Lewis, a lawyer by profession and the deputy leader of the N.D.P., listen to the conversation on another line if he would like to do so.

Pearson had told me a week or two before that he was concerned about whether Spencer had been fairly treated when he was dismissed from the civil service and that he intended to review the whole file himself. Later he told me he had done so. I admired his motives, and I could understand what lay behind his statement in the House respecting an inquiry. But naturally it caused immediate comment.

It seemed unthinkable that the Prime Minister himself should telephone Spencer who, it was assumed, was or had been a Soviet agent. And it seemed extraordinary that he would invite David Lewis of the New Democratic Party to listen in on the conversation. But even more astonishing was Pearson's agreement to the holding of a judicial inquiry into one aspect of the Spencer case – his dismissal from the civil service – after saying on February 23 that he agreed with Cardin this would not be a useful thing to do. Moreover, he did so on the very day that Cardin, Pennell, and Marchand had reiterated that there would be no such inquiry. This cut Cardin's legs from under him. Much was made of this on Monday, March 7, when debate was resumed on the justice department's Estimates.

Maurice Lamontagne came to see me the following day and said Cardin intended to resign; that Cardin was a hero to the members of the Quebec caucus who were delighted with the way he had stood up to Mr. Diefenbaker and brought the Munsinger case out in the open; and that Marchand and other French-Canadian ministers planned to resign with Cardin as they felt Pearson had let him down very badly. Maurice and I agreed that if Marchand and other French-Canadian ministers were sufficiently incensed, as they seemed to be, the only alternative if the government was not to be defeated, would be for Pearson to resign as Prime Minister in favour of someone else. Maurice said that Cardin was coming to see him and urged that Marchand and I should join them and plead with Cardin to accept some compromise solution of the problem. I protested that, like Lamontagne, I was no longer a member of the cabinet and that in any case this was something that should be settled by the French-Canadian members of the party. But Maurice persuaded me that, as Cardin and I had considerable respect for one another, I should join him and Marchand in trying to avert what appeared to be a calamity of major proportions for the Liberal Party.

We spent several hours with Lucien Cardin that evening. To begin with, he was quite determined. Pearson had let him down. He had done the same thing to Guy Favreau. Lucien was fed up with politics and intended to resign. Marchand made it clear that he would go with him and that meant that most of the French-speaking ministers from Quebec would do the same.

Maurice and I argued that this simply could not be allowed to happen. Pearson could not possibly accept the resignations of Marchand and most of the French-speaking members of the cabinet. Rather than this he would have to resign himself, leaving no opportunity for any of us to consider who might be the best man to succeed him. After a great deal of discussion, Lucien said he could see the logic of our analysis. His only wish was to get out of politics, but he would agree not to resign immediately.

When Cardin mentioned "the Monseignor case," he was really referring to the case of Gerda Munsinger, a German lady of easy affections, an alleged agent of the Soviet Union who had had an affair with Pierre Sévigny, Associate Minister of Defence in the Diefenbaker government. The question was whether Diefenbaker had been sound in judgement in not dismissing Sévigny from his post on the grounds he might have become a security risk.

More than a year previously, when I was a member of the cabinet, some ministers, who had become exasperated with Diefenbaker's tactics and his attacks on Favreau, Lamontagne, and Tremblay, had suggested to the Prime Minister that bringing this case into the open would be a way to get back at him. While I knew nothing about the details of the case referred to, I remember saying that we had not entered politics to engage in sordid tactics of that kind and that we should not even think of doing such a thing. I remember being quite indignant about the suggestion. But, while I could not condone it, I could understand the feelings of Lucien Cardin and some of the other Quebec ministers. They had watched Diefenbaker destroy one after another of their colleagues. Cardin was the current target, and he decided to fight back with any weapons he could lay his hands on.

The result was another judicial inquiry, this time by Mr. Justice Wishart Spence of the Supreme Court of Canada. The newspapers had a field day, especially when Gerda Munsinger, who was said to have died some time before, was discovered by Robert Reguly of *The Toronto Star* in Munich very much alive and kicking. The same Reguly had discovered Harold Banks on the New York waterfront in 1964 after he had skipped his bail in Montreal.

While Mr. Justice Spence censured Diefenbaker in his report, no more damage was done to him in the eyes of the public than was done to the Liberal Party for resurrecting an incident that had occurred several years before. It was looked upon as dirty politics and was not appreciated by the public even though they seemed to enjoy all the salacious details of what had happened.

It was rumoured, for example, that another ex-cabinet minister had also got to know the lady rather well, but it turned out he had only taken her to lunch on two occasions. Gene Whelan, the Liberal Member for Essex South, came back to Ottawa one Monday after spending the weekend at his home in Amherstburg to report he had been talking about this to two die-hard Tory farmers. They said they had always favoured the ex-cabinet minister in question as the successor to Mr. Diefenbaker. "But not no more. Any man who would spend money giving lunch to that kind of woman, and couldn't get no farther, don't deserve to be Prime Minister of Canada!"

Twenty thousand copies of my book, *A Choice for Canada*, subtitled "Independence or Colonial Status," were published in May 1966 and it created quite a stir. One chapter of the book discusses foreign policy in a somewhat cautious fashion. In the light of later controversies, however, my views about the war in Vietnam and about Canadian defence policy are relevant. I suggested that Canadians should do everything within their power to help the Americans extricate themselves from their predicament in Vietnam before it was too late. We should do everything possible to mobilize world opinion to stop the escalation of the war. "Canada should not hesitate to express her concern over what is happening in Vietnam. . . . This is one of the occasions when Canada should be prepared to risk the displeasure of the United States by speaking out, if there is any chance that our speaking out would do some good."

I wrote that "Canada's defence policy should flow naturally and logically from the foreign policy that she adopts." At one time it could be argued that having a reasonably large and well-equipped defence force

REPRINTED WITH PERMISSION THE TORONTO STAR

helped us to retain our independence. But times have changed and if this argument had any validity in the past, I argued, it had none any longer. With the overwhelming power of nuclear missiles concentrated in the hands of the United States and the Soviet Union, the size of our armed forces becomes somewhat redundant. My view was that we should continue to fulfil what should be a declining role in NATO; we should make a useful contribution to NORAD, if this is possible; and we should have available for peace-keeping purposes a hard hitting well-equipped mobile force that is ready to go anywhere at the United Nations' bidding. In concluding these views about defence policy, I expressed the hope that "in the kind of world we live in, we should be able to look forward to some gradual reduction rather than an increase in our defence forces and defence expenditures."

In discussing Canada's balance of payments and the ways in which we had been financing our huge deficits on current account with the United States, my book asserted that, in the past, it was sensible for Canada to "borrow" foreign capital in order to speed the development of the economy. It would be sensible for us to continue to do this in the future but, ideally, to a somewhat lesser extent. I pointed out that the United States did this in the nineteenth century. It imported capital in those days in the form of borrowings which it was able to repay out of future earnings. In this context, "future earnings" means a surplus of merchandise exports over merchandise imports less all the "invisible" items, including interest charges on past borrowings. Canadians are far from this position. "We cannot even earn enough on our merchandise trade (exports minus imports) to pay the interest charges on past borrowings. It will be a long time before we can hope to earn enough to begin repaying the borrowings themselves."

In *A Choice for Canada,* I made some suggestions about what might be done about foreign control of our industries and resources and about our balance of payments situation. I recalled that there were those who saw no problem in the snowballing of foreign investment in Canada, even if it led eventually to economic union with the United States. I contended that "this would be a disaster for Canada, that in such circumstances most of the industrial expansion needed would take place south of the border, and that hundreds of thousands of young Canadians would be forced to seek employment in the United States. Inevitably, this would mean a reduction in the standard of living of many Canadians who stayed behind. This is what we must prevent."

On the broad question of foreign control of Canada's economy, I wrote that the public should expect politicians in all parties, and leaders in all fields, to state their positions. "The future of our country depends upon what we decide to do about it. It is my hope that our leaders and a great majority of Canadians in all provinces will decide our independence is worth fighting for."

Quite apart from my book, I had created a good deal of discussion within the party with a speech on May 7, 1966, during the course of the annual meeting of the Liberal Party of Ontario, in which I raised questions respecting the aims of the party and the direction in which it should go. After talking about the Tories and the N.D.P., I went on to say that it would seem the Liberal Party had three choices:

> One: We can adopt a cautious and conservative approach and try to compete with what may become a more united and potentially rejuvenated Conservative Party – a party which in the future may be expected to adopt more traditional attitudes and policies.
> Two: We can adopt deliberately and forthrightly a left of centre set of policies clearly stated and agreed to. I would include in this a firm determination to reverse the present trend towards ever-increasing foreign control of our economy – in other words, a firm determination to keep Canada free and independent.
> Three: The Liberal Party can waffle in between these two positions in the hope that by so doing, no one will be offended. This is what may happen if, as a party, we have not agreed upon what we stand for – or if we wish to try to be all things to all men.

I expressed the fear that the Liberal Party might adopt this third course, a waffling approach, without ever consciously realizing or admitting it was doing so. In my view this might prove fatal. I said it was quite true that sometimes in the past the Liberal Party had been ambivalent in its approaches, and sometimes with success. But now news travels with the speed of light and times have changed. I submitted that people were looking for direction, for clarity and for leadership. The Liberal Party would not be able to provide this if it were to take one line one day and an opposite line the next. I stated that I did not believe a waffling, indecisive Liberal Party would be able to compete successfully with the N.D.P. or with a reorganized Conservative Party under the kind of leadership that would be available when Mr. Diefenbaker retired. I did not believe a Liberal Party that was unsure about its course and indefinite about its policies could attract and hold the support of people under forty who were looking for new ideas and new approaches. Nor did I believe the Liberal Party could survive by adopting a clearly conservative approach. This could be done more naturally by a reorganized Conservative Party under traditional Tory leadership. I recalled that such attitudes of mind had not worked with the Liberal Party in the 1950s. They had led to the defeat in 1957, which some of us had predicted several years before. "Such attitudes of mind – negative, cautious, indecisive – would have the same result again."

> Canadians are crying out these days for leadership. By this I mean they are seeking fresh and clear ideas and a firm program for making the most of the tremendous future that can be ours in Canada. . . . The Liberal Party has always stood and must always stand for an enlightened and independent "Canadianism" in the best sense of that term. Today this means policies, measures and approaches designed to safeguard the independence of our country. If we do not take a stand on this, it will be too late for the Liberal Party or any other party to do anything very much for Canada.

Despite the fact I was no longer a member of the cabinet, Mike Pearson spoke to me on several occasions during the winter of 1966 about who would be best qualified to succeed him as leader of the Liberal Party. He said if I were interested he would do what he could to help me. Nothing conclusive was decided, but on June 9 he asked me to lunch, during the course of which he invited me to rejoin the cabinet as Minister of Transport. I said I was not interested in a heavy administrative job like transport which would tie me down. My interest was in the formulation and implementation of broad policy. But quite apart from that, I pointed out that my return to the cabinet would have much wider implications which we then proceeded to discuss.

I said the first issue was the whole question of policy, and reminded Pearson that I had just written a book, *A Choice for Canada*. He said he agreed with the views expressed in the book, although he would favour some broad international arrangement with regard to trade if this ever became practicable. I reminded him that he had agreed with my views in the summer of 1960, before I had decided to enter politics. I said that the issues I believed in would have to be threshed out before I could seriously consider returning to the cabinet.

The second major issue was the succession. I reminded Pearson that two months or so previously he had asked me if I was interested in the leadership because, if so, he could help me. I said I had not taken him up on this because I did not think he had thought it through and I did not know whether I wanted it. I said I could think of many reasons why I was not suited for the job. At the same time, I did not think certain cabinet ministers who were aspirants for the leadership were suited either.

I suggested to Pearson that, if I returned to the cabinet, it would be interpreted to mean that I would seek the leadership on his retirement and that he thought I was the best man for it. Pearson had not thought about this, although he agreed I was quite right. In these circumstances I said both of us should do some heavy thinking, following which we should meet again with enough time to talk things through.

We agreed to have dinner together on the following Tuesday, June 14. When we met, Pearson said he realized now that if I returned to the cabinet in any capacity it would be interpreted to mean he thought I was the logical man to succeed him. He promised to think things through and to get in touch with me by the end of July. I did not hear from him again.

For a period of about six months I had given considerable thought to going after the leadership when the Prime Minister retired. Most politicians probably do the same thing at one time or another. But I did not do anything about it. My friends in the party insisted that if I wanted the leadership I should stop talking about such controversial subjects as the increasing foreign ownership of Canadian resources and Canadian business enterprises. I agreed that their advice was good but I was not prepared to accept it. I felt too keenly about the foreign ownership question to let it drop.

Moreover, I believed very seriously that in the best interests of the country, as well as of the Liberal Party, the next leader should be a French Canadian, if one could be found who was qualified and whose reputation had not been compromised in the public mind. I felt also that, if possible, the next leader should be in his forties or early fifties. I was sixty years of age, which is too old to take on the toughest job the nation has to offer. While I did not believe that any of the principal candidates being talked about – Martin, Hellyer, Winters, Sharp – were what was wanted, I kept hoping that someone else would turn up in time.

Quite apart from the question of the leadership, I had grown increasingly out of sympathy with the change in emphasis of the government's financial and economic policies. I was not enjoying life in Ottawa where I had little to do, and by the middle of the summer had concluded that my best course was to give up my seat and retire from politics. I did not think I should do this before the end of the year, however, and decided that before then I would give voice to my opinions both in a series of speeches in September and at the Liberal convention in October.

Ross Thatcher, the Premier of Saskatchewan, had decided to organize a meeting of more or less hand-picked Liberals from the Western provinces to decide on the line of policy the West should plump for at the National Liberal Conference in October. Thatcher had been a CCF'er, but some years previously had proclaimed himself a Liberal and soon afterwards was chosen as the leader of the party in his province. I had refused to go along with his importunities when I was Minister of Finance, which had incensed him. And he was bitterly opposed to the policies I had advocated in my book *A Choice for Canada*. He accused me publicly of being "the most dangerous socialist in Canada."

His meeting was held in Saskatoon on Friday and Saturday, August 12-13. It so happened that I had been invited to address the Saskatoon Rotary Club on Monday, August 15. I had accepted the invitation which I thought would be a good preliminary to my speech-making tour of Western Canada. Also, I thought if I arrived in Saskatoon on the Sunday afternoon, I would have an excellent opportunity to comment on the resolutions passed at the Thatcher conference.

But when Thatcher heard I was to speak to the Saskatoon Rotary Club, he gave instructions that the invitation should be withdrawn, and this was done. No contrary views were to be expressed in Saskatchewan while the reactionary-minded Premier remained the boss there. Joey Smallwood had done exactly the same thing a few years earlier, when Donald Fleming turned up to address the Rotary Club in St. John's. Thatcher was smarter. He did not wait until the meeting was in progress, so there was no bad publicity to worry about.

I began my tour in the fall of 1966 with a speech to the Women's Canadian Club in Edmonton on September 13. I spoke about *A Choice for Canada,* and the criticisms of it. I said I was well aware that there were people who did not believe it mattered who owned Canadian resources and businesses, or that a very high degree of foreign control of Canadian resources influenced in any way Canadian government policies or Canada's independence, economic or political. These people were sincere in their opinions. But, based on thirty years' experience in professional practice and in business and some experience in government, I was convinced that they were wrong.

I said that in my book I had given a number of examples in support of my conviction. But it was not the kind of question that could be proved empirically to everyone's satisfaction. I did not believe it needed to be, since most people realized what was going on and could see the takeover of Canadian resources taking place. They could feel it and could sense its implications. There would not be so much interest in this issue – and the mail I was receiving, the space given to it in the press, and the time devoted to it on the air attested to this interest – unless a great many Canadians were seriously concerned about it.

Later that evening I spoke to a Liberal Party meeting in Calgary which was well attended. The question period went on for a long time, and before leaving to spend the night with Muriel and Harry Hays, I had confirmed the fact that there were fewer Liberals in Calgary who shared my views than there were in Edmonton or in British Columbia.

246

While I continued to stress the independence issue throughout my tour, I also raised some other questions. In a speech to the Canadian Clubs of Port Arthur and Fort William, I talked about inflation and the importance in any attempt to deal with it of not bringing on or aggravating a downturn in the economy. While I had taken pains in drafting this speech to point out both sides of the dilemma with which the government was confronted, it was interpreted in the press as an attack on Mitchell Sharp, especially over the Medicare issue, and to an extent, upon the government. There was some truth in this:

> Quite frankly, I am not happy about the decision to postpone Medicare. The argument that Medicare should be put off in order to combat inflation will not stand up upon reflection. On the other hand, the decision is being hailed as a great victory by those who are opposed to Medicare in any form at any time. I believe Parliament should proceed with the Medicare legislation this fall and be prepared to implement it as soon as it has been accepted by a number of provinces representing a majority of the population – or some alternative along these lines. If a majority of the provincial governments are not prepared to go ahead with Medicare – perhaps because they feel their electors are not prepared to pay for it – quite obviously it cannot, and should not be forced upon them. But after all that has been said about Medicare in the last few years – including the clear intimation it would be proceeded with this fall – it seems to me the onus should be placed squarely on the provincial governments if it is to be deferred. . . .
>
> Moreover, the government has been accused of adding to the inflationary pressures by acquiescing in some degree to labour's high wage demands. Whether this accusation is fair or not is beyond the point. There is much that is not fair in politics. The fact is that the public seems to think the government was responsible for certain very generous wage settlements this spring and summer which set a pattern, more or less, for wage negotiations everywhere.

The wage settlements referred to were those with the Seaway operators in Montreal and the Montreal longshoremen. The Seaway operators were granted a twenty per cent increase retroactive to January 1, 1966, and an additional ten per cent in January 1967. The longshoremen received an increase of forty cents an hour retroactive to January 1, 1966, plus an additional fifteen cents an hour on January 1, 1967, and a further twenty-five cents an hour on May 1, 1967.

The next day in Sudbury, I spoke about the role of the central government but also mentioned Medicare and the independence issue. Then after a ten-day break in Toronto and Ottawa, I visited the West Coast where I spoke to the students at Simon Fraser University, the University of British Columbia, and the University of Victoria. On my return I spoke to a meeting of students at the University of Toronto on October 6. I concluded my speech to them with these words:

> We can drift into a kind of colonial or satellite status without protest or complaint. That is what is happening now. But if the members of your generation and the generation ahead of you prefer to have something to say about the future of our great country – if you want to share in its development – if you want an exciting life with plenty of adventure – if you are not afraid of taking the kind of responsibility that goes with the power to make decisions – then I say to you . . . let the people in Ottawa know how you feel and what you want.
>
> Let me amplify that statement. I would like to see four or five hundred of you go to the Liberal Party convention in Ottawa next week – and tell the Liberal politicians what kind of Canada you want. Believe me, it would make quite a sensation if you did.

In addition to these prepared addresses, I spoke to meetings of local Liberals, answered questions, gave press conferences, appeared on television, and participated in some open-line radio programs. As a result, my tour and the views I was expressing were well publicized not only in the places I visited but throughout the country.

There had been a strenuous debate about Medicare in caucus. Mitchell Sharp had submitted that the proposal should be indefinitely postponed in an effort to combat inflation. Maurice Lamontagne and I had argued that this was blatant nonsense. The program would create some budgetary difficulties but it was not inflationary. We reminded Sharp that it had always been understood that new taxes would have to be levied to pay for this important program. But we pointed out that this problem, if it were one, was not something that was immediate. We said the Medicare legislation should be passed by Parliament effective July 1, 1967, as had been promised, but like the hospital insurance plan before it, the legislation should not become operative until a majority of the provinces representing a majority of the population had approved it. Obviously this would take some time. The caucus was strongly behind Maurice and me on this issue which placed the government in something of a spot, especially as Sharp had been making statements to the press, and someone had leaked what had been going on in caucus.

In the end, the government decided to go ahead with the Medicare legislation, but to make it effective on July 1, 1968, instead of 1967. This was the worst possible solution. Instead of becoming effective on July 1, 1967, the anniversary of Confederation, but not operative until approved by a majority of the provinces, it was to become effective one year later automatically in those provinces that approved it. While the legislation was passed in this form, Sharp, right up to the end of the Pearson government, continued to oppose the scheme for one reason or another and to advocate amendments to it or a further deferral of its implementation.

Some time during the summer, I had talked to my friend Andrew Thompson, the Leader of the Liberal Party in Ontario, about the National Liberal Convention to be held in Ottawa on October 10-12. Thompson agreed with my views about Medicare and the independence issue and said there was a lot of support for my position throughout Ontario. He promised to line up delegates to the convention from the province who were sympathetic to my views and would be prepared to back me. Unfortunately, although I did not know about it, Andy became seriously ill and was not able to organize the Ontario delegates as he had intended. He came to the convention against his doctor's orders, and made a valiant effort, but by that time it was too late to compete with the bloc from Western Canada.

On August 12, Western Liberals had met in Saskatoon to draft a united approach to the development of new federal policies. At the Saskatoon conference, they went on record in support of attracting more foreign capital, a North American free-trade area, and larger oil exports to the United States. Two resolutions endorsing the Canada Development Corporation were killed in committee. Although the Liberal Party in Western Canada had been able to win a total of only six of 192 Prairie seats in four previous federal elections, the 460 Western delegates came to the October policy conference in Ottawa determined, as *The Winnipeg Free Press* put it, that "the West's voice will be heard and heeded."

At the October conference, Andy Thompson led the attack on the government's decision to postpone Medicare, pointing out that the Liberal Party had a solemn commitment to begin it by July 1967. Sharp defended the decision claiming it would seriously undermine the position of the country and the budgetary position of the government. Eventually a compromise resolution was agreed on which regretted the cabinet's decision but affirmed the determination to go ahead with Medicare not later than July 1, 1968.

Meanwhile, the Western delegates led by Ray Perrault of British Columbia and Gil Molgat of Manitoba had begun to flex their muscles. Carefully organized and voting in a bloc, they rammed through a resolution in favour of a North American free-trade area. Subsequently, both the Prime Minister and Sharp threw cold water on the idea and made it clear they would not be bound by it.

I did not speak on either the free-trade resolution or Medicare, since I was holding my fire for the debate on foreign investment and the issue of Canadian independence. In May, at the time of publication of *A Choice for Canada,* Sharp had claimed that he held more or less the same views on the independence issue as I did. He desired a sovereign Canada and recognized that political sovereignty implied a larger measure of economic independence than Canada possessed. But by October he had reversed his stand on the desirability of controlling foreign investment in Canada. Under these circumstances the press billed the policy conference as a confrontation between Sharp and Gordon.

When the issue of foreign investment came before a workshop group on Tuesday, October 10, Western delegates rejected a proposal calling for measures to be taken to reverse the trend towards foreign ownership and control in Canada, and substituted the resolution on foreign investment they had adopted in Saskatoon. When the issue was raised in plenary session, Donald Macdonald, who was acting as a kind of floor manager on my behalf, ran into procedural difficulties. The issue provoked a heated debate which I, among others, felt could be damaging to the party. Accordingly, it was arranged that about thirty delegates representing both sides of the question should meet in the evening under the chairmanship of Maurice Lamontagne to work out a compromise.

The compromise suggested included nearly all the points that Macdonald and I had been putting forward. Sharp agreed to this and suggested that he move the compromise resolution with me as seconder. The object was to arrive at something that everyone could go along with and, since the resolution covered ninety per cent of what I had been asking for, I thought this would be quite satisfactory. However, after Sharp had made his proposal, Mike McCabe, his Executive Assistant, shouted: "You should not move that resolution, Mr. Minister." Nevertheless, both Lamontagne and I were left with the clear impression that Mitchell agreed with the comprehensive resolution even though, on Mike McCabe's advice, he decided not to move it.

But once again there was a procedural debate, and the various points were put through in a piecemeal fashion, instead of in the form of a comprehensive resolution as had been agreed to. The Sharp forces managed to persuade the press that this was a great victory for Mitchell and a devastating defeat for me. And this was the way the press played it.

The press generally agreed that Sharp had emerged as the strong man of the Liberal Party and, hence, as a major contender to succeed Pearson. But a poll of 150 delegates at the end of the conference named Paul Hellyer, who had not been particularly prominent during the discussions, as the man most likely to win the leadership when the time came. Although the press generally lauded the rank-and-file participation in the process of policy making, some were less than entranced by the failure of the conference to chart a new course for the Liberal Party. *The Toronto Star,* for example, had its expectations of bold policies dashed. "We were hoping for a new vision of Liberalism which would inspire Canadians in the years ahead. All that emerged was a dull grey ghost of a once-great party."

I was not particularly concerned about the outcome of the conference in any personal sense, as I was planning to get out of politics completely before the year was over.

I made one more public speech in 1966 to the Advertising and Sales Club of Toronto on October 25. This was a commitment I had made some time previously and I used the occasion to talk about a free-trade area with the United States. I began by stating that there were a great many English-speaking Canadians who expected Canada to become part of the United States in the not too distant future. These persons believed that absorption or integration of Canada by the United States was inevitable and we should get it over with as soon as possible. Included among those holding such views were some members of the financial fraternity and many business leaders, some of whom, when scratched, turned out to be Americans or Canadians who worked for American concerns. Certain newspaper proprietors also held these views.

I pointed out that there were those who were in favour of a North American free-trade area, in spite of the fact that, if implemented, this proposition would almost certainly result in some kind of merger with the United States. "We would be foolish," I said, "to sacrifice our economic independence – and complete free trade with the United States would mean just that – without, at the same time, working out the terms of political union." The concept of free trade with our southern neighbour appealed particularly to people in the West and in the Atlantic provinces. It was supported by the Canadian-American Committee, by some university economists, and probably by some of the members of the Economic Council of Canada, powerful groups whose influence is persistent and pervasive. These people argued that, if implemented over a period of years, the disrupting effects of free trade with the United States would be mitigated at least to some extent. There were others, however, who feared that the net result in the long run would be much the same.

The last time there had been a strong push in Canada for free trade with the United States was in 1947. The negotiations were said to have been carried out in secret by a small group of civil servants headed by John Deutsch reporting directly to the Prime Minister. No hint of what was going on was given to the public. Apparently the negotiations were proceeding well when Mr. King, perhaps recalling what happened to Sir Wilfrid Laurier in the reciprocity election of 1911, decided to call the whole thing off. "Let us hope," I said, "that, once again, it will be realized in time that while most intimate relationships have a pleasant and useful part to play in life, the complete integration of the lives and working habits of two animals so different in size and character as an elephant and a mouse – or, if you will, a beaver – would not be likely to work out to the best advantage of the beaver."

I suggested that sooner or later Canadians would have to choose whether they wanted to make more of the decisions that affected their lives, even if this meant taking the kind of positive action many people shrank from. "I do not believe," I declared, "this decision can be put off much longer." I reminded the audience that half the eligible voters in the next election would be under thirty-five years of age and the younger generation should be more concerned with the outcome than my own. "I urge all of you," I concluded, "but especially those in the younger age groups, to study these questions carefully, to resolve your choice for Canada, and having done so, to let your Members of Parliament and the members of the government know what your wishes are."

CHAPTER FOURTEEN

Return to the Cabinet

Terms on which I rejoined the government; return was a mistake; a divided cabinet; ways in which cabinets can function effectively; establishing the Watkins Task Force; the Mercantile Bank affair; correspondence with the Prime Minister about my position; contemplated resignation and reasons for its deferment.

By the end of October 1966, it began to get about that I was intending to retire from politics at the end of the year, and pressures were put upon me not to do so. The members of the Ontario caucus invited me to a "surprise" dinner on November 9 (which Keith Davey warned me about beforehand). It was an emotional affair, with many references to what I had done in helping to reorganize the party and with the members urging me not to resign my seat in Parliament.

In replying to the speeches at the dinner, after thanking those present for their concern and friendly feelings, I warned them of my fears about the future for the Liberal Party, especially in Ontario. This was along the lines of my speech at the annual meeting of the Liberal Party of Ontario six months previously. The majority of those present seemed to agree with me.

I spent very little time in Ottawa during the remainder of the year. I heard by the grapevine that members of the caucus were urging Pearson to recall me to the cabinet but, quite frankly, I was in two minds about this. I had had my fill of Ottawa and politics. I did not agree with the views of Mitchell Sharp or with the way he went about things. And it was clear that Pearson would be relieved if I were off the scene. But I was flattered by the anxiety of my friends and by the extent of the following I seemed to have within the party. Moreover, I was loath to give up on the independence issue if there were still a chance to do something about it.

Towards the end of November the Prime Minister called me on the telephone. He referred to the lobbying by most of the members of the Ontario caucus to persuade him to persuade me not to resign my seat, and invited me to come to Ottawa to have lunch with him on November 30 to talk things over. I did so and he made it clear that despite the importunities of the Ontario Members he was not going to ask me to rejoin the cabinet. One paragraph of my notes of our conversation reads as follows:

> He said that when we talked last spring he had hoped I would return to the cabinet in the fall. However, while he did not disagree with the speeches I made this fall, in view of the way they were played up in the press, he could not ask me to return to the cabinet in which Sharp is a member! I emphasized I was not asking to go back to the cabinet or for anything else. Mike agreed.

I presumed this was the end of the matter, but Maurice Lamontagne telephoned me on December 15 to say that at a party the night before, in the hearing of four reporters, Pearson had asked Lamontagne when he was going to come back to the cabinet. Maurice said he intended to press Benson, Marchand, and MacEachen to urge Pearson to invite me back at the same time.

Benson also called to say he intended to speak to the Prime Minister who, he suspected, had no realization of the political implications of my forthcoming resignation from Parliament. He said he did not see any real difficulty in my returning to the cabinet in any position insofar as issues were concerned. I explained it was not my ambition in life to return to the cabinet and that I intended to give up my seat between Christmas and New Year's.

Benson called me again a few days later, after seeing the Prime Minister, and Keith Davey came to see me. Both of them said Pearson would now like me back as a Minister without Portfolio to take responsibility, among other things, for organizing the work of the cabinet which was in something of a mess. Davey reported that Pearson had said that if I took on the things he had in mind, I would, in reality, be a sort of Deputy Prime Minister. This interested me, but I told him and also Benson that I would not even consider such a proposal unless the government was prepared to move on the independence issue. Pearson called me the next day; he said he was very keen that I should return to the cabinet; he asked me to give him an opportunity to talk to me about it before I took any step that would be irrevocable. I agreed to see him in Ottawa on December 29, but after what he had said to me when I had last seen him on November 30, I did not expect anything would come of it. So I made plans to give up my seat. This involved preparing a formal letter to the Speaker and a long letter, originally dated December 29, 1966, to Lex Thomson, the President of the Davenport Liberal Association.* Neither letter was sent, but the draft of

*See Appendix 5.

my letter to Thomson set out my feelings at the time. I pointed out that the main issues which had influenced me to enter politics were: the high level of unemployment; the need for new and amplified measures of social security; and the need for policies to counter the excessive foreign control over the Canadian economy and resources if Canada was to avoid a satellite status. Much had been done in the first two areas. Unemployment had been greatly reduced and social security coverage had been increased by the Canada Pension Plan, the Canada Assistance Act, increased old-age pensions, student loans, a national labour code, and Medicare would become effective July 1, 1968. However, I felt that the government's approach to the foreign investment issue was neither positive nor consistent with election statements, and in my present position there was nothing I could do about it.

I said that, in these circumstances, I had decided I should not in good conscience continue to sit in the House. While Pearson had invited me to become a Minister without Portfolio, I could not be a member of a cabinet which was not prepared to act on the foreign control issue, and I had advised him to this effect.

Much to my surprise the meeting with the Prime Minister on December 29 went quite differently than I had expected. While Pearson had made it clear in our previous conversations that he did not want me back in the cabinet because, among other things, it would cause trouble with those ministers who were conservatively inclined, he had apparently concluded that he would be in even worse trouble with the Ontario members of the caucus and other elements in the party if I were to give up my seat. In any event, we had a good discussion over a long luncheon. He said he would like me to organize the work of the cabinet and to help with the business of the party. Part of the notes I made of our conversation are reproduced here:

> I said if I went back to the cabinet (and I repeated several times my present plan is to resign) it would be interpreted to mean:
> (a) The government was concerned about the foreign control issue and was prepared to do something about it; and
> (b) Mike as leader of the party was ready to acknowledge the unhappiness of the "progressive wing" of the party.
>
> I added I was surprised at the number – and types – of people who were urging me not to resign and said I presumed they were writing to him also. He agreed.
>
> I mentioned my "White Paper" idea [on the independence issue]. He was intrigued and asked me to give him a memo on it. I promised to do so.

I said there were many questions to settle before I could consider rejoining the cabinet and that I would not come back in a junior post, *i.e.*, Minister without Portfolio because this would defeat the very impression he wants to create. . . .

I reminded Mike that at one of our last meetings he had said he could not ask me to rejoin the cabinet with Sharp there. He said he thought things had changed. (I presume he meant my position in the party is stronger than he thought.) I said everything would have to be ironed out with Sharp; that I was not prepared for any more conflict. . . .

It was agreed that I should give the Prime Minister a memorandum outlining my ideas for a White Paper on the independence issue and that I should talk to him again on January 3, after he had had a chance to consider it and go over it with Sharp. In the interval, I was to consider carefully the various responsibilities I was being asked to undertake. These included:

(a) General supervision of the work of the cabinet;
(b) Membership on a ministerial committee consisting of Marchand, Sharp, the House Leader (MacEachen), and possibly the Deputy House Leader (Pennell) and myself, which would meet daily to plan and organize government business and the business of the House;
(c) Improved public relations and communications;
(d) Liaison between cabinet and caucus;
(e) Liaison between cabinet and the National Liberal Federation;
(f) Chairman of a group of representatives from the cabinet, caucus and the Federation to plan the long-term policies of the Liberal Party.

The intention was that I should be responsible for organizing the work of the cabinet, the work of the House (as a member of a small ministerial committee), and the work of the Liberal Party organization. Taken together, these were important responsibilities and I became intrigued with the idea of returning to the government on these terms.

In addition to the responsibilities enumerated by the Prime Minister, I had stipulated that I should be chairman of a ministerial committee responsible for drafting a White Paper on the independence issue.

I recognized, of course, that I was being invited to rejoin the cabinet because of my following within the party and not because the Prime Minister wanted me to come back. Pearson knew that I disagreed with Sharp's policies, and particularly with his lukewarm attitude on the independence issue. And as Pearson had made very clear to me on November 30, the last thing he wanted in the closing year of his leadership was any kind of controversy within the cabinet. While I had a strong feeling of obligation to my supporters in the party, and while I felt keenly about the importance of doing something about the independence issue, this was the time for me to get out of Parliament if I was not going to rejoin the government on suitable terms. I was no more anxious than Pearson was to get involved in controversy with Sharp or anyone else. And so I believed it was imperative to get things settled and confirmed in writing if I was to go back.

Pearson called in Benson, Pennell, and MacEachen to act as go-betweens. Because of the situation in the cabinet and the personalities involved, they persuaded me to accept the position of Minister without Portfolio until the end of January, when Guy Favreau was to resign and I would become President of the Privy Council. They approved a draft of a letter which I had prepared for the Prime Minister to write me, setting out the terms on which he had suggested I should rejoin the government. These included the various responsibilities referred to above, together with the chairmanship of a small ministerial committee to review the structure of industry in Canada with reference to the independence issue.*

I had lunch with Pearson on January 3, and, according to my notes, "I gave him my draft letter which he said was quite satisfactory." He gave the same assurance to Benson the next day according to a handwritten note I made on my copy of the draft: "Before joining Mike in a press conference today, Benson advised me that Mike had approved this draft and would send me a signed letter in these terms tomorrow. W.L.G. 4/1/67."

I discussed a number of things with Pearson at the luncheon meeting on January 3, including the importance of having a talk with Sharp in order "to avoid any possibility of conflict in the future." The three of us got together at 5:00 P.M. that day at Sussex Drive. Sharp said he was very much in favour of my returning to the cabinet, which he thought would be "good politics." I replied that we were meeting to make sure that if I did return there would not be areas of conflict between us. We started in to discuss the banking legislation, and I said that, while I disagreed with the proposals respecting the interest rate, I acknowledged this was now a *fait accompli* for all practical purposes, as Sharp's revised bill had been presented to Parliament the previous July. I said I assumed from what I had read that there would be no compromising on the subject of the Mercantile Bank. Pearson and Sharp agreed this was a correct assumption.

I then brought up the question of agencies of foreign banks. Sharp said that he had announced in the House that he would be receptive to any recommendations of the banking committee in regard to this. I said I could

*See Appendix 6.

not go along with this. Pearson said this would mean a retreat and gave the impression that he was completely sympathetic to my view. I asked Sharp about developments in the field of security legislation and was satisfied with what he told me. I said I presumed there would be opportunities to discuss budget proposals ahead of time, and he agreed.

We then went on to discuss the importance of agreement between Sharp and myself if I returned to the cabinet and I said the way to ensure this was for Sharp and me to talk things over in advance. After we left the house, Sharp continued to talk about the importance of our not disagreeing in public on any points of policy. I repeated that the answer to the latter problem was for us to make up our minds to see something of each other and to discuss things ahead of time.

Sharp then said that he thought he should inform me that he had advised his supporters that he would stand for the leadership. I said that while the Prime Minister had told him that I did not intend to run again, nothing was certain in politics and that I hoped the party would arrive at some kind of consensus about Pearson's successor before the time came. I made it clear that while my present intention was not to run again, this would depend upon circumstances.

The next day, January 4, there was a good deal of backing and filling, with Benson, Pennell, and MacEachen continuing to act as go-betweens. While the Prime Minister repeated both to me and again to Benson that he was in full agreement with the draft letter of January 3 setting out what my responsibilities were to be, he did not want to make the letter public. He said he did not wish to give any indication that I had been in disagreement with government policy on the foreign control issue up to that time. I thought this was understandable enough from the Prime Minister's point of view although, in retrospect, I should have insisted that the letter be made public there and then.

Pearson and I had lunch together again on January 4, and according to my notes:

We referred to the previous evening's conversation with Sharp. I said I felt it was inevitable that Sharp and I would find ourselves in disagreement from time to time about government policy; that he [Sharp], instinctively and understandably, takes the civil service approach while I am inclined to question the conventional wisdom of the Ottawa establishment. . . .

I said that of the matters discussed last night there were two things which should be faced up to. First and most important is the question of permitting agencies of foreign banks to locate in Canada. I said that really this was something that Mike would have to handle himself, but that I would [supply him with] a memorandum privately which I hoped would give some of the reasons why this would be undesirable. I also mentioned that it would be a simple matter to get Herb Gray, the Chairman of the Committee, not to bring forward any recommendations on this matter. . . .

I said the second question, and one of much greater importance, was the proposed White Paper, because there is no doubt in my mind that Sharp and I are not in agreement on this question of foreign control. I reminded him that I feel deeply about this question and that it is only because we had agreed to issue a White Paper on it that I was willing to come back to the cabinet. I did not want there to be any misunderstanding about the strength of my feelings on this issue. . . .

It seemed evident to me – and also I believe to Benson, Pennell, and Mac-Eachen – that if I was going to be President of the Privy Council, responsible for the work of the cabinet, for liaison with the party's political apparatus, and for the various other matters referred to in the draft letter of January 3, 1967, and if at the same time I was to work closely with the Prime Minister, I would be a Deputy Prime Minister in all but name. According to my notes, this is how Pearson had described the position I was to fill to Keith Davey before Davey came to see me on his behalf on December 20. It was on this assumption that I rejoined the cabinet.

The Prime Minister and I attended a press conference together at 4.30 P.M., January 4, when he announced my return to the government. Naturally enough, the reporters asked questions respecting possible differences of opinion between me and other members of the cabinet, especially on the independence issue. This part of the transcript reads as follows:

QUESTION: Sir, Mr. Gordon, unlike other Cabinet Ministers, has written a book in which he said –

THE PRIME MINISTER: I've written two books. Nobody ever paid any attention to my books. Nobody would even buy one!

QUESTION: In the book he sets out some specific feelings that he had about government policy. Are we to assume that his rejoining the cabinet outdates those policies in the mind of the government itself?

THE PRIME MINISTER: Mr. Gordon has expressed quite clearly in his book his views about national policies and Mr. Gordon and I and Mr. Sharp talked about national policies last night and we find, as indeed we found ourselves when we previously worked in the Government, in very close accord in regard to Canadian national policy.

QUESTION: Mr. Prime Minister, at the Liberal Meeting there was much made on the so-called confrontation between Mr. Sharp and Mr. Gordon. Has this matter –

THE PRIME MINISTER: There was much made by you – by you I mean in the generic sense. I can only repeat, Mr. Gordon and Mr. Sharp worked together in the cabinet for quite a long time with me and we got on pretty well together.

QUESTION: Sir, do you plan to provide any more work for any other out-of-job cabinet ministers?

THE PRIME MINISTER: That is a leading question which I refuse to follow.

QUESTION: We ask Mr. Gordon if it is true ... that he would resign from Parliament if he did not come back into the cabinet.

THE PRIME MINISTER: Do you want him to answer that?

MR. GORDON: I was considering resigning. I feel very strongly on this question of greater control of the Canadian economy. I have talked to the Prime Minister and Mr. Sharp and I think we are in complete agreement as to the best approach to this very thorny problem. There is no difference between us. I think this is fair. We had a long discussion on this. I am just delighted about the general approach that the government is going to follow and it will be announced at the appropriate time. This is not the time to do it. I am just delighted about it.

QUESTION: Your return then does coincide with a policy change or that's what it amounts to –

THE PRIME MINISTER: No, it doesn't. We have never, as a government, felt that the policies for the maximum Canadian control of Canadian economic development and Canadian resources should not be a primary objective of Canadian government policy. We've also felt – and Mr. Gordon has felt this – that this kind of thing has to be reconciled with the need for Canadian capital and indeed foreign capital for Canadian development. These are the things we have to reconcile.

MR. GORDON: If I might just add this – if I did have any misgivings on this subject in recent months they have been cleared up by the conversations I have had with the Prime Minister and with other members of the Cabinet.

QUESTION: Mr. Prime Minister, is it fair to assume then that new specific proposals are in the offing?

THE PRIME MINISTER: We have quite a legislative program, some part of which deals with this vital issue. It is a vital issue. It is an issue of far-reaching importance. It is going to require, and is receiving, a great deal of study and examination and as a result of that examination, in due course, we will be announcing new measures, but that is not for the immediate weeks ahead. We have certain things we have to get through before prorogation of this particular session. The Canada Development Corporation is one item in this program we are going to proceed with. It has been on our legislative list now for some time and we hope to get it through as soon as we can.

The reporters must have called Sharp after the press conference, and apparently he denied that any new policies were contemplated in connection with the independence issue. This was interpreted as a conflict between him and myself before I had even got started. Some ministers, including Winters, McIlraith, and Connolly, who had not been informed in advance about my return to the cabinet, complained bitterly about it. And according to the grapevine, Sharp, who had been advised and had sat in on some of the discussions, was having second thoughts. Pearson, who hated any kind of disagreement, was unhappy and kept putting off telling the cabinet what he had asked me to do.

Sharp and I met with the Prime Minister at Sussex Drive at 8.30 P.M. on the evening of January 17 to discuss the revision of the Bank Act and particularly the question of agencies of foreign banks. Sharp said he was working on an amendment to prevent the Mercantile Bank from circumventing the proposed legislation. The main conversation was about the agency question. I was against allowing foreign banks to establish agencies in Canada. Sharp agreed that Rasminsky was not in favour of allowing agencies of foreign banks to establish in Canada, but implied Rasminsky did not feel this to be a major issue. I was left with the impression that Sharp would speak to Herb Gray, the Chairman of the Committee on Finance, Trade, and Economic Affairs and accept my advice in the matter.

Robert Winters joined us at 9:00 P.M. and we had a long discussion of the proposed review of the foreign control issue. Sharp and Winters made it clear they were opposed to the proposed review as they did not think the issue was important. They urged me to take on several big administrative jobs, including housing. I did not reply except to say I had not asked to come back to the cabinet. The Prime Minister had come to me at the last possible moment and invited me to do a number of things, including the chairmanship of a cabinet committee to look into the foreign control issue. I added that Sharp had been present during the discussion. Winters told me after the meeting that he might have to resign. I urged him not to. My notes of this meeting are included as an Appendix.*

Bob Winters, who was a pleasant, honest man, did not resign from the cabinet, but continued to be unhappy about the government he had joined following the 1965 election. I expect the main reason for his disenchantment was the general lack of organization and of control over the business of the cabinet. The improvement of this condition was one of the important responsibilities Pearson had asked me to undertake, but Winters did not know this. Bob and I had always got along well together, and some months later we agreed that even though we differed on policy matters there was no reason why we should not continue to be personal friends. We

*See Appendix 7.

went fishing together to cement the bargain.

Apart from everything else at this time, I was feeling very badly about Maurice Lamontagne. The Prime Minister had asked him to rejoin the cabinet and I had assumed he would be doing so at the same time as I did. However, some objections were raised, and at the last minute the invitation to Maurice was not proceeded with. Part of a letter dated January 4, 1967, which I wrote to Pearson about this, reads as follows:

> Maurice has a knowledge of economics and sometimes a useful scepticism of official thought that is not matched by anyone in the cabinet. He is an original thinker and his assistance would be invaluable in the work you have asked me to supervise in connection with a long-term program for the Liberal Party. I believe it was Maurice who suggested that this work should be undertaken in the first place.
>
> Maurice had hoped that at the appropriate time you would appoint him to the presidency of the Privy Council, the post that has been suggested for myself. I agree that this would be an appropriate post for me, given the various responsibilities you have asked me to assume. Nevertheless, I wish to make it perfectly clear that if another suitable portfolio cannot be found for Maurice, I would be more than willing to stand aside in his favour.
>
> The purpose of this note is to say how very seriously concerned I am about all this. Maurice has done a lot for you and for me over a long period of time. We must consider his feelings and his pride. . . .

By the end of January I was thoroughly sorry I had agreed to return to the cabinet. By that time I realized this had been a serious mistake. The various undertakings which Pearson had given to me and had confirmed in writing were not lived up to, and I became involved in a series of disagreements with Sharp, including the one over the Mercantile Bank, which I would have preferred to have avoided.

I soon found that there was a very different atmosphere in the cabinet I had rejoined in January 1967 from the one I had resigned from fourteen months previously. The leadership contenders – especially Martin, Hellyer, Sharp, and Winters – were openly vying for position and were distrustful of one another. There was no air of camaraderie or team spirit. Cabinet meetings were disorganized. There was little or no discipline, and the leaks from ministerial offices, one in particular, were damaging to the government and sometimes to individual cabinet colleagues. While Pearson continued to spend long hours in his office and was still as bright as ever when he addressed his mind to some particular issue, he was getting noticeably older, and his authority as a caretaker Prime Minister was often challenged.

I do not mean that discussions in cabinet were always acrimonious. Frequently we had a good deal of fun together. But it was harder to arrive at a consensus. On many issues it would seem that Sharp, Winters, Hellyer, Pickersgill, Laing, McIlraith, and Connolly would line up on one side, while Benson, Marchand, LaMarsh, Pennell, MacEachen, and I – and later, Trudeau, when he joined the cabinet in April – would find ourselves together on the other. The probable position of the other members of the cabinet, including that of the Prime Minister, was less certain.

Under our system of parliamentary government there are two alternative ways in which cabinets can function effectively. The first of these is for important policy initiatives to come from the Prime Minister, with the other ministers tending to accept them without much criticism or question. This means choosing ministers who have no strong views on policy issues and are content to accept the lead of the Prime Minister. The second approach is the formation of a cabinet in which the Prime Minister and the other principal ministers see eye-to-eye on most issues, at least in principle. This is the better of the two alternatives, in my opinion.

In the first Pearson government, there usually was a consensus among the more active ministers, and a great deal was accomplished. Those who adopted more negative attitudes were outnumbered. The trouble with the second Pearson government was that the cabinet received no firm lead from the Prime Minister, while there were wide differences of opinion on policy matters and in political philosophy among the members of the cabinet. Those who believed in change and a positive line of action and those who believed in maintaining the *status quo* were more or less evenly divided. Inevitably this gave the advantage to the ones in favour of the *status quo*. There was not the same fear of a defeat in Parliament as there had been prior to the 1965 election, but it was obvious the government was tired and on the whole was not responsive to new ideas or to proposals that called for change.

I had had considerable influence in the first Pearson government because of my standing in the party and my position as Minister of Finance. I had expected to have much the same position when I joined the new government. But as I have intimated, there was considerable opposition to my return by the conservative wing of the cabinet and their like-minded followers in the party, in the press, and in business circles. This upset the Prime Minister and his method of dealing with the situation was simply to avoid implementing his undertakings. Perhaps he felt his own position was not strong enough to permit him to do so, but if this was the case he never mentioned it to me. I had difficulty in getting him to

announce his intention of establishing a task force on the foreign investment issue which would report to a small cabinet committee with me as
chairman. Sharp, Marchand, Turner, and Roger Teillet were to be the
other members of the committee. Pearson had asked Winters to serve on
the committee, but he refused as he was opposed to the whole idea. Then
there was considerable discussion and argument about the composition of
the task force itself, which was resolved only when I agreed to include on it
any competent economist whom any member of the cabinet suggested.
This was done. Melville Watkins of the University of Toronto was
appointed to head the task force, the other members being Gideon Rosen-
bluth of the University of British Columbia; Ed Safarian, formerly of the
University of Saskatchewan but now with the University of Toronto;
Abraham Rotstein of the University of Toronto; Stephen Hymmer of Yale
University; Bernard Bonin of the University of Montreal; Claude Masson
of Laval University, and William Woodfine of St. Francis Xavier University. Fortunately, all eight members of the task force were good people and
they managed to submit a unanimous report. Nevertheless, some of the
ministers continued to be unhappy.

I had expected to be appointed President of the Privy Council by the end
of January 1967. But Guy Favreau was ill and no one, least of all myself,
wanted to disturb him in any way until he was appointed to the Quebec
Superior Court in April. The result was that I continued to be a Minister
without Portfolio until April 4 when I was sworn in as President of the
Privy Council. The Prime Minister did not inform the cabinet about any of
the other things he had asked me to do and none of them were ever implemented. Naturally I protested about this. A note of a conversation with the
Prime Minister on February 9, 1967, reads: "I said I would be back from
Jamaica on March 13 and would be asking Mike when I will be asked to
take on the other responsibilities discussed when I returned to the cabinet.
Mike said Favreau would be leaving by then – that I would be appointed
to the Privy Council – and that the rest would follow."

I raised the matter again several times, after my return from Jamaica
and the row over the Mercantile Bank matter had subsided. Finally on
April 27, I wrote the Prime Minister a formal letter. In it I referred to our
understanding that the Privy Council staff would be turned over to me "in
order to give me a base to work from," something that Gordon Robertson,
the Clerk of the Privy Council and Secretary to the Cabinet, was opposed
to. It was obvious to me, however, that I would need this staff if I were to
do a proper job of organizing the work of the cabinet. I said that with this
staff I was quite prepared to take on housing and the Company of Young
Canadians in addition to the matters referred to in our correspondence

when I rejoined the government. After protesting that any further delays were surely unnecessary, I wrote, "After thinking the matter over since our conversation yesterday, I feel I should ask you now, without further delays, to implement the various proposals and undertakings you made to me last January or, alternatively, to explain to me why you are not prepared to do so. At the same time the necessary Order-in-Council under the Transfer of Duties Act should be approved making me President of the Privy Council in fact as well as title."

I did not hear from Pearson for nearly three weeks. In the interval, at a dinner at Government House on May 10, he referred to my letter and said he must reply to it. My recollection is that he added it was a hard letter to answer. Eventually he did reply on May 16. I felt the timing of his letter was significant, coming as it did the day before a special cabinet meeting which had been called to discuss a speech I had made about the war in Vietnam which had attracted wide attention.

The Prime Minister's letter was a long one, but he failed to deal directly with the main points that I had raised in my letter to him of April 27. In his letter Pearson referred to the staff of the Privy Council office and suggested I should be able to get along with my personal ministerial establishment. I had tried once before to operate without proper departmental or civil service backing. This was at the beginning of the first Pearson government in April 1963, when I had agreed to proceed with the budget preparations without the promised assistance of Bob Bryce. I had no intention of making the same mistake again. In his letter, the Prime Minister suggested that my main concern on returning to the cabinet had been the question of foreign ownership and control and that, accordingly, an inquiry into this matter had subsequently been launched. He felt this was his major commitment to me. He referred again to housing and the Company of Young Canadians and also to a number of other possible projects that I might undertake. But he said nothing about his proposal that I should be responsible for the work of the cabinet or, as a member of a small ministerial committee, for the work of the government and of the House. He did refer, rather casually, to his proposal that I should be responsible for the political activities of the Liberal Party, but assumed "that we can leave this matter aside for the moment." Pearson ended his letter on a critical note: "Also, the press and radio reports of your speeches on Friday and Saturday last on foreign policy suggest that you went well beyond anything we have discussed – let alone decided – in the Cabinet as to what we should do about NORAD, NATO and U.S. policy in Vietnam. But this is another matter with which I will deal separately."

While this criticism had some validity, it seemed a bit out of place in this particular letter, especially as the matters referred to were to be discussed at a special cabinet meeting the next morning. It was obvious from the Prime Minister's letter that the undertakings made to me when I rejoined the government were not going to be implemented, either because Pearson had changed his mind about them or because his own position was not strong enough to force them through. Naturally, I considered resigning from the cabinet immediately. But three days before receiving Pearson's letter, I had made the speech about Vietnam which he had referred to in his letter (and which I shall discuss in Chapter Fifteen). This had created quite a furore, and I was not prepared to resign until this had subsided. Another reason for not resigning in May 1967 was the conviction that, if I did so, the report of the task force on the foreign investment issue would never see the light of day. I expected the report would be ready in September and decided to stay until that time. But it took considerably longer to complete it than had been expected. And by September, both the situation in Quebec following Charles de Gaulle's visit and the lack of cohesion in the government were most disturbing. I decided to stay on a little longer.

Soon after I had rejoined the cabinet at the beginning of 1967, I had a serious disagreement with Sharp over an attempt by the First National City Bank of New York to secure special exemptions for its subsidiary, the Mercantile Bank of Canada. I have described the visit of Mr. James S. Rockefeller and Mr. Robert MacFadden, the President and a Vice-President of Citibank, to my office in July 1963. At that time Mr. Rockefeller said that Citibank had intended to acquire the shares of Mercantile from Dutch interests but that no firm commitment had been made. I advised Messrs. Rockefeller and MacFadden not to proceed with the transaction and said that if they did go ahead with it, since they were now aware of the Canadian government's view in the matter, the government would not consider they would be entitled to exemption from any legislation in respect of foreign ownership of Canadian chartered banks that might be enacted in the future. Disregarding this advice, Citibank concluded its deal and purchased all the outstanding shares of the Mercantile Bank.

On September 22, 1964, I stated in the house that the forthcoming amendments to the Bank Act would include provisions that not more than twenty-five per cent of the shares of any Canadian bank could be held by non-residents and that no single person or associated group (of residents or non-residents) could hold more than ten per cent of the shares of any bank. These provisions would be made retroactive to that date. A further provision was included in the revised Bank Act which was presented to Parliament on May 6, 1965, the effect of which would be to restrict the future growth of the Mercantile Bank as long as Citibank retained more than a twenty-five per cent interest in it. This provoked strong reactions from

266

Citibank, from the U.S. State Department, and from some senior officers of the Canadian Chartered Banks who feared American retaliation. The proposed revisions to the Bank Act died on the order paper when Parliament was dissolved for the election of November 1965.

In the spring of 1966, the issue of the Mercantile Bank flared up again when I published the account of the meeting in July 1963 with Messrs. Rockefeller and MacFadden in my book *A Choice for Canada*. There was an immediate denial of my version of the story by Robert MacFadden, then President of the Mercantile Bank, who stated to the press on May 11 that "our understanding of what transpired at the meeting with him is not in accord with his." Two days later, I rose on a question of privilege in the House of Commons and attempted to refer the issue to a Commons committee to which the two public officials concerned, on whose account of the meeting with Messrs. Rockefeller and MacFadden my story was based, could be called on to confirm what had transpired. The Speaker deferred his ruling on the point of privilege but permitted the tabling of the memorandum about the meeting on July 18, 1963.* While subsequently the Speaker ruled that my privileges as an M.P. had not been infringed by Mr. MacFadden's statement, the tabling of the memorandum achieved my purpose as it was widely reported in the press.

New proposed revisions to the Bank Act were presented to Parliament on June 20, 1966, by Mitchell Sharp, the Minister of Finance. The bill received first reading on July 7, but no further action was taken until the fall. The bill received second reading on October 6, and was referred to the Standing Committee on Finance, Trade and Economic Affairs. Public hearings before the committee began early in November and continued well into 1967.

Pressures on the Canadian government to change the proposed revisions to the Bank Act restricting foreign ownership of the shares of Canadian banks intensified in 1966. Two notes were received from the American government protesting against the legislation. Neither of these notes, nor a copy of the Canadian government's reply, was made public. I was not aware of their contents until they were included as appendices to *The Distemper of our Times* by Peter C. Newman which was published in the fall of 1968. It is true that I was not a member of the cabinet when these notes were exchanged, but in view of my interest in this matter it is surprising I was not informed about them after I returned to the cabinet on January 4, 1967. I am sure this was not done deliberately. Perhaps it was an indication, however, of the state of disorganization of cabinet business at the time.

*See Appendix 3.

Despite the complaints and protests referred to, the bill that was presented to Parliament in 1966 left intact the 1965 proposals to limit the holdings of any one person or associated group (resident or non-resident) to ten per cent of a bank's outstanding shares and the holdings of all non-residents together to not more than twenty-five per cent. Under the proposed provisions, any bank which had more than twenty-five per cent of its shares held by one shareholder would not be allowed to hold assets in excess of twenty times the amount of its authorized capital. The effect of this amendment was to limit the assets of the Mercantile Bank to $200 million, unless Citibank divested itself of seventy-five per cent of its shares.

The situation was further aggravated in December 1966 by remarks made by the United States Ambassador to Canada at a closed-door seminar sponsored by the School of Advanced International Studies of Johns Hopkins University, Baltimore. Walton Butterworth took the occasion of a general discussion on United States–Canadian economic relations to launch a sharp attack against the provisions of the proposed banking legislation and against the Canadian government's policies respecting foreign ownership and control. In doing so, he is alleged to have made some uncomplimentary remarks about me personally, despite the fact I was not then a member of the cabinet. Word of Mr. Butterworth's attack leaked to the press, and in January 1967 a *Washington Post* story quoted unnamed senior Canadian officials as charging that Mr. Butterworth had employed hamhanded methods and thrown his weight around at the December seminar and that some felt his usefulness in Ottawa had ended. The U.S. State Department was quick to defend their representative stating that "he had been following instructions from the Department of State and carrying them out with complete propriety."

In any event, it was reported in the press that the dispute between Canada and the United States over the Mercantile Bank had become the most serious one since the Diefenbaker government's refusal to accept nuclear warheads for missiles and other carriers. A Republican Congressman from New York went so far as to introduce a bill to provide United States federal control over "Canada's multi-billion dollar banking empire in the United States."

On January 24, 1967, the Committee on Trade, Finance and Economic Affairs heard representations from the two representatives of Citibank and Mercantile, James S. Rockefeller and Robert MacFadden, protesting the proposed revisions to the Bank Act. During the testimony the two bankers admitted that they had come to Ottawa in 1963 expressly to inform the Canadian government of the takeover of the Mercantile Bank by Citibank, but had failed "to get the message across" to me as Minister of Finance or to Louis Rasminsky, the Governor of the Bank of Canada. They admitted that Rasminsky had indicated to them before the takeover that neither he nor the government would be happy about it. Nevertheless, they did not believe it necessary to consult with me as Minister of Finance before completing the deal. Later their visit to me on July 18, 1963, was described as purely a courtesy call to inform me of their purchase of Mercantile. They conceded in their evidence to the committee that the agreement to take over the Mercantile Bank from its Dutch owners was subject to the approval of all the governmental authorities concerned. However, Citibank interpreted this to mean the Dutch and United States governments and did not consider it necessary to obtain Canadian government approval.

Perhaps the most damaging evidence to the cause of Citibank was a memorandum of Mr. MacFadden's, clearly stating with respect to the deal to take over Mercantile that they had agreed with Louis Rasminsky to "clear it with the Minister of Finance" before making any final commitment. The memorandum recorded that the deal had not been completed when he and Mr. Rockefeller saw me in July 1963. This was corroborated by Rasminsky's own testimony before the committee on January 30, 1967.

My feelings in the Mercantile Bank affair were very clear. I was opposed to opening the door to the American banks. I believed that if Citibank was permitted to establish itself in this country on a large scale through its subsidiary, the Mercantile Bank of Canada, it would be very difficult to prevent the entry of other American banks. Moreover, it seemed to me somewhat naïve for Canadians to feel sorry for Citibank, whose officials, as evidenced by their statements to the parliamentary committee, had simply not told the truth about what they had said either to Louis Rasminsky, the Governor of the Bank of Canada, or to me when I was Minister of Finance. And quite apart from this, the whole subject had been discussed before I agreed to rejoin the government. Both Pearson and Sharp had declared that no changes were contemplated in the revised Bank Act to alter the then-existing provisions respecting the Mercantile Bank except one that was designed to plug a loophole. If they had not given me this assurance, I would not have returned to the government.

I was astonished, therefore, when, on February 9, 1967, the Prime Minister told me that Sharp wanted to make a deal with Citibank under which it would be given a three-year run to expand the operations of Mercantile beyond the limits provided for in the bill, but on the understanding that over this period seventy-five per cent of its shares would be sold to Canadians. The remaining twenty-five per cent would allow Citibank to maintain effective control of Mercantile. No one else was permitted to hold more than a ten per cent interest in a Canadian bank. When I protested, Pearson said he would get Sharp and me together to discuss the matter.

I did not hear from Sharp but on February 20 the Prime Minister informed me that Sharp had seen him and had decided not to make any changes in the proposed legislation respecting the Mercantile Bank. Two days later, however, on February 22, when I was away in Winnipeg, Bryce Mackasey, the Liberal Member for Verdun, moved an amendment in the Committee on Finance, Trade and Economic Affairs – obviously with the knowledge and approval of the Minister of Finance – giving Mercantile a period of five years in which to expand to a profitable size before Citibank was obliged to cut its ownership to twenty-five per cent. The amendment passed the committee unanimously and went into the draft bill for report to the House of Commons.

Later it transpired that Mackasey had decided to undertake an independent effort of conciliation by going to New York to visit the Citibank officials. According to Mackasey, as reported by the press, the trip was taken with the knowledge of the Prime Minister and Sharp but without their official sanction. According to his own reports, Mackasey succeeded in getting Mr. Rockefeller to reconsider the stand he had taken at the committee meetings when he had refused to consider the possibility of selling any shares of Mercantile to Canadians.

On my return to Toronto from Winnipeg late on February 22, I was called by the press to ask for comments about the changes recommended by the Committee on Finance, Trade and Economic Affairs. I said I had no comment to make and tried to reach Sharp on the telephone without success. At 11:00 P.M. I called the Prime Minister and told him I felt I had been badly let down. I said I would catch the early plane to Ottawa in order to attend the cabinet meeting next morning, but thought it important for him to see me and Sharp ahead of time. I made it quite clear that I could not stay in the cabinet unless further changes were made – that is, rescinding the Mackasey amendment.

I saw Mr. Pearson about 9:00 A.M., February 23, and later had a conversation with both him and Sharp. I felt that if concessions were to be made to Mercantile, as proposed in the Mackasey amendment, then at the same time it should be written into the law that no increase in the capital of any bank would be granted unless it complied with all the conditions that apply to other banks. In the case of Mercantile, this would mean that Citibank's interest would have to be reduced to ten per cent. But Sharp was adamant. He would make no concessions whatever.

I mentioned to the Prime Minister that at the root of the issue was the fact that Sharp would like to see American banks operating in Canada and that, in my opinion, if we allowed Citibank to come here in a big way, sooner or later we would have to allow others in as well. I also mentioned that Sharp wanted to let agencies of foreign banks operate in Canada and that I disagreed with this. I made it clear that if Sharp remained adamant and if cabinet supported him, I would submit my resignation on two counts: first, that the firm commitments which had been made to me when I re-entered the cabinet had been repudiated; and, second, that in my opinion this decision respecting the Mercantile Bank would have a symbolic significance insofar as the whole foreign control issue was concerned.

Later that morning the matter was discussed in cabinet. No agreement was reached, and the subject was referred to an informal group of ministers for further consideration. A number of us met in the Prime Minister's office the next day, that is, February 24. Present, in addition to the Prime Minister, were Sharp, Winters, Marchand, Benson, Martin, and myself. After a long discussion it was agreed that an amendment would be made to the Bank Act to the effect that no bank in Canada would be permitted to increase its capital if any shareholder had or was about to acquire more than a ten per cent interest in the bank.

Later that evening, Benson, Sharp, and I met in Benson's office to discuss ways of implementing the decisions arrived at earlier that day. We discussed various possible plans, but Sharp argued the matter all over again and repudiated the understandings arrived at that morning in the Prime Minister's office. Eventually we worked out the following compromise:

(a) The bill to be amended to provide that no shareholder of any bank would be able to acquire any additional shares of that bank under any circumstances if his holdings exceeded ten per cent of the capital.

(b) The bill to be amended respecting the five-year extension period so that the time limit for the adjustment could be extended beyond December 31, 1967, by the Governor-in-Council, provided that such extension did not exceed five years.

(c) A resolution to be passed by cabinet providing that no extension of time would be granted beyond December 31, 1967, unless prior to that date Citibank has given substantial evidence that it intended to sell seventy-five per cent of its shares to Canadians.

(d) A resolution to be passed by cabinet providing that the capital of Mercantile would not be increased until Citibank's interest had been reduced to ten per cent.

It was my understanding that, while the two cabinet resolutions would not be made public, the government's intentions, as recited therein, would be communicated to the Citibank people.

Sharp agreed to the first two proposals noted above but not to the proposed cabinet resolutions, on the grounds that they anticipated a prospective decision. I felt that the cabinet resolutions were important if for no other reason than that we should not place Citibank in a preferred position *vis-à-vis* Canadian banks. Benson indicated that he would support these resolutions and felt it likely that a majority of cabinet would do the same. He undertook to mention this matter to the Prime Minister, as I was leaving the next day for a short holiday to Jamaica. I did not learn until later that the amendments that had been agreed to were formally approved by cabinet on February 28.

To my surprise, and despite the concessions I had made, the controversy over the Mercantile Bank was not finished. While I was vacationing in Jamaica, speculative stories began to appear in the press to the effect that Sharp was going to win the battle over the Mercantile bank affair. I was kept informed by telephone, both by the people in my own office and by Larry Pennell who, on March 2, advised me to return to Ottawa. I heard that Beland Honderich, the publisher of *The Toronto Star,* said Sharp's supporters were insisting he should win this "fight," as otherwise his leadership hopes would be dead. He thought I should return to Ottawa. I did so on Sunday, March 5.

The situation was further aggravated when stories of the disagreements in cabinet between Sharp and me appeared in the press. Sharp was reluctant to acknowledge the compromise of February 24, approved by cabinet on February 28, since he believed it would appear that he had bowed to pressure in cabinet. Reports of what he said in Toronto on Saturday, March 4, appeared in the papers of the following Monday. The following are two excerpts:

> There has not been and will not be any change in principle in Ottawa's policy toward the Mercantile Bank of Canada, Sharp said in Toronto on Saturday.
>
> The principle of the Government's policy is, as recommended to and adopted by the Commons Finance Committee that First National City Bank of New York must sell seventy-five per cent of its shares in Mercantile within five years, he said.
>
> "There will be no changes in principle," Mr. Sharp said when interviewed. "The only changes I have heard of are changes in detail, not in principle."
>
> Asked if a change in the percentage of shares Citibank would be required to sell would be a change in principle or detail, he replied: "That would be a matter of principle. . . ."
>
> "As far as I know it's not going to be changed. There is no suggestion that it be changed. I've heard of no changes and I am the Minister of Finance."
>
> *The Globe and Mail,* March 6, 1967

Meanwhile Finance Minister Mitchell Sharp returned [to Ottawa] from a weekend in Toronto where he drew a battle line with Gordon in unyielding terms. . . .

Gordon wants Mercantile shares sold to Canadians before the bank could grow bigger and he wants First National City Bank of New York . . . to eventually sell ninety per cent of its Mercantile holdings. Sharp favours giving the bank five years to sell only seventy-five per cent of its shares while continuing normal development to increase their value.

It's believed Gordon won a majority of the cabinet over to his views at the meeting. . . .

In a Toronto interview Saturday Sharp denied that Gordon won key concessions at the cabinet meeting concerning Mercantile's growth.

"I've heard no suggestion of any change and I'm the minister of finance," he told reporters. "If it were changed from 25% to 10% that would be a matter of principle. The only changes I have heard of are in details, not in principles."

When told of reports that Gordon had swayed the cabinet to his side, Sharp retorted: "You shouldn't listen to gossip."

The Toronto Star, March 6, 1967

There was a flaming row in cabinet on Tuesday, March 7. After reviewing the events of February 23 and 24, I stated what I believed to be the substance of the issue. Very simply, the problem was foreign control. Everyone knew my view. Sharp had been saying more or less the same things publicly but with increasing lack of conviction complicated by the leadership race. The Mercantile question was symbolic for three reasons: Were we to give way to intensive pressures including those from the U.S. State Department? Were we to clear the way for the full scale entry into Canada of U.S. banks? Were members of the cabinet to be able to trust each other's commitments?

I was not unmindful of the fact that Sharp had tried to make changes after I left for Western Canada on February 21. When I returned unexpectedly for a cabinet meeting on February 23, he had had to back down. Then when I was away again, this time in Jamaica, press reports seemed to indicate that the new formula which had been agreed to before I left was not going to be implemented. I did not like this. Some of us met with the Prime Minister on the evening of March 7 to try to settle the matter. In addition to the Prime Minister, Benson, Sharp, Marchand, and I were present. Eventually Benson was again given the thankless job of working out a final solution which he presented to me in a memorandum on March 9. The substance of the proposal was as follows:

(a) The two amendments approved by the cabinet on February 28, 1967, were to be introduced into the House by private members.

273

REPRINTED WITH PERMISSION THE TORONTO STAR

"Hi!"

(b) If difficulty arose we would agree to a further amendment to section 75(2)(g) (the five-year extension period) whereby any Order-in-Council must be tabled in the House for fifteen days before it becomes effective and any ten members may arise and require a debate on the subject matter.

(c) The Minister of Finance would state that if a request for extension under section 75(2)(g) is received from the Mercantile Bank, this will be granted for one year, provided they indicate their intentions to move to operate within the spirit of the legislation.

(d) The matter of an increase in capital of the Mercantile Bank would not be considered by cabinet at the present time, but would await an application from Mercantile for such an increase. It was not anticipated that such an application would be made for at least two or three years. The Minister of Finance could, therefore, indicate if the question arose that it was a hypothetical question.

274

(e) When the resolutions are introduced in the House, the government would indicate that it would support these resolutions and no members of the cabinet would in any way try to influence any changes or variations to the amendments as agreed upon by cabinet.

(f) There would be no discussions with the press or comments outside the House by any of the parties involved concerning these particular amendments.

I had a telephone call on March 10, 1967, from Beland Honderich who said that he knew the real story of what was going to happen and also that I could say nothing. I told him I was not in a position to make any comment. He replied that he knew this, but that he merely wished me to know his sources of information in Ottawa were pretty good. He added that he knew all about the recent argument, but in the meantime was running the story that was being put out by the Sharp people – that is, that Sharp had won the battle. Honderich said that naturally his only concern was that there should be no slip-up next week when the bill went to the House of Commons.

PERMISSION TORONTO SUN

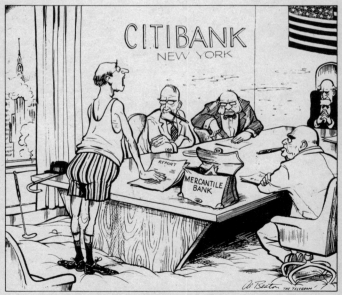

"The dealings with our friendly northern neighbour are almost settled."

Bill No. C-222 respecting banks and banking was considered by the House on Wednesday, March 15, 1967. Debate on the bill continued for five days, during which time two amendments of substance were made, that is, the two changes that had been approved by cabinet on February 28. The first, moved by Bryce Mackasey, prohibited any shareholder, resident or non-resident, who owned more than ten per cent of the shares of any Canadian bank, from adding to his holdings. The second, moved by Milton Klein, another private member, amended the controversial section 75(2)*(g)* whereby the fixed five-year period of grace provided in the bill for the disposal of shares of banks which had more than twenty-five per cent of their shares held by one resident or non-resident shareholder was made dependent on specific action by the Governor-in-Council.

These amendments more or less successfully disposed of the points for which I had been fighting.

CHAPTER FIFTEEN

Foreign Policy and Defence

The White Paper on defence, 1964; the war in Vietnam; leaks from the cabinet; a NATO meeting in Luxembourg; the NORAD agreement; questions to be answered about defence and foreign policy.

In January 1963, Pearson had announced that if elected the Liberals would accept tactical nuclear weapons for our armed services in order to live up to Canada's commitments. At the same time, he pledged that a new Liberal government would re-examine all aspects of our foreign and defence policies. There was some discussion of this in the first year of the new Pearson government, and Paul Hellyer undertook to prepare a White Paper on defence policy. He presented his first draft to the Prime Minister early in 1964, and Pearson forwarded a copy of it to me for comment.

The draft contemplated a substantial build-up of the services and, in consequence, a considerable increase in defence expenditures. In addition, towards the end of the White Paper, it was proposed that the three services be unified. To me the whole idea of spending a great deal more money on defence was nonsensical, both because I failed to see what Canada could gain or could accomplish by having a larger or better-equipped military establishment and because I felt the money could be spent to greater advantage in other ways. I wrote a long memorandum to the Prime Minister about this on February 12, 1964, setting out what my views were – and still are – on defence policy. In my memorandum I said that, in the opinion of many people, including myself, the prospect of all-out war with the Soviet Union was less than it had been some years before. If there should be a war, it would almost certainly be a thermonuclear war in which Canada's contribution would be insignificant. In these circumstances I believed it was difficult to generate much enthusiasm for large expenditures on defence. I went on to say that Canada's relative position in the Western World had changed very considerably from what it had been in the immediate post-war years and in the early 1950s. In the ten years following the end of the war, the countries of Western Europe were tired and beaten, while Canada was enjoying a great period of development and prosperity. We were, therefore, in a position to give leadership in the Western Alliance and to exert a greater influence among our Allies than would normally have been expected for a country of our size. But these conditions no longer prevailed. Europe had made a remarkable recovery while in the last seven or eight years Canada's economic performance had not been distinguished. I believed Canadians sensed the fact that, as a nation, we were not as important in the scheme of things as we once thought we were. "I, for one, have thought for some time that the Europeans should assume a greater responsibility for the defence of Western Europe and that Canada's commitments there should be very substantially reduced."

My memorandum suggested that the Prime Minister, perhaps more than any other English-speaking Canadian, appreciated the existing tensions in Canada, and the difficulty of holding the country together. But I questioned whether we would succeed in doing this "unless we can solve our economic problems (especially unemployment), and unless the provinces, and particularly Quebec, are placed in a position financially where they can spend more money on the kind of things that should be given top priority, of which I would rate education as number one."

I went on to say that one of the root causes of our economic difficulties in recent years, including high levels of unemployment, had been the very large deficits on current account in our balance of payments. We had all agreed that bringing our current account transactions into balance should be given a top priority in our economic policies. Substantial expenditures in Europe, in connection with defence, and heavy expenditures for weapons and equipment in the United States, would make it much more difficult, if not impossible, to solve our balance of payments and, therefore, our economic and unemployment problems.

I pointed out in the memorandum that unless there was some kind of emergency it would be very difficult to increase materially the over-all level of taxation in Canada. This meant that if the provinces were to be placed in a position where they could spend more money on such things as education, certain tax revenues or portions of tax fields must be made available to them. But, I pointed out, "The federal government is caught in something of a strait-jacket. I do not believe that in present economic conditions (excluding for the moment the special situation in Eastern Canada) the federal government should increase the present deficit. This means we shall not be able to do more for the provinces financially unless we are prepared to cut expenditures."

I said I knew something of the difficulties of cutting expenditures, having participated over a period of two months during the fall of 1963 in the efforts made by Treasury Board to reduce the departmental estimates. In practical terms I believed that we would be able to reduce appreciably the level of federal expenditures in only two ways: by resisting the continual requests and proposals for new expenditures; or by a major reduction in expenditures on defence.

I suggested that the "government could make no greater contribution to the future of this country than by diverting several hundred million dollars per annum from defence to the provinces, to be spent primarily on education." My memorandum concluded with a request to talk to the Prime Minister about the broader implications of defence policy before any conclusions were arrived at concerning the draft White Paper for "once it is approved, or even acquiesced in in principle, there will be no turning back."

We had a number of meetings at Sussex Drive to discuss the draft White Paper. Paul Hellyer was unhappy about the feelings of those present, including the Prime Minister's, that his plans should be cut back, and that the strong opinions about defence and foreign policy which were expressed in the draft paper should be softened. I thought he would resign, but he decided to accept the views of the Prime Minister and other members of the cabinet. In the end, Pearson asked Tom Kent to try his hand at a new draft. Tom did so, featuring the proposed unification of the services and soft-pedalling the proposals for expansion and for increasing defence expenditures.

Following these meetings, Hellyer spoke to me about the annoyance of his officials in the defence department over the questions raised from time to time by Treasury Board officials concerning the details of the defence expenditures. He submitted that the Treasury Board staff could not hope to be well informed about many of the items that they challenged. I thought it important for the Treasury Board officials to be kept advised not only about current expenditures but also about contemplated programs that would affect the level of expenditures in the future. Hellyer accepted this as reasonable. We then agreed on the total budget for the defence department, with an escalation clause of two per cent per year. We agreed that the defence department should be given wide latitude as to how they wished to spend the money to be allotted to them, always providing they kept within the over-all budget. Among other things this arrangement kept Paul and me out of one another's hair.

Apart from this discussion about the White Paper on defence early in 1964, there was seldom any serious discussion in cabinet about defence or foreign policy, which most ministers were content to leave to the Prime Minister and Paul Martin. However, despite Pearson's great interest and experience in this field, no changes in policy were made or new initiatives of any consequence taken during the five years in which he was Prime Minister. The only exception was the acceptance of nuclear warheads under American control for our troops in Europe and for the Bomarc missile bases in Canada. We agreed to send a peacekeeping force to Cyprus in 1964, but this was in accordance with established policy and not a new development.

Paul Martin was extremely careful about anything he said about the war in Vietnam, and seemed to go out of his way to avoid ruffling the feathers of the Americans, especially those of Dean Rusk, the Secretary of State. I remember telling Pearson, after a trip to Washington to attend a meeting of a Joint Ministerial Committee on Defence, that I was impressed with the obvious competence and lucidity of Robert McNamara, the Secretary of Defence, but that Rusk struck me as a pedestrian version of the late John Foster Dulles.

I felt that Canada should protest more vigorously than it had done about what was going on in Vietnam, and I had said so in my book *A Choice for Canada* which was published in May 1966. Since writing it, I had become increasingly concerned about the devastation and the terrible cruelties inflicted on the inhabitants of that country who had been involved in almost continuous war for several generations. Moreover, as a member of the Canadian government, I felt an urge to express my own horror and revulsion about the escalation of the war. I did not agree with Paul Martin's statements on the subject which, while sometimes hard to interpret, seemed on the whole to support the policy and actions of the United States.

Pearson usually went a bit further than Paul Martin in his public utterances on the Vietnam war, but he also tended to qualify and becloud what he had to say. However, on April 2, 1965, at Temple University in Pennsylvania, where he went to receive an honorary degree, Pearson, in a carefully hedged speech, advocated a cessation of the bombing of North Vietnam in these words: "There are many factors in this situation which I am not in a position to weigh or even know. But there does appear to be at least a possibility, in my view, that a suspension of air strikes against North Vietnam *at the right time* might provide the Hanoi authorities with an opportunity, if they wish to take it, to inject some flexibility into their policy without appearing to do so as the direct result of military pressure."

After his speech at Temple University, Pearson went on to see President Johnson, who gave him a very cool reception. Nevertheless, in speaking about Vietnam in the House of Commons on May 10, 1967, the

Prime Minister referred to his "increasing anxiety in regard to Vietnam" and to the fact that "the possibility of early negotiations has receded and a quick military victory is not possible, nor a military solution." He went on to say that "all we can do as Canadians [is] to bring our worries and anxieties to the notice of those who are more immediately and directly involved in the hope that our advice and counsel will be of some help to them. I am thinking particularly of Washington. . . ."

I had a word with Pearson that evening at a dinner at Government House and congratulated him on his speech in the House. I mentioned that I planned to make a speech about Vietnam myself within a few days, something I had wanted to do for a long time. I had written to the Prime Minister earlier that day about a conversation I had had with Professor James Steele of Carleton University who held strong views about the Vietnam situation. In that letter, I had referred to the speech I was going to make and had promised to send copies both to him and to Paul Martin.

My speech in Toronto on May 13 was to the Arts and Management Conference of Professional Women.* I began by saying that I proposed to speak about the war in Vietnam "not as an expert who presumes to know what should be done to end it nor as a member of the Government responsible for foreign policy, but just as an ordinary Canadian who is deeply troubled by what is going on." A good part of the speech quoted statements by world leaders and those prominent in public life in the United States who had expressed concern about the Vietnam war.

I said that the United States had not sought its present awesome responsibilities as the leader of the Western World and that it had found itself in a position where the government was forced to make decisions quickly and often without adequate information. Sometimes mistakes had been made, and when this had happened the United States had become committed to policies that seemed to go from bad to worse. "Governments, like individuals," I said, "do not like to confess to errors or to change policies once embarked upon. When this happens, one can always hope that something will turn up which will justify the original decision."

I suggested that the United States had become enmeshed in a bloody civil war in Vietnam "which cannot be justified on either moral or strategic grounds." I said that if left to the Vietnamese themselves, it was questionable whether the civil war could be settled without more bloodshed because these people had a reputation for toughness and they had been fighting continually throughout the lives of several generations. "It might not be any worse for the Vietnamese to be allowed to fight things out

*See Appendix 8.

among themselves than it is to be bombed, burned and exterminated by a foreign power."

From Canada's standpoint, I said, there were four "grave dangers" in the Vietnam situation. The first danger was that the conflict might reinforce a natural distrust of all westerners and of all white people on the part of millions of non-whites throughout the world. The second danger was that Russia and China might become reconciled as a result of their opposition to the United States in Vietnam. The third danger was that further escalation of the war might lead to the direct involvement of Red China. Finally, there was the "gravest danger" that, if the United States used nuclear weapons, the Russians would retaliate immediately, something "no thinking person dares to contemplate."

The closing words of my speech were a plea to stop the bombing. "I hope Canadians in all walks of life and in all political parties – including especially Mr. Pearson and Mr. Martin – will continue to do everything in their power to press the Americans to stop the bombing. If we fail to do this, we must be prepared to share the responsibility of those whose policies and actions are destroying a poor but determined people. We must share the responsibility of those whose policies involve the gravest risks for all mankind."

This speech attracted a great deal of notice in the press and on the air. Examples of the editorial comment follow:

Walter Gordon's statement on Vietnam opens the way to a debate on fundamentals. Not only does he fear that the war will spread, to engulf the world in a global conflict, but, equally important, that it is not based on moral principles. Instead, it constitutes unilateral intervention by the United States in a civil war that should be none of its business. . . .

The government faces a serious challenge. It must either accept or repudiate Mr. Gordon's views. If it repudiates them, the principle of cabinet solidarity may require that Mr. Gordon resign; public differences cannot be tolerated on so vital a foreign policy issue. If the government accepts his views, it should state its position with clarity.

The Ottawa Citizen, May 16, 1967

Mr. Pearson's answer may not be enough to discourage speculation that Mr. Gordon said what the P.M. would like to say if he felt free to do so. . . .

The Montreal Star, May 15, 1967

Mr. Gordon is calling for an end to Canadian niceties, of under-the-counter discussions, of our supposed quiet diplomacy. He is demanding instead a forthright effort by the Canadian government to join in trying to put a halt to the "unhappy errors" of the United States. We must applaud and support Mr. Gordon for his honesty and courage. . . .

The Montreal Star, May 16, 1967

For the Prime Minister, the trouble with that speech of Walter Gordon's about Vietnam is that a lot of people are going to agree with it.

The Globe and Mail, May 16, 1967

There have been hints that many, perhaps most, of Mr. Gordon's cabinet colleagues share his misgivings about American policy. But they have gone along with the Prime Minister's reasoning that a publicly neutral stance would give Canada's diplomacy a better reception in Washington and a better chance to promote peace negotiations. To date, this circumspect policy has borne no fruit. We hope that instead of demanding Mr. Gordon's resignation, Mr. Pearson and the cabinet will come around to his position.

The Toronto Star, May 16, 1967

Pearson at Temple University and in the House of Commons had gone much further than Martin had ever done in urging the United States to stop the bombing of North Vietnam. Despite this and the fact that Pearson and Martin did not always agree between themselves, they continued in the main to be strong protagonists of a policy of "quiet diplomacy." And in view of their long experience, they appeared to adopt a kind of "mother-knows-best" approach with regard to foreign policy which, as I have said, was seldom raised in cabinet. Perhaps for these reasons, as well as others, they were annoyed that anyone else should express views on a subject that they considered to be their sole prerogative. And while I had told Pearson I was going to make a speech about Vietnam, he had not seen the text nor, for that matter, had he asked to do so.

In any event, the reaction in Ottawa to my speech seemed to be one of intense indignation that a member of the cabinet not responsible for foreign policy – I was not responsible for anything at that time – should have presumed to speak out on this subject. This was the feeling in Ottawa, despite the fact that the subject in question was troubling the consciences of a great many people not only in Canada but throughout the world.

I was informed on Monday morning, May 15, that Paul Martin was trying to line up support to have me fired from the cabinet. A special meeting was called for Wednesday, May 17, to discuss the question. The Prime Minister was tired and very critical of me. He began by reading a statement he had prepared about the Vietnam issue which included these words: "We hope the U.S.A., as the strongest of the warring parties, will take the initiative by bringing the bombing to an end and demanding that talks begin at once for an armistice and a settlement." Because of this sentence, I said

I could accept the statement despite its criticism of myself. Pearson wished to make it clear to the press that I had been criticized and disciplined.

At the beginning of the meeting Pearson had managed to concentrate the discussion on the issue of cabinet solidarity rather than on the substance of my speech. He could not very well criticize me for the views I had put forward because, in the course of private conversations with me, he had been severely critical of the way Canadian policy in this field had been expressed. In fact, Pearson stated he agreed with ninety-eight per cent of what I had said in my speech. But strictures based on the theory of cabinet solidarity could not very well stand up when Sharp and sometimes Winters expressed publicly their own views on other subjects, like the independence issue, which were contrary to those held by many of their colleagues. Moreover, it was difficult to talk about cabinet solidarity at a time when there was little cabinet secrecy. If ministers and their staffs were permitted to leak the details of cabinet discussions to the press, how could anyone pretend there could be cabinet solidarity?

In any event, except in Ottawa, few people seemed to be primarily concerned about the principle of cabinet solidarity. What they were disturbed about was the horror of the war in Vietnam, and they responded with relief when someone in a position of seniority protested against it in language everyone could understand. I do not know exactly how many letters I received about my speech because some of them were sent on behalf of several people. I do know that I signed some twelve hundred letters of acknowledgement, to people in all parts of Canada, and that the mail received was over ninety-seven per cent in my favour. This was an extraordinary amount of mail and an extraordinarily high degree of support for any cabinet minister to receive on any single issue. And, of course, the Prime Minister, Paul Martin, and others received many letters and telegrams in favour of the position I had taken.

And so the criticism directed at me by the Prime Minister and other members of the cabinet began to abate almost before it started. Of more importance, the government began to be more outspoken in its views about the Vietnam situation. Within a few months Martin himself would begin to urge the United States to cease the bombing unilaterally.

The question of cabinet secrecy or the lack of it was a matter of considerable concern to many of us especially when it became evident that one or more ministers were deliberately leaking stories to the press. The matter was raised one day by Joe Greene, who had succeeded Harry Hays as Minister of Agriculture and was one of the most popular members of the House of Commons. After a distinguished career in the Royal Canadian Air Force, he obtained a law degree and moved to Renfrew, Ontario, a small town in the Ottawa Valley, where he practised his profession and soon began to take an interest in politics. He acquired a "Valley" accent and developed a considerable likeness in appearance, mannerisms, and oratorical style to his hero, Abraham Lincoln. One could never be quite sure when one encountered Joe whether he was about to give his interpretation of a small-town, country lawyer, or a rather persecuted Abe Lincoln, or of a combination of the two.

At the funeral service for Georges Vanier, the distinguished and much-beloved Governor General, members of the cabinet were expected to wear formal clothes. This meant quite a run on the local outfitter whose stock was limited. Joe turned up in a morning coat of decidedly old-fashioned cut and a stove-pipe hat that must have been at least one hundred years old. He was Abe Lincoln to a tee. Larry Pennell whispered to me that *The Man from Illinois* was playing at the Renfrew Theatre which was advertising there would be a personal appearance that evening. Joe had discovered that for an extra two dollars he could keep his clothes until the following morning.

But Joe is shrewd as well as entertaining and on occasion can go right to the heart of things. When the Prime Minister was complaining about the leaks from cabinet, Joe interrupted to say it would be a very simple matter to stop them. Looking directly at a certain minister, he said, "We all know where the leaks come from. If one of our colleagues were to receive a sentence of five years in the penitentiary, I expect the whole problem would be resolved." After a rather pregnant silence, we proceeded to discuss another subject.

On another occasion, I raised the question of cabinet leaks but in a lighter vein. One morning before cabinet began, several ministers commented on an article by Peter Newman which had appeared in *The Toronto Star* and other newspapers the previous day. Newman, an extremely talented writer as well as an able and industrious reporter, had quoted with remarkable accuracy what was said by a number of ministers at a recent cabinet meeting. This was still the topic of conversation when the Prime Minister arrived. I asked him if it would not be a kindness to give Newman a chair on the grounds that it was most uncomfortable for him to have to crouch for several hours under the table while cabinet meetings were in session. I was delighted to notice two ministers looking surreptitiously under the table to see if Peter was really there.

The day before I made my speech on Vietnam on May 12, 1967, I had spoken to a group of younger businessmen who were attending a course at the University of Western Ontario about the great prospects that lay ahead for them "if" certain things did or did not happen, including developments in our defence policy. In this speech I suggested that quite apart from what might happen as a result of the war in Vietnam, Canadians would soon have to begin to reassess their own foreign and defence policies. Both the NATO and NORAD treaties would be up for renewal or renegotiation within a year or two. We might wonder whether Canada should continue to maintain air squadrons and a brigade group in Europe. The French did not want us; the countries of Western Europe were now prosperous enough to maintain their own defence establishments if they wished to; both the United States and Britain had stated their intentions to withdraw some of their troops from Europe. In these circumstances what was the "sensible thing and the right thing for Canada to do?"

I said that the situation with respect to NORAD was not yet clear. Thus far, the U.S. Secretary of Defence had not agreed with the recommendations of the Joint Chiefs of Staff to embark upon an extensive and highly expensive anti-missile program for the protection of American cities. But if the views of the Chiefs of Staff should prevail in the end, we would have to decide whether we should participate in the program in an effort to protect Canadian cities despite the enormous expenditure involved. "The alternative for a country of our size may be to opt out of the contest altogether on the grounds that if there should ever be a nuclear war between the United States and the Soviet Union, there would be nothing effective we could do about it anyway."

My speech concluded with the suggestion that in circumstances such as these Canada instead of stepping up her defence budget considerably "might decide to concentrate her efforts on the maintenance of mobile peace-keeping or peace-restoring units to be available to the United Nations on the shortest possible notice. . . . Our new unified forces should be well suited to this task."

Things had settled down in cabinet after the row over my Vietnam speech and the volume and character of the mail that it provoked. Martin invited me to attend a NATO meeting of foreign ministers with him in Luxembourg in June in view of my questioning attitude respecting Canada's contribution to that alliance. Liz and I went with him and we had a pleasant trip. This included having dinner with George Brown, the British Foreign Secretary, an intelligent and engaging character, if an irreverent and unpredictable one. It also included, at Martin's urging, a private meeting of all the foreign ministers to talk about the situation in Vietnam. Paul began the discussion and concluded by urging the United States to stop the bombing of North Vietnam. It was an excellent presentation and took courage. Dean Rusk replied somewhat superciliously and proceeded to slap Paul down. In doing so he made it clear that, when it comes to foreign policy, the United States sees things in blacks and whites; there is nothing between, certainly no place for grey. Britain was dependent on the United States for the preservation of the pound and was therefore officially supporting U.S. policy in Southeast Asia. So George Brown remained silent, which was quite an unusual achievement for him. No one else said anything. Later I asked Couve de Murville, the French Foreign Minister, why he had not come to Martin's assistance. He replied with a smile that "the General" had stated France's views about Vietnam a short time before. There was nothing more to say.

This meeting left me with two impressions. The first was that, with the exception of France, how dependent all the members of the NATO alliance were upon the United States and how fearful they were of saying anything that would offend senior American officials. The second was a confirmation of my view that, without the full support of France, NATO was unlikely to recover its former viability. The meeting gave me the impression of an aging bureaucracy trying desperately to retain the privileges and vested interests of its members. It seemed to have about it the smell of moth balls.

I do not mean by this that Canada necessarily should pull out of NATO altogether. Overt action of such a kind would have disadvantages that could and should be avoided. But I believe we should take steps to reduce our contribution to NATO in terms of troops and in terms of weapons that are equipped with nuclear warheads. Given the difference in our relative power and influence, the argument that a reduced Canadian involvement in NATO might weaken the resolve of the Americans to stay in Europe seems hardly worth discussing.

While in Luxembourg, we stayed in one of the smaller hotels. Paul Martin worked at a desk by the window of a room on the second or third floor. When his speech for the opening session was finally completed, it was placed on this desk. Suddenly the wind changed and several pages of the speech were blown out the window. A few minutes later we were intrigued by the spectacle of several of the more junior members of the Department of External Affairs scrambling over the Luxembourg rooftops in hot pursuit of the missing pages. They reported later and in triumph that all sheets of the Minister's deathless prose had been recovered and the speech successfully reassembled.

The question of renewing the NORAD agreement came up in cabinet in the late summer or early fall of 1967, in the form of a proposal to authorize Arnold Heeney, the Canadian Chairman of the Permanent Joint Board on Defence, to inform his American colleagues that Canada would renew the NORAD agreement. I protested that we should be given a great deal more information before giving the impression to the Americans that we were prepared to renew the agreement more or less automatically. In particular, I submitted that we must take the stand from the beginning that we would not participate in the contemplated anti-missile program. This latter point was agreed to. It was also agreed that we should insist upon the inclusion of a suitable clause with regard to termination. Moreover, cabinet was assured that Canada would not be committed in any way by allowing Heeney to discuss the matter with the Americans and, in the process, to find out what they had in mind. Despite this assurance Heeney told me later that he felt the Americans were quite right in assuming that Canada would renew the NORAD agreement when cabinet authorized him to discuss the matter with them, subject to the reservation noted.

When the matter was referred to cabinet again in February 1968, with a recommendation that the agreement be renewed, I argued that it would be wrong to bind the next government in this way on a matter of such importance. I thought that there should be a public debate about renewing NORAD before a decision was made, and that no action should be taken by the Pearson government in its final weeks in office. The matter was held up until after I resigned from the cabinet on March 11. It was then brought up again and approved at a time when everyone was preoccupied with the leadership contest and without the public debate I had advocated. Perhaps this reflected a more or less helpless feeling respecting Canada's options in the fields of foreign policy and defence.

I believe there are several questions that should be answered in considering Canada's defence and foreign policies. Will it make sense for Canada in the 1970s to maintain troops in Europe? Should we continue to supply air squadrons to NORAD and thus participate in a policy we have no say in formulating? Would it make any sense, as many of us thought it would when we were developing new policies for the Liberal Party in 1960 and 1961, for Canada to forswear the use of nuclear weapons, tactical or otherwise? Would there be any great disadvantages for us if we took a somewhat more independent line in our foreign and defence policies? I suspect the answers to these questions will depend upon whether we believe that in the kind of world we live in Canada can retain any vestige of independence. If we cannot, if for all practical purposes we acquiesce in the assertion that we are a dependency or a satellite of the United States, then would it be more sensible for us to join that great country if it would have us, and having done so try to influence the policies that it pursues? These are all questions that have still to be decided.

CHAPTER SIXTEEN

Retirement from Politics

Some issues for discussion; the situation in Quebec; proposed cabinet reorganization; retirement of L. B. Pearson; the choice of a successor; budgetary difficulties; the question of Medicare again; defeat in the House on February 19, 1968; the dollar crisis of 1967-68; the Watkins Report; my resignation.

I considered resigning from the government in May 1967 but decided to put off doing so until the row over my Vietnam speech had subsided and until the White Paper on the independence issue had been completed. The paper took longer to finish than had been expected, and it was not until ten months later, on March 11, 1968, that I felt I could properly leave a government with which I had been feeling increasingly out of sympathy.

By the end of the summer of 1967, it seemed improbable that Pearson would be able to carry on as Prime Minister much longer. He was over seventy and, except perhaps in physical terms, had aged noticeably in the past four years. He was disillusioned by his inability to obtain an over-all majority, and seemed to have lost the interest he once had in policy issues and political strategy. He was no longer able to control the cabinet. He had been preoccupied during the summer with the Centennial celebrations, including innumerable banquets and conversations with visiting heads of state. While they were exhausting, he seemed to enjoy these formal occasions. But in the main he gave the impression that he was just going through the motions and doing his best to avoid trouble by putting things off and not facing up to anything of importance.

During the controversy over the Vietnam affair, I had complained that, during the preceding four and one-half months since I rejoined the cabinet, there had been no opportunity whatever to discuss important issues. Cabinet meetings were devoted not primarily to the consideration of broad policy but mainly to matters which for the most part could be described as "housekeeping." Pearson had agreed that this was valid criticism and that

289

something should be done about it. He wrote all ministers to this effect on May 26, 1967, and later raised two issues which he felt should be considered: the question of scholarships and other forms of student aid, and the Canada Development Corporation. I commented on both these matters in a letter of reply dated June 1, 1967, but to my knowledge no discussion ever took place about scholarships, certainly not in cabinet while I was a member of it. Before I rejoined the government it had been agreed that the Canada Development Corporation would be proceeded with, but this promise was not implemented.

In my letter of June 1, I raised three other issues which I thought should be discussed. The first of these referred to the monopolistic activities of Max Bell's F. P. Publications chain. Bell's empire then included important newspapers in Victoria, Vancouver, Lethbridge, Calgary, Winnipeg, Ottawa, and *The Globe and Mail* in Toronto. It was said on good authority that his company was dickering for *The Montreal Star*. In my letter I wrote: "Rather than attempting to do anything about this after the event, I wonder if it would not be preferable to inform F. P. Publications that, if they should acquire any more newspapers or other news media, the matter will be referred to the [Restrictive Trades Practices] Commission." Nothing was ever done about this to my knowledge.

My letter urged that there should be some discussion of a floating exchange rate for the Canadian dollar, something advocated by most academic economists. I recalled that, in 1962, Mr. Diefenbaker and Donald Fleming, the Minister of Finance, under pressure from the International Monetary Fund, had agreed to adopt a fixed exchange rate and to impose a program of austerity. At that time Pearson, as Leader of the Opposition, had committed himself not to oppose this although I, for one, had felt this decision was "most unfortunate." When we had assumed office in April 1963, it was much too soon to contemplate any change. "Now, however," I wrote, "enough time had elapsed to reconsider this question." We would be doing so at a time [June 1967] when we were not under pressure and when the repercussions of any change might be much less severe than during a time of crisis. I said that I knew very well that "the Bank of Canada would strenuously oppose any thought of reverting to a floating rate; nevertheless the matter is sufficiently important to review the pros and cons."

In my letter I referred also to some brief comments in cabinet that morning about NORAD and NATO, when it was agreed that both subjects should be fully discussed in the very near future. I said I thought this was important and urged that not only should there be a discussion but "a willingness to review and reconsider policies which may not now be quite so valid as when originally adopted."

Charles de Gaulle paid his visit to Quebec in August 1967. In September, René Lévesque unequivocally espoused the cause of separatism. Marchand, Trudeau, Benson, and I got together to discuss these developments, which we took very seriously.

When cabinet met at 9.30 A.M. on September 21, I urged that we should put aside our other business to discuss the Quebec problem in the light of Lévesque's pronouncement. Pearson said he would prefer to do this later in the day. It was one of those marathon meetings, however, and it was not until about 4.30 P.M. that we managed to get down to a discussion of the Quebec situation and the possible reaction to it in English-speaking Canada.

The next day, September 22, I wrote the Prime Minister reminding him that in the speech he made in December 1962 he had shown a sympathy and understanding for what was happening in Quebec that no other English-speaking leader had demonstrated. And since becoming Prime Minister I believed that he and the government had gone out of their way to meet the legitimate claims of Quebec despite some rebuffs by Quebec leaders, despite a steady rising of their demands and a continual changing of their positions, and despite some lack of understanding on the part of certain French-Canadian leaders to reactions in English-speaking Canada. I said, "I have thought, and have often said publicly that your understanding of Quebec and your efforts to hold the country together has been the single most important contribution you have made during your period as Prime Minister." I went on to say that, if all this effort were not to be lost, a new and more positive stance would be called for. Although the reaction in English-speaking Canada to recent statements from Quebec had thus far been quiet and moderate, I did not think its importance should be underestimated.

My letter postulated that Réne Lévesque's unequivocal espousal of separatism, Jean Lesage's initial reaction to it, and Pierre Laporte's vaguely expressed views on the subject had followed a series of incidents that had been disturbing to people who lived in other parts of Canada. Lesage's speaking tour of the West and of Northern Ontario two years ago had not been well received, and his behaviour on that occasion had not been forgotten. Since then, de Gaulle's visit and all the talk at the Tory convention about *les deux nations* had managed to keep the subject alive, especially in the West. "And now we have France, for all practical purposes, transferring her normal diplomatic relations from Canada to Quebec."

The only really positive response from any Quebec leader to René Lévesque thus far had been the unequivocal statement of Eric Kierans. I wrote that, in a long telephone conversation two nights previously, Kierans had told me he thought that Lévesque would be resoundingly defeated at the provincial Liberal convention the following month. I thought we should give Kierans credit for persuading Lesage to come out with a second statement "which seemed to me to be almost exactly opposite to what he had said the first time." In any event, Lesage's position was "anything but strong." In view of this confused situation and the vacuum that seemed to exist, I believed that "the federal government should be prepared to step into the breach and give a lead. Obviously the main burden would have to fall on Jean Marchand and the Quebec ministers, but they should know where they stand and that the rest of us are prepared to back them."

Pearson spoke to me about my letter and left no doubt that he considered the Quebec situation very serious, even if he seemed unable to come to grips with it. At the next meeting of caucus, he referred to what was happening in Quebec and to the reaction in the rest of Canada. He told the caucus it was the most serious situation to face us in the one hundred years of our existence, and raised the question of Canada's ability to continue as a state.

The dangerous situation in Quebec made it imperative that some attempt should be made to pull things together and to effect a reorganization of the cabinet. I drafted a long memorandum dated October 3, 1967,* describing the situation as I saw it and suggesting what should be done about it. I discussed it with Pearson in some detail over an extended luncheon meeting.

I submitted that Canadians were deeply troubled about the possible break-up of the country and were looking for strong leadership, and this at a time when the government was giving the impression of being weak and uncertain. I suggested that this impression of weakness stemmed from many causes. In the first place, the Liberals received only forty per cent of the popular vote in the 1965 election and our support since then, according to the opinion polls, had fallen off still further. At the same time, the recent Conservative convention and the election of Robert Stanfield as the new leader of that party had made its mark upon the public.

Then I raised the economic situation and the failure of the government to give the impression that it knew how to handle the difficulties it must contend with. In particular, I referred to the lack of control over expenditures and the fear of inflation which, I argued, was being aggravated by the kind of speeches Sharp had been making. I mentioned also the housing problem and the need to do something about it, the rising level of interest rates, and the uncertainties about what the government intended respecting the Carter report on taxation.

I pointed out that inevitably the unofficial leadership race had created

*See Appendix 9.

292

frictions, and stated that as far as I could tell there was no consensus in the party at that time as to the best man to succeed Pearson as Prime Minister. I went on to say that the most important cause of present frustrations in the cabinet was the confusion about areas of responsibility and authority and the way in which the time of busy ministers was being wasted. The work of the cabinet needed to be completely overhauled, and the Prime Minister should stop trying to do everything himself. I added that the frustrations in the cabinet were reflected in the caucus by absenteeism and lack of discipline.

In the light of these circumstances, and the importance of resolving the Quebec situation and the constitutional question before another election, I suggested tentatively that the leadership race should be called off; that Pearson should carry on for another year; but that he should confine himself to helping Marchand with the Quebec problem and negotiating new constitutional arrangements with the provinces.

In my memorandum I proposed that the work of the cabinet should be reorganized "in a way that will not flout all the elementary principles of organization." One senior minister should be made responsible for organizing the work of the cabinet and for reviewing carefully all proposals before they were presented. He should also be the chairman of a proposed new policy committee. The present cabinet committee system was time wasting and the number of committees should be reduced to five: a new policy committee; a committee on the Quebec situation (under Jean Marchand); the Treasury Board; the special committee of council responsible for certain routine matters; and a legislation committee which should assume full and final responsibility for all bills. In addition, *ad hoc* committees should be established from time to time to study particular problems.

Many of the matters at present brought to cabinet should be settled by the ministers themselves, in some cases after consultation with the chairman of the policy committee, or by the Treasury Board. The policy committee – which, in addition to the chairman and the Prime Minister, should include the Secretary of State for External Affairs, the leader of the Quebec caucus, the Minister of Finance, the President of the Treasury Board, the Minister of Justice, and the House Leader – should meet daily and should deal with all questions involving policy. I argued that if the principal ministers were to meet together every day they would soon begin to present a more united front to the House and to the public. The full cabinet should meet once a week only and should devote most of its time to political matters rather than administration. Three senior cabinet ministers should be designated as Deputy Prime Ministers in order to give them the necessary authority and standing. These should be Martin, Marchand, and the chairman of the proposed policy committee. Concurrently with these proposals, some important changes should be made in the membership of the cabinet.

I also proposed that we should take initiatives to get the attention of the House and of the public off the current economic situation. This could be done by introducing social legislation dealing with such subjects as divorce, the use of contraceptives, abortion and capital punishment, the White Paper on foreign investment, the Canada Development Corporation, and legislation dealing with broadcasting and election expenditures. I concluded that it was vitally important to the government to get busy on the constitutional issue and the situation in Quebec; to develop a new housing policy; to reverse the present trend in interest rates even if this meant bringing pressure on the chartered banks; and to reduce prospective expenditures so that the next year's budget would be defensible.

Pearson said he could find no fault with my diagnosis as set forth in the memorandum or with the proposals for dealing with the situation. He agreed that he would have to reorganize the government if he were to stay on as Prime Minister. We talked very frankly about the capabilities of the members of the cabinet and what positions they might fill. I suggested five or six, including myself, who might be encouraged to retire by Christmas, which would do a lot to clear the air. I said I hoped to leave by November if, as I then expected, the White Paper on foreign investment was finished.

At the end of our conversation, Pearson said he would like two or three days to think things over and would probably want to see me over the weekend. However, I did not hear from him for nearly three weeks. At that time he told me it was obvious that the cabinet should be reorganized along the lines I had suggested but that he could not proceed to do this if he were going to leave in the near future. I interpreted this to mean that he was not up to the reorganization job and that he should be encouraged to say when he was proposing to retire.

In another talk with the Prime Minister on November 8, I reminded him that early in October I had suggested he stay on to resolve the constitutional issue, but only if there were a major reorganization of the government. Pearson admitted he was not up to this. If that were so, I urged him to get out as quickly as possible. He replied that he might do so when he got back from Europe in December.

This was a disheartening period for members of the government. We seemed to be having innumerable and inconclusive meetings about the financial situation. Sharp had reopened the Medicare question and morale was low. Prior to the formal opening of a cabinet meeting on November 20, but with the Prime Minister in the chair as usual, I questioned Sharp about publicly reopening the Medicare issue without cabinet approval. It was clear he did not have much support for having done so. After reviewing the political situation, I pointed out that all of us had put everything we had into reorganizing and revitalizing the Liberal Party a few years ago and that I assumed we were all disturbed and unhappy about what was happening to it. I submitted that the party was in bad shape and that uncertainties about the Medicare issue were not helpful. In a sense the government was disintegrating and the same thing would happen to the party if we were not careful. In these circumstances we should make some hard decisions.

As a start I submitted that, on his return from Britain, Pearson should tell us what he planned to do. It was his decision and whatever it was all of us would accept it, but the present public discussion of his plans was bad for everybody, himself included.

As I had mentioned to the Prime Minister privately some seven weeks previously, I brought up the point that if we wished to improve our public image, there would have to be major changes in the cabinet; that there should be a new approach on policy with less emphasis on the financial situation; and a new and sparkling housing program. I spoke at some length and closed on a personal note. I explained I was going into hopital for an operation on the vertebrae in my neck and would be away for some time.

The Prime Minister did not like me speaking out so frankly. But after ticking me off rather mildly for what I had said about himself, he stated that he would announce his plans when he got back from England. Benson and Marchand came to see me after the cabinet meeting before I left for Toronto to enter St. Michael's Hospital. They said I had expressed what everyone was thinking about Pearson and his plans and that it needed saying.

Just before my operation, Dr. William Horsey, the surgeon, came to see me. He said that another doctor, a strongly partisan supporter of the Progressive Conservative Party, had expressed a keen interest in my case and had offered to take over and perform the operation. Bill Horsey and I agreed it would be unfair to put such temptation – that is, my neck – in the other doctor's way.

Pearson called me on December 14 after his return from England while I was convalescing, to say he intended to advise cabinet that morning that he planned to leave and that he was informing Senator John Nichol, the President of the National Liberal Federation, to that effect. He said he would carry on until his successor could be chosen at a convention. I said I felt he was making the right decision.

In his years as a diplomat, Pearson made a host of friends throughout the world and established a reputation for himself that is not likely to be equalled by any other Canadian in our lifetime. Twice he was considered for the position of Secretary General of the United Nations, of which he had been President in 1952-53. I have no doubt that he would have made a tremendous success in that post if the Russians had not blocked his appointment on both occasions. As it was, his career as a diplomat and as Canada's foreign minister was brought to a close with the winning of the Nobel Peace Prize in 1957, a fitting climax to almost thirty years of brilliant service in this field. Pearson was less successful as a politician partly because he had to stay on too long, and partly because domestic issues, apart from that of national unity – and the kind of people who are concerned with them – did not interest him as much as international affairs and the personalities he came in contact with as a prominent performer on the world stage. He did not begin to learn his political ABC's until late in life. Despite this, he did a courageous job in opposition and in guiding the Liberal Party to recovery after the defeats of 1957 and 1958.

Moreover, the achievements of his first government under the most difficult of circumstances were phenomenal. Pearson is entitled to much of the credit for what was accomplished during the two and a half years of the first government he headed. But the failure to obtain a majority in the 1965 election seemed to undermine his spirit and his confidence. He was not the same thereafter. The achievements of the second Pearson government were limited. And, strangely enough, the greatest failure of both his governments was in the field in which the Prime Minister himself was most experienced. In five years in office, no changes of importance were made in Canada's foreign policy or defence policy. It is true that the armed forces were unified in a single service, but this was more a matter of organization than of strategic policy. When he made his speech in January 1963 on the use of nuclear weapons, Pearson stated that Canada's defence and foreign policies would be thoroughly revised when the Liberals came to power. Unfortunately, this was not among the accomplishments of the two governments he headed.

As a rule, when it was a question of an issue he could study objectively and on its merits, Pearson would come down on the side of the small "l" liberals. But his father and his grandfather, despite the fact they were Methodist preachers, had been strong Tories. While intellectually Pearson was a liberal, in emotional or instinctive terms he sometimes seemed to have inherited the conservative leanings of his forbears, a schizophrenic attitude that could be disconcerting. This was particularly manifest when he had been listening to the advice of his contemporaries in the financial and business world. Like others in politics and in the civil service, Pearson was impressed by successful businessmen, especially it sometimes seemed with those who had retired or were approaching retirement age. It was unfortunate that Pearson could not have retired himself in 1965, at the end of his first government. His last two and a half years in office was not the best period in his long life of service to his country.

If there is a moral to this, I expect it is that except in the most unusual circumstances no one should be encouraged to assume or to retain the most difficult and onerous job in Canada – the position of Prime Minister – after·he has passed the age of normal retirement. Pearson did have the vitality and the endurance to enable him to do this successfully to begin with, but he simply could not keep up the pace. I do not know of anyone of that age in any country who could. Perhaps Winston Churchill, Konrad Adenauer, Charles de Gaulle, and Mao Tse-tung were the last exceptions to prove this rule, and there are many who would question whether even they succeeded in so doing.

During the summer and fall of 1967, Marchand, Benson, Trudeau, and I, and occasionally Pennell, began to meet for lunch or dinner to discuss the problems of the government and in the party and what, if anything, could be done about them. Our conversations ended inevitably with a discussion about who would be the best man to succeed Pearson when the time came. We thought Marchand should be the one, but he was diffident about his own capabilities and always insisted it was not the job for him. A few kites were flown about Benson but, despite his abilities, these did not proceed to fly. I was not young enough for the job, my health was not good enough, and I had become too controversial a figure, especially in Western Canada. Trudeau at that time was little known within the party and was thought to be too inexperienced, with only a few months in the cabinet behind him.

Nevertheless we kept on meeting. Our best guess in September 1967 was that Paul Martin would win a leadership convention at that time if the four of us got behind him. We toyed with this idea but could not get enthusiastic about it. For one thing, Martin was even older than I was, and we felt the next leader should be much younger. We also discussed the desirability of asking Pearson to stay on for a short time as the titular head of a reorganized government – in view of the threatening situation in Quebec following de Gaulle's visit in the summer and René Lévesque's espousal of the separatist cause. But while I discussed this suggestion with Pearson on October 4, it soon became clear that even he had his reservations. In these circumstances, Benson, Trudeau, and I continued to urge Marchand to contest the leadership both because we felt it was the turn for a French-Canadian and because Benson, Trudeau, and I had a high opinion of his many qualities. Marchand protested that he neither wished to become Prime Minister nor thought he had all the necessary qualifications for the job. He did say, however, that he felt a French Canadian should be among the contestants at the leadership convention when the time came. He thought this should be Trudeau, despite the fact that in the fall of 1967 Trudeau's stock was not too high in Liberal Party circles in Quebec. This was because he had spoken out forthrightly on the constitutional question and had ridiculed those who were advocating a "special status" for his province. Trudeau was urging linguistic equality throughout Canada so that French Canadians should have an equal chance to flourish and to prosper anywhere throughout the country. But he argued that this should be done within the Canadian federation, with Quebec on the same footing as all the other provinces.

Just before Christmas 1967, Marchand admitted very tentatively that if no one else from Quebec would consent to be a candidate he just might be persuaded to run. However, he emphasized again and again that he did not wish to do this, that he did not feel his English was good enough, and that in his view his knowledge of finance and world affairs was insufficient to qualify him for the position of Prime Minister.

About this time I made a number of inquiries among prospective delegates from Ontario to the forthcoming leadership convention and informed Marchand I was satisfied that he could win the leadership provided he announced his candidacy within the next few weeks. He promised to call me about this after Christmas.

According to my notes, he called me on December 28 or 29:

Marchand called me at "Seldom Seen" from Montreal where he had been attending Maurice Rinfret's funeral.

He said he had not called before because he had not made up his mind about the leadership. He said his wife was much opposed and while this was not the only factor, he had serious reservations about contesting it.

He said the Quebeckers seem to think some French Canadian should be a candidate and that Trudeau's [political] standing had improved and they might get behind him.

He said he was going to Florida and would be thinking this over. He will get in touch with me as soon as he gets back – about January 13.

My impression is that Marchand will not be a candidate. The longer he leaves it, the more difficult it will be. People are getting committed.

Despite this impression, in answer to a question by a journalist early in January 1968, I stated that my choice for the next leader of the Liberal Party would be Jean Marchand. This attracted considerable attention and I received a lot of calls about it. Marchand spent a short holiday in Florida and I am sure he canvassed the situation very carefully. When I saw him on his return, he was still firmly of the opinion that some French Canadian should be a candidate. But he was equally firm that Trudeau would make a better Prime Minister than he would.

A series of meetings of a cabinet sub-committee was held in January 1968 to discuss the line the federal government should take at a federal-provincial conference in February on the constitutional question. I was much impressed with the way in which Trudeau presented his proposals and with his firmness in resisting suggestions that would have modified his recommendations in order to appease the provinces. He had made the same impression on me during the fall by the way in which he handled a cabinet sub-committee which was created to consider his recommendations for changing the grounds for granting divorces. In both cases it was clear he had studied the subject thoroughly, and that having made up his mind about the right approach he was prepared to fight for it.

I had a pleasant personal conversation with Trudeau in late January 1968. I reminded him that we had both done our best to persuade Marchand to contest the leadership and that I had stated publicly that if he did so I would support him. I mentioned, that after checking things fairly carefully in Ontario in December, I was reasonably confident that Marchand could win the leadership, although whether or not he could go on to win the election that would follow it sooner or later was something no one could predict. I believed that he could do so. I said if Marchand did win the leadership I would feel obligated to stay with him and to run in the next election, despite the fact that I was not at all sure my health was up to it.

I told Trudeau that if Marchand remained firm in his decision not to seek the leadership, and if Trudeau decided to go after it, I would support him to the best of my ability. However, I said that in these circumstances I did not wish to obligate myself to run in the next election, primarily because after my operation it was very difficult for me to work as hard as I was used to. In the course of the conversation, I said I was not certain that Trudeau could win the nomination. (How wrong I was!) At that time, he was not nearly as well known as Marchand. However, I said I was inclined to agree with Marchand's opinion that if Trudeau did win he might very well make the better Prime Minister.

Trudeau agreed that the best thing would be for Marchand to seek the leadership. He said that if Marchand refused to do so he was not at all sure that he could be persuaded to go after it. He referred particularly to his inexperience and to the fact he had been in the cabinet for only nine or ten months at that time. He also questioned his ability to rouse public support in the way we both felt Marchand was capable of doing. (How wrong *he* was!) In any event, he said he did not intend to think about the matter seriously until after the federal-provincial conference, which he felt to be of prime importance. He could not allow his attention on this to be distracted by other considerations at the moment.

Trudeau said he understood my own position. He agreed that I had assumed some kind of obligation insofar as Marchand was concerned. But he recognized that I had no such obligation in regard to himself, if by chance he should be the one to go after the nomination and to win it. He said he could fully appreciate my reasons for feeling I should retire from politics. It was a most friendly conversation conducted with the utmost frankness, and I felt we fully understood each other.

Trudeau's performance at the federal-provincial conference on February 5-7, all of which was televised, was quite superb. He seemed controlled, sure of himself, extremely lucid and articulate, and very firm. In the course of the proceedings he engaged in a debate with Daniel Johnson, the Premier of Quebec and the leader of the Union Nationale, the political party that Trudeau and Marchand had opposed for many years. Johnson was good, but Trudeau won hands down. Overnight Trudeau was recognized as a new and talented television performer and obviously a major prospect in the leadership stakes. On February 16, he formally announced he would be a candidate, a candidate that it would be very difficult indeed for anyone else to stop. On March 25, on *Front Page Challenge*, the television program with one of the largest audiences in Canada, I stated in answer to a question that Trudeau was my choice for leader. But apart from that I did not take any part in his campaign.

I was asked, of course, how I could support Trudeau for the leadership in view of the fact he was supposed to be lukewarm on the independence issue about which I have always held strong views. I do not know whether Trudeau had thought deeply about this question. I do know that, after reading *A Choice for Canada*, he came to see me and said he agreed with it. And I gained the clear impression that he approved in principle the proposals contained in the Watkins Report. It is quite true that he played down this whole question during the leadership campaign. But while I was disappointed about this, I acknowledged that from his standpoint it was "good politics" to do so at that time.

One of the greatest mistakes of the second Pearson government which was elected in November 1965 was its failure to control expenditures, and hence its inability to keep the government's finances in a sound condition. The Glassco Commission had recommended in 1962 that responsibility for supervising expenditures should be removed from the Department of Finance and placed under a separate minister working out of the Privy Council office and reporting to the Prime Minister. I had serious reservations about this proposal. In my view, a second minister should be appointed for this purpose, but he should work directly with the Minister of Finance, as is the case in Britain. I recommended that he should be designated Associate Minister of Finance and President of the Treasury Board. In this way the ultimate responsibility of the finance department for the state of the national finances would be preserved. It seemed to me impractical to load this added burden on the Prime Minister, who had much too much to do already. This argument about who should be responsible for controlling expenditures continued throughout the period when I was Minister of Finance, with the Prime Minister periodically bringing up the subject of separating the Treasury Board from its connections with the finance department. My views on the subject can best be expressed by quoting one paragraph from a letter to the Prime Minister, dated February 17, 1965:

> I think it is generally accepted that the Minister of Finance in our system should have primary responsibility for coordinating the various financial and economic policies of the Government subject, of course, to the overall responsibility of the Prime Minister and Cabinet. To do this successfully, the Minister of Finance must have some control both over policy aspects of raising revenues and over the level of Government expenditures. To separate these functions would be to require a Minister of Finance to do the job that is expected of him and to take the responsibility for it with one hand tied behind his back.

While I was minister, the Department of Finance took a direct interest in the preliminary spending estimates for the coming year. The preliminary figures for the year 1964-65 – the year beginning on April 1, 1964, and ending March 31, 1965 – became available for discussion purposes in late August 1963. They were reviewed in detail at a series of meetings as a result of which the plans and programs of the various departments for the coming fiscal year were kept down to reasonable levels. As things turned out, the budgetary deficit for that year was only some $39 million, the best showing since 1956-57, when there had been a surplus of $282 million. This was not fortuitous.

Louis Rasminsky, the able Governor of the Bank of Canada, had written to the Prime Minister on August 27, 1963, about the importance of keeping our expenditures under control and thus keeping costs in line. Pearson had referred his letter to me for comment. In reply, I said that I agreed with Rasminsky's views, about which he had talked to me beforehand, except those in connection with the proposed Canada Pension Plan. On this point my letter reads as follows:

In our conversation, Rasminsky suggested that it would not be necessary to increase the amount of the Old Age Security payments if the Pension Plan did not go through. . . . I did not find him convincing on this point but in fairness it was one that he had not been thinking about prior to our conversation. The Pension Plan is being undertaken as a matter of social priority to which the Government, Parliament and large sections of the public all attribute great importance notwithstanding some inevitable costs.

I pointed out to Rasminsky that there are some political and social considerations that cannot be overlooked especially by a Liberal Government. If we were foolish enough to concentrate our whole attention on economic considerations, we would not only lose our own following but also fail to achieve the ultimate objectives to which apparently we all subscribe. . . .

It seemed to me we should go ahead with badly needed social measures like the Canada Pension Plan, and later Medicare, but in doing so we should make proper provision for paying for them and should not be afraid to raise taxes for the purpose.

We had the same problem over spending programs in the summer of 1964, and I spent a great deal of time persuading ministers to reduce their preliminary estimates for the coming year, 1965-66, by some $200 million. Again the deficit was held down to some $39 million, despite a very substantial reduction in personal income taxes.

The following summer, just before the beginning of the 1965 election campaign, I asked George Davidson, the Secretary of the Treasury Board, to prepare by early in November suggestions as to how the preliminary expenditure programs for the year 1966-67 could be cut by $200 million, $400 million, or $600 million. My hope was to present a budget for the coming year which would be in balance, or nearly so.

With my departure from the government, however, the Treasury Board was separated from the Department of Finance. Whether this had anything to do with it or not, the budget for the year 1966-67 contemplated an increase in expenditures of nearly ten per cent and a deficit of $150 million – this despite a substantial increase in taxes and a strong plea for restraint. In actual fact, the deficit that year turned out to be $428 million. In the budget for the following year, which was presented on June 1, 1967, Mitchell Sharp, the Minister of Finance, forecast a somewhat slower rate of growth than in 1966, a modest increase in unemployment, and "a somewhat smaller increase in prices than last year, with some further squeeze on profits." He forecast a deficit for the year 1967-68 of $700 million. (The actual deficit turned out to be almost $100 million more.)

302

Within a very few months of the presentation of his budget, however, Sharp became obviously worried not only about the government's budgetary position but also about inflation and the stability of the Canadian dollar which was under pressure. He began to urge the cabinet to agree to a mini-budget to be presented in November or December, which would impose a substantial increase in taxes. At the same time he made a number of public statements about the need to cut the preliminary spending estimates for the year 1968-69 and about the weak position of the Canadian dollar, including predictions as to what would happen if his recommendations, including a further postponement of Medicare, were not accepted.

There was no disagreement in cabinet in the fall of 1967 about the need to bring the government's finances under control. Everyone knew that the financial community was losing confidence and that it was becoming increasingly difficult for the government to sell its bonds. We were fully aware, also, that the Canadian dollar was under pressure. Some of us believed, however, that the lack of confidence in the government's fiscal measures was being aggravated by the kind of speeches Sharp was making, not to mention the very large deficit that had been forecast in the June budget. Quite apart from this there were differences of opinion respecting the nature and the timing of the corrective measures to be taken.

We had a long discussion in cabinet on October 24 about what should be done. Most of the ministers expressed opinions. Several more meetings were devoted to the same subject, and I decided to summarize my own views in a long letter to the Prime Minister dated November 7, 1967.* In it I said that I believed we had magnified the problem by talking too much about the need to cut expenditures and about the problem of selling government bonds. I did not intend to minimize the difficulties that confronted us, but only wished to say again what I believed should be done about them. According to a memorandum circulated by the Prime Minister on November 2, if further action were not taken we would face a budget deficit of $635 million for the year 1968-69. I said that in my opinion this would be quite indefensible if we believed that the next year would be a reasonably good one in terms of economic activity and employment. In these circumstances, I thought "we should plan for a balanced budget according to traditional methods of accounting, or as close to this as may be practicable."

I suggested, therefore, that cabinet should approve: the various reductions in expenditures outlined in the memorandum of November 2 or suitable alternatives which, after revisions and discussions, might amount to $100 million; that additions to the civil service be frozen (subject to an

*See Appendix 10.

understanding that the ceiling could be pierced in cases where this was demonstrably important); and that most departments should be required to reduce their dollar estimates by, say, five per cent of variable or controllable expenditures. I anticipated that these proposals would produce additional savings of perhaps $150 million. If both proposals were carried out, it should result in a reduction of the estimated deficit to about $400 million.

My letter suggested that we should face up to a further cut in the Estimates of the Department of National Defence, even though this would entail a reduction in our contributions to NATO. I admitted that this suggestion involved a number of broad questions which other members of the cabinet might not be willing to consider. If this were the case, I suggested that additional revenues might be raised by the advancement of the dates on which corporation income taxes were payable. I recalled that we had made the first step in this direction in the budget for the year 1963-64. The second step could produce something of the order of $300 million for the fiscal year 1968-69.

In my letter I advised against an early announcement of what we proposed to do – it was only five months since the last budget had been presented. Instead, I suggested that we plan to introduce the next budget in February on the same day as the Estimates were brought down. I thought it would be "unwise" to introduce a refundable tax on individuals since, if this were done, it would reduce the ordinary man's take-home pay and in the existing climate of wage negotiations "might well provoke further demands for increased wages." I thought we should make an early announcement of our intentions respecting the Carter Commission's tax proposals, especially about increasing the taxes of the oil industry, the mining industry, and the life insurance industry, as advocated by the commission.

My letter concluded with the observation that the recent policies of the two largest Canadian chartered banks, in my view, had "had something to do with the general rise in interest rates in Canada." I said it was "indefensible for the heads of two chartered banks, in order to ensure that the total assets of their institutions should exceed $7 billion at their year end (October 31, 1967), should be permitted to bid for deposits in the way they have done in recent months." I thought it might be desirable for the Minister of Finance to explain publicly and in detail just what had been going on in what was essentially a monopoly field. I suspected that he would be warmly applauded if he were to introduce legislation "which would ensure that this sort of thing could not be repeated."

Some people felt that, with his Calvinist background, Mitchell Sharp was not only willing and anxious to wear a hair-shirt himself but that he would not be satisfied until everyone else was doing the same thing. He seemed obsessed with the idea that the only proper way to raise the additional revenues that were needed was by an increase in personal income taxes, which was bound to be politically unpopular. And quite apart from the question of its popularity or otherwise, a tax of this kind was bound to aggravate the demands of the trade unions.

One reason why Sharp failed to obtain the support of his cabinet colleagues was the absence of a consistent line on the expenditure question. For example, when a new wheat agreement was being negotiated in Geneva at the same time as the Kennedy Round of tariff cuts, no one foresaw the possibility that wheat prices might fall between the date when the current agreement expired on July 31, 1967, and the new one became effective eleven months later on July 1, 1968. But the price of wheat did fall, and Winters supported by Sharp, the cabinet's most outspoken advocates of what Winters called "fiscal integrity," proposed that the government should guarantee a price of $1.95 per bushel (basis No. 1 Northern at the head of the Lakes) until the new agreement became effective. No one could estimate with any accuracy what the cost of this subsidy would amount to. Winters said there was a commitment to give this guarantee, but was unable to explain when this was made or to whom it had been given. Naturally, Winters and Sharp were twitted about this proposal and it was pointed out to them that a firm commitment had been given about Medicare and the necessary legislation approved by Parliament; nevertheless Sharp wished to reverse this. Winters, while he had serious reservations about Medicare, agreed the government was committed to that program. Benson, the President of the Treasury Board, did his utmost to hold the line on government expenditures, but he did not have the necessary authority or the final say when it came to politically sensitive issues like the wheat subsidy.

Throughout the fall of 1967, Benson and I had argued that rather than introduce a mini-budget in the fall, it would be better to bring in an early budget for the year 1968-69 which should be balanced or should call for a modest surplus. We thought this would be more effective than doing the job in bits and pieces. We were opposed to an increase in personal income taxes and preferred the alternatives suggested in my letter to the Prime Minister of November 7, 1967.

Sharp's support in cabinet and in caucus was weakened further by his desire to put off Medicare until some future date. He had argued this during the summer and early fall of 1966 on the grounds that the program would be inflationary. Lamontagne and I had challenged this in caucus and successfully demolished his argument. When Sharp raised the question of Medicare again, in the early fall of 1967, he argued that it should be deferred for budgetary considerations rather than as an offset to inflation. This was a sounder argument, but those who favoured Medicare and felt we were committed to it asserted that it had always been understood that additional taxes would have to be levied to pay for Medicare, and that if this were done the problem would be taken care of.

Towards the end of 1967, Sharp shifted his ground again, arguing that we should not go ahead with Medicare because this would mean raising taxes in Quebec and all the other provinces to pay for Medicare in, say, Ontario. He thought this would have grave consequences on the negotiations in connection with the Constitution. Sharp got more support for this argument than for the others, including a public statement by Hellyer at a convention of the Nova Scotia Liberal Association in early January 1968 that the starting date for Medicare should be reviewed. (I was reminded of Hellyer's strictures about cabinet solidarity at the time of my speech on Vietnam in May 1967.) Then, on January 12, the Prime Minister who, by this time, was thoroughly preoccupied with the forthcoming constitutional conference, announced that the government would take another look at the Medicare plan. In the end, while everybody was made to look extremely silly, the proposal to defer Medicare again was defeated, mainly by MacEachen, Marchand, Benson, and myself.

Later still, Sharp raised the subject yet again, this time on the grounds that abandoning or deferring Medicare would show the government was taking its responsibilities seriously and thus help to support the position of the Canadian dollar. By this time, no one was prepared to reopen the subject for this or any other reason.

Some time in November, Sharp obtained approval to introduce a mini-budget on November 30. Many of us were worried about the proposed five per cent surcharge on personal incomes, which we thought would be difficult to get through the House. But Sharp was opposed to the alternative ways of raising the necessary revenues that had been suggested, and he remained committed to his own proposals. The bill to impose a surtax on personal incomes had a difficult passage through the House. On February 6, it received second reading by a vote of 84 to 73, which should have been a warning. I arrived in a half-empty House at about 5:30 P.M. on Monday, February 19, to find the bill was in committee. Someone ran over to ask me if I would speak in order to keep things going until the 6:00 P.M. adjournment, as we did not want to risk a vote. I agreed to this immediately, provided it would be satisfactory to Sharp if I spoke about the financial and economic situation in general terms. I was not anxious to speak in favour of the proposed increase in personal income taxes, which I had opposed so strenuously in cabinet. Sharp sent me a message that this would be quite in order and I made some notes for my speech. But I was not called upon to deliver it. Instead, to my surprise, at about 5:45 P.M., word was passed around that we had a comfortable majority and it had been decided to let the bill go to a vote, which the Liberals won by only 65 to 62. It was a near thing, and a grave risk to have taken. But at 6:00 P.M. we adjourned, assuming the danger was over until the bill came up for third reading later in the week.

I was sitting in the parliamentary restaurant having dinner when the bells began to ring at about ten minutes after eight. This was perplexing, and I proceeded to the Chamber with other members to find out what was going on. We discovered that at 8:00 P.M., when the House was called to order, Sharp and Bernard Pilon, the government Whip, had decided, against the advice and instructions of the House Leader, Allan Mac-Eachen, that it was safe to consent to having third reading of the contentious bill called immediately. It was a fateful decision. The bells rang for well over an hour while the opposition rounded up all the members they could find. Finally the vote was called, and the government was defeated 84 to 82. Later it turned out that two Liberal members, who were in Ottawa, refused to come to the House to vote as they were opposed to the proposed tax increase.

When the House adjourned at 10:00 P.M., we held a cabinet meeting in Winters' office. He was Acting Prime Minister in the absence of Pearson, who was holidaying in Jamaica, and Paul Martin, who was away campaigning. Various alternative courses of action were discussed. It was suggested that we could ask for a new vote of confidence, that Pearson could resign and recommend that some other Liberal be asked to form a government, or that Parliament could be dissolved and an election called for some appropriate date after the leadership convention.

The fact of the matter was that the government had been defeated on a major money bill, and by accepted constitutional practice it was no longer entitled to stay in office. I believe that if Robert Stanfield, the Leader of the Opposition, had felt more sure of his position, he could have forced a dissolution. In that event it would have been much more difficult for Trudeau to win the next election, even with less than an over-all majority.

Pearson was telephoned in Jamaica and agreed to return immediately. A day or two afterwards, I was informed that Sharp had offered to resign but was told this would not help. It was decided the government should ask for a vote of confidence and then introduce a new version of the old finance bill. There was considerable argument about the contents of the bill, with several ministers refusing to face the facts of political life. The government had taken a proper shellacking. It had lost its credibility and there were limits to what it could do in the circumstances. On top of all this, we were threatened with an exchange crisis. What should we do?

In the end, after much heated argument in cabinet, the government obtained its vote of confidence and obtained approval of a new finance bill which provided a three per cent surtax (instead of the originally proposed five per cent) on personal and corporation incomes, a speed-up in corporation income-tax collections, a further cut in government spending for the fiscal year 1968-69 of $75 million, a freeze on increases in the civil service, and the establishment of a prices and wages review board.

There was continual concern about the stability of the Canadian dollar during the fall of 1967, and especially in the early months of 1968. In a letter to the Prime Minister on June 1, 1967, when the Canadian dollar was quite strong, I had urged that there be some discussion of the advantages and disadvantages of reverting to a floating exchange rate. I spoke to him about this again on October 30, and reminded him of his chagrin in June 1962 at being talked into going along with Rasminsky's pleadings to support the fixed exchange rate and the austerity program which was necessary in order to get the support of the International Monetary Fund. This, in my view, had been a great mistake. A year later, not wishing to contemplate a second devaluation within a period of fourteen months, we had had to agree, as the price of being exempted from the American interest equalization tax, that our reserves would not exceed the then existing ceiling. This placed Canada in something of a strait-jacket. I argued that the subject of a floating exchange rate was one that was at least entitled to some serious discussion.

The Canadian dollar continued to weaken in the early months of 1968, and this was brought up in cabinet on several occasions. I felt this was extremely dangerous, as much of what went on in cabinet at that time was soon known to various journalists and the public. I urged the Prime Minister to hold a smaller meeting of those interested to discuss the situation in detail, and in particular to determine what our best course would be if we were suddenly confronted with devaluation. Finally, I wrote to him again on February 27, after I had submitted my resignation but before it was accepted.

In that letter I suggested that there were three courses open to us if it became apparent that we could not sustain the present value of the Canadian dollar. We could appeal to the International Monetary Fund for help; we could ask the American government to guarantee the present fixed rate of exchange; or we could adopt a floating rate. As to the first of these options, I said:

I am opposed to going to the IMF for help. The rate of exchange for the

308

Canadian dollar is not under attack primarily because it is too high in terms of general economic conditions in Canada. It is under attack because of the uncertain world situation, because of President Johnson's program for safeguarding the U.S. dollar and because of our inherently vulnerable position in respect of sudden withdrawals of funds by U.S. corporations from their Canadian subsidiaries. It can be argued, as Mr. Sharp does, that the situation is aggravated because costs in Canada have been increasing at too high a rate. While I do not disregard this factor in the situation, nevertheless I do not think this is the main reason for the current weakness in the exchange situation. But if we appeal to the IMF, that institution might well exact a price as they have done in the past. I do not believe we should place ourselves in this position.

For more or less similar reasons, I was against asking the American government to guarantee the rate of exchange for the Canadian dollar. Moreover, I suggested that "such a move would be another clear indication of our subservience or dependence on the U.S.A. I do not consider this to be either necessary or desirable."

Despite the fact that on February 27 both Pearson and Sharp said they were opposed to appealing to the American government for help, just two days later, Sharp and Rasminsky went to Washington to explain our situation and, according to my notes: "The Americans were startled by the extent of the problem – but I gathered the impression they will guarantee or support the Canadian dollar." How they planned to do this I was not able to find out.

As one would expect, the Bank of Canada was a strong advocate of the International Monetary Fund, and its officers were very much opposed to those who might suggest it would be in Canada's best interest to adopt a floating exchange rate. Some of the senior civil servants not connected with the Bank recognized that a case could be made in favour of a floating rate, an opinion that was held by a majority of academic economists and by some commercial bankers. But the bank was firmly opposed to considering such a course.

There is an implication here that only certain top officials know what is best or should know what is best. This surely is unacceptable. If it were true that the academic economists in Canada and some of the commercial bankers did not know all the arguments in favour of a fixed exchange rate, and this was the inference, then surely it should be the obligation of the Ottawa authorities to see they were informed. Speaking personally, I am against an assumption that laymen, including academic economists and commercial bankers, should be protected against knowing too much about international monetary matters, just as I think the philosophy of "quiet diplomacy" has had its day in international affairs. Such matters are too serious to be left entirely to the experts.

The report of the task force on foreign investment took considerably longer to complete than had been expected. I wrote to the Prime Minister about two matters which had a bearing on the work of the task force on November 7, 1967,* at which time I said, "I now expect that a draft will be ready for consideration by the cabinet committee or by cabinet itself by the end of November." This again proved to be too optimistic. The report was not completed until January 1968. One of its main proposals was that a special agency, or a branch of one of the existing departments, should be created, reporting directly to a minister, to co-ordinate all policies dealing with foreign-controlled companies in Canada. These companies should be required to respect Canadian aspirations and to behave in a manner consistent with Canadian economic and political goals. The agency or branch should assume responsibility for the present guiding principles program. This program, which is now a voluntary one, should be made mandatory and extended to cover information respecting the operations of the companies in question.

The report recommended that much fuller information should be provided to the public respecting the activities of corporations, particularly large corporations, regardless of their ownership, and that anti-combines and tariff policies should be used to maintain and increase competition, regardless of ownership of the firms involved. It recognized that "there is a special need to maintain a strong Canadian presence to countervail foreign private economic power and foreign government power."

In order to improve the efficiency of Canadian industry, the report proposed that certain industries should be rationalized. Although it was suggested that Canada should continue to promote multilateral tariff reductions, it was recommended that steps should be taken "to limit any tendencies under free trade for the locus of private decision-making to shift outside Canada," and to ensure that over-all Canadian employment did not "suffer in the short-run and the long-run."

The report proposed that positive steps should be taken to block the intrusion into Canada of United States law and policy applicable to American-owned subsidiaries with respect to freedom to export to Communist countries, with respect to anti-trust law and policy, and to balance of payments policy. Legislation along these lines has been enacted in The Netherlands. The report also proposed "that American balance of payments guidelines, controls and surveillance machinery, insofar as they affect the

*See Appendix 11.

behaviour of American-controlled subsidiaries in Canada, be counter-vailed by Canadian guidelines of an operational nature to foreign-owned subsidiaries and by the requisite surveillance machinery."

The report stated that "there is a need to ensure Canadian participation in the benefits of foreign direct investment and a Canadian presence in the decision-making of multi-national enterprises." In specific terms, it recommended that: the tax authorities should "exercise caution in granting special tax arrangements to industries predominantly consisting of foreign-owned firms"; the Canada Development Corporation should be created; and that stronger incentives should be provided to encourage large corporations, including foreign-owned subsidiaries, to offer their shares for sale to Canadians.

The report was much longer than had originally been intended and because of its form and style did not lend itself to being transformed into

REPRINTED WITH PERMISSION THE TORONTO STAR

a White Paper. In the circumstances, I thought the best thing would be to table the report and refer it for discussion to a standing committee of the House. I discussed this with the Prime Minister on January 31, and said I would like to table the report when the constitutional conference was over, and hoped the cabinet would agree that it should be referred to a standing committee. I suggested that the government should approve in principle the proposals contained in the report.

Pearson told me he had read the report and could see no reason why cabinet should not approve it in principle. However, a number of ministers were opposed to doing this. Winters did not believe the report should even be tabled on the grounds it might upset the financial markets. Sharp took the stand, which he repeated publicly, that the report was only the expression of the personal views of a group of professors and had no bearing on government policy. Some other ministers felt that, while the report should be tabled, it would be unwise to give the impression that the government approved it. The Prime Minister did not press his own views in cabinet.

As a result, I tabled the Watkins Report on February 15 and said it would be referred to the Standing Committee on Finance, Trade and Economic Affairs. It was made quite clear, however, that cabinet had not approved it either in principle or in detail. I had remained in the cabinet in the hope that I could persuade the government to commit itself to the recommendations of the eight economists who comprised the task force. I had not succeeded. My only consolation was the knowledge that if I had not stayed on it would have been most unlikely that this important report and its very useful proposals would ever have been made public.

I had been wanting to leave the cabinet since May 1967 when it became clear that the terms on which I rejoined the government were not going to be implemented. Once the report of the task force was published, there was nothing to keep me any longer – especially as the cabinet had failed to approve the report at least in principle. Accordingly, I submitted my resignation on February 19, four days after the report was tabled, to take effect as soon as was convenient, but in any event within the next two or three weeks. February 19 was the day the government was defeated in the House and, naturally, I did not wish to embarrass anyone by insisting that my resignation should be announced immediately.

However, there was one thing before cabinet that I was not prepared to go along with. This was the extension of the NORAD agreement, which I believed should be the subject of a full public debate and certainly should not be approved quietly in the dying days of the Pearson government. I was not prepared to stay in the cabinet if this agreement was going to be approved. I did not hear anything officially about my letter of resignation until March 1, when Pearson wrote accepting my resignation, the exact timing to be settled on my return to Ottawa on the following Monday. This suited me. I thought it would be much better for my resignation to become effective before I was asked to participate in the approval of a policy I was opposed to. My friends in the cabinet did not necessarily agree with my decision to resign as quickly as possible. According to a note dated Sunday, March 3:

> Trudeau called from the Royal York this morning. Benson was with him. Trudeau said he was afraid if I left, Marchand might go too – as he is very upset about his bill (*re* the CNTU). He said he hoped the four of us could get together on Monday or Tuesday. I'm not sure there is anything to be gained by this.

However, when I returned to Ottawa the next day, the Prime Minister asked me to stay on until the expiry of the three-week period stipulated in my letter, at which time my resignation would become effective. This I agreed to.

Mitchell Sharp, with whom I had had a number of disagreements over policy issues, wrote me a pleasant letter when my resignation was announced.

I did not stand for re-election in the general election of June 25, 1968.

Afterthoughts

Disappointments; writing my memoirs; Canadian Corporate Management Company Limited; Committee for an Independent Canada; appearances before the Prime Minister and the Standing Committee on Finance, Trade and Economic Affairs; article in Maclean's Magazine; *the composition of federal governments; The Canada Studies Foundation; Massey College and York University; death of Mike Pearson;* Storm Signals; *the fabulous party.*

I was in poor health when I decided not to run again in the 1968 election. The operation on my neck had been successful but I had not recovered from it fully and, from time to time, was still in considerable pain. Pierre Elliott Trudeau, the new Prime Minister, invited me to join his cabinet but, while I had supported him for the leadership against such conservatives as Winters, Hellyer, and Turner, and against Paul Martin who was not as young as he once was, I had misgivings about being able to work with him successfully.

I was disappointed because I had not been able to persuade the Liberal Party as a whole about the importance of reducing foreign economic control in Canada or to keep Mike Pearson persuaded on this issue. I had left an interesting professional practice to help reorganize the Liberal Party after 1958 and to help make my friend Mike Prime Minister. But in the course of six years in Parliament, in opposition as well as in minority government, my long friendship with Pearson had gradually come unstuck. This left me saddened and somewhat disillusioned with the gentle game of politics.

I was sixty-two years of age, too old to return to professional practice in the way I had enjoyed it in the past, and finished with active politics, but too young to sit around and watch the trees grow. I decided on two things, to write my political memoirs while things were still fresh in my mind and to return to the business world. I did the former during the summer and early fall of 1968 and then revised the manuscript slightly in the summer of 1969. While doing this, I had every intention of publishing the book more or less immediately, but upon reflection decided this should not be done for the time being. Then one day, late in 1970, Denis Smith, a political scientist and distinguished scholar, came to see me at the suggestion of Mel Hurtig, the Edmonton publisher. Smith said he wished to write a book about me in the context of the politics of the sixties and requested access to my papers. I had not met him before and he was not a member of the Liberal Party. I thought these considerations should guarantee his objectivity insofar as I was concerned. So with some trepidation I agreed to his request. He wrote a generous biography which was published two years later as *Gentle Patriot*.

Concurrently, back in the summer of 1968, I joined my friend Larry Bonnycastle at Canadian Corporate Management, a company I had organized after the Second World War and which Bonnycastle had managed with intelligence and skill for nearly twenty years. Together it took us about six months to analyze in detail the company's prospects and potential, its various interests and personnel, and, having agreed upon our conclusions, we proceeded to implement them over the next few years with considerable success. In this, we were assisted by Val Stock who became President in 1972. Bonnycastle and I have continued our active participation in the management as Chairman and Vice-Chairman of the Board.

Early in 1970, two friends of mine, Abraham Rotstein, an economist at the University of Toronto, and Peter Newman, editor-in-chief of *The Toronto Star* and subsequently editor of *Maclean's Magazine*, had lunch with me to talk about that perennial subject, the growing foreign influence over the Canadian economy, the Canadian independence issue. Following this discussion, we decided to form the Committee for an Independent Canada and proceeded to enlist the sponsorship of a wide cross-section of well-known Canadians from all walks of life and all regions of Canada. Jack McClelland and Claude Ryan became the first Co-Chairmen, to be followed by Eddie Goodman, a prominent Conservative, and Mel Hurtig, at the time a left-wing Liberal. Hurtig was succeeded by Robert Page, a professor at Trent University and a Conservative. He, in turn, was succeeded by Dave Treleaven and Bruce Willson. Dorothy Petrie, Flora MacDonald, and Barbara Daprato were among the early Executive Directors.

The objective of the C.I.C. was simply to focus attention on the issue by speaking about it to all kinds of audiences. In this, with great help from the media, we were successful. In my capacity as the first Honorary Chairman,

I made some fifty speeches in the six months ending May 1971. The various Chairmen and Flora MacDonald made many more. It was agreed at the beginning that the C.I.C. should be strictly non-partisan. The purpose of the Committee was to inform Canadians of what was happening, to focus attention on the issue, and then to leave it with the politicians. There was no thought of starting a new political party which could never have been successful. It was not intended originally to keep the C.I.C. going for any extended period.

Since the C.I.C.'s founding in 1970, an increasing number of Canadians have become aware of the extent of foreign control of the economy and of the implications of this control. This assertion is confirmed by all the recent opinion polls and surveys.

In June 1971, between sixty and seventy members of the Committee assembled in Ottawa to meet the Prime Minister and present a petition signed by 170,000 Canadians urging that action be taken to regain economic control of the economy. Mr. Trudeau sent word that he would prefer to meet with a smaller group which would make it easier to discuss the matter in more detail. This was agreed to but, naturally, with some disappointment on the part of those who had come to Ottawa at their own expense and would not have the opportunity of meeting the Prime Minister. It was decided that those who would meet with Mr. Trudeau should include Jack McClelland, our Chairman, Eddie Goodman, Mel Hurtig, Flora MacDonald, myself, and two or three others. McClelland began with a statement along the following lines:

Mr. Prime Minister:

It has been suggested that ours is a pressure group and that is true. But we are not a political organization in any sense of the term. Our Committee was formed to provide a focus for the views of those Canadians who are concerned about the dominating influence of foreigners – mainly Americans – over all phases of our lives. We felt this could best be done if we emphasized the non-partisan character of our group and this has proved to be the case.

Essentially, we represent a large number of Canadians who believe the present excessive foreign control of our industry and resources and the extent of this foreign influence in our cultural and social affairs to be one of the two most critical issues facing Canada today. (The other is the question of Quebec.) Naturally, we are aware that a government charged with responsibility for all things must concern itself on a priority basis with such crucial matters as unemployment, inflation, constitutional issues, regional disparities, social welfare, external relations, long-term development. It is our view not only that these problems may be better solved within the context of a common and united goal of economic independence but that it is the only framework in which any of these issues can be satisfactorily resolved in the long term.

One of the unstated purposes of the C.I.C. has been to present our views and findings to you prior to the introduction of whatever policies may result from consideration of the Honourable Mr. Gray's report on foreign ownership.

I am going to ask Miss Flora MacDonald, our Executive Director, to read a few paragraphs from our brief, after which we shall ask Mr. Gordon to enlarge upon it. Then if you wish, we shall be happy to answer any questions.

According to my notes, we all agreed it was an excellent interview and that the Prime Minister seemed most receptive. My notes record that "on the substance of our submission, we urged the importance of giving the proposed government agency broad powers to supervise the operations of foreign-controlled companies in Canada and spent quite a bit of time on what the agency should be expected to do." During the course of the discussion, Trudeau "referred to some private correspondence he had with me recently. In that correspondence, he had reiterated the fact that he still agreed with me on the foreign control issue." I found this heartening.

According to my notes of the meeting, Trudeau said he felt the Committee had done a fine job in focusing public attention on this issue and hoped it would continue in existence. He said the government was now considering Herb Gray's report and that they would be coming forward with a policy statement soon (by which we thought he meant that September). He said he felt it would be helpful to the government in getting its proposals accepted if spokesmen for the Committee in different parts of Canada were prepared to express their views thereon. "All of us came away feeling that we had had an excellent hearing and that the government will produce a policy statement within the next few months. We felt also that the attention and pressure exerted by the C.I.C. had been well worth while."

But nothing happened and we heard no word from Mr. Trudeau.

In the following year, the creation of the Foreign Investment Review Agency was announced. This new agency deals only with takeovers and new investment proposals which together in an average year account for only a small fraction of the annual increase in foreign investment in this country. The annual increase is mainly accounted for by the expansion of existing foreign-controlled companies in Canada.

On a later occasion I appeared before the Standing Committee on Finance, Trade and Economic Affairs, on June 13, 1972, to protest the provisions of the bill to create the Foreign Investment Review Agency. The following is a portion of my submission:

I was a member of the delegation from the Committee for an Independent Canada that submitted the Committee's views on the Canadian independence issue to the Prime Minister in June 1971. We had an excellent discussion with Mr. Trudeau which lasted for more than an hour and which covered the whole subject. The Prime Minister assured us that the government was on the verge of announcing a strong policy for dealing with the problem of foreign control of the Canadian economy. He urged the Committee to stay in being so that people would be available in all parts of Canada to support the government's position and to assist public opinion in focusing upon it. We left the Prime Minister feeling that, at long last, a Canadian government was about to tackle this vital issue.

The Committee proceeded to raise the funds needed to stay in business and waited patiently for Mr. Trudeau to announce the government's "strong policy." Finally, at the beginning of last month, it was announced in effect that the Prime Minister no longer thought it was important to do anything at all significant to contain the increasing control of our economy by foreigners or, in other words, to do anything meaningful about the Canadian independence issue. The government rejected the findings and proposals of the Gray Report. The whole matter was taken out of the hands of Mr. Gray, who is concerned about the increasing foreign control of our economy, and turned over to Mr. Pépin.

Apparently, the government does not propose to do anything about this vital issue other than the provisions of this Bill which could prevent some takeovers if Mr. Pépin, the minister responsible, is so minded. But, from what he has said to an audience of American businessmen and to others, one may be forgiven for assuming the minister will not be so minded very often.

Later in an interview the Prime Minister confirmed that this is all there is to be; that there is nothing up his sleeve. I believe he added that he – and presumably other members of his party – are prepared to be judged by this decision.

Bill C-201, as I am sure all members of the Committee will acknowledge, will not reduce the level of foreign control over the economy. The extent of foreign control will continue to grow – as it has in the past – through the expansion of existing Canadian subsidiaries of foreign parent corporations. This is by far and away the most important source of growth. For the most part, this expansion has been and will continue to be financed by the retained earnings of these Canadian subsidiaries including the generous depletion and capital cost allowances they receive.

Second, the extent of foreign control will continue to grow as a result of new developments promoted in Canada by foreigners. I believe the government was right, in present circumstances of high unemployment, not to restrict new developments that will provide new job opportunities. However, as I am sure we all know, there are other and more effective ways of reducing unemployment if that is really our primary objective.

Finally, the extent of foreign control will continue to grow as a result of takeovers of existing Canadian enterprises. But this represents only about 10%, more or less, of the total growth of foreign control in most years. And this, of course, is the only area that Bill C-201 touches on. Moreover, its provisions are subject to the discretion of the Minister of Industry, Trade and Commerce. There has been no suggestion that the Minister will stop all takeovers. Quite the contrary. Therefore, this particular Bill will not affect the continuing growth of foreign control of our economy except perhaps in a very minor way. It is completely inadequate by itself to deal with the Canadian independence issue. And we are told that nothing else is planned.

It is ironical that while most of the growth in the foreign control of our economy is financed by the retained earnings of Canadian subsidiaries of foreign corporations, part of the funds required are being provided by our own banks and other Canadian lending institutions. In this way, Canadian savings are used to help foreigners increase their control of the Canadian economy.

This may be as good a place as any to emphasize that it would not be wise for Canada to shut out all inflows of foreign capital, particularly capital that comes here for investment in bonds and other fixed-term securities. We can pay off this kind of obligation at some time in the future. It is not this type of foreign capital investment that constitutes a threat to Canada's continued independence.

With the greatest respect, Gentlemen, I suggest to you that this Bill may confuse some members of the Canadian public into believing that Members of Parliament are really and seriously concerned about the Canadian independence issue and are doing something important about it. This will not be the case. I would urge the Committee, therefore, to recommend some changes that would strengthen Bill C-201 and thereby make its provisions more meaningful.

I have quoted from the above submission at considerable length because I believe the views expressed therein are still pertinent. The fact is that foreign control and influence over the Canadian economy has proceeded and is still proceeding apace. I am as firmly convinced as I ever was that unless we regain control of the Canadian economy we shall gradually and imperceptibly lose an increasing measure of our political as well as our economic independence. I believe that a majority of Canadians now sense this.

I expect all those who met with Mr. Trudeau in June 1971 and then heard nothing from him except the announcement of the government's rather pathetic intention to establish what later became the Foreign Investment Review Agency felt as frustrated and let down as I did. In my case, I wrote an article for *Maclean's Magazine* which appeared in the September 1972 issue, prior to the general election one month later. The article, under the heading "Last Chance for Canada," began:

> The spring of 1972 may turn out to be the beginning of the end for Canada.
>
> The unrest and unhappiness that appear to be increasing in Quebec were highlighted this spring by some serious labour disturbances. And in May, I was shocked by the federal government's repudiation of the Gray Report and the complete inadequacy of its legislation for coming to grips with the Canadian independence issue. If whoever is called upon to head the Canadian government after the next election is unable to settle the problems of Quebec and Canadian independence within the next four years, it may be too late to do anything about them. . . .

After discussing the issue, I went on to quote what Mr. Trudeau had written some years previously:

> It is difficult to understand why the Trudeau government decided to adopt a do-nothing – or practically nothing – stance on independence. In *Cité Libre* as far back as 1958, Mr. Trudeau wrote: "Shall we suffer passively our situation of economic domination? It would be better to be annexed outright by the United States than be exploited without limit."
>
> From what he has said subsequently, there has been nothing to suggest that he had changed his mind about this basic issue; that is, until quite recently.

I went on to refer to our meeting with the Prime Minister in June 1971 and concluded the article with these words:

> In all probability, therefore, this will be the last time that ordinary Canadians – those of us who are not or are no longer actively engaged in politics – will have a chance to influence the way our country is to go.
>
> In these circumstances, it is vitally important for us to insist that all candidates in the election state clearly and without equivocation where

they stand on the two issues I have been writing about. It is even more important that we know where the party leaders stand, without any hedging or vague promises. In Mr. Trudeau's case, Canadians are entitled to ask what he will do if he is re-elected to head another government – and for an explanation of his failure to do more than he has about these two basic issues during the past four years. I hope the Prime Minister will give us convincing answers to these questions. Apart from everything else, this would resolve my personal dilemma as a long-time member of the Liberal Party and perhaps that of others who may think as I do. If Pierre Trudeau does not announce some major changes in his policies, I expect some of us will decide, on the day of the election, that we must put the future of our country first.

In a separate piece in the same September 1972 issue of *Maclean's,* I advanced some views about Quebec:

> With the notable exception of Lester B. Pearson and his talented adviser Maurice Lamontagne, most Canadian prime ministers and their colleagues have tended to treat Quebec as if it were a province like all the others. But this has never been the case. Quite apart from the question of language, Quebec has always been subject to the civil code inherited from France, while the English-speaking provinces have followed the common law of Britain. There are also wide differences in culture and ways of thinking between French- and English-speaking Canadians. These differences, as well as the natural fears and frustrations of French Canadians about the preservation of their identity, should be acknowledged and respected by all English-speaking Canadians concerned about the future of our country.

After discussing a number of possibilities for meeting the views and aspirations of Quebeckers, I concluded my article with these words:

> But if there is a chance that a more flexible and understanding attitude toward Quebec under a formula of this kind would reduce the tensions in that province to some meaningful extent and thereby reduce the threat of separation, should it not be tried? Especially when separation includes the possibility of civil conflict? It seems unlikely that we shall be able to avoid a breakup of our country indefinitely if we continue to pretend that Quebec is a province like all the others. Why not admit that she is different before, not after, we are confronted with a national catastrophe?

My views about Quebec are very different from those held by Mr. Trudeau, at least as he expressed them in conversation with me. His assertion at that time that Quebec is a province like all the others and must be so treated flies in the face of all the facts.

Canadian governments, like governments in other countries, reflect the characters, the personalities, the drives, and the personal objectives of the prime ministers who hold office from time to time. Ideally, if the Prime Minister comes from English-speaking Canada, he should have a French-speaking Quebecker as his chief lieutenant. If the Prime Minister is from Quebec, he should have an English-speaking second-in-command. Between them, the Prime Minister and his chief lieutenant should have an intuitive understanding of the thinking and responses of people in the two quite different sections of our country. No English-speaking Prime Minister should ever believe he fully understands the subjective feelings of Quebeckers. And no French-Canadian Prime Minister, no matter how bilingual he may be, should think he fully appreciates the peculiar and often somewhat illogical ways in which Canadians in other parts of the country react and arrive at their conclusions. I believe this idea of true partnership at the top between the Prime Minister and his chief lieutenant is an essential factor in any truly successful federal administration.

Secondly and again ideally, the cabinet should include one or more people who have a real understanding of business and finance. Otherwise, the responsible ministers and the cabinet as a whole will be completely dependent upon their senior civil servants and the top officials of the Bank of Canada. In the days of Mackenzie King, there were people in the cabinet like Charles Dunning, C.D. Howe, and later Layton Ralston and Louis St. Laurent who had had extensive connections in business circles. They may have tended to be a bit conservative as a result, but at least they understood the implications and probable effects of the various policy proposals made to cabinet. And in their day, they could rely on Clifford Clark and Bill Mackintosh at the Department of Finance, Norman Robertson at the Department of External Affairs who had a deep understanding of international finance and economics, and Graham Towers at the Bank of Canada. The advice of these men was always sound and could be trusted by the ministers. There have been many able and dedicated men and women in the senior echelons of the civil service and the Bank of Canada since those days. But, with the exception of Bob Bryce, they have not had quite the very exceptional talents and imagination of the men referred to. So I repeat that, ideally, a successful Canadian government should include one or more members with a broad understanding of finance and economics. If it should happen that the Prime Minister himself has had some experience in these areas, so much the better.

Thirdly and ideally, a Canadian cabinet should include someone who is sympathetic to, and preferably who is identified with, organized labour. And it should include several women. Obviously, it should have representatives from the various regions of the country, although I do not consider

322

it essential for every single province to be represented. As a progressive-minded liberal, I should add that at least a majority of the members of any cabinet formed by the Liberal Party should be forward-looking and innovative in their thinking. And I would hope they would hold strong views on the Canadian independence issue.

If the kind of people I have indicated, especially a principal lieutenant who is an acceptable leader from Quebec, for example, or from English-speaking Canada as the case may be, and someone with some personal experience and understanding of business and finance, are not available among the members elected from time to time, the Prime Minister should consider looking outside his parliamentary group for men or women with the necessary qualities. Mackenzie King did this in 1941 when he brought in Louis St. Laurent, and Pearson tried with less success with Guy Favreau. Diefenbaker brought in Wallace McCutcheon through the Senate. While approaches such as these could not be pursued too often, upon occasion they could be very helpful.

Finally, if a cabinet is to operate well, if its members are to work in harmony, they should all feel a true sense of loyalty to the Prime Minister and be prepared to support him no matter what the circumstance. And this sense of loyalty should be reciprocated by the Prime Minister to his colleagues.

In this context, let us look at the strengths and weaknesses of the men who have held the office of Prime Minister in the last forty-five years and the difficulties they have been up against.

R.B. Bennett, whose Conservative Party came to power in 1930, was a hard-driving, self-confident, direct, and forthright corporation lawyer who towered above his cabinet colleagues and who obviously called the shots. He was doomed to failure by the fact he came to office at the beginning of the Great Depression. No one could have survived that period. Bennett's government started attacking massive unemployment by doing the wrong things; cutting expenditures and preaching parsimony. But in fairness to Bennett, it should be remembered that in those pre-Keynesian days no one else seemed able to suggest credible alternatives, at least to begin with. But Bennett was an intelligent as well as a hard-driving man and, under the influence and with the help of his brother-in-law W. H. Herridge, he was finally converted to more appropriate policies. In his last year as Prime Minister, he proposed a far-reaching set of progressive policies which were incorporated in legislation. It was too late in the day, however, to save his government, which was defeated in 1935. Subsequently, nearly all his progressive legislation was ruled to be unconstitutional.

There was no one in Bennett's cabinet who approached him in power or influence, and he did not have a strong French-Canadian lieutenant. His principal advisers were Bill Herridge, an Ottawa lawyer, Rod Finlayson, his secretary, and O. D. Skelton, whom Mackenzie King had appointed Under Secretary of State for External Affairs some years before but who managed to gain Mr. Bennett's confidence. If there were other advisers of importance, I do not know of them. Nor do I know about the question of loyalty in the Bennett cabinet. Harry Stevens, the Minister of Trade and Commerce, resigned over a disagreement and later left the Conservative Party in 1934 to form the Reconstruction Party. But considering the desperate economic conditions of the 1930s, it is surprising there were not more resignations and upheavals. Perhaps this was due more to Mr. Bennett's powerful personality than to any feeling of personal affection or loyalty for him.*

Mackenzie King was a very different type of man, wily, tortuous, and skilful at playing one political enemy or one cabinet colleague off against another. (The distinction may be only a matter of semantics!) He always seemed afraid of Arthur Meighen, a great debater. But after Meighen's departure and Bennett's defeat, King was confronted with a succession of relatively ineffectual opposition leaders and he made the most of it. King, while a devious character with some peculiar habits and beliefs, as has later come to light, had a real understanding of Canadian politics. He relied implicitly on Ernest Lapointe, his Quebec partner and lieutenant. And when Lapointe died, he insisted on another French-Canadian second-in-command of equal stature and ability. He passed over his French-Canadian colleagues in the cabinet and brought in Louis St. Laurent, a brilliant lawyer from Quebec who knew little about politics but was to show he could learn quickly.

King put together a series of strong cabinets including such men as Lapointe, and later St. Laurent, Charles Dunning, C. D. Howe, J.L. Ilsley, J.L. Ralston, and later, Douglas Abbott and Brooke Claxton. And he was blessed with some of the ablest civil servants we have ever had, O.D. Skelton, W.C. Clark (a most imaginative man), Norman Robertson, Mike Pearson, Graham Towers, and Arnold Heeney, among others, and he relied upon their advice and policy proposals. In addition to having first-

---

* Mr. Bennett always dressed in formal attire; morning coat, striped trousers, and a large, black waistcoat covering his well-developed paunch. He was not what in these days might be described as a "swinger." Nevertheless, there is a story about him, no doubt apocryphal, striding into the stenographers' pool in the East Block one Christmas Eve. There was some mistletoe over the door and coming the other way was a pretty young stenographer. According to the story, Bennett grabbed her and kissed her soundly on the lips. Then holding her off away from his ample paunch, he demanded, "What did you think of that, young lady?" To which the young typist is said to have replied, "More of an honour than a pleasure, Prime Minister."

class men around him in Ottawa, King kept in touch with a great number of friends and advisers across the country with whom he maintained constant touch by telephone and correspondence. These were his political antennae, of vital importance in the days before opinion surveys.

Apart from the preservation of national unity, which must always be a top priority with prime ministers, King was determined to change Canada's colonial status *vis-à-vis* Great Britain. In this he was successful only to fall into the trap of encouraging a similar status for us *vis-à-vis* the United States.

With his intense preoccupation with political survival, King was always reluctant to embrace new ideas and new policies. He preferred to move slowly or, it often seemed, not to move at all. And yet in fairness, he was persuaded by Clifford Clark, supported by Bill Mackintosh, to introduce some important social legislation towards the end of World War II, including unemployment insurance and family allowances.

When it came to loyalty, King seemed to rely primarily on fear and, upon occasion, on his ability to play one minister off against another. While his ministers appreciated his ability to get himself and them elected, few had any real affection for him. I knew two who thoroughly despised him.

Mackenzie King is not likely to go down in history as a Great Canadian Hero. To be revered by successive generations, a Canadian political leader must surely have more important, more inspiring aims and objectives than mere political longevity.

Louis St. Laurent who succeeded King as Prime Minister in 1948 was a man of very different stamp. He was intelligent, well-organized, charming, courteous, and respected by everyone who came in contact with him. C.D. Howe was obviously his chief lieutenant in English-speaking Canada but, in addition, he had other able cabinet colleagues including Brooke Claxton, Doug Abbott, Walter Harris, and Mike Pearson. And he still had Clifford Clark and Graham Towers at Finance and the Bank of Canada. He presided over the government and supported Pearson during Canada's greatest period in international affairs and, despite a somewhat conservative background and experience, he had a curiosity and an open mind about domestic policies. As I pointed out in Chapter Four, he became interested in the critical views that I put forward in 1955 about current economic policies and, as a result, appointed the Royal Commission on Canada's Economic Prospects.

Mr. St. Laurent's colleagues were always intensely loyal to him, and I am sure these sentiments were reciprocated. To me, Louis St. Laurent was the greatest of Canada's prime ministers in the last fifty years. I have no personal knowledge of the ones who came before that!

Mr. St. Laurent fought the election in 1957 when he was seventy-five years old and virtually exhausted both mentally and physically. The Liberals had been in office for twenty-two years, a period that had included the last years of the depression and the six years of World War II. It was time for a change, and John Diefenbaker was elected at the head of a surprised Conservative Party. He remained Prime Minister from June 1957 until April 1963.

Diefenbaker, a Prairie lawyer and rhetorician, was a great performer, both on the stump and in the House of Commons which he dominated for nearly six years. But he had no sense of organization, no personal knowledge of business or finance, no one in his cabinet who knew much about these things either until he brought in Wallace McCutcheon, and no outstanding French-Canadian lieutenant. As a result, the Diefenbaker government was quite incapable of dealing with the economic and other problems the country was confronted with from 1958 until the end of his term in office.

It was a one-man government and it is doubtful if many of his more senior cabinet colleagues, apart from Gordon Churchill, Howard Green, Alvin Hamilton, and J. Waldo Monteith, had any deep feelings of personal loyalty to him; or, for that matter, if he had for them. In the end, he went down to defeat following a series of revolts and resignations by his colleagues.*

Lester B. Pearson became Prime Minister of a minority Liberal government in 1963 after a rugged six years in opposition which followed the devastating defeats of 1957 and 1958. He was deeply conscious of the fact that he did not have a chief lieutenant from Quebec who was accepted in that province. With this in mind, he persuaded Guy Favreau, a wonderful,

---

* In the second volume of his memoirs, Mr. Diefenbaker wrote: "One of the ironies of recent Canadian history is that Walter Gordon, a man whom I had met only for a few minutes when he delivered to me his Royal Commission Report, had stated that he decided to do everything in his power to make Mr. Pearson Prime Minister because he hated me and feared that my policies would wreck Canada!" What a strange man Mr. Diefenbaker is. It is quite true that I thought his policies were disastrous but I am certain I never said I hated him. In fact, I do not believe I have ever said I hated anyone. I do not use that kind of language. But speaking of Mr. Diefenbaker's strangeness, his suspicions, and his fears that anything said could be used against him in the future, I remember, when I was a member of the opposition in the fall of 1962, Mr. Diefenbaker, then still Prime Minister, shaking his forefinger at me and shouting that I personally had cost him twenty-five seats in the 1962 election. That was quite a compliment to any politician in my position and I felt flattered. But when some time later I went to check what he had said in *Hansard*, I could find no record of it. In those days, Cabinet Ministers were shown the preliminary drafts of the *Hansard* record – the "blues" – and given a chance to correct grammatical errors or, in Diefenbaker's case, to punctuate his long, involved sentences and even to add a verb or two where these had been omitted. It was understood, however, that changes should not be made that would in any way change the sense of what was said. In this case, Mr. Diefenbaker or someone in his office had simply deleted his comment altogether.

generous-hearted man and a former civil servant, to run in the 1963 election. Favreau was elected but he knew little about politics and got into a series of difficulties which undoubtedly destroyed his health. He died in 1967, beloved by all of us who knew him well.

Pearson's colleagues in the cabinet, with few exceptions, had great loyalty and affection for him, despite the fact they recognized his weaknesses, and despite the fact that Mike's loyalty to his colleagues in return was sometimes uncertain and inconsistent. Nevertheless, his first minority government accomplished many things in its turbulent two-and-one-half years in office from 1963 to 1965. His second minority government was less successful but it did manage finally, after many delays, waverings, and some changes of mind to get health insurance on the statute books.

In spite of his ambiguous attitudes at times, and his less-than-consistent support for particular policies, Pearson at heart was a confirmed Canadian nationalist. And he was progressive in his thinking when it came to social legislation, as the accomplishments of his government clearly showed.

Pearson was as intelligent as any of our prime ministers have been and was wittier, more entertaining, and more fun to be with than any of them. These great human qualities should not be overlooked by future historians.

Pierre Elliott Trudeau was elected Leader of the Liberal Party in April 1968 and won a resounding victory in the general election that followed in June of that year. Before the election, Bob Winters decided to retire permanently from politics and Paul Martin became Government Leader in the Senate and later High Commissioner to the United Kingdom. In 1969, Paul Hellyer resigned from the cabinet and from the Liberal Party. In 1971, Eric Kierans, the Postmaster General, who also had been a leadership contender in 1968, resigned from the cabinet. Ben Benson resigned as Minister of Finance in 1972, to be succeeded by John Turner. While Turner was not looked upon as Trudeau's chief lieutenant for English-speaking Canada in any official sense – there seemed to be more a feeling of rivalry and suspicion than of partnership between them – he was clearly the heir apparent if anything should happen to the Prime Minister. And quite obviously he wanted that position when the time became appropriate. But Trudeau is still Prime Minister, after nine years in office, and John Turner is engaged in a new legal and business career at which he should do well. Such are the upsets of politics.

There is still no English-speaking second-in-command. Trudeau, who is highly intelligent and completely bilingual without being attuned intuitively to the way English-speaking Canadians think, has tried to fill both roles himself. He has not been successful in so doing. He simply does not comprehend the reactions of people in English-speaking Canada. And so, from time to time his government has been in trouble.

In its first four years in office, the Trudeau government adopted a conservative stance supported in cabinet by four of its strongest members, Drury, Sharp, Turner, and the Prime Minister himself. On the advice of the Bank of Canada, restrictive policies were introduced in late 1969 and early 1970, with the result the economy was slowed and many people became unemployed. The objective of these policies was, of course, to contain inflation and in this they were more or less successful. No doubt, the Bank's officials were pleased with these results but, in political terms, the Trudeau government was all but defeated at the polls, getting 109 seats in the October 1972 election to 107 seats for the Tories and 31 for the N.D.P.

Trudeau faced up to this defeat and managed to survive a minority position for eighteen months, thanks in part to a much less arrogant attitude and the skilful work of Allan MacEachen who had been appointed House Leader. At the same time, Trudeau was preparing for the next election with the help of Senator Keith Davey whom he seconded as Chairman of his Campaign Committee.

Thanks to Keith Davey's masterly political direction and the government's more sensitive response to popular wishes and demands during the period of minority government, and also to opposition leader Robert Stanfield's inability to explain his price-and-wage control proposals, the Liberals won a resounding victory in July 1974, winning 140 seats in the election.

Trudeau is said to be more than careful about his personal expenditures and finances. But this has not been reflected in the level of expenditures of his government. During the past eight years, the expenditures of the federal government and the number of federal civil servants have increased phenomenally, and this has led to record government deficits. To the extent these have been financed by the Bank of Canada through increases in the money supply, this has contributed to the high rates of inflation from which we have been suffering.

It can be argued that because of the present cabinet committee system, and the division of responsibilities between several ministers in the same general fields, especially in economic matters, no one seems to be in full charge except, of course, the Prime Minister himself. The result has been poor administration of the economy and government expenditures that have got out of control.

Trudeau seems to have the loyal support of the present members of his cabinet but, since he became Prime Minister in 1968, most of the original English-speaking members have gone for one reason or another – Martin, Hellyer, Kierans, Benson, Gray, O'Connell, Stanbury, Haidasz, Turner, Richardson, Drury, and Sharp. Not all these questioned Mr. Trudeau's leadership or were disloyal to him. John Turner, in particular, was always meticulous in his support of the Prime Minister while a member of the cabinet. But the fact remains there have been a great many changes in the membership of Mr. Trudeau's governments.

Trudeau loyally supported his friend Jean Marchand without whom he could not have been elected leader of the Liberal Party. And he has supported some others, including Gérard Pelletier, now Ambassador to France, and Jean-Pierre Goyer, the Minister of Supply. However, he has shown less understanding of the feelings of some of those who have been dropped from his cabinet. Some of these men may not have been among the government's strongest ministers. And some of them have received or presumably will receive new appointments. But others have been dropped and are languishing on the back benches. Surely some other positions could have been found for them if for no other reason than to assuage their natural sensitivities.

Shortly before the founding of the Committee for an Independent Canada, A.B. Hodgetts asked me to become Chairman of The Canada Studies Foundation. Hodgetts, a much-beloved and very able school teacher, had written *What Culture? What Heritage?* which was published in 1968. It is a report of the most thorough investigation ever undertaken into the teaching of Canadian studies in the schools across the country. And it demonstrated a woeful ignorance about Canada on the part of both teachers and students. As stated in the first report of The Canada Studies Foundation:

> It is appropriate to remind ourselves periodically that The Canada Studies Foundation was established to carry forward the ideas of Mr. Hodgetts following his report in 1968 – *What Culture? What Heritage?* – on the way in which Canadian studies are taught in our primary and secondary schools. The purpose of the Foundation is to attempt, with the co-operation of active teachers in our secondary schools and a number of academic advisers from our universities, a new approach which is designed to excite the interest and the co-operation of both teachers and students. Essentially, it is a pilot project and its activities should be completed within a five-year period. It is hoped that if the new approaches sponsored by the Foundation are successful, they will be taken up by the ten provincial Departments of Education after that time and applied on a more widespread scale throughout the whole educational system.

The Canada Studies Foundation was a pilot project financed to the extent of nearly two million dollars over a five-year period by individuals, corporations, and private foundations. This private funding enabled the Foundation to obtain more than another million dollars from the Canada Council, the Secretary of State, school boards, teachers' federations, universities, etc. Quite apart from such essential financial support, the Foundation benefited enormously from the time and enthusiasm of a dedicated lot of school teachers in every province. All the projects sponsored by the Foundation have involved teachers and students from more than a single province. We were particularly pleased that teachers and students from the Province of Quebec were prepared to participate whole-heartedly in the work, despite language and other difficulties.

As was to be expected, Birnie Hodgetts, the Director of the Foundation for the whole five years, was the heart and soul of the organization and generated most of its ideas. He provided the inspiration which successfully resulted in attracting university professors, school teachers, and the students who became actively engaged in working together on the projects sponsored by the Foundation. His contributions were of paramount importance. The Foundation could not have existed, let alone succeeded, without him.

My role as Chairman was to help raise the necessary finances and to do some of the liaison work with governments. In addition, in the course of many meetings, I had a chance to meet and talk with a considerable number of dedicated teachers and, on some occasions, with their students. It became crystal clear that both teachers and students are desperately anxious to have more opportunities to learn about our country. And I was reinforced in my conviction that Canadians want this country to remain free and independent in the future. At the end of the pilot period, responsibility for the Foundation's continued operations was assumed by the Council of Ministers of Education and the Secretary of State.

Birnie Hodgetts succeeded me as Chairman with Paul Lacoste, the Rector of the University of Montreal, continuing as Co-chairman. Paul Gallagher, who has been associated with the Foundation from the beginning, succeeded Hodgetts as full-time Director.

Concurrently with these activities, I was given opportunities to see something of what is happening in post-secondary education in this country. In April 1973, Robertson Davies, the Master of Massey College in the University of Toronto, invited me to become a Senior Fellow of the College. And in September 1973, I was appointed Chancellor of York University, a position that carries with it membership on both the Board of Governors and the Senate of the University. I have enjoyed both of these associations.

I had not seen Mike Pearson in the more than four years since I left Ottawa in March 1968, except casually at two or three large receptions, and once on a plane trip. But in November 1972, I began to hear stories that he had cancer and did not have long to live. Barbara Ward, whom I had seen recently in Chicago, George Ignatieff, and John Aird all told me they had been in touch with Mike and that he would like to see me. I also felt I would like to see him again before he died. Accordingly, after checking with Patsy Hannah, Mike's daughter, I went to Ottawa on November 28, 1972. My note about this reads as follows:

> I found him in better shape than I had been led to believe. Clear in his head, witty, and quite reconciled to whatever may be in store. He said he was due for another set of chemical treatments in the hope the cancer may be contained. He did not appear to have much hope of success, however.
>
> I congratulated him on the first volume of his memoirs. He said someone else would have to complete the remaining two volumes. He is trying to complete his recollections of certain events and individuals but stated he would not have time to do the necessary checking.
>
> Mike quite obviously was pleased to see me. He said he was troubled by two things that happened when he was P.M. The first was about Favreau. Pearson came very close to acknowledging he had been in the wrong in not stating Favreau had spoken to him about Rouleau-Rivard, etc.
>
> The second matter as he put it was the way he and I had "drifted apart."
>
> I stayed with him for 30-40 minutes. He kept on pressing me not to leave – but I had been warned that he gets tired very easily.
>
> If it helped him to see me again – and our conversation was very easy; no strain – I am glad I went.

I cannot pretend to have forgotten some of the things that happened between Mike Pearson and me a decade ago. As Minister of Finance, I had taken a long and ferocious beating in the House of Commons over the 1963 budget, made more difficult by the failure of Pearson as Prime Minister to support me, if not in the House then at least in cabinet. The substantive provisions of that budget had proved to be successful with the result that unemployment had been reduced very considerably. This was what the Liberals had been elected to accomplish. Nevertheless, I had become thoroughly unpopular with the business community and this made life difficult, not only for me but also for Pearson and his government. He would have been quite entitled, therefore, to ask for my resignation and appoint a new Minister of Finance more acceptable to business if he believed that this was called for. I had told him that, if he felt this to be politically desirable, I would resign and not stand for re-election in the next election.

What, in my opinion, Pearson was not entitled to do was to urge me to run again, presumably because at the time I had a considerable following within the Liberal Party, and assure me I would continue to be Minister of Finance, while at the same time he was telling members of the business community, including Robert Winters, that I would not continue in that position.

Nor do I believe there was any justification for Pearson to ask me to return to the cabinet in January 1967 on the basis of certain firm commitments and then repudiate the commitments without an explanation of any kind. I still cannot forget these Mike Pearson's actions in these matters.

Having expressed these personal feelings, I shall go on to say that Mike Pearson was a much more complex character than the general public ever realized. In retrospect, I believe he will go down in history, not only as a witty, humorous, and in many ways a lovable human being, but as one of Canada's great men, and certainly as one of the country's greatest public servants. He won the Nobel Prize for Peace in 1957 for his handling of the Suez affair, something no other Canadian has done. He was always at his best in a crisis and never lost his head. Late in life, he proved to be a courageous and resourceful political leader in the way he brought the Liberals back to power in five years, following their devastating defeat in the 1958 election. Under his term of office as Prime Minister, Canadians obtained a respectable social-security base on which to build. He, personally, directed the long, drawn-out fight for the Canadian flag. With it all, he remained modest, unassuming and always very much a Canadian.

Pearson died on December 27, 1972.

By the end of 1974, I found myself becoming increasingly concerned with what was happening in the world and with Canada's place in it. Accordingly, I wrote *Storm Signals,* which was completed in May 1975 but not published until October of that year. Among other subjects, the book deals with the Canadian independence issue and what to do about it. In it I suggested that members of Parliament in a free vote should express by resolution the view that the foreign owners of the larger Canadian subsidiary companies should gradually, over a period of ten years, sell out to Canadians. I suggested that such larger Canadian subsidiary companies should include all those with assets in excess of $250 million, there being only thirty-two of them at the end of 1973.

I went on to suggest that the House of Commons resolution should spell out the stages in which control of these thirty-two companies should be transferred. This should be done as follows:

Stage one: To take place within a year or eighteen months and apply to companies in the resource sector with total assets in excess of $2 billion. Imperial Oil would be the only one to qualify. The quoted market value of the seventy per cent of its shares held by Exxon was about $2.25 billion at the end of March of 1975.

Stage two: To take place within three years and apply to companies in the resource sector with total assets exceeding $1 billion. Only two companies would be involved: Gulf Oil Canada and Shell Canada. The quoted market value of the approximately seventy per cent of the shares of these companies owned by their foreign parent corporations would amount to about $1.5 billion.

Stage three: To take place within five years and apply also to companies in the resource field with assets exceeding $500 million. These would include Texaco Canada, Canadian International Paper, Amoco Canada Petroleum, Pacific Petroleums, Westcoast Transmission, and Falconbridge Nickel. The shares of two of these are not quoted on the stock exchanges. However, at a rough guess, the six companies together might be worth about $2 billion.

Stage four: To take place within seven years and apply to manufacturing and commercial companies with total assets exceeding $1 billion. These would include Ford of Canada Ltd., General Motors of Canada Ltd. and Anglo Canadian Telephone. Total quoted market value of Ford and Anglo Canadian on March 31, 1975, was approximately $600 million. GM Canada's shares are not listed, but their net book value according to the company's balance sheet on December 31, 1973, was $443 million. Taken all together, these three companies might be worth about $1.25 billion.

Stage five: To take place within ten years, and apply to all other foreign-controlled companies with total assets exceeding $250 million. These would include: Chrysler Canada Ltd., Canadian General Electric Co., IBM Canada Ltd., Canadian Industries Ltd., Rothmans of Pall Mall Canada Ltd., Petrofina Canada Ltd., Rio Algom Mines, BP Canada Ltd., Du Pont of Canada Ltd., Crown Zellerbach Canada Ltd., Canada Cement Lafarge, B. C. Forest Products, Husky Oil, Interprovincial Pipe Lines, Hudson Bay Mining & Smelting, Texaco Exploration Canada Ltd., Hudson's Bay Oil & Gas, Imasco, Genstar and the Canadian assets of I.T.&T. As a guess, the total value of this group might amount to about $4.5 billion.

Altogether, these estimates total $11.5 billion, but I suggested that, to be on the safe side, the total be placed at $15 billion to be paid by Canadian investors (not the Canadian government) over a ten-year period. This amount should be well within Canada's financial capabilities. The advantages of this proposal would be that:

1. No legislation would be required and there would be no need for sanctions. Obviously, if the proposed resolution by Members of Parliament was ignored, the government would have to take action at some later date. But this would seem to be unlikely.
2. Only thirty-two companies would be affected.
3. The companies would not be nationalized.
4. It would be left to the foreign owners to decide how to go about selling the shares of their subsidiaries to Canadians.
5. They would have plenty of time to work things out.
6. For all practical purposes, the transfer of ownership of these thirty-two large companies would resolve the foreign control issue. The remaining seven or eight thousand smaller foreign-controlled companies in Canada would not be involved in any way.

I have pointed out in subsequent speeches that this proposal, at least to begin with, could be limited to companies in the resource industries or even to the larger foreign-owned Canadian oil companies.

Storm Signals went on to suggest that the tax rate for Canadian-controlled companies should be ten percentage points lower than the rate for other companies. In other words, if the normal rate of tax for companies were fifty per cent, the rate for Canadian-controlled companies would be forty per cent. It also suggested that Canadian-controlled companies should be permitted to amortize their capital expenditures against taxable income at any rate they might determine. These suggestions were intended to give Canadian-controlled companies an advantage over their foreign-controlled competitors who have them at a disadvantage in so many ways.

These proposals for resolving the problem of foreign control of the Canadian economy fell on deaf ears in Ottawa, as had earlier suggestions for dealing with this problem.

While *Storm Signals* was not primarily concerned with short-term issues, it was published just after the government's anti-inflation program was announced. Naturally enough, the latter was the main subject of discussion at the time. Whatever the reasons, *Storm Signals* received a mixed reception. *The Globe and Mail* invited Ed Broadbent, the leader of the N.D.P., to review it for them. It was not one of his best efforts. Professor Anthony Scott, a charming man who was a member of the research staff of the Royal Commission on Canada's Economic Prospects and is now a professor of economics at the University of British Columbia, was critical in a review in *The Vancouver Sun*. This was to be expected from a neo-classical economist with somewhat stereotyped views. Professor Myron Gordon of the University of Toronto, writing in *The Canadian Forum*, was most complimentary. The book provoked no comments in Ottawa political circles to whom it was primarily directed. Such is the fate of authors who hope to change the course of history!

I am a reasonably optimistic person and I would prefer to end this book on a hopeful note. Canadians are a fortunate people. We have a high standard of living. We have most of the natural resources that are essential for the future well-being of future generations. We are reasonably peaceable in temperament, and we do not covet the resources or the possessions of other peoples. But we are a naïve people in many ways. By this I mean we tend to think that others, including foreign businessmen who control resources or business enterprises in our country, should be taken at face value; that their representatives in Canada have our best interests at heart rather than those of their employers in other countries. Perhaps we are too satisfied with the phenomenal improvement in our living standards since the days of the Great Depression and World War II; perhaps we are too comfortable. Whatever it is, we seem to acquiesce in a kind of somnolent unthinking continuation of policies that can lead to our gradual absorption by the United States, first economically and then inevitably politically.

If Canada is to survive as a reasonably independent, separate state over the long term, we must learn to administer our economic affairs with greater skill. We have not been doing this in recent years. We must remain united. In other words, long-term solutions must be found that will keep Quebec contented and within Confederation; if Quebec should separate, it would mean the end of Canada within a decade or two. Long-term solutions must be found also that will improve federal-provincial relations as a whole and delineate more clearly the responsibilities of each. Above all, Canadians must learn to stand on their own feet, not in any belligerent fashion, but at the same time with a sense of confidence and determination. This means a resolution of the problems inherent in so much foreign control of the economy. If the Canadian independence issue is not resolved, we shall lose our economic independence and eventually our political independence also.

There is no reason why these fundamental problems cannot be resolved. But it will take courage on the part of our political leaders, a better understanding of the basic issues, and a firm determination to see they are resolved no matter what the consequences.

Some time in 1975, my friend Beland Honderich said that he and some of my other friends were going to stage a surprise party for me. He said they intended to do this whether I liked it or not but not to worry. They knew I did not like formalities or to listen to a lot of speeches. It was to be a fun occasion. In the end, the party took the form of a great dinner at the

Royal York Hotel on my seventieth birthday, January 27, 1976, at which between eight and nine hundred guests were present. It was wonderfully well organized down to the smallest details. The usual formalities and pomposities of such occasions were kept to a minimum. Bee had gone to endless trouble over a period of several months, as had the other members of his committee. This is what I had to say about them:

> I am especially grateful to Bee and to the members of his committee for all the hard work and kindly thought that went into the planning of this occasion.
>
> Bee Honderich is a man of high principle and great integrity and I am lucky to have had him as a true friend for many years. His friendship and his support have meant a great deal to me.
>
> Keith [Davey] is another loyal friend who has always been there when help and support were needed and I have a real affection for him.
>
> The same is true of the other members of the committee: Bill Dimma, the new president-elect of *The Toronto Star*. Eddie Goodman, that "Red Tory" who is always cheerful and optimistic and whom one day I hope we'll see graduate from the back rooms to the front lines of politics. Alex MacIntosh is another lawyer but this time a Liberal from Nova Scotia. They say it was an early diet almost solely consisting of fish that accounts for his wisdom and exceptionally good judgement. For many years, he has advised me on legal matters, political matters, and business matters, and also on my personal affairs. But above all he is a very good friend. Maurice Lamontagne, Pauline Jewett and Harry Hays (who isn't able to be with us this evening), all of whom did tremendous jobs in the old Pearson days in Ottawa. It's a great pleasure to see them and some of the others who worked together at that time – Judy LaMarsh, Edgar Benson, Jean Marchand and Larry Pennell, as well as many others. Alderman William (Bill) Kilbourn is another member of the committee who, as a History Professor at York University, was the most inspiring teacher my son John ever had. I only wish John could have been with us this evening. Gordon Hughes, a great tennis player, a wise political counsellor, and a very good friend. Abe Rotstein and Peter Newman who invited me to join them in founding the Committee for an Independent Canada. Since then, Abe has progressed from economics to philosophy. Very soon now he will be telling us all about his researches. They are startling and I suspect their publication will establish Abe as one of the leading thinkers of his generation. Peter has, of course, written that great Canadian best-seller *The Canadian Establishment*. If anyone here is worth $100 million and was left out of the book, I suggest he speak to Peter after dinner. I am

sure he will put him in the next edition. And Hartland Molson who has been my close friend ever since we used to get into mild trouble together as teenagers. I don't have to add that was a long time ago. We are much more cautious and careful these days.

I would like to mention one other person who I believe was a kind of *ex-officio* member of the committee. That is my brother Duncan, a friend as well as a brother. He has helped me through many difficulties over the years and I am very grateful to him.

Keith Davey acted as Master of Ceremonies and did a superb and very witty job. Peter Newman wrote a much too laudatory piece about me that was incorporated in the program for the dinner. He included some anecdotes that appear in this book for which I can only offer my apologies. I was presented with a cartoon that Duncan Macpherson had drawn especially for the occasion. And Bee Honderich announced the establishment

Seventieth Birthday Party Cartoon
REPRINTED WITH PERMISSION THE TORONTO STAR

of an annual lecture series in my name at three different Canadian universities commencing in the 1976-77 academic year. In acknowledging this great and unique honour, I said:

I am deeply honoured by the proposed series of lectures that Bee has told us about. This is a great tribute, not so much to me personally as to all Canadians who love their country and who want to keep it as free and as independent as is possible in the kind of world we live in.

I am deeply grateful to Bee Honderich for this and to all those who contributed to it.

The evening concluded with some marvellous entertainment provided by Judy Armstrong, Frank Augustyn, Dave Broadfoot, Jack Duffy, Maureen Forrester, Don Harron, Karen Kain, Catherine McKinnon, and Tink Robinson. Fen Watkin conducted the band and the program was produced and directed by Norman and Elaine Campbell.

The only sad note to the evening was that Liz could not be present. She was in hospital with a broken hip that had become infected. As I said:

Most of us have our ups and downs in life, and, of course, Liz and I are no exceptions. During my – I should say our – down periods, Liz has always been there with her support and sound advice. And in our up periods, she has been there to keep my feet as close to the ground as possible. If she were here tonight, she would be telling me that I've spoken long enough. She is a very remarkable person, and very special.

Naturally, I am disappointed and many of you are disappointed that Liz could not be with us. But, as I said earlier, she is very much here in spirit. On her behalf as well as mine, let me thank all of you from the bottom of our hearts for this absolutely smashing party.

It was the greatest, the most marvellous party I have ever been to. Once again, let me say how grateful I am to all those who arranged it and to all those who attended. What a wonderful note on which to end these memoirs.

Appendices

**1. Part of a letter to The Honourable L.B. Pearson
dated March 9, 1960,
outlining my views on a variety of policy issues.**

Personal
Dear Mike:

Following the chat we had the last time I was in Ottawa – when you cheered me up considerably – I have tried to analyse my own thoughts and situation because I think you are entitled to know where I stand and what my plans are. And I sense from what Scott [the new National Organizer] said to me last week that you would like to know what I propose to do. With this in mind and in order to avoid the possibility of misunderstanding, it may be useful if I write down how I feel about things.

To begin with, as I have said before, I would like to do anything I can to help you become Prime Minister in two or two and a half years' time if there is any practical chance of this becoming possible. To be honest, I am not sure there will be a chance of achieving this so soon. As I suggested to you last November, this will depend primarily on Diefenbaker and on the times. To a lesser extent, it will depend on you, the people you get around you, the enthusiasm that you and they inspire, the kind of programme or platform the Liberals agree upon, the way it is presented and upon the kind of organization that can be developed and the kind of candidates that can be secured.

From a personal standpoint, I shall hope that the programme will tend to be leftish, imaginative, reasonably clear cut and that it will discard as many as possible of the old theories and beliefs that are no longer relevant. If it does not do these things, I doubt if the Liberal Party will regain power for some years to come despite the mistakes that Diefenbaker may make between now and the next election.

I can say without any reservation that I would like to serve under you as Minister of Finance. The job would intrigue me both because I would enjoy participating as a senior Minister in Canada's international negotiations and because I would like to help you tidy up our present domestic policies or lack of them. At long last, I seem to have got my gout under control with the result that I feel better than I have for many years. And I think Liz would be willing to go along if things should turn out this way; as you know, I would not make the move without her blessing and approval. However, all this is somewhat academic as there are two questions about which I still am very doubtful. The first one has to do with issues and the second with the not inconsiderable task of getting both me and the Liberal Party elected.

I am still not sure that my views on freer trade, on integration with the United States, on the need for a greater degree of direction and control of the economy by Ottawa or on defence policy would be acceptable to most Liberals. I tried to spell out how I feel about the first subject in my speech to the Ontario Federation of Labour on February 13 – which was not very different from the views expressed in the report of the Royal Commission. I am against "high" tariffs but I think we shall need "more" not "less" secondary industry throughout all of Canada if we are going to lick chronic unemployment. To me, the objectives of reducing many of the "higher" tariff rates and, at the same time, of having more secondary industry are not necessarily incompatible. In fact, I believe just the opposite.

However, as I think you know, I would be very hesitant about a policy of all-out free trade – even on some regional basis like the North Atlantic Area – unless I was more certain than I now am of where it would lead and the extent of the disruptions that would be involved. . . .

I am unhappy about the gradual economic and financial take-over by the United States, or rather by the owners of United States capital, that is taking place and if I were in public life I expect I would wish to urge some modest steps to counteract what is presently going on in this direction. As I have said at other times, I would prefer us to go in one direction or the other knowing what is happening and what we are trying to do about it. . . .

I doubt if the question of a strong central Government is one on which there would be any serious differences of opinion. I might want to go farther and faster in this direction than some people but I expect this would be more a question of degree than one of principle.

On the question of defence policy, I am becoming more of the opinion that Canada should begin to take an independent line and should stop pouring money down the drain. I do not profess to know too much about this subject or all of its implications, but I assume that this line of thinking might lead to the cancellation of the NORAD deal and thus to a full dress argument, or showdown, with the Americans. . . .

I dare say you will think the doubts that I have raised concerning the above issues are not so very different from the doubts that everyone has felt who has considered these matters seriously. This may be true about defence policy and the need for a strong central Government. I think I am more concerned, however, about the trade question and integration with the United States where I lack the instinctive convictions that most people of the Liberal persuasion seem to have. . . .

Yours sincerely,

The Hon. L. B. Pearson,
House of Commons,
Ottawa, Canada.

2. "Whither Canada – Satellite or Independent Nation?"

Remarks to the National Seminar,
National Federation of Canadian University Students,
at the University of British Columbia,
Monday, August 29, 1960

You have invited me to open the discussion on the broader aspects of "Research, Education and National Development," a subject that is comprehensive in scope but at the same time a bit elusive in its outline. One may ask: Research of what kind, for what purpose, and for whom? Education of what kind, for what purpose, and for what proportion of our high school graduates? National Development of what kind, for what purpose, and for whose benefit? If we can answer these questions, if we can come to some measure of agreement about our broad objectives, then perhaps we may begin to come to grips with the subject for discussion. But without such agreement, without some definition about goals and objectives, I doubt if we should get very far. So I shall begin my remarks with a somewhat discursive review of some existing trends and some of the problems of the Canadian economy as I see them. Having done this, I shall indicate my own personal views about what the broad objectives of Canadian policy should be. And finally, I shall try to indicate my conception of the roles that research, education and national development should play, given the broad objectives of policy that I shall try to outline and define.

In the fall of 1956, nearly four years ago, the Royal Commission on Canada's Economic Prospects submitted its Preliminary Report. Its Final Report was completed a year later. The Commission's conclusions were predicated upon certain arbitrary assumptions or premises – that there would not be a nuclear war; that there would not be a serious depression like the one in the thirties, or prolonged periods of mass unemployment; and that our governments would pursue sensible, flexible policies designed to meet changing economic and political conditions at home and abroad.

On the basis of these premises, the Commission put forward some tentative and very carefully qualified estimates of what economic conditions in Canada might be like twenty-five years hence, *i.e.,* in the year 1980. These estimates were considered at the time to be rather optimistic. They indicated that twenty-five years from now Canada's population might have increased to about 27 million; that the Gross National Product might be tripled; and that per capita net incomes should have increased quite substantially. In addition to these forecasts, the Commission noted a number of important economic trends and suggested that the structure of the Canadian economy might change over the twenty-five year period in various ways. I should like to remind you of some of these conclusions.

The rapid movement of people from the farms to the cities and towns that has occurred since 1939 may be expected to slow down, and in fact has already done so to a considerable extent. But as a percentage of a much larger civilian labour force, the number of people engaged in agriculture in 1980 may be no more than 6% or 7% of the total compared with over 30% before the war. In twenty years' time, about 80% of the population may be living in urban centres. It is a simple fact that Canadians are no longer agricultural and rural in their way of life. We are now, and will become increasingly, an urbanized industrialized society with very different problems, objectives, needs and values from those that preoccupied us as recently as even twenty years ago.

I might add in parentheses that I am impressed by the great inflow of people who have come from Europe since the end of the war to live in my hometown of Toronto. Most of these people are gay and intelligent as well as hardworking. They will make a real contribution to Canadian life in the years to come, and already they are beginning to wield considerable influence, as they should do. They are city people for the most part, and they will not be content for long with the traditional solemnity, particularly on Sundays, that Toronto was noted for in the past, or with the general drabness and lack of beauty in our public buildings and institutions that we have inherited from a different age. Those of us who were born in this country have a great deal to learn from these newcomers about living in big cities, about how to get the most enjoyment out of life, and in terms of entertainment, of friendship, of neighbourliness and close-knit family ties.

The fundamental change to which I have referred, the shift from the farms to the cities and the fact that people now have appreciably higher incomes and much more leisure time, has posed challenging problems for our municipalities, many of which have not yet been settled. These problems will not be resolved, I think, until there is a clearer definition of the respective responsibilities of the municipalities and the provinces for the costs of social services of all kinds, and also probably for the cost of education. The financial difficulties of the municipalities will have to be recognized one of these days by the two senior levels of government in this country, and something done about alleviating them.

The changed way of life in an urban industrial society has brought with it a need for the kinds of collective security measures against unemployment, against sickness and other calamities, and for old age that are now beyond the capabilities of the individual to handle by himself. This has meant a great deal more activity on the part of government at all levels than was necessary or desirable when the country was in a more primitive stage of its development. Many people are inclined to deplore this trend, without perhaps fully realizing the changed conditions that mainly are responsible for it. But I suggest to you that increased governmental activity in the areas I have mentioned is both necessary and inevitable in the new kind of society in which we now live in most parts of Canada. Certainly I can see no prospect of a reversal of the present trend.

In its report, the Commission forecast a considerable expansion of our highly important natural resource industries and the refining and primary manufacturing activities based upon them. There are some things we can do to encourage development in this important sector of the economy – for example, we should not permit the exchange rate for the Canadian dollar to get too high, as this tends to raise the costs of our export products in terms of foreign currencies – but in the last analysis, the expansion of these industries will be dependent mainly upon the demand in other countries, primarily in the United States, for industrial raw materials. The rate of increase in this demand is not likely to be an even one, and as a result, we shall probably have to face periods when there is surplus capacity in this sector. There is surplus capacity now, and there are those who think this condition may prevail for some time to come. But over a span of years, the resource and primary manufacturing industries can be expected to expand, and should continue to provide employment for about 10% to 12% of the labour force.

It is not always appreciated that, if Canada is to be prosperous and if we are to have a high level of employment, it is important also that our secondary industries flourish and expand their operations. In 1955, these industries accounted for 22% of the total output of the country (compared with 17% in the case of the resource and primary manufacturing industries and 13% for agriculture). They provided employment for 20% of the labour force (compared with 11½% for the resource and primary manufacturing industries and 15% for agriculture). According to the Commission's forecasts, it is to be hoped that these secondary industries will continue to provide employment for about one-fifth of the labour force, and that by 1980 they will account for about one-quarter of the total output of the economy.

I am emphasizing these facts because many of our secondary industries are in trouble these days. And there are a few people who do not seem to worry about this very much. In fact, one hears it suggested sometimes that Canada should concentrate her main attention on our great resource industries, which for the most part are relatively efficient, and let our secondary industries more or less go by the boards. This is a dangerous concept. It is not a case of the resource industries or the secondary manufacturers. We need them both. And we cannot hope to have high levels of employment in Canada unless all the major sections of our economy, including secondary industry, are doing well. We should, of course, continue to emphasize the great importance of our resource industries and do everything possible to ensure that their costs of production remain competitive in world markets. But as I have said, the rate of activity in the resource industries, even if their costs remain competitive, will depend to a very considerable extent upon conditions beyond our own control, *i.e.,* upon the demand in other countries, principally in the United States, for our exports of industrial raw materials.

The rate of expansion of the secondary manufacturing industries, on the other hand, will depend upon the growth of the domestic market and the share of it that these industries can secure. This, in turn, will depend in the long run upon the relative efficiency of these secondary industries and upon their ability to keep their costs of production down and competitive with imports. I for one am very much against high rates of tariff protection. And I see no reason why such rates should be excessive if steps are taken to maintain the exchange rate for the Canadian dollar at realistic levels, if money is relatively cheap and reasonably available, and if our tax and fiscal policies are designed to encourage growth. But whether we like it or not, some moderate protection will be needed if Canadian secondary industry is to prosper and to provide employment for a substantial proportion of the total working force. This is one of the facts of Canadian economic life that there is just no escaping.

Another trend that was referred to by the Commission was the pattern and the volume of our foreign trade. It seems probable that a high proportion of our exports and of our imports will continue to flow to and from the United States, and that, for the most part, our exports will consist of industrial raw materials. Canadians would prefer it if the pattern of our foreign trade – both exports and imports – was more widely diversified. And if the United States would change its tariff policy so that we would have a better chance to process our raw materials in Canada and export the finished products. But as of this moment, the prospects of these events happening do not seem very great.

We hear a lot these days about the potential effects on Canadian exports of the European Common Market, and sometimes, that we should explore the possibilities of establishing a Common Market or a free trade area on the North American continent. In my opinion, we should rejoice if, as a result of the Common Market, the countries of Western Europe become more prosperous. For one thing, this should provide an obstacle to the spread of Communism. And in the long run, this increased prosperity may result in increased exports to that area from Canada of such things as newsprint and some of the base metals.

But we should think twice before concluding that the same approach would be desirable on this continent. After all, some of the keenest promoters of the common market idea in Europe have political union as their ultimate objective, a union – incidentally – in which not one of the present countries would wield a dominating influence. A similar approach on this continent might have a very different result if eventually it led to some kind of political union between Canada and the United States. In our case, because of our much smaller size, this would really mean absorption by the United States. This is a prospect which I, for one, would not look upon with relish – not that I am in any way anti-American – but just because I think Canada has something to contribute to this weary, troubled world as a separate, independent nation with no axe to grind at the expense of any other country anywhere.

In this connection, the Commission had quite a lot to say about the extent to which Canadian industry is owned and controlled by non-residents, mostly by citizens or corporations in the United States. Foreign investment has been helpful in the rapid development of our country, and we have gained a great deal through the connections that many of our larger companies have with their parent companies in the United States and elsewhere. These benefits include access to management know-how, technological developments and research, and, in the case of many of our primary industries, to assured markets for their products. But, looking at the picture as a whole, I think we have allowed this trend to go too far. There is no other country in the world, to my knowledge — certainly no country that is as fully developed economically as Canada — which has so much of its industry controlled by non-residents. We shall have to reverse the present trend if we really wish to maintain our identity as a separate nation on the North American continent.

This may be an appropriate place to remark that the attitudes of Canadians about our economy differ somewhat from those of our American friends about the economy of the United States. In that country, there is greater and more vocal insistence upon the advantages of "free enterprise" and upon the subsidiary role that government should play. In Canada – which is sometimes referred to as an economic anachronism – governments have always played an important and sometimes a dominant role in economic affairs. This has been the case from the beginning, as even a cursory reading of the history of the CPR will show. We have come to accept the concept of public ownership in Canada in certain fields: the CNR, the TCA, the Hydro Commissions of Ontario and Quebec, the CBC, the National Film Board, the PGE, the Canadian Wheat Board, are a few examples of what I mean. The cooperative movement is steadily gaining ground. While there is no element of public ownership here, nevertheless the co-operative method of doing business is not exactly what people have in mind when they talk about the advantages of "private enterprise" or "free enterprise" with their connotations of untrammelled competition and a free market economy.

In the so-called private sector, many of our largest companies which wield a dominating influence in their respective industries are controlled and directed, not by individual Canadians but by people who reside outside our borders. To this extent, Canadians do not make the day-to-day decisions in the economic sphere. Again, this is hardly what we mean when we talk about "free enterprise." Certainly, it is not "free enterprise" in any national sense insofar as Canadians are concerned.

There are, of course, large sections of Canadian economic life that still are relatively free. Small businessmen, professional men and farmers can still be independent up to a point, and speaking as one of them, I hope this will long continue. But taking the economy of the country as a whole, I suggest the term "mixed enterprise" rather than "free enterprise" would be a better way of describing it. Like the majority of Canadians, I dislike too much government interference, too much bureaucracy, too much red tape. And too much government control will always be particularly obnoxious in a Federal State like ours with its great differences in points of view and in the nature of the economies of the different provinces. But I am afraid that, in the age in which we live, governments – provincial as well as federal – must be prepared to take the initiative and to give a lead upon occasion if Canada is to remain free and independent and if we are to have a high level of employment throughout the country.

This brings us to a basic question about which we should make up our minds before we can discuss intelligently the most appropriate policies for Canadians to pursue. And that is, the importance that we attach to retaining our economic and political independence – or as much independence as is possible for any single nation in this shrinking world of powerful super-states.

There are tremendous pressures upon us to integrate the Canadian economy more and more with that of the United States. Hardly a day goes by, it seems, that some Canadian company is not purchased by a large U.S. corporation or by its subsidiary in Canada. Hardly a day goes by without someone making a speech or writing an article suggesting a "continental approach" to one or other of our economic problems; or asking if it is possible or if it really makes sense for a small country like Canada to struggle to remain free and separate from an enormous neighbour with ten times her population and fifteen times the value of her annual output.

The fact is that in recent years, whether we like to admit it or not, Canada has been losing steadily a considerable measure of her independence, both economically and politically. If we are sensible, we should decide either to accelerate the pace of further integration with the United States, politically as well as economically, or alternatively, take steps without delay to reverse the present trend. Either course, in my opinion, would entail difficulties and some unpleasantness. Free trade with the United States on any appreciable scale – even if the Americans were willing to consider this – would bring about a great disruption of Canadian industry and serious unemployment, certainly during an extended period of readjustment and probably for longer. And if this was not accompanied by moves in the direction of some sort of political union or affiliation, we might find ourselves in a very difficult position if, at some later date, some new Administration in the United States decided to abrogate the arrangement.

On the other hand, we could not hope to reverse the present trend and to regain some of our lost independence without paying some sort of price in terms of a less rapid rise in our standard of living, though not, I think of greater unemployment. (This is a price, incidentally, that Canadians have always been prepared to pay, ever since Canada became a nation, when the situation was explained to them.) Furthermore, we could not hope to accomplish our objective quickly. To be successful, we would have to work at it for many years and with great determination.

While a case can be made for either of the courses I have mentioned – faster integration with the United States or the regaining of our independence – I submit that there is no excuse whatever for failing to face up to the dilemma in which we find ourselves today. To do nothing, to refuse to recognize the situation that confronts us or to admit its implications, will lead inevitably to our becoming a more or less helpless satellite of the United States. (The great majority of Canadians might never fully realize just when or how this happened.) Like many other people, I have thought a great deal about this issue. Having done so, I for one am prepared to say without any qualification that I hope Canadians will choose to regain a greater measure of economic independence than we now have. I believe we could be successful in this endeavour over the next decade or so if we really put our minds to it.

When it comes to foreign policy and defence, however, I cannot subscribe to the thesis of James Minifie that Canada should go neutral. Is it conceivable that we could remain neutral if a war took place between Russia and the United States? I think not. In the first place, there is the matter of geography, and it seems unlikely that the antagonists would oblige by going around or even over us, any more than Germany did in the case of Belgium in 1914 and 1939. But, quite apart from this, the Americans are our friends – our very best friends – even if at times we may find their attentions a little overpowering. And the Russian Communists are not our friends, let us remember. We do not like their system, and we want no part of it. So, to me, it is idle to think we could remain neutral even if we wanted to if war should break out – and it would be nuclear war – between these two great powers.

This does not mean, to my mind, that we should become subservient to the United States or to anyone, for that matter. The United Nations and the NATO alliance are the cornerstones of Canadian foreign policy and should remain so. But, speaking personally, I feel less certain about NORAD and about the use of nuclear weapons that are not under Canadian control. Despite all the words – many of them contradictory – that have been uttered about the NORAD arrangement that was entered into so hurriedly and obviously without much serious consideration in the summer of 1957, it seems to boil down to the fact that Canada has contributed a few squadrons to the American Air Force. Much publicity has been given to the fact that a Canadian airman is Deputy Commander of the NORAD Force, and that both the President of the United States and some unspecified official of the Canadian Government (possibly the Prime Minister) must give joint approval before any shots are fired in anger. I find these explanations unconvincing. To me, it seems farcical to suggest that, in a grave emergency, retaliatory measures would be delayed while the officials in question were located, the situation explained to them, and their approval given to repel attack.

347

Similarly, if Canadian defence forces are to be equipped with nuclear arms, including nuclear warheads for the Bomarc missile, I think a decision to use such arms and warheads should be made by the Canadian authorities and by them alone. I do not think this should be contingent upon the approval of the American authorities, or jointly by the Americans and the Canadian Prime Minister. If these are the conditions, I would prefer to see us get along, at least for the time being, without weapons that are not within our own control.

To refer back to the Commission and its forecasts, I am still optimistic about what Canada can accomplish over the long term if we manage our affairs intelligently. What we need, I think, is to agree upon the objectives that Canadians should aim for, and then to develop the policies that we should follow in an effort to achieve them. In thinking about a consistent set of policies, there are of course many different tests or yardsticks against which proposals can be measured. For example,

(1) Will they result in more jobs and less unemployment?
(2) Will they cause inflation?
(3) Will they make a real and substantial contribution to the defence of the Free World or of North America?
(4) Will they result in a further loss of Canadian independence, or the reverse?
(5) Will they benefit the people of Canada as a whole, or just particular groups or classes or sections of the country?
(6) How will they affect personal incomes and the cost of living?
(7) Will they tend to create difficulties for us at some future time?
(8) Will they benefit people in depressed sections of Canada, or people in other countries who are less well off than we are?

All these tests, and many others that could be added, are important. And all of them should be considered carefully before particular policies are decided upon. It will be quite apparent, of course, that some of the tests that I have mentioned are not mutually exclusive. For instance, a broad program of public works may help to relieve unemployment, but in some way it must be paid for and this may reduce personal incomes or increase the cost of living or cause inflationary pressures, either now or in the future.

Or, to take another example, excessive borrowing in the United States by municipalities when the Canadian dollar is at a premium may solve an immediate problem. But such borrowings may have to be paid off in the future at a time when our dollar is at a discount. In such event, the additional costs involved will have to be paid by somebody. In other words, we are not likely to arrive at policies that will meet all tests successfully or that will please everyone.

But in deciding upon the best course for Canada to follow in the years immediately ahead, it seems to me there are two factors above all others that will be of paramount importance. In the first place, the threat of serious and possibly chronic unemployment is beginning to frighten and to haunt us. I am not exaggerating. The fact is that when 4.7% of the civilian working force are unemployed and seeking work in July – in the middle of the summer – we can be reasonably certain that the number of people who will be without jobs next winter will be very high indeed. This problem will not be solved by rhetoric and exhortations, or by *ad hoc* measures of relief. It needs to be thought through, first of all, and then we shall have to adopt policies that are designed to correct the situation over the long term – even if they may offend some of our most deeply held and long-established myths and prejudices.

In the second place, as I have suggested, if we really do wish Canada to retain her separate identity as an independent nation, we will have to re-examine our present defence and foreign policies and do something about stopping and then reversing the trend under which such a staggering number of our most dynamic industries have fallen into foreign hands.

It follows from what I have been saying that, in considering the pros and cons of any policy proposals, there are two tests above all others that should be kept very much in mind, viz.,

Will the proposed policy result in more jobs and less unemployment?
Will the proposed policy result in a further loss of Canadian independence, or the reverse?

Now, where does all this lead us from the standpoint of research, education and national development? Well, I think the discussion so far should help to place these highly important questions in perspective. If we decide we want to recapture some of our disappearing independence and if we succeed in this attempt, all kinds of research work will be required in Canada. If, however, we are content to let the present trend continue under which more and more of our industry is coming under the control of non-residents, then I expect that a large proportion of industrial research will continue to be done elsewhere. There would still be need for fundamental research of various kinds in our universities and research institutes. But if it becomes apparent that Canada is going to come under the domination of the United States – either because Canadians don't care or don't know how to stop the present trend – an increasing number of our better scientists and research people in all fields may understandably decide to find places for themselves in other countries.

In the same vein, if Canadians are determined to remain as free and as independent as possible, we shall have an urgent incentive to improve our educational facilities at all levels and to make it both possible and desirable for a larger percentage of our highschool graduates to go on to university. In particular, we shall have to take much greater care to see that no really bright boy or girl is dissuaded from continuing his or her education after highschool because of financial considerations or because he or she has not been inspired or informed about the advantages of higher education.

It would be my hope that, in the future, an increasing number of Canadians will be encouraged to seek and to accept positions of responsibility in all parts and sections of our increasingly complex society. In addition, it will be important that more Canadians – and particularly more Canadians who have had a good education or who have risen to prominence in business, in organized labour, in farming, or in other pursuits – should be willing to express their views about public affairs and should not be afraid to identify themselves with the political party of their choice. Government at all three levels is becoming increasingly difficult and complex. The decisions taken by our government leaders affect all of us. We cannot expect these decisions to be necessarily wise or enlightened if our most talented but sometimes most fastidious citizens shun politics as something that is beneath their dignity.

As to national development, I would like to see this country twenty years from now with a population of 27 or 28 million people; with a considerably higher standard of living; with plenty of opportunities available for all who seek to work in a mixed enterprise economy as at present; with a considerable measure of decentralization of day-to-day economic decision-making in the private sector, but with a great deal more of our basic industries in Canadian hands; with a more rounded and complete program of social security benefits; with the responsibilities and the functions and the revenue sources of the provinces and municipalities better defined and more adequate for their needs; with greater cultural and recreational facilities for an urban people who have more free time in which to enjoy a rich and abundant life; and with a better educated people, taking a greater interest in public and community affairs.

I would hope that twenty years from now there may be less emphasis than there is today on material values. I am in favour of competition and I believe in the profit motive – but it should not be the only motive if our objective is a well-balanced, rounded, happy, and at the same time interesting and stimulating life for a people who can be proud of their accomplishments, their independence, and of their influence in the world for good. These are some of the things that seem to me important when we talk about Canadian development.

In conclusion, let me say that I make no apologies for this interpretation of Canadianism, or if you like, Canadian Nationalism. I have no anti-British or anti-French or anti-American or anti-European feelings. On the contrary, these people in particular are our very best friends, both in terms of their countries who are our allies and as individuals. But just as a Britisher or a Frenchman or an American is proud of his country, so I am of ours. I want to see Canada remain as free and independent as it is possible for any single country to be in this interdependent world. I want to see all Canadians share in a more prosperous, abundant, and satisfying way of life. But I hope we will not concentrate all our energies and our whole attention upon that intangible abstraction the economists call the Gross National Product. I would like to see us do more to help our fellow-citizens who are less well off than we are or who live in those sections of our country that are relatively depressed. I would like to see us do more to help people in less fortunate countries than our own. And finally, I want to see Canada take her place in the community of nations as one of the most influential and respected of all the so-called middle powers.

3. Memorandum of the interview with James Stillman Rockefeller of Citibank about the Mercantile Bank of Canada, July 18, 1963.

MEMORANDUM ● Government of Canada

Confidential

TO: The Minister
FROM: C.F. Elderkin
SUBJECT: The First National City Bank of New York   DATE: July 18, 1963
and
The Mercantile Bank of Canada

The Minister held an interview in his office at 12 noon today attended by Messrs. Rockefeller and MacFadden representing the National City, and by Messrs. Bryce and Elderkin.

Mr. Rockefeller said that National City had made an arrangement with the shareholders of Mercantile to acquire the shares of the latter bank, but that no firm commitment had been made. He said his people considered that Canada was one of the more important countries in the financial world, that they would like to participate in its growth and that he had asked for this interview to obtain the viewpoint of the Government with respect to the proposed purchase.

The Minister said that he was glad to have the opportunity of expressing the views of the Government regarding the proposed transaction as he considered it of great importance. He stated that, while he had a very high regard for the National City, he was going to be quite candid in explaining some of the objections to the proposed purchase.

He said that owing to rather unique circumstances it was possible for National City to acquire a banking subsidiary in Canada through what amounted in effect to a loophole in the law which required that bank charters be approved by Parliament. There is nothing in present Canadian legislation to prevent the transfer of Mercantile shares to another non-resident group. This could enable a non-resident bank to establish a subsidiary here which could be expanded into a large foreign-owned banking institution, unless subsequent action is taken. If National City enters the Canadian banking field by this method, it is very probable that other American banking corporations would want to do so as well, but in that case charters would have to be obtained.

It is highly unlikely that a charter would be granted by this Parliament for a bank that was to be non-resident controlled. Not only would the Government not be in favour of such action, but both of the minor parties have expressed opposition to an extension of foreign control in financial institutions. The Minister emphasized that the situation now is different from that in 1953 when the Mercantile received its charter. Since that time, the Royal Commission on Economic Prospects has recommended that control of Canadian chartered banks (and insurance companies, Mr. MacFadden noted) should be in the hands of Canadians and it suggested that appropriate action be taken to prevent control passing to non-residents.

The Minister also referred to the matter of relations between Bank of Canada and the chartered banks which had been discussed with the Governor of the Bank.

Problems might arise in carrying out monetary policy if a foreign-controlled bank was prevented from co-operating because of laws or regulations in the country of the parent. Mr. Rockefeller said that this presented no problem as any branch or subsidiary of theirs would be entirely governed by the laws of the country in which it was licensed or chartered. He said that National City had always maintained good relations with the Bank of England but the Minister said circumstances here were quite different. He was told there had been one instance when American anti-trust legislation appeared to interfere with the central bank's attempt to control credit here. Moreover at times there have been difficulties over United States Treasury attempts to extend foreign asset control regulations into Canada through the banks.

The Royal Commission on Banking and Finance is expected to report before the end of the year. The Minister said it is quite possible that the Commission will have some recommendations regarding foreign participation in Canadian banks. The Bank Act will be up for revision in 1964 and the Government then will have to decide what it will do in respect of this particular matter.

In response to a question, Mr. Rockefeller was told by Elderkin that it was the practice to revise the Bank Act every ten years and that the Act was each bank's only charter; it would be possible to stop a bank carrying on business when the revised Act comes into force if its charter were not continued thereby. The Minister remarked that while he himself might not have volunteered this information, no doubt Messrs. Rockefeller and MacFadden were quite aware of it. Mr. Rockefeller recalled that the licences of Canadian banks to do business in New York State come up for renewal annually.

At one stage, Mr. Rockefeller said that National City would prefer to operate in Canada through a branch rather than by means of a charter and asked if this could be permitted as it was in many other countries and, with some restricted powers, in certain American states. He was told it has always been considered the best policy in Canada to have commercial banks chartered and subject to uniform legislation.

The Minister said that it would normally be unfair to apply retroactively any legislative restrictions on control of banks by non-residents, but since the National City people were now aware of the Government's views about the possibility of their acquiring the shares of the Mercantile, the Government would not consider that they would be entitled to exemption from any legislation in respect of foreign ownership that might be enacted in the future.

In conclusion, the Minister said that if the National City proceeded with its plan, it might tend to encourage restrictive legislation and advised Messrs. Rockefeller and MacFadden not to proceed with their proposed action. Mr. Rockefeller then said, "In other words, if we do so, it will be at our own peril." The Minister said that he would not have volunteered this expression but that he thought Mr. Rockefeller had sized up the situation correctly.

The interview was conducted on a very amicable basis, but left no doubt as to the views of the Government on this subject.

Copy to: Deputy Minister of Finance
          Governor, Bank of Canada

4. Memorandum to Mr. Pearson on election possibilities.

Personal   *Copy*
                                        Original delivered to
                                        L.B.P. on Dec. 31st

Memo to L.B.P.   Dec. 30th, 1964
re Strategy

1. The first thing to be decided (tentatively) in our present situation is whether or not it is in our interests to have an election this year (*i.e.*, 1965). As I see it the pros and cons (in reverse order) are as follows:

Cons

- The public doesn't want an election.
- There would be some objection to an election before redistribution becomes effective.
- It would be very difficult to raise the money. (This will be true for all parties.)
- I'm sure another national campaign is the last thing in the world you personally would wish to contemplate.

Pros

- We could not survive another year like 1964.
- We could win an election now (according to the December – pre-scandal – survey). The alleged scandals should not make too much difference if handled firmly.
- We need Diefenbaker this time – and he may not be around indefinitely.
- We should strike while economic conditions are favourable.
- It will be most difficult if not impossible for us to deal successfully with a host of major issues as a minority government, *e.g.*:
  * The Carter Commission report on taxation. This will pose some awkward and controversial questions.
  * Our tax arrangements with the provinces.
  * Banking legislation.
  * Transportation.
  * Unemployment insurance.
                         et cetera.

It seems to me these various considerations lead to the clear conclusion there should be an election in 1965 (provided a new survey in say February indicates we could win it). If you agree the next question is whether it should be in June or September. I would be inclined to the earlier date for the following reasons:

- Having decided on an election (if you do), we should get on with it. Otherwise we will lose our drive. And we will be hurt if the House business bogs down again.
- The economy is in good shape now.
- Diefenbaker.
- I would prefer to go before not after the Carter Commission report is published.

2. If you are thinking of a June election the business for the remainder of the Session might include the following:

- Canada Pension Plan.
- Opting Out Bill. (This will not be easy.)
- Labour Standards Act. (There could be a delaying tactic in the Senate.)
- Third reading of the Insurance Trust and Loan Act. (This is quite important.)
- Possibly an Act to extend the Bank Charters (again) if it doesn't seem likely we can get the Revised Bank Act through in time.
- Possibly the Budget. (I am checking the procedures to see if the Budget can be brought down before the end of *this* Session if that seems desirable.)

For public consumption we could indicate that the Budget Bills (and Resolutions) would be dealt with at the next Session. In practice they would be dealt with after the election.

The next Session could begin as soon as the Budget Debate was concluded. The Speech from the Throne could be the election manifesto. (It might include a long term program for Health Care – Davey's idea. This will come up inevitably if there is an election and we might as well take the initiative.)

Having had the Speech from the Throne, Parliament would be dissolved without debate for an election in June.

3. Once you decide (tentatively) on whether there is to be an election (and the date) some other things will begin to fall in place. The first of these – and one on which work should be done while we are away – is the Budget. Some of the questions involved here are:

- Tax cuts.
- Legislation dealing with the periodicals.
- Canada Development Corporation.
- Possibly limited tax exemptions for campaign contributions (see below).

4. Whether or not there is to be an election, it will be imperative for you to show firmness – especially between the time you get back, Jan. 16th and when Parliament reassembles.

There are some obvious things to be done regardless of the timing and contents of the Dorion report. I do not see how you can wait for it. Some of the things I am thinking of include:

(a) A major reorganization of the Dept. of Citizenship and Immigration under a new Minister who would command wide public support. I have in mind Paul Hellyer, Sharp or Nicholson in that order.
     If Hellyer would take it on, it would do more than anything else to convince people you mean business (and incidentally would boost his long-term prospects!).

(b) A major Cabinet reorganization. The more comprehensive and spectacular this is, the better. I suggest it should include a big reshuffle of Parliamentary Secretaries as well as Ministers.
     I hope you can announce this before the end of January so that Ministers will have a chance to get the feel of their Departments before the House meets.

(c) You as Prime Minister should make all important announcements from now until the election, *e.g.*, the proposed Federal contribution to a trunk highway system in the Atlantic area.

(d) You might write a letter (to be published) to the Joint Chairmen or to all the members of the Pension Committee urging them to complete their work by February 16th. This would emphasize your personal interest in and sense of urgency about the Canada Pension Plan.

(e) You might stage a meeting with the Committee on Election Expenses for later in the month – to be followed by a proposed Code of Procedure for M.P.s including a prohibition against M.P.s (and Senators?) accepting professional retainers of any kind involving business with the Government. This would be aimed at the lawyers and should be well received by the public.

You might also fly a kite about election expenses. For example, you might suggest that pending the report of the Election Committee campaign contributions should not exceed, say, 1% (or less) of the previous year's taxable income – and might be deductible for tax purposes. If well received, this could be incorporated in the Budget.

5. There are a number of matters in connection with planning an Election Campaign which should be dealt with more or less immediately if you decide on a June election. These include:

(a) The question of Sharp running in Winnipeg.
(b) The problem of campaign contributions – and some kind of settlement of the Montreal situation in this regard.
(c) Grooming candidates to replace Members who do not plan to stand again.
(d) And a thousand other things.

W.

5. Draft letter to A. T. Thomson concerning my resignation.

[This letter was not sent.]
HOUSE OF COMMONS
Canada

Ottawa 4,
29 December,
1966.

Mr. A. T. Thomson,
President,
Davenport Liberal Association,
c/o Yorktown Paint & Chemicals Ltd.,
1181 Bloor Street West,
Toronto 4, Ontario.

Dear Lex:

We have had several conversations in the last few months about whether I should continue to represent Davenport in the House of Commons. As you know, the main issues which influenced me to enter politics originally were: *(a)* the high level of unemployment at the time and the need for expansionary economic policies to reduce it; *(b)* the need for new and amplified measures of social security; and *(c)* the need for policies to counter the excessive foreign control over the Canadian economy and resources in its present concentrated form through parent-subsidiary company relationships. I believe the last of these issues is fundamental if Canada is to remain independent and avoid a kind of satellite status.

The policies introduced in 1963 to expand the economy and reduce unemployment were successful. Finding a job, which was the main concern of many people in Davenport and throughout Canada from 1959 to 1963, is no longer a serious problem except in the Atlantic region. Moreover, a great deal of progress has been made since 1963 in improving our social security coverage in Canada. The Canada Pension Plan; the Canada Assistance Act; increased Old Age Pensions; Student Loans; a National Labour Code; and Medicare, to become effective by July 1, 1968, are considerable achievements. While all of us were not happy about the reasons given for deferring Medicare for one year, at least the legislation approving this important measure has now been passed.

I do not believe, however, that the present emphasis and attitudes of the Government respecting the kind of measures that are required to deal with the foreign investment issue are sufficiently positive, or that they are consistent with statements made at the time of the last election. During the past year I have done my best to keep this issue before the public. But in my present position, which was not anticipated at the time of the 1965 election, there is nothing I can do about bringing appropriate legislation for dealing with this matter before Parliament.

In these circumstances, I have been considering whether, in good conscience, I should continue to sit in the House of Commons. After the most careful thought and the benefit of much advice, I decided I should not do so, and informed the Prime Minister of my intention to resign. After several discussions he invited me to rejoin the Cabinet as a Minister without Portfolio with no assurance that the Government would proceed with the kind of legislation on the foreign control issue which I believe is needed. In view of my strongly held convictions on this subject I could not become a member of the Cabinet under such conditions. I have advised the Prime Minister to this effect and given the Speaker formal notice of my resignation as a Member of Parliament.

This was a hard decision for me to take for many reasons. I know that some people who feel as strongly as I do about the need to reverse the present foreign control of the Canadian economy will not agree with my decision. In their view I should retain my seat despite the fact that as a private member I could do nothing effectively about this issue. Moreover, an occasion might arise when I would feel compelled to vote against the Government. I wish to avoid this eventuality. In personal terms, my resignation means that I shall see much less of the true friends who worked with me in helping Mr. Pearson rebuild the Party following the defeats of 1957 and 1958. These friends include many of the present Liberal Members of Parliament. It means seeing less of the great many friends I have made in Davenport during the four-and-one-half years it has been my privilege to represent the people of that riding. Nevertheless, after weighing all the conflicting arguments and considerations, I believe I am doing the proper thing.

I shall never be able to thank you adequately for all you have done for me both as President of the Association and as Campaign Manager in the 1965 election. I feel the same way about Joe Grittani, who was Campaign Manager in 1962 and 1963, and about John Stroz and Alex MacIntosh who preceded you as President. I am equally indebted to Andy Thompson and Olga Riisna who have been the heart and soul of our organization, to all the present and past members of the Executive, and to everyone who worked so hard and so successfully in the hard fought campaigns of 1962, 1963 and 1965. I shall always value the warm friendship of each one of you, just as I shall always be grateful for the wonderful support given to me by the people of Davenport.

With my most grateful thanks and best wishes for the future,

Yours sincerely,

W. L. Gordon: BH

**6. Draft letter from the Prime Minister setting out terms for
rejoining the government.**

Handwritten remarks at top of this letter:
"Before joining Mike in a press conference today, Benson advised me that Mike
had approved this draft and would send me a signed letter in these terms tomorrow.
W.L.G. 4/1/67"

Ottawa 4, January 3, 1967

Dear Walter:

With reference to our conversation and your letter and enclosure of December 29,
it is my hope that you will rejoin the cabinet and assume the following responsibilities:

(1) Chairman of a small committee (say, three or five) to draft a White Paper
dealing with the corporate structure of Canadian business, of the Canadian
economy and the review or supervision of monopolies. After consideration
by the cabinet as a whole, the White Paper would be made public and
referred to the parliamentary committee on Finance, Trade and Economic
Affairs for full public discussion and debate. Appropriate legislation would
be introduced following such public discussion.

(2) General supervision of the work of the cabinet, including some screening of
the various matters now being brought before cabinet and following up to
see that cabinet decisions are acted upon promptly.

(3) Membership on a small ministerial committee which I propose to set up
and which will meet daily to plan and organize legislative and governmental business and which will also have as members Messrs. Marchand, Sharp
and the House Leader; possibly also the Deputy House Leader.

(4) The planning and organization of political tactics, in particular putting into
effect methods of improved communications and public relations.

(5) Liaison between the cabinet and the caucus.

(6) Liaison between the cabinet and the National Federation; particular concern with general party organization, especially in Ontario.

(7) Chairman of a Ministerial Caucus and Federation group to plan the long
term policies of the Liberal Party.

In all of these activities, I would expect you to work closely with me and to
report directly to me.

We have had some discussion about the exact post to which you would be
appointed. Naturally with the responsibilities outlined above you would be looked
upon as a senior member of the cabinet. However, we have both agreed that you
could not carry out these various responsibilities effectively if, in addition, you
were to take on a portfolio which carried with it heavy day-to-day responsibilities. I
expect that there will be some changes in the cabinet before the end of this month
when the present session should be concluded. At that time you would be
appointed to one or other of the cabinet posts we have discussed together. In the
meantime, if you wish to get ahead with the various matters referred to above, and
in particular with the preparation of the proposed White Paper, you could serve as
a Minister without Portfolio for the next three weeks or so.

7. Notes of meeting with Messrs. Pearson, Sharp, and Winters on agencies of foreign banks and proposed review of foreign control; attached memo.

18 January 1967

Mike, Sharp and I met at 8.30 P.M. last evening to talk about the Revision of the Bank Act and particularly the question of agencies of foreign banks. Sharp said he was working on an amendment to prevent the Mercantile from circumventing the proposed legislation.

The main conversation was about the agency question. I did most of the talking – it was all low key – and made the points outlined in my memo of January 16, 1967, attached. I gave a copy to Sharp. Sharp agreed that Rasminsky was not in favour of allowing agencies of foreign banks to establish in Canada but implied Rasminsky did not feel this is a major issue. There was no other comment about my presentation and I was left with the clear impression that Sharp will speak to Herb Gray and accept my advice in the matter.

Winters joined us at 9 P.M. and we had a long (until 10.45) discussion of the proposed review of the foreign control issue. The following points were made:

(a) Sharp suggested that in *my* own interests I should not be connected with the enquiry. (He obviously believes it will be a reflection on himself for not moving in this matter.)

(b) Sharp made it clear he does not consider this a real major issue.

(c) Mike asked if I really believe there is a danger that in 10 - 15 years if we do nothing it will be too late. I said I did.

(d) Sharp and Winters argued I should accept some or several big administrative jobs. I said I was not interested. Mike brought up C.M.H.C. The others agreed. I did not comment.

(e) I repeated several times that I had not asked to come back to the Cabinet; that my plans were all set to retire; that I was not exactly fascinated by what goes on here; that Mike had come to me at the last possible minute presumably because he thought it wise to do so from a political point of view; that he asked me to do various things including the Chairmanship of a Cabinet Committee to look into the foreign control issue preparatory to the issue of a White Paper; that because of my keen interest in this issue I agreed to come back with the Government; and that the understandings and agreement were confirmed in writing.

I mentioned that Sharp had been present during a discussion on policy which dealt with the above matter in some detail. Winters said he had not known about it. I pointed out it is the P.M.'s prerogative to ask people to join the Cabinet and no one else's. No argument on this.

(f) There was a lot of talk about the reaction of the business community. I told Winters that I had been a member of the business community in Toronto for 30 years and the only thing I was sure of is that one cannot generalize on what businessmen think; some feel one way on this issue – others think the opposite.

(g) When it was clear I would not give in Sharp suggested Mike should head the enquiry instead of me. This would be ridiculous and contrary to the agreement but I did not say so.

(h) There is no doubt that (a) Sharp and especially Winters are strongly opposed to doing anything (Sharp would go along with a whitewash approach), (b) that . . . . (c) that nobody really gives a damn.

(i) At one stage Sharp asked that the enquiry be tied to the Convention resolutions.

(j) On the way home Winters told me he would have to reconsider his position, *i.e.,* whether he would resign. I urged him not to do so.

(k) This morning, 9.45 A.M., I spoke to Mike on the telephone. He felt it was useful to have had the talk last night; and that now he would go ahead. He plans to get approval from Cabinet tomorrow and suggested he might then put out a press release. I said I thought this was preferable to a statement in the House which would provoke debate.

I referred to Sharp but pointed out he had not objected to the proposition when the three of us got together before I rejoined the Cabinet. I said I supposed Winters might resign. He agreed but said he did not think he would.

I also said it would be a mistake to tie the enquiry to the Convention resolutions. It must be kept non-partisan.

9.50 A.M.   18/1/67

ATTACHED MEMO:
RE: AGENCIES OF FOREIGN BANKS

If the government is to prepare a report, and later a White Paper on the structure of Canadian industry and the effects which foreign control and the parent-subsidiary company relationships have on this, it would be inconsistent to prejudge the issue by allowing agencies of foreign banks to be established in Canada. It would also be inconsistent, it seems to me, to take a hard line about the Mercantile Bank and at the same time to open things up for all other foreign banks by permitting them to establish agencies here.

There are other reasons why this should not be done, including the following:

1. Presumably Canadian agencies of foreign banks would not be permitted to accept deposits from residents in Canada. Their head offices would, however, make U.S. dollar loans to Canadian entities (especially to Canadian subsidiaries of foreign corporations) and the borrowers, if they sold the resulting U.S. dollars, would acquire Canadian funds for their operations.

This could present serious problems for the Canadian authorities who, at the time, might not wish either to acquire U.S. dollars or to see an increase in Canadian dollars taking place. This kind of thing would quite likely occur at times of monetary restraint in Canada and if so, would be in conflict with what the Canadian Government and the Bank of Canada were trying to accomplish.

It seems probable that most of the business of the agencies of foreign banks would be with Canadian subsidiaries of U.S. corporations. To the extent that this made resources available to such Canadian subsidiaries in periods of tight money, it would give the subsidiaries a decided advantage over their Canadian competitors, quite apart from defeating the purposes of a restrictive monetary policy in

Canada. Moreover, if the policy in question should conflict at any time with U.S. government policy and thus lead to a withdrawal of support, it could have serious effects upon Canadian monetary and exchange policy.

It seems clear, therefore, that the establishment of Canadian agencies of foreign banks on any scale would reduce the influence and the authority of the Bank of Canada both in the exercise of monetary policy and in its role on behalf of the government in the field of exchange policy.

2. If foreign banks were permitted to establish agencies in Canada, they might be expected to operate them in several, or in most, of the ten provinces. Having done so, they would concentrate on the cream of the business; *i.e.*, the accounts of the larger Canadian subsidiaries of foreign concerns. While competition in the banking business is desirable per se, it would be difficult to justify placing agencies of foreign banks in a preferred position.

They would be in a preferred position for the reasons indicated, and also because they would be under no pressure to serve the population as a whole. There would be another advantage in the fact that they would be wholly owned by the foreign banks in question, whereas under the proposed revisions of the Bank Act there will be severe restrictions on any concentration of ownership of the established banks.

3. Much has been said about the fact that Canadian banks have been permitted to establish agencies in New York state and about the desirability of a reciprocal approach by Canada. But the two situations are not at all comparable. New York is the financial capital of the world and there are strong reasons why, because of this, foreign banks in all countries should be permitted, in fact, encouraged, to establish agencies or branches there.

Moreover, if the larger U.S. banks were permitted to establish agencies in Canada, these could not be restricted to any one centre; *i.e.*, Montreal or Toronto. It is inconceivable that they would not be allowed to set up offices in each of the provinces if they wished to do so. This means that one agency office in New York would be balanced by perhaps ten offices in Canada.

It will be appreciated that the business done by agencies of Canadian banks in New York is a very small fraction indeed of the total banking business in the United States. If, on the other hand, U.S. banks were permitted to establish agencies in Canada and these agencies secured the cream of the domestic business; *i.e.*, the business of Canadian subsidiaries of U.S. concerns, they would over the years obtain an appreciable amount of the total banking business in Canada. This, of course, would be placed with their head offices in the United States, the profits would be recorded by such head offices and no taxes would be payable in Canada.

4. It is argued that if we do not permit agencies of foreign banks to be established in Canada, the United States will retaliate. Much has been said about the proposed Javits bill in this connection. However, the power over banking in the United States is shared between the federal and state governments. Most, or at least many of the states, do not permit foreign banks to operate within their borders in any form. It seems doubtful, therefore, whether the Javits bill, even if passed, would have very

much effect. It might do so in New York, but this might depend on the reactions of the Legislature of New York State.

5. It should be appreciated that most of the fuss over this matter has been stirred up by the First National City Bank of New York and its concern about its Canadian subsidiary, the Mercantile Bank. There is great competition among the principal New York banks. The senior officers of at least one of these institutions have intimated privately that they would be happy if Canada takes no action in this matter; *i.e.*, if Canada does not permit agencies of foreign banks to be established and restricts the operations of the Mercantile Bank in the manner being proposed. These people point out that if the situation is opened up, then whether they like it or not, all the principal New York banks (and presumably other U.S. banks as well), will be forced to open agencies in Canada.

6. *Conclusion.* This issue of permitting foreign banks to establish agencies in Canada has far greater implications than may be realized. It is a step that, once taken, could not be reversed. If Canadians are seriously concerned about retaining a reasonable measure of control of their own economy, then no action should be taken in this matter at the present time and without a great deal more study. Perhaps the best solution would be to suggest to our people on the Committee on Finance, Trade and Economic Affairs that they should recommend that further study and consideration be given to this question over the next year or so and that no action should be taken in the meantime.

8. "The War in Vietnam." Speech to the Sixth Arts and Management Conference of Professional Women, May 13, 1967.

I would like to speak to you today about the war in Vietnam – not as an expert who presumes to know what should be done to end it nor as a member of the Government responsible for foreign policy – but just as an ordinary Canadian who is deeply troubled by what is going on. I share this concern with a great many others in this country including the Prime Minister, the Secretary of State for External Affairs, Members of Parliament on all sides of the House, university teachers and people in every walk of life.

This same concern is felt by people in other countries including U Thant, Secretary-General of the United Nations, and His Holiness the Pope. It is shared by many highly placed Americans who have had the courage to speak out or to demonstrate against the present policies of their government. I am thinking of Senator William Fulbright, Chairman of the Foreign Relations Committee of the U. S. Senate, Senator Robert F. Kennedy, Senator George McGovern of South Dakota, retired generals James M. Gavan and Matthew B. Ridgway, Reverend Dr. Eugene Carson Blake, General Secretary of the World Council of Churches, Walter Lippmann and Martin Luther King, as well as by a galaxy of university teachers and many others.

I am told that the great mass of Canadians are not really interested in this war in far-off Asia; that they feel safe and comfortable and are looking forward to visiting Expo and to the Centennial celebrations. If this be true then surely it is the duty of their leaders in every field and especially of those in politics to bring home to them the inherent danger to all of us of what is going on in Vietnam. That is what I propose to try to do today.

No Canadian likes to criticize the United States or the policies of its government. The Americans are our friends and neighbours and our relationships with them are warm, varied, and extensive. Moreover, we would be wholly dependent on our American allies if there should be an attack on North America. This was brought home to us with shocking clarity in October, 1962, when the late President John F. Kennedy insisted that the Russians dismantle the nuclear bases they were establishing in Cuba.

We know also that the United States did not seek her present awesome responsibilities as the leader of the Western World. She now finds herself in a position where her government is forced to make decisions quickly and often without adequate information. Sometimes mistakes are made and when this happens the U.S. becomes committed to policies that seem to go from bad to worse. Governments, like individuals, do not like to confess to errors or to change policies once embarked upon. When this happens one can always hope that something will turn up which will justify the original decision.

But where does this leave the individual who is convinced that present policies are wrong, morally and in every other way? As I have said, many distinguished Americans have had the courage to speak out against the war in Vietnam. Should Canadians, who are just as horrified by what is going on as these Americans, speak out as well? Or should we keep silent on the grounds that it is not our affair; that we are not involved in any direct way ourselves – except, of course, as members of the

International Control Commission; that it could be dangerous for us as a nation or as individuals to criticize the U.S. Government; that in Canada's dependent or semi-satellite position *vis-à-vis* the U.S., the better part of wisdom would be silence?

I suppose the answer to these queries depends upon our individual consciences and our concept about the kind of world we live in. It was the general reaction against old-fashioned views of colonialism and imperialism which left France without support in her war in Indo-China in the late forties and early fifties.

It was the feeling that governments should not any longer act unilaterally that caused so much criticism of Britain and France over the Suez affair in 1956 and of the Russian intervention in Hungary in the same year. The U.S. was on the side of the angels then.

Perhaps it is similar feelings which more recently have provoked criticism of U.S. policies in Santo Domingo and Vietnam. Whatever the reasons I believe all of us have a duty to record our concern – our growing horror if you will – over what is going on in Vietnam. If the present policy ends in disaster – the extermination of millions of unfortunate Vietnamese, or possibly global nuclear war – our failure to speak out against what is happening will always remain on our consciences – if by chance we happen to survive – and so it should.

Dr. Blake, as reported in *The New York Times* of April 27, recently put this far more eloquently than I can:

> It is increasingly a unilateral policy and less and less supported by the peoples and governments who have been our allies in resisting Communist aggression. Our course has all the elements of high tragedy. More like Hamlet or King Lear than Macbeth or Julius Caesar, unable to distinguish friend from foe, caught in a dilemma which makes any decision increasingly difficult, the United States seems to be stumbling on towards final disaster.

> Our high ideals more and more suspected by our best friends among the nations, we find our position successfully attacked by our enemies and we find ourselves more and more isolated from our friends.

> Even those governments who share our fear of Communist aggression dare not fully and publicly support us because of the almost hysterical fears of their people of what we will do next.

> In the second place our Vietnam policy is wrong because we cannot win. By this I do not mean we cannot obliterate Vietnam, north and south. We have the military power to do just that. But when the swamps of the Mekong delta are filled up with dead Vietnamese and when the flower of our youth lies dead with them, what victory will have been won?

> Force cannot obliterate ideas. The more force we use the weaker become our best ideals. The picture of a great and wealthy nation mobilizing each month more and more of its unparalleled technological might to bring a tiny, long suffering, dark skinned nation to capitulation means clearly that the more we win the more we lose and each American soldier dead or wounded is a useless sacrifice.

To me it seems that U.S. policy in the Far East has been a succession of unhappy errors beginning with a gross misconception of the weakness and corruption of the Chiang Kai-shek regime in China and then failure to appreciate the relative strength of Mao Tse-tung's Communist government which took power in 1949.

I paid my first visit to the Far East in 1954. The late Carroll Binder, a well-known American publicist and the Editor of the *Minneapolis Tribune*, was on the same trip and on his return recorded his opinions in his newspaper. He had this to say about U. S. policy:

> I cannot recall one informed person with whom I talked during hundreds of conversations who personally accepted the underlying premise of United States policy towards China – that the present regime is a transient one which in due course will be replaced by one with which the United States can treat.
>
> Regardless of the position that is taken officially and despite personal antipathy towards Red China, every person with whom I have talked during the past five weeks takes it for granted that the present regime will endure a long time.

And again:

> The present United States policy of acting as though the Red regime is a transient one and of supporting Chiang's feeble but provocative sallies against the Red regime is regarded as amateurish and potentially dangerous by virtually everyone I met on this journey.
>
> It is believed to be based on short-sighted domestic political considerations instead of the long-term interest of the United States and other free nations. The United States is poorly situated to influence the course of world affairs at a critical juncture of history so long as a large part of the free world has so little confidence in its attitude towards China and China's neighbours.

I remember quoting Mr. Binder in a speech some twelve years ago and then remarking:

> All I can say is that, like Mr. Binder, I did not meet one person in the Far East who agreed with present United States policy. They all thought the present Communist government would remain in power in China for a long time. And accordingly that present United States policy is wrong. Most of the people we talked with were sensible enough to agree that no nation as important as the United States can be expected to reverse her policies overnight. Changes, if they are to come, must come gradually as and when public opinion becomes prepared for them. And certainly the recent series of provocative acts by the Chinese Communists makes it more difficult for the United States to modify her Far Eastern policy – even if her principal leaders were disposed to do so. (I might add that many of the people we talked with thought the present foreign policy of Communist China is deplorable. They blame this largely on the ignorance of the Communist leaders about the rest of the world.)

Since that time U. S. policy towards Red China has hardened steadily. The same is true – even more true perhaps – of Red China's attitude towards the United States. At the official level the leaders of both nations seem to have reached an almost pathological stage in their reactions to each other.

At the same time the Chinese have become engaged in an ideological conflict with the Soviet Union, formerly their principal ally, and in what appears to be serious upheavals at home. The U.S., for its part, has become enmeshed in a bloody civil war in Vietnam which cannot be justified on either moral or strategic grounds.

Senator George McGovern made a speech in the U.S. Senate recently about U.S. policy in Vietnam, parts of which were reported by *The New York Times* as follows:

> Our deepening involvement in Vietnam represents the most tragic diplomatic and moral failure in our national experience. The mightiest nation in history – a nation with a glorious democratic tradition based on the dignity and brotherhood of man – is with allegedly good motives devastating an impoverished little state and ravishing the people whose freedom we would protect.
>
> In the process we are sacrificing many of our bravest young men, wasting valuable resources, and threatening the peace of the world. We are being pulled step by step into a jungle quicksand that may claim our sons and the sons of Asia for years to come – a fearful path which our ablest generals have warned against for decades. "Anyone who commits American forces to a land war in Asia," said the late General Douglas MacArthur, "ought to have his head examined."

Senator McGovern went on to say:

> Communism is a force hostile to American ideals, but we do not meet its challenge by forcing an American solution on a people still in search of their own national identity. Mao Tse-tung may have claimed that "power grows out of the barrel of a gun," but that has not been the chief source of American power in the world, and it does not answer the basic yearning of the people of Asia. After all the dead are counted – American and Vietnamese – and the countryside is laid waste, we will have accomplished nothing. Having sown the wind, we shall reap the whirlwind.
>
> We fight in Vietnam not for any enduring objective; rather, we fight because of a highly questionable notion that this is the only honourable course. Implicit in our Vietnam involvement is an assumption that we may be ordained to play God in Asia by settling the struggle and determining the ideology of the people of that continent.

In the May issue of *The Progressive*, the Senator wrote in the same vein:

> We seem bent upon saving the Vietnamese from Ho Chi Minh even if we have to kill them and demolish their country to do it.

And again:

> Many of the Senate's most influential members, including the chairmen of powerful committees, have believed for years that the United States made a serious mistake in intervening in Vietnam – first by trying to defeat the Vietnamese independence struggle led by Ho Chi Minh against imperial France, and second, by fostering a divided Vietnam leading to civil conflict after the expulsion of the French.

Vietnam is a country of some thirty million people who have been resisting external aggression for centuries. First it was the Chinese. Then about one hundred years ago the French established control over the country. The Japanese took over for a short time during World War II and then the French again. Since the expulsion of the French in 1954 there has been civil war and more recently ever increasing intervention by the United States.

There are said to be about three million Catholics and about twelve million Buddhists in the South. There is no way of telling how many actual Communists there are (*i.e.*, members of the party) under Ho Chi Minh in the North or in the Vietcong. But there can be little question that the Vietnamese are intensely nationalistic and wish to retain their independence.

If left to the Vietnamese themselves it is questionable whether the civil war could be settled without more bloodshed. These people have a reputation for toughness and they have been fighting continually throughout the lives of several generations. However it might not be any worse for the Vietnamese to be allowed to fight things out among themselves than it is to be bombed, burned and exterminated by a foreign power.

As a Westerner, as a citizen of a country that has such close and friendly connections with the United States – military alliances as well as trade, financial, cultural and social ties – I feel sick at heart at what is going on. One is constantly reminded of the bombing, the use of napalm, the policy of defoliation and the effect this must have, not only on the lives, but on the thinking of the local population.

It would be quite unfair to blame American troops for what is happening. They are obeying orders, as is their duty. Unfortunately, in a war like this, there are bound to be acts of barbarism on both sides. In this war, the strongest nation in the world has taken sides in a savage civil struggle and is using its tremendous power to force the other side to quit. If the escalation of the war continues, as seems probable, and the North Vietnamese do not give up soon, one may wonder if the United States will be driven to use nuclear bombs or to spread germs or exterminating chemicals.

You may think this is exaggerated. If so would it be too much to ask the President of the United States to give a categorical undertaking that the U.S. will not use nuclear bombs or germs or life destroying chemicals under any circumstances?

From Canada's standpoint the grave dangers in the present situation are fourfold:

1. The present conflict may reinforce a natural distrust of all Westerners and of all white people on the part of millions of non-whites throughout the world. We may know that in their hearts, ordinary Americans are good, generous and kindly. But after what is happening in Vietnam, how can we expect Asians or Africans to believe this? And how can we expect them to differentiate between one white nation and another?

2. The second danger is that Russia and China may become reconciled as a result of their opposition to U.S. action in Vietnam. Senator Robert Kennedy, a critic of U.S. policy, is quoted in *The New York Times* of April 26 in this connection:

> Senator Kennedy backed the warnings of Senators McGovern and Fulbright about the effect of expansion of the war, saying:
> I had a visitor, a rather important visitor, from the Soviet Union during the last week, and he spoke about the Berlin crisis of 1961 and the Cuban crisis of 1962.

He admitted quite frankly that those two efforts by the Soviet Union had driven the allies and NATO countries – France, Germany, the United States, and England and other countries – very closely together in a way that they had not been in the past.

He said that is what is happening in Southeast Asia today. He said: "Through the efforts of the United States, you are accomplishing what we thought impossible, because you are bringing Communist China and Russia back together again."

3. The third danger that could result from a further escalation of the war is the direct involvement of Red China. If it seemed likely that North Vietnam was going to be defeated, it is quite possible that China might decide to intervene. Apart from everything else, this might be one way in which the Chinese leaders could suppress the present uprisings in their own country which may include the possibility of civil war at home.

Probably the U.S. could defeat Red China with the use of nuclear weapons if the Russians did not come to China's rescue – but what then? Having achieved victory, how could the U.S. police a nation of seven or eight hundred million people? And quite apart from that, would not all civilized people be revolted by a nuclear conflict which might involve a hundred million casualties?

4. Finally, there is the gravest danger that if the United States used nuclear weapons, the Russians would retaliate immediately. That is something which no thinking person dares to contemplate.

What should be done in present circumstances? I have read the suggestions put forward by U Thant, by our own Prime Minister, by the Honourable Paul Martin, by General Gavan, and by other thoughtful and informed Americans. They do not differ in essentials. Let me quote what Senator McGovern proposed in the speech previously referred to: .

> I recommend now as I have in the past, but with a new urgency and a deeper concern, that we:
>
> Stop the bombing, North and South, end the "search and destroy" offensive sweeps, and confine our military action to holding operations on the ground. A defensive holding action in the South as advocated by Generals [James M.] Gavin and [Matthew B.] Ridgway could be pursued while determined efforts are being made to negotiate a cease-fire. It is the bombing of North Vietnam that presents the greatest obstacle to a settlement and the greatest danger of involving Russia or China in the war.
>
> We should clearly state our willingness to negotiate directly with the Vietcong with some recognition that they will play a significant role in any provisional government resulting from a cease-fire and a negotiated settlement.
>
> We should use what influence we have to encourage a more broadly based civilian government in Saigon. A government willing to start discussions with the other side looking toward arrangements to end the war.
>
> We should advocate an international presence to police a cease-fire, supervise elections, provide an umbrella for the resettlement of Vietnamese concerned about their safety, and arrange for the withdrawal of all outside forces and the conversion of military bases to peacetime uses.

There can be no certainty that a course along these lines would work out satisfactorily. Hanoi might be suspicious of any new proposals and refuse to negotiate on any terms. The U.S. military commanders, on the other hand, have argued that cessation of the bombing will give the North Vietnamese opportunities to re-establish their communications and to bring up supplies. But surely it would be preferable to face these very real difficulties than to continue on a course that is so fraught with danger.

I hope Canadians in all walks of life and in all political parties – including especially Mr. Pearson and Mr. Martin – will continue to do everything in their power to press the Americans to stop the bombing. If we fail to do this, we must be prepared to share the responsibility of those whose policies and actions are destroying a poor but determined people. We must share the responsibility of those whose policies involve the gravest risks for all mankind.

9. Memorandum on current difficulties.

Private and Confidential

Ottawa, October 3, 1967.

The Position of the Government at the Present Time

Canadians are deeply troubled about the possible break-up of the country and are looking for strong leadership. This comes at a time when the Government gives the impression of being weak and uncertain. This is due to several causes, some deep rooted, others more superficial. These causes include:

(a) The fact that we have a minority government which obtained only 40 per cent of the popular vote in November, 1965, and whose support since then has fallen off still further.

(b) The fact that for the time being at least, the Tory Party has been rejuvenated under Stanfield who appears to be what many people have been seeking. It may be that he is overrated; that he will not show up so well when he appears in the House of Commons. But it would be very foolish to take this for granted. A great many ordinary people who have been looking for new leadership have identified themselves with Stanfield and will vote for him in the next election no matter what happens in the meantime.

(c) The economic situation is uncomfortable and the Government is not giving the impression that it knows how to handle the difficulties that confront us. In particular –

    (i) People are complaining about high taxes and rising living costs as they always do in good times. The Federal Government is blamed even if the taxes complained about are primarily municipal real estate taxes and provincial sales taxes.

    (ii) Lack of control over expenditures, something that cannot be corrected quickly. We should talk less and do more about this.

    (iii) There is the fear of inflation which may easily be aggravated by the kind of speeches and public statements Ministers have been making.

    (iv) The housing crisis. The Government must indicate its concern more convincingly and take new and forceful initiatives in this area.

    (v) High and rising interest rates.

    (vi) Uncertainties about the Carter report. Conflicting statements by Ministers are not helpful. A simple announcement that we do not propose to implement the report but will feel free to amend the existing tax law from time to time may be the best solution.

(d) The Liberal Government has given the impression of becoming increasingly conservative in its attitudes. In the process, we have given the public a confused impression of what we stand for. The more conservative elements in the cabinet, both because of their numbers and the portfolios they hold, exert a dominating influence, one that tends to be deadening and unimaginative. And yet, left to themselves, the individuals in question would have no chance against Stanfield in an election.

(e) Inevitably, the unofficial leadership race in the Liberal Party has created frictions and some suspicion – perhaps quite unfair – that one or more of the

370

contenders have on occasion allowed their personal ambitions to affect their judgement about public policy.

(f) There is no consensus in the Party as to the best man to succeed Mr. Pearson, although Paul Martin's support is greater than that of any of the others.

(g) Members of the Cabinet are not working well together and as a result, tend to make contradictory speeches and pronouncements. There is no team spirit any longer, and some of the personal irritations have become public knowledge. There will always be differences of opinion about public policy in any cabinet but, if properly handled, there is no reason why this should lead to the kind of situation that has developed in the present cabinet.

By far the most important cause of the frustrations that exist at present is the confusion about areas of responsibility and authority and the way in which the time of busy Ministers is wasted. The work of the Cabinet and Cabinet Committees needs to be completely overhauled and the responsibilities of Ministers more clearly defined.

Present frustrations and confusions are accentuated by overlapping authority and by reversals of and retreats from firmly agreed policy positions. The Prime Minister is the ablest member of the Cabinet, but his tendency to take on far more himself than any one man can handle is not an answer to the problem.

Some Ministers make no bones about the fact that because they cannot work effectively under existing conditions they intend to retire at the first available opportunity. Others, while intending to stay until the next election, do not propose to run again. And, quite frankly, there are one or two more whom the Cabinet would be better off without. This is an unhealthy situation which can spell serious trouble.

(h) The frustrations in the Cabinet are reflected in the caucus where the symptoms are evident in absenteeism and lack of discipline. Morale is at a low ebb in the Cabinet, in caucus and throughout the Party. Everywhere people sense that if there should be an early election we would be badly beaten.

* * *

I do not believe the foregoing is exaggerating the present position of the Government and of the Liberal Party. We could be defeated in the House if we are not very careful. But surely it is imperative to resolve the Quebec situation and the constitutional issue *before* another federal election campaign in which all kinds of passions could be aroused and damaging statements made?

What should we do in these circumstances and in the light of the Quebec situation?

I wish to submit the following proposals:

1. We should call off the leadership race. This would be a great blow to Paul Martin who, in the ordinary course of events, should win it. But he would probably agree if he felt it desirable in the country's interests and if some public recognition were made of his standing in the Party.

2. There is no doubt that most Liberals would like Mr. Pearson to carry on for another year at least. If he is willing to do this, he should announce his intention publicly at the earliest opportunity. He should say that he plans to devote almost his whole attention and effort to helping Marchand with the Quebec situation

and in negotiating new constitutional arrangements with the provinces. This should take precedence over everything else in an attempt to reach an agreement by next summer.

3. It might be wise to relieve Jean Marchand of his departmental responsibilities until the Quebec situation is resolved. It will require his whole time and attention in the interim.

4. The work of the Cabinet should be reorganized in a way that will not flout all the elementary principles of organization. (I used to practise in this field professionally and can assert that many of the frustrations referred to on pages 4 and 5 are the result of bad organization.) There should be some division, or differentiation, according to rank and authority, and greater regularity in the way policies are developed and approved. In particular:

(a) One senior Minister should be made responsible for organizing the work of the Cabinet, including a careful review of all proposals before they are presented. He should be the Chairman of the proposed Policy Committee (see below).

(b) The present Cabinet committee system is time wasting and should be reduced to the following:
   – A new Policy Committee (which, in effect, might become a sort of Inner Cabinet);
   – A Committee on the Quebec situation – under Marchand;
   – Treasury Board;
   – Special Committee of Council to deal with routine matters;
   – Legislation Committee – which should assume full and final responsibility for all Bills;
   – Ad Hoc Committees established from time to time to study particular problems.

(c) Many of the matters now brought before Cabinet should be settled by the Ministers themselves (in some cases, if they so wished, after consultation with the Chairman of the Policy Committee) or by Treasury Board.

(d) Three Deputy Prime Ministers should be designated in order to give them the necessary authority and standing. These should include Paul Martin, Jean Marchand and the Chairman of the Policy Committee.

(e) The Policy Committee which, in addition to the Chairman and the Prime Minister, should include the Secretary of State for External Affairs, the Leader of the Quebec Caucus, the Minister of Finance, the President of the Treasury Board, the Minister of Justice and the House Leader, should meet daily for an hour or an hour and a half – say, from 9.30 A.M. to 11 A.M. This Committee should deal with all questions involving policy.

   If the principal Ministers met together for a short time each day, they should soon begin to present a more united front to the House and to the public.

(f) The full Cabinet should meet once a week only (say, at 11 A.M. on Tuesdays) and should devote most of its time to political matters rather than administration.

(g) Concurrently with the other proposals, some important changes should be made in the composition of the Cabinet.

5. Initiatives should be taken to get the attention of the House and the public off

the current economic situation. The following subjects should be introduced as soon as possible:

- Social legislation, including divorce, the use of contraceptives, abortion and capital punishment.
- Foreign investment, including the C.D.C. and the White Paper. (Public concern about this issue is increasing.)
- Broadcasting.
- Election expenses.

6. In addition, it is vitally important for us to:

- Get busy on the constitutional issue and the situation in Quebec.
- Develop a new housing policy. Some Minister, preferably someone who knows something about the subject, should be placed in full charge with instructions to come up with a policy that will produce 200,000 starts in 1968 at substantially below present cost levels.
- Take steps to reverse the present trend in interest rates (even if this involves some indirect pressure on the banks about the way they are operating at present).
- Reduce our prospective expenditures so that next year's budget will be defensible.

* * *

Our primary objective should be to resolve the uncertainties surrounding the Quebec situation within a year. If we can do that, we can retire – or be defeated – with clear consciences. But of course if we are successful in this objective, the Liberal Party will deserve to be re-elected.

However, without a drastic reorganization along the lines suggested we are not likely to succeed in anything. It would be a case of waiting for the axe to fall which would not be a pleasant prospect.

WLG

10. Letter to Mr. Pearson on the financial situation.

November 7, 1967.

Personal and Confidential

The Right Honourable Lester B. Pearson,
Prime Minister of Canada,
Ottawa.

Dear Mr. Pearson:

Following the discussion of the financial situation at Cabinet today, it was agreed that we would be given an opportunity to study your memorandum of November 2nd and then to discuss the problem again on Thursday. I thought you might like to have my views ahead of time and I am writing this letter to you accordingly.

In the first place, I believe we have magnified the problem by talking too much about the need to cut expenditures and the problem of selling Government bonds. I do not wish to minimize the difficulties that confront us. I only wish to say again what I believe should be done about them.

According to your memorandum of November 2nd, if further action is not taken we would face a budget deficit of $635 million for the year 1968-69. In my opinion, this would be quite indefensible if we believe that next year will be a reasonably good one in terms of economic activity and employment. In these circumstances, I think we should plan for a balanced budget according to traditional methods of accounting or as close to this as may be practicable.

I would suggest, therefore, that Cabinet should approve the following:

(a) The various reductions outlined in the memorandum of November 2nd, or suitable alternatives thereto which, after revisions and discussions, might amount to $100 million.

(b) In addition I would suggest that additions to the Civil Service be frozen (subject to an understanding that the ceiling could be pierced in cases where this was demonstrably important) and that all departments – or most departments – should be required to reduce their dollar estimates by, say, 5% of variable or controllable expenditures. I would hope that these proposals would produce additional savings of perhaps $150 million.

The items referred to under (a) and (b) above should reduce the estimated deficit to about $400 million.

My personal view is that we should face up to a further cut in the estimates of the Department of National Defence, even though this would entail a reduction in our present contributions to NATO. I recognise this involves a number of broad questions which other members of Cabinet may not be willing to go into at this time. If this is the case, I suggest that additional revenues be raised by the advancement of the dates on which corporation income taxes should become payable. My recollection is that we made the first step in this direction in the budget for the year 1963-64. The second step could produce something of the order of $300 million for the fiscal year 1968-69.

In discussing this matter this morning Mr. Sharp raised the question of the liquidity of Canadian corporations. While I agree that this is a matter of importance, it is difficult for me to see why corporations should not be required to pay

374

their income taxes on the same basis as individuals.

This proposal, if applied in full, could come close to producing a balanced budget.

In addition to the foregoing, I have had some discussion with Mr. Benson (another Chartered Accountant) about the desirability of combining the Old Age Security revenues and expenditures with the government's other revenues and expenditures for budgetary purposes. If this were done, it should produce another $100 to $150 million. My recollection is that a step in this direction was made in the budget presentation for the year 1963-64.

It is true that this proposal would not mean any savings in terms of cash, but it would make it possible to improve the budget presentation. In fact, if all these suggestions were accepted, it would mean that the Minister of Finance could budget for a surplus for the year 1968-69, something that has not been done for many years.

I have a number of other points which I should like to mention in this general context:

1. I would be against an early announcement of what we propose to do. Instead I would like to see us plan to introduce next year's budget in February, 1968, and, as I have said, I would like to see us budget for a surplus. I think it would be important for the budget to be brought down on the same day as the estimates. The latter would undoubtedly show substantial increases in projected expenditures over the corresponding figures for the previous year, which if announced by themselves would be damaging to public confidence. If, however, this were reported on the same day as the budget, which indicated either a balance or a surplus, then it would be this latter fact that would attract the most attention.

2. In any event, I think it would be unwise to introduce a refundable tax on individuals. If this were done it would reduce the ordinary man's take-home pay and in the present climate of wage negotiations might well provoke further demands for increased wages.

3. As I have said before, I think we should make an early announcement of our intentions respecting the Carter Commission proposals. I would hope it would be possible at the same time to say what we propose to do about increasing the taxes of the oil industry, the mining industry, and the life insurance industry as proposed by the Commission. (In fact, such taxes could go some distance in paying for Medicare.)

I am not at all clear why it has been necessary for us to take so long in arriving at conclusions respecting the broad principles recommended by the Carter Commission and also the taxes on these three industries.

4. I was disturbed by Mr. Sharp's remarks this morning about the control which the Bank of Canada may be in a position to impose, directly or indirectly, upon the government in these matters. Since the amendment of the Bank of Canada Act, it is surely clear that the Government and not the Bank must take responsibility for monetary policy in Canada. We are fortunate to have as able a man as Mr. Rasminsky as Governor of the Bank of Canada. Nevertheless it would be indefensible if ever again the Canadian Government accepted the premise that it is the Central Bank and not the Government that sets policy in this area.

I should add in this connection that the recent policies of the two largest chartered banks have been irresponsible and in my view have had something to do with the general rise in interest rates in Canada. I quite agree that this has not been the main cause for the increase in interest rates. Nevertheless, I think it is indefensible for the heads of two Chartered Banks, in order to ensure that the total assets of their institutions should exceed $7 billion at their year ends (October 31, 1967), should be permitted to bid for deposits in the way they have done in recent months. It might be desirable for the Minister of Finance to explain publicly and in detail just what has been going on in what is essentially a monopoly field. I suspect that he would be warmly applauded if he introduced legislation which would ensure that this sort of thing could not be repeated.

To sum up, I believe the Government should make every effort to come up with a balanced budget, or close to a balanced budget in the coming year. I would like to see this accomplished as far as possible by reductions in prospective expenditures. But realistically, I acknowledge that if we do not cut Defence expenditures, substantial additional revenues will also be required. I have suggested two ways in which this objective could be realized. I expect that others may have additional suggestions which should be considered.

I am sending a copy of this letter to Mr. Sharp.

Yours sincerely,

11. Letter to Mr. Pearson *re* the Watkins Task Force.

Ottawa 4,
November 7,
1967.

PRIVATE AND CONFIDENTIAL

The Right Honourable L. B. Pearson, P. C., M.P.,
Prime Minister,
Ottawa, Ontario.

Dear Mr. Pearson:

Quite apart from the question of the government's finances and expenditures, two matters were mentioned at cabinet today which disturbed me.

Mr. Martin raised the question of the postal rates to be charged to *Time* and *Reader's Digest*. He implied that there has been, and may be expected to be, further strong pressures from the United States against charging rates to these two periodicals that are in any way different from those charged in the case of Canadian periodicals. I am informed that after I left a previous cabinet meeting recently, a decision was taken to adjust the rates which it had previously been decided to charge *Time* and *Reader's Digest* in a way that would be less burdensome to these two periodicals.

I should think it is highly probable that when this legislation is before Parliament, the government will be asked to disclose and to justify the element of subsidy which will still apply in the case of *Time* and *Reader's Digest* after the introduction of the new rates. If this subsidy is substantial, I should think we would be in for trouble.

The other matter was the brief reference to the Canada Development Corporation. At the time of the discussions in late December, 1966, about my return to the cabinet, it was understood that this legislation would be referred to in the Speech from the Throne – and this was done – and would be proceeded with during the current session. There was no suggestion that an entirely new concept of the Canada Development Corporation would be considered and I felt entitled to assume that we were talking about the Canada Development Corporation in the same terms as the one which I had previously put forward on behalf of the government when I was Minister of Finance.

In September Mr. Sharp spoke to me about some quite new and different ideas he was considering which, if agreed to, would have little relation to the previous concept of the Canada Development Corporation except the retention of the name. Naturally I pointed this out to Mr. Sharp, as well as my opinion that the new proposals were subject to serious weaknesses. While he promised to discuss this matter with me again as soon as he returned from certain meetings in South America at the end of that month, I have not heard from him and I would like to know where matters stand.

I raise these two matters with the proposed White Paper on foreign investment and the structure of industry in Canada very much in mind. I had hoped that the White Paper would be ready for consideration by cabinet some weeks ago, but it has taken longer to put the ideas of the Task Force down on paper than was originally contemplated. I now expect that a draft will be ready for consideration by the cabinet committee or by cabinet itself by the end of November.

I should add that according to a recent survey, a copy of which I shall be glad to give you, there is no question that the Canadian public is disturbed about the issue of foreign control of Canadian industries and Canadian resources and believes the government should be doing more about this. I hope very much that the proposed report of the Task Force will provide the government with an approach which will be acceptable and which will be pressed forward vigorously.

However, the two questions referred to at the beginning of this letter have caused me some concern. If there is any doubt in your mind about the willingness of the government to press forward with the proposed White Paper, then I should appreciate being informed of this at your earliest convenience.

Yours sincerely,

12. THE FIRST PEARSON GOVERNMENT
(22 April 1963 to 18 December 1965)

Prime Minister	Rt. Hon. Lester B. Pearson	22 Apr 1963 - 18 Dec 1965
Minister of Agriculture	Hon. Harry W. Hays	22 Apr 1963 - 18 Dec 1965
Minister of Citizenship and Immigration	Hon. Guy Favreau	22 Apr 1963 - 2 Feb 1964
	Hon. René Tremblay	3 Feb 1964 - 14 Feb 1965
	Hon. John R. Nicholson	15 Feb 1965 - 18 Dec 1965
Minister of Defence Production	Hon. Charles M. Drury	22 Apr 1963 - 18 Dec 1965
Secretary of State for External Affairs	Hon. Paul J.J. Martin	22 Apr 1963 - 18 Dec 1965
Minister of Finance and Receiver General	Hon. Walter L. Gordon	22 Apr 1963 - 10 Nov 1965
Minister of Fisheries	Hon. Hédard Robichaud	22 Apr 1963 - 18 Dec 1965
Minister of Forestry	Hon. John R. Nicholson	22 Apr 1963 - 2 Feb 1964
	Hon. Maurice Sauvé	3 Feb 1964 - 18 Dec 1965
Minister of Industry	Hon. Charles M. Drury	25 Jul 1963 - 18 Dec 1965
Minister of Justice and Attorney General	Hon. Lionel Chevrier	22 Apr 1963 - 2 Feb 1964
	Hon. Guy Favreau	3 Feb 1964 - 29 Jun 1965
	Hon. Lucien Cardin	7 Jul 1965 - 18 Dec 1965
Minister of Labour	Hon. Allan J. MacEachen	22 Apr 1963 - 18 Dec 1965
Minister of Mines and Technical Surveys	Hon. William M. Benidickson	22 Apr 1963 - 6 Jul 1965
	Hon. John Watson MacNaught	7 Jul 1965 - 18 Dec 1965
Minister of National Defence	Hon. Paul T. Hellyer	22 Apr 1963 - 18 Dec 1965
Associate Minister of National Defence	Hon. Lucien Cardin	22 Apr 1963 - 14 Feb 1965
	Hon. Leo A.J. Cadieux	15 Feb 1965 - 18 Dec 1965
Minister of National Health and Welfare	Rt. Julia V. LaMarsh	22 Apr 1963 - 18 Dec 1965
Minister of National Revenue	Hon. John R. Garland	22 Apr 1963 - 13 Mar 1964
	Hon. Edgar J. Benson	29 June 1964 - 18 Dec 1965
Minister of Northern Affairs and National Resources	Hon. Arthur Laing	22 Apr 1963 - 18 Dec 1965
Postmaster General	Hon. Azellus Denis	22 Apr 1963 - 2 Feb 1964
	Hon. John R. Nicholson	3 Feb 1964 - 14 Feb 1965
	Hon. René Tremblay	15 Feb 1965 - 18 Dec 1965
President of the Privy Council	Hon. Maurice Lamontagne	22 Apr 1963 - 2 Feb 1964
	Hon. George J. McIlraith	3 Feb 1964 - 6 Jul 1965

	Hon. Guy Favreau	7 Jul 1965 - 18 Dec 1965
Minister of Public Works	Hon. Jean-Paul Deschatelets	22 Apr 1963 - 11 Feb 1965
	Hon. Lucien Cardin	15 Feb 1965 - 6 Jul 1965
	Hon. George J. McIlraith	7 Jul 1965 - 18 Dec 1965
Secretary of State of Canada	Hon. John W. Pickersgill	22 Apr 1963 - 2 Feb 1964
	Hon. Maurice Lamontagne	3 Feb 1964 - 18 Dec 1965
Solicitor General of Canada	Hon. John Watson MacNaught	22 Apr 1963 - 6 Jul 1965
	Hon. Lawrence Pennell	7 Jul 1965 - 18 Dec 1965
Minister of Trade and Commerce	Hon. Mitchell Sharp	22 Apr 1963 - 18 Dec 1965
Minister of Transport	Hon. George J. McIlraith	22 Apr 1963 - 2 Feb 1964
	Hon. John W. Pickersgill	3 Feb 1964 - 18 Dec 1965
Minister of Veterans Affairs	Hon. Roger J. Teillet	22 Apr 1963 - 18 Dec 1965
Minister without Portfolio	Hon. W. Ross Macdonald (Senator)	22 Apr 1963 - 3 Feb 1964
	Hon. René Tremblay	22 Apr 1963 - 2 Feb 1964
	Hon. John J. Connolly (Senator)	3 Feb 1964 - 18 Dec 1965
	Hon. Yvon Dupuis	3 Feb 1964 - 21 Jan 1965
	Hon. Jean-Luc Pépin	7 Jul 1965 - 18 Dec 1965

13. THE SECOND PEARSON GOVERNMENT
(18 December 1965 to 6 July 1968)

Prime Minister	Rt. Hon. Lester B. Pearson	18 Dec 1965 - 20 Apr 1968
	Rt. Hon. Pierre Elliott Trudeau	20 April 1968 - 6 Jul 1968
Minister of Agriculture	Hon. John J. Greene	18 Dec 1965 - 6 Jul 1968
Minister of Citizenship and Immigration	Hon. Jean Marchand	18 Dec 1965 - 30 Sep 1966
Minister of Consumer and Corporate Affairs	Hon. John N. Turner	21 Dec 1967 - 6 Jul 1968
Minister of Defence Production	Hon. Charles M. Drury	18 Dec 1965 - 6 Jul 1968
Minister of Energy, Mines and Resources	Hon. Jean-Luc Pépin	1 Oct 1966 - 6 Jul 1968
Secretary of State for External Affairs	Hon. Paul J.J. Martin	18 Dec 1965 - 20 Apr 1968
	Hon. Mitchell Sharp	20 Apr 1968 - 6 Jul 1968
Minister of Finance and Receiver General	Hon. Mitchell Sharp	18 Dec 1965 - 20 Apr 1968
	Hon. Edgar J. Benson	20 Apr 1968 - 6 Jul 1968
Minister of Fisheries	Hon. Hédard Robichaud	18 Dec 1965 - 6 Jul 1968
Minister of Forestry	Hon. Maurice Sauvé	18 Dec 1965 - 30 Sep 1966
Minister of Forestry and Rural Development	Hon. Maurice Sauvé	1 Oct 1966 - 6 Jul 1968
Minister of Indian Affairs and Northern Development	Hon. Arthur Laing	1 Oct 1966 - 6 Jul 1968
Minister of Industry	Hon. Charles M. Drury	18 Dec 1965 - 6 Jul 1968
Minister of Justice and Attorney General	Hon. Lucien Cardin	18 Dec 1965 - 3 Apr 1967
	Hon. Pierre Elliott Trudeau	4 Apr 1967 - 6 Jul 1968
Minister of Labour	Hon. John R. Nicholson	18 Dec 1965 - 20 Apr 1968
	Hon. Jean-Luc Pépin	20 Apr 1968 - 6 Jul 1968
Minister of Manpower and Immigration	Hon. Jean Marchand	1 Oct 1966 - 6 Jul 1968
Minister of Mines and Technical Surveys	Hon. Jean-Luc Pépin	18 Dec 1965 - 30 Sep 1966
Minister of National Defence	Hon. Paul T. Hellyer	18 Dec 1965 - 18 Sep 1967
	Hon. Leo A.J. Cadieux	19 Sep 1967 - 6 Jul 1968
Associate Minister of National Defence	Hon. Leo A.J. Cadieux	18 Dec 1965 - 18 Sep 1967
Minister of National Health and Welfare	Hon. Allan J. MacEachen	18 Dec 1965 - 6 Jul 1968
Minister of National Revenue	Hon. Edgar J. Benson	18 Dec 1965 - 17 Jan 1968
	Hon. Jean Chrétien	18 Jan 1968 - 6 Jul 1968

Minister of Northern Affairs and National Resources	Hon. Arthur Laing	18 Dec 1965 - 30 Sep 1966
Postmaster General	Hon. Jean-Pierre Côté	18 Dec 1965 - 6 Jul 1968
President of the Privy Council	Hon. Guy Favreau	18 Dec 1965 - 3 Apr 1967
	Hon. Walter L. Gordon	4 Apr 1967 - 11 Mar 1968
Minister of Public Works	Hon. George J. McIlraith	18 Dec 1965 - 6 Jul 1968
Registrar General of Canada	Hon. Guy Favreau	18 Dec 1965 - 3 Apr 1967
	Hon. John N. Turner	4 Apr 1967 - 20 Dec 1967
Secretary of State of Canada	Hon. Julia V. LaMarsh	18 Dec 1965 - 9 Apr 1968
	Hon. Jean Marchand	20 Apr 1968 - 6 Jul 1968
Solicitor General of Canada	Hon. Lawrence Pennell	18 Dec 1965 - 19 Apr 1968
	Hon. John N. Turner	20 Apr 1968 - 6 Jul 1968
Minister of Trade and Commerce	Hon. Mitchell Sharp	18 Dec 1965 - 3 Jan 1966
	Hon. Robert H. Winters	4 Jan 1966 - 29 Mar 1968
	Hon. Charles M. Drury	20 Apr 1968 - 6 Jul 1968
Minister of Transport	Hon. John W. Pickersgill	18 Dec 1965 - 18 Sep 1967
	Hon. Paul T. Hellyer	19 Sep 1967 - 6 Jul 1968
President of the Treasury Board	Hon. Edgar J. Benson	1 Oct 1966 - 6 Jul 1968
Minister of Veterans Affairs	Hon. Roger J. Teillet	18 Dec 1965 - 6 Jul 1968
Minister without Portfolio	Hon. John J. Connolly (Senator)	18 Dec 1965 - 20 Apr 1968
	Hon. John N. Turner	18 Dec 1965 - 3 Apr 1967
	Hon. Walter L. Gordon	9 Jan 1967 - 3 Apr 1967
	Hon. Jean Chrétien	4 Apr 1967 - 17 Jan 1968
	Hon. Charles R. Granger	25 Sep 1967 - 6 Jul 1968
	Hon. Bryce S. Mackasey	9 Feb 1968 - 6 Jul 1968
	Hon. Paul J.J. Martin (Senator)	20 Apr 1968 - 6 Jul 1968
	Hon. Donald S. Macdonald	20 Apr 1968 - 6 Jul 1968
	Hon. John C. Munro	20 Apr 1968 - 6 Jul 1968
	Hon. Gérard Pelletier	20 Apr 1968 - 6 Jul 1968
	Hon. Jack Davis	26 Apr 1968 - 6 Jul 1968

Index

Abbott, Douglas C., 34, 51, 56, 324, 325
Abraham, Nelson W., 232
Adenauer, Konrad, 297
Agricultural-implement industry, 18-19
Aird, John B., 94, 95, 119, 132, 331
Alexander, A. V., 53
American Empire, The (de Riencourt), 165-6
Anderson, David, 92-3, 124
Anderson, Rod, 138
Andrew, Geoffrey C., 58
Annis, Arthur, 167
Area Development Agency, 142
Argue, Hazen, 100, 103
Armstrong, Judy, 338
Arthur Young and Co., 22
Arthur Young, Clarkson, Gordon and Co., 22
Artuso, Vic, 232
Asquith, H. H., 154n.
Asselin, Edouard, 201, 202
Atlantic Development Board, 135, 142
Attlee, Clement R., 53
Augustyn , Frank, 338
Automotive agreement, 163, 166-72, 206, 217
Automotive industry, Tariff Board inquiry into, 18-20
Axworthy, Tom, 207

Babcock Wilcox, 20
Bailey, Gerry, 23-4
Balance of payments, 36, 141, 142, 158-9, 160-3, 166, 167, 170, 180, 242, 278
Balcer, Léon, 191
Balfour, St. Clair, 207-8
Balfour family, 20
Ball, George, 160-2, 163-5, 170
Bank Act revision, 179, 203, 208-14, 220, 235-6; ceiling on interest rates, 208, 209-10, 235-6, 257; question of

"near banks," 208, 210-11; non-resident ownership, 211-14, 218, 266-76; agencies of foreign banks, 257, 258-9, 261, 270; notes of meeting (January 1967), 359-62
Bank interest rates, 304; and see Bank Act revision
Bank of Canada, 27, 30-2, 36, 42, 77-8, 109-10, 213, 236, 290, 309, 328
Bank of Canada Act revision, 179, 203, 208
Bank of England, 25, 26, 32
Banks, Harold, 193, 240
Baring Brothers, 25
Barrow, Irving, 94, 118
Basic Motion Timestudy (Bailey and Presgrave), 23
Basilian Fathers, 106
Baxter, Clive, 146
Beattie, J. R., 157-8
Bell, Max, 206, 290
Bell, Raymond, 107
Bennett, R. B., 17, 18, 21, 27, 323-4
Benson, Edgar J. (Ben), 100, 112, 151-2, 175-6, 177, 254, 257, 258, 259, 263, 271-2, 273-4, 291, 295, 297, 304, 306, 313, 327, 328, 336
Bernhardt, Prince, 160
Bessborough, Earl of, 27
Bilak, Jerry, 232
Bilderberg Group, 160
Binder, Carroll, 58
Bladen, Vincent W., 166
Bolik, Horst, 232
Bomarc missiles, 89; and see Defence policy
Bonin, Bernard, 264
Bonnycastle, L. C. (Larry), 26, 315
Borden, Henry, 33
Borden, Sir Robert, 15
Bosa, Peter, 232
Brewin, F. Andrew, 197
Bridges, Sir Edward, 52
Broadbent, Edward, 334
Broadfoot, Dave, 338
Brown, George, 286, 287
Bryce, R. B. (Bob), 35, 46, 61, 137-8,

383

About the author

Born in Toronto in 1906, Walter Gordon was educated at Upper Canada College and the Royal Military College. From 1935 to 1963, he was a partner in Clarkson Gordon & Co., chartered accountants.

Gordon was called to Ottawa many times in the 1930s, '40s and '50s, working for government inquiries and on business-related problems. In 1955, he suggested a royal commission on Canada's economic prospects, and the government responded by asking him to chair what proved to be a landmark investigation into the country's economic future.

In 1958, he became actively involved in the Liberal party when Lester Pearson became leader, and in this book he tells of his work organizing the party and running for office in 1962. From 1963-65, he was finance minister in the Pearson government, and he served again in the cabinet in 1967-68.

He returned to the business world as chairman of Canadian Corporate Management Company Limited. In 1970, he was a founder of the Committee for an Independent Canada. He is now the chairman of the Canadian Institute for Economic Policy, an independent public policy institute which publishes studies of current economic policy issues.

Walter Gordon is the author of three other books: *Troubled Canada* (1960), *A Choice for Canada: Independence or Colonial Status* (1966) and *Storm Signals: New Economic Policies for Canada* (1975). He is also the subject of a biography, *Gentle Patriot*, by Denis Smith.

Other Canadian Lives you'll enjoy reading

Canadian Lives is a paperback reprint series which presents the best in Canadian biography chosen from the lists of Canada's many publishing houses. Here is a selection of titles in the series. Watch for more Canadian Lives every season, from Goodread Biographies. Ask for them at your local bookstore.

Something Hidden: A Biography of Wilder Penfield
Jefferson Lewis

The life story of a world-famous Canadian surgeon and scientist — written by his journalist grandson who has portrayed both the public and the private sides of Penfield's extraordinary life of achievement.

"One of the most valuable and fascinating biographies I have read in many years." — Hugh MacLennan

Canadian Lives 1   0-88780-101-3

Within the Barbed Wire Fence
Takeo Nakano

The moving story of a young Japanese man, torn from his family in 1942 and sent with hundreds of others to a labour camp in the B.C. interior.

"A poet's story of a man trapped by history and events far beyond his control." — *Canadian Press*

Canadian Lives 2   0-88780-102-1

The Patricks: Hockey's Royal Family
Eric Whitehead

A first-rate chronicle of the four-generation family of lively Irish-Canadians who have played a key role in the history of hockey for more than 70 years.

"A damn good story." — Jack Dulmage, *The Windsor Star*

Canadian Lives 3   0-88780-103-X

Hugh MacLennan: A Writer's Life
Elspeth Cameron

The prize-winning bestseller that chronicles the life of one of Canada's most successful novelists.

"This impressive biography does justice to the man and his work." — Margaret Laurence

Canadian Lives 4   0-88780-104-8

Canadian Nurse in China
Jean Ewen

The story of a remarkable young adventurer who went to war-torn China in the 1930s, met all the heroes of the Chinese Revolution, and survived the terrors and dangers she encountered with her ironic sense of humour intact.

"A remarkably candid book by a no-nonsense nurse."
— Pierre Berton

Canadian Lives 5   0-88780-105-6

An Arctic Man
Ernie Lyall

Sixty-five years in Canada's North — the story of a man who chose the Inuit way of life.

"The main reason I decided to do a book about my life in the north is that I finally got fed up with all the baloney in so many books written about the north." — Ernie Lyall, in the preface.

Canadian Lives 6   0-88780-106-4

Boys, Bombs and Brussels Sprouts
J. Douglas Harvey

One man's irreverent, racy, sometimes heart-breaking, account of flying for Canada with Bomber Command in the Second World War.

"Tells more about what it was like 'over there' than all of the military histories ever written." — *Canadian Press*

Canadian Lives 7   0-88780-107-2

Nathan Cohen: The Making of a Critic
Wayne Edmonstone

A giant of a man, a legend, Cohen had a vision of what Canadians could achieve in the arts and entertainment — and he convinced both audiences and artists that Canadian work should and could equal the world's best.

"A man of vision, prophecy and insight." — *Ottawa Revue*

Canadian Lives 8   0-88780-108-0

The Wheel of Things:
A Biography of L.M. Montgomery
Mollie Gillen

The remarkable double life of the woman who created Canada's best-loved heroine, Anne of Green Gables.

"A perceptive and sympathetic portrait of a complex personality." — Ottawa *Journal*

Canadian Lives 9   0-88780-109-9

Walter Gordon: A Political Memoir
Walter Gordon

The gentle, passionate patriot who became an Ottawa insider and fought for his principles in a cabinet of politicians all too ready to abandon theirs.

"Valuable insight into our political history and a revealing portrait of the man himself."
                    — CBC newsman Norman Depoe

Canadian Lives 10   0-88780-110-2

Troublemaker!
James Gray

The memoirs of a witty, warm-hearted, irreverent newspaperman who witnessed the golden age of Western Canada, 1935-1955.

"A book of great immediacy and appeal — wise and extraordinarily revealing about ourselves." — Jamie Portman, Southam News Services

Canadian Lives 11   0-88780-111-0

When I Was Young

Raymond Massey

One of Canada's most distinguished actors tells the story of his aristocratic youth as the offspring of the most Establishment family of Toronto. The first of his two-volume memoirs.

"An urbane, humour-inflected and sensitive recollection."
— *Victoria Times-Colonist*

Canadian Lives 12   0-88780-112-9

Having trouble finding a copy of a book in this series?

If you're having difficulty finding a copy of a book in Goodread Biographies' Canadian Lives series, send us a stamped, self-addressed envelope and we'll put you in touch with a bookstore that stocks all titles in the series.

Write to:
Goodread Biographies
333 - 1657 Barrington Street
Halifax, Nova Scotia
B3J 2A1

Be sure to enclose a stamped, self-addressed envelope with your letter.

Printed in Canada

g